TEACHER'S MANUAL TO

CASES AND MATERIALS

CORPORATIONS AND OTHER BUSINESS ORGANIZATIONS

TENTH UNABRIDGED AND CONCISE EDITIONS

by

MELVIN ARON EISENBERG
Koret Professor of Law
University of California at Berkeley

JAMES D. COX
Brainerd Currie Professor of Law
Duke University Law School

FOUNDATION PRESS
2012

THOMSON REUTERS

© 2012 By THOMSON REUTERS/FOUNDATION PRESS

      1 New York Plaza, 34th Floor

      New York, NY 10004

      Phone Toll Free 1–877–888–1330

      Fax 646–424–5201

      foundation–press.com

Printed in the United States of America

ISBN 978–1–60930–046–3

Mat #41179626

Table of Contents

Chapter 1

Agency: The Sole Proprietorship

Chapter Overview: We customarily include in the first class a quick review of the course syllabus. We find the students are reassured by this thumbnail sketch; they are uninitiated in the field and their unease is salved by seeing the forest at the outset before they are expected to navigate among the trees. The materials in this casebook are modular; that is, they have been purposely edited, written and assembled so that you can teach the materials in the order that *you* prefer and not the order preferred by the casebook authors.

The material in this chapter can be covered in two days; if you prefer to move faster through this chapter you may consider assigning the two principle cases, *Morris Oil Co. v. Rainbow Oilfield Trucking Co.* and *Tarnowski v. Resop*, with discussion and lecture filling in the material in Note on the Agency Relationship.

Section 1.   The Sole Proprietorship

An interesting point here is that there are a lot of sole proprietorships, but note they account for a very small part of the multi-trillion dollar GDP. A sole proprietorship does have organizational problems of making sure that all employees are engaged in carrying out the objectives of the firm. The difference from what follows in later chapters is that there are no co-owners to add to these problems, i.e., organizational and operational issues among owners as well as within the workforce. As the note material makes clear, even a sole proprietor will view there to be some distinction between the firm and her own assets and activities. A second reason for considering the sole proprietorship a business organization is that it employs agents. Hence many of the same issues that we see in other business forms are present in the sole proprietorship: how decision making is structured; who has authority; liability of parties; and conflicts of interest between its agents and the firm/owner. We will see, therefore, that in many areas fiduciary obligations, expectations of owners and the underlying concepts and approaches are fairly consistent across all forms of doing business.

Why are some businesses that have but a single owner, i.e., sole proprietorships? There are some fairly obvious answers: some owners prefer to not share authority over the organization's business, the business cannot sustain more than a single owner (i.e., the expected profits are not sufficient to be divided, as this would be insufficient to reward each owner for the risk and burdens of being an owner), and some tasks are non-delegable, e.g., being an artist, and hence do not have the same attraction for co-ownership. But even a sole proprietorship can have agency costs of the type captured in the Jensen & Meckling excerpt.

Section 2:   Agency

In the background of the material that follows is the large question: why do we permit individuals to enter into binding contracts through their agents. From the answer to this question flows the principles of agency law studied in the section of the material.

A.   The Authority of an Agent

Morris Oil Co. v. Rainbow Oilfield Trucking, Inc.,

The case introduces the questions whether Rainbow as an agent of Dawn and, if so, did Rainbow have authority to bind Dawn on the fuel purchases used in the agency?

Dawn had a "certificate of public convenience" which allowed its holder to transport goods in New Mexico. Dawn entered into an agreement with Rainbow whereby the latter would operate under Dawn's certificate of convenience," using its truck to engage in transporting items in the oilfields of New Mexico. Dawn would bill for all services and collect the all revenues from the operation, retain a fee of $1000 a month (rent for the certificate) plus a percentage of the revenues, and would remit the balance to Rainbow. Rainbow was to pay its own operating fees and "operations utilizing fuel were to be under the direct control and supervision of Dawn."

Ultimately Rainbow went bankrupt, but not before running up a bill to Morris for gasoline delivered for the trucking business. Morris then learns of Dawn, presents his claim, it is denied, even though there remains $13,000 on hand from which the payment could be made. Morris sues.

The case provides an opportunity to integrate into the facts and reasoning of the case the material under Note on the Agency Relationship. The questions the case poses related to that note material are:

1. What supports any conclusion that Rainbow was Dawn's agent?

2. Was this a case of actual or apparent authority?

3. Was this a case of an undisclosed principal?

4. Did Dawn ratify Rainbow's actions by the bills it did pay or by asking Morris to forbear and indicating that payment would be forthcoming?

The court finds there is an agency. Citing paragraph 4 of the Dawn-Rainbow agreement, Rainbow had the authority, within the "ordinary course of business" to "create any debt or liability." And the court holds that their private understanding does not affect the rights of third parties. We might wonder if it is not inconsistent to say that Rainbow is an independent contractor but also to recognize that in that capacity has the power to bind the principal on contracts within the ordinary course of the business. But note their agreement stated that all operations, "including fuel," were to be under Dawn's "direct control." This seems to cut against actual authority in Rainbow to purchase fuel.

Note the court treats this not as apparent authority, but one of an undisclosed principal. That is, Rainbow never purported to act other than on its own behalf. Thus, we cannot use the reasonable expectations based on agents similarly situated since Morris did not believe that Rainbow as an agent. Thus, the issue is whether Rainbow's actions are "usual" in the discharge of the business of delivering goods in the oil fields of New Mexico.

The second/alternative basis for liability is that Dawn ratified. Here the court emphasized that when Dawn was fully aware of Morris's claim that he assured Morris that payment would be forthcoming. How strong is the case for ratification here? The crucial finding is that Dawn's representative (acting within his authority presumably) said that payment would be made after learning of the material facts underlying the claim. This fits within the scope of ratification.

So, was this the right result? Why? We might view the question of who should bear the risk of the maverick or rogue agent? Rainbow acted in breach of his agreement to Dawn (although we might question whether Dawn really believed that this business could be run without fuel being acquired on credit). The doctrine of both apparent authority and undisclosed principals each hold that the principal is in the best position to absorb the risk. This no doubt facilitates commerce as third parties are more willing to enter into transactions if they don't have to incur the risk not only that their known counterpart is an undisclosed principal but that the contract would not be enforceable against the true principal even if it is the type that is customary for a business.

A clear understanding of actual versus apparent authority is useful. Here you might try an approach one of us uses to illustrate the difference between actual and apparent authority. Draw a triangle with the top being the location of the principal and the bottom left the agent and the bottom right the third party. Note that on the Principal-Agent slope is actual authority, it arises from what the principal communicates director, either expressly or by implication, to the agent. On the Principal-Third Party slope authority arises from what the principal communicates to the third party, i.e., apparent/ostensible authority, by among other means of holding out to the third party that the agent has the authority that agents in similarly situations customarily have.

B.   The Agent's Duty of Loyalty

The Agent's Duty of Loyalty and Jensen & Meckling, The Theory of the Firm

What is meant by agency costs? How can the costs be controlled? These are the subjects of Jensen and Mecklings classic article. First, how might an agent visit costs on the principal that the principal did not bargain for when retaining the agent? Well, the agent could steal. He could divert business opportunities to himself. The agent may engage in suboptimal contracting on behalf of the principal, e.g., paying too much for goods purchased from friends or practicing nepotism instead of hiring the most qualified individuals. The agent may take long lunches and quit early. There are lots of ways an agent can cause agency costs. Students may be asked what their understanding of monitoring, bonding, and residual loss are. Some examples of monitoring are video cameras in warehouses holding valuable goods, auditors of public companies, trustees of universities, inspectors general of government agencies. Some examples of bonding are pay that is linked to long-term performance and licensing of professionals and certain trades. What are residual costs? They are the slippage in the system which is not efficient to prevent at all costs.

Tarnowski v. Resop

This case illustrates way in which the agent can be a rogue. The plaintiff retained the defendant to locate and investigate a route, or chain, of coin-operated music machines (a/k/a "juke boxes"). Defendant represented that he had found a route with 75 such locations which would produce about $3,000 a month. The plaintiff took the plunge, investing $11,000 as a down payment against the slightly more than $30,000 purchase price. It turned out that the defendant had not investigated very well, there were only 47 locations at some of those locations there was no machine, and at others they were only older machines. And it turns out that the defendant did not do his work very well because he was paid secretly by the sellers of the route. The plaintiff brought suit against the sellers and recovered $9,500 on the $10,000 judgment against them. He then moves against the defendant and is successful.

The court held: "the principle that all profits made by an agent in the course of an agency belonging to the principal, whether they are the fruits of performance or the violation of an agent's duty, is firmly established and universally recognized....It matters not that the principal has suffered no damage or even that the transaction has been profitable to him....The transaction was nothing more or less than the acceptance by the agent of a bribe to perform his duties in the manner desired by the person who gave the bribe. Such a contract is void. This doctrine rests on such plain principles of law, as well as common business honesty, that the citation of authorities is unnecessary.

"If an agent has received a benefit as a result of violating his duty of loyalty, the principal is entitled to recover from him what he has so received, its value, or its proceeds, and also the amount of damage thereby caused, except that if the violation consists of the wrongful disposal of the principal's property, the principal cannot recover its value and also what the agent received in exchange therefore."

How was the principal harmed by the agent's misconduct? What justifies making the agent disgorge the gains flowing from his misbehavior here? Note, students should be asked whether the recovery here is greater than the plaintiff's loss? That is, it appears the defendant lied to the plaintiff and thereby induced the plaintiff to purchase the rights to several locations for $11,000. Those purchases were unwound in other litigation, in which the jury awarded plaintiff $9.500. Presumably, this made the plaintiff whole (likely also that he collected some moneys from the machines/locations that were legitimate). The instant suit recovered the payments the vendor made to the defendant. This point emphasizes that the recovery here is premised not on harm, but discouraging agents from breaches. Thus, what result here if the plaintiff had gotten exactly what he bargained for, i.e., 75 locations that could be expected on average to yield $3,000 a month, but there was evidence of secret payment by the vendors of those locations to the defendant? We would expect the same result to be reached. The outcome is based not on the harm to the principal but on the lack of fidelity by the agent.

Reading v. Attorney–General

Reading, a sergeant in the British Medical Corps, picked up some extra change by standing in the bed of a truck smuggling whisky and brandy into Cairo. His presence allowed the truck to enter the city without being inspected. He did this several times, earning about £ 20,000 for his efforts. The money was seized and he sued to recover the sum. He was unsuccessful in the face of the following reasoning:

> "[I]f a servant, in violation of his duty of honesty and good faith, takes advantage of his service to make a profit for himself, in this sense, that the assets of which he has control, or the facilities which he enjoys, or the position which he occupies, are the real cause of his obtaining the money, as distinct from being the mere opportunity for getting it, that is to say, if they play the predominant part in his obtaining the money, then he is accountable for it to the master. It matters not that the master has not lost any profit, nor suffered any damage. ….In my opinion any official position, whether marked by a uniform or not, which enables the holder to earn money by its use gives his master a right to receive the money so earned even though it was earned by a criminal act."

It should be noted that Reading's abuse was the abuse of using his position of authority, or rather legitimacy - which position was conferred on him by his principal, as embodied in his uniform - for private gain.

RASH V. J.V. INTERMEDIATE, LTD

The block quote sets for the twin justifications for requiring the disloyal agent to give up her ill-gotten gains.

What result if the agent's disloyalty is actually helpful to carrying out an aspect of the agency? On this consider Restatement Third § 8.05, Illustration 1. "P, who owns a stable of horses, employs A to take care of them. While P is absent for a month, and without P's consent,

A rents the horses [for his own personal gain] to persons who ride them. Although being ridden is beneficial to the horses, A is subject to liability to P for the amount A receives for the rentals."

Chapter 2

A Primer on Accounting and Finance

Chapter Overview: Most law students have no familiarity with accounting and finance. Unfortunately for them, the world in which they are preparing to enter as professionals, regardless of whether the area of specialization is commercial, domestic relations, or litigation repeatedly call on a knowledge of the fundamentals of accounting and finance (e.g., the distinction between a balance sheet and income statement, the difference between revenue and income, and the meaning of present value). The curriculums of most law schools include accounting for lawyers and corporate finance classes. Those classes, unfortunately, tend to be more heavily populated by the students committed to entering a commercially focused career; thus, many students whose future careers will require a knowledge of accounting and finance do not prepare themselves by enrolling in an introductory accounting or finance course. Ah, youth is indeed wasted on the young. Moreover, cases studied in the standard business organizations class also depend on a working familiarity with accounting and finance. And, the "efficiency of markets" is fairly common parlance in the business world and, for that matter, leading business organization cases. For these reasons, we added to the Tenth Edition of the casebook as a free-standing chapter materials focused on the rudiments of accounting and finance. We believe the materials in this chapter are optional, although students at some point in the class need to understanding the tenets and qualifications of the Efficient Market Hypothesis (covered in the closing section of this chapter). Because we have prepared the book so that all materials are modular so that there is no particular progression required, this chapter can be skipped or added later, or parts of it added later in your own course. You might also consider covering this chapter in an optional set of two or three classes; although doing so runs the risk of all such anti-paternalism; it likely would mean those most in need of the material will not be exposed to it.

Section 1. An Introduction to Accounting and Financial Statement

We suggest emphasizing and raising the following in this first section:

1. What is the meaning of "debit"? "Credit"? Perhaps phrasing this, "which is better, a debit or a credit?" The answer of course is, like all good law school questions, "it depends." Debit and credit refer only to the left-side and right-side of the account; whether it is good or bad to have a debit (credit) depends on the particular account.

2. Students might be asked to verbalize what is the difference between the items on the left-hand (debit) side of the Tutt balance sheet and the right-hand side? In the case of Tutt, each of the items listed as an asset has a physical quality. Would this necessarily be a requirement for something to be deemed an asset? No, consider a license to use a patent. If you paid $500 for such a license and could use if for a year, would that be an asset? What we later see in the discussion of the "matching convention" is that an asset is an item recorded at its cost that is expected to contribute to future operations. What distinguishes every item on the right-hand side of the balance sheet is the lack of any physical character. Items whose normal balance is on the

rights side of the balance sheet are the sources by which the business used to acquire the assets listed on the left-hand side of the balance sheet. Thus, we have a rudimentary understanding of the balance sheet. It reflects items owned (albeit perhaps by borrowing to acquire the item) that are available to use in the operation of the business; it reflects the liabilities that have been incurred both to acquire assets and more generally in the operation of the business; and it reflects the owner's portion of the sources of funds committed to the business.

3. Why might we think of the balance sheet as a "snap shot" and the income statement as a "movie"? The balance sheet speaks as of a particular *date* and the income statement covers a *period* of time.

4. What is the difference between "Professional Income" and "Rent" as to Tutt? Which would he prefer to have more of?

5. Why don't we see Professional Income on the June 30th balance sheet ? What is the link between the income statement and the balance sheet? Why did Proprietorship increase from $1000 to $1525? The answers are that Professional Income is a component of measuring how well Tutt's practice did in June. The revenues of his business are Professional Income and he incurred several expenses to produce those revenues. When netted, Tutt came out ahead, and this adds to his ownership, equity, in the sole proprietorship. The net gain is the $525 increase.

6. What is the difference between cash and accrual basis accounting? Why does the latter have more judgment attached to it? Note here that accounting is not a science but filled with judgments, estimates and assumptions.

7. It may be good to ask a student to verbalize what is the meaning and purpose of matching expenses to revenue"? Why might we believe that the "assets" on the balance sheet can really be seen as expenditures waiting to be assigned as expenses to a later period? These questions go to the heart of accrual accounting: matching the expenditures (whether by paying cash or taking on debt) incurred with the revenues they generate. To illustrate, assume fiscal statements are prepared only on the calendar year basis. On July 1st, $12,000 is paid for 12 months of rent. How much of fiscal year A should be burdened by this and how much in fiscal year B? Similarly, what if a machine is acquired on July 1st and its expected life is 5 years. The firm paid $1000 cash and incurred a $4000 non-interest bearing note to pay for the machine. How much of this should be charged to year 19A? What happens to the amount that is not charged as an expense to 19A?

8. What is meant by the expression "revenue must be realized before it can be recognized"? This is the credo of the "realization convention" and it means that before we can record on the income statement a sale or professional income there must be shipment of the goods purchased or rendition of the services for which revenue is to be recorded. Thus, assume that a shoe store receives payment from a customer for a specially designed pair of shoes. Can it record the receipt as a "sale" and thus include the amount received among its revenues on its income statement? What if it had the shoes in stock but the customer paid for the shoes with a promissory note and not cash?

9. Students should be asked what is meant by the cost convention? Why not use fair market value instead of cost?

10. A review of the problem on inventory accounting is useful. If you wish a joke, try the old accounting joke: there are four methods of accounting for inventory: average, FIFO, LIFO and FISH (the latter, the hallmark of the failing firm, "first in, still here").

11. Emphasize that the illustrations involving depreciable assets and inventory reflect that there is a good deal of assumptions, judgments and estimates in reporting under GAAP.

It is useful to identify that the metrics of accounting are set by FASB and the regulation of auditors, at least for public reporting companies (and post Dodd-Frank registered broker-dealers) is by the PCAOB.

Section 2. Present Value: Its Utility and Calculation

A. Techniques of Determining Present Value

A reasonable place to begin is to ask a student why s/he would prefer $5 today compared to receiving $5 in a year. This gets into what s/he would consider as reasonable compensation for delaying a year and, more importantly, what considerations would inform the determination of what would be reasonable compensation for delaying receipt of the money. We can list a few: 1) forsaking current consumption (which would include opportunity costs of other investments of that sum, e.g., bank might pay 3% annually); 2) risk of non-payment, and 3) erosion of purchasing power of dollar via inflation. In combination, such factors form the discount rate, the amount by which the future payment is reduced to yield the present value of that future payment.

Next, you can move through what each of the three tables do: compound (interest on interest) interest to yield future value; present value of a future payment; and present value of an annuity (go idea to define an annuity). What is a perpetuity? **Note Errata, infra Page 13 of TM.**

From there, the problems can be used to demonstrate not just the mechanics of present value tables but more importantly the analysis that is needed to identify just what is going to be discounted.

Problem 1: The bond has a future value ($1000) and an 8-year annuity ($100 annually). Given a discount rate of 8 percent, the bond's present value is:

Terminal value at end of 8 years	.540	x	$1000=	$540
8-year annuity	5.747	x	100=	574.70
Present Value				$1,114.70

If the bond can be purchased for $1050, this would more than meet the investor's constraints, since an even greater return than the demanded 8 percent will be received. That is, with an 8 percent discount rate, the bond is worth $1,114.70 to the investor. Because the bond can be purchased for less than that amount, the investment is a good deal per the investor's assumption of an 8 percent discount rate.

Students need to be reminded that the most important part of the above calculation is identifying the timing and amount of future cash flows, plus determining an appropriate discount rate. As to the timing and amount, the maxim in finance is "cash is king" meaning that is what ultimately gets valued. In the problem, we determined the bond produces two cash streams: one yearly and one at the end of 8 years. There amounts are given and after that the balance is mechanical.

Problem 2:

Students can ask how to determine the overall cash flow of oil leases. It is 40 years at an estimated amount of $30,000 per year. This means the present value of the oil leases at the discount rate is as follows:

8.244 x $30,000 = $ 247,320

How then to calculate the charitable remainder? It would be the above figure less the present value of the ten years that the nephew is expected to live. The present value of the life estate is determined as follows:

5.650 x $30,000 = $ 169,500

Therefore, the value of the charitable remainder is $ 77,820 ($247,320 – 169,500). Students may be asked why the present value of the last thirty years of the oil leases is less than one-half the present value of their first ten years? This reflects the compounded effect (the opposite of compounding of interest) that takes its toll in the out years. Thus, one lesson that can be learned (aside from it being better to take the life estate over the balance of the annuity) is that it likely does not make a lot of sense to invest too much time worrying about the far out years when estimating future returns for a present value calculation. The near years, say 5 to 10 years, is what is important in this calculation's reliability.

B. Stock Valuation Model

There are many sophisticated models for pricing equity securities. For this primer we are content to introduce one of the simplest of the models, the capitalized earnings model where the expected (constant) earnings are divided by the appropriate capitalization rate. Students should be asked what the difference is meaning between a "discount" and "capitalization" rate. These terms are, to be sure, used interchangeably, but technically the former is for a finite, and the latter for an infinite, return.

Section 3.   What Is Risk and Diversification

Students can be asked how the comparison between Investment A and B explains the meaning of risk? Risk refers to variance, not expected return (the latter being the average of outcomes with each potential outcome weighted by the probability of it occurring). Such variance can be mathematically measured and this is captured in the standard deviation calculation (see this reference made in the following excerpt). Students can then be asked why it is important in valuing a future payment to know its risk? Simply put, this is done to adjust the compensation for the uncertainty of receiving the future payment. Using the *Joy v. North* examples, students can be asked which is the better investment? It is not possible to answer this question because we don't know their respective returns. That is, while Investment A is riskier, its return should be higher, and if high enough to compensate the investor for the risk of its acquisition, may appropriately be preferred over the less risky Investment B. These are matters of judgment. Hence, in the real world, if one is complaining about improvident decision-making by managers, we might ask whether courts or managers should be the arbiters whether Investment A provides sufficient rewards to merit its acquisition? This seems to be the essence of the business judgment rule, discussed later in the casebook.

What then do we learn from the Jackson, et.al. excerpt? It builds on the thought that is in the background of the preceding discussion, namely that investors demand a higher return for higher risk securities. What appears to be related to risk aside from return? It is firm size, namely that smaller firms are more risky than larger ones (likely reflecting that bigger firms likely have multiple products/revenue streams that are uncorrelated, i.e., big firms are themselves diversified).

What then does this excerpt have to do with the expression, "don't put all your eggs in one basket?" This is the point emphasized in the celebrated Markowitz article, namely that risk can be reduced by diversification, so that this ultimately procures returns that are higher, but less risky overall. Note the statistics about how truly very little diversification can reduce substantially portfolio variance.

What then are the insights of the Capital Asset Pricing Model (CAPM)? It really tells us that the *expected* return for any security is the combination of the risk free rate (short-term government T bills), plus a premium for risk. The latter is made up of two components: the degree to which macro-economic forces influence the individual firm's return (stock price change plus dividends paid over a discrete time period) and the random developments within that firm's operations. The former is referred to as systematic risk and the latter to unsystematic or firm-specific risk. Theory holds that diversification can eliminate the influence of unsystematic risk. Thus, what is important in investing on a portfolio basis is not the total risk of a security being considered to be added to the portfolio, but rather that security's Beta, the measurement of how its return moves with the market as a whole, so we can assess its impact on the overall risk of the portfolio. More precisely, on a portfolio basis, the relevance of an individual stock is its impact on the overall Beta of the portfolio.

Corporations and Other Business Organizations

We thus believe the students should carry away from this subsection of the materials the following:

1. What is Beta? It can and is observed, being the co-movement of a particular stock's return against a market (e.g., S&P Industrial 500 Index);

2. Risk is driven by market-wide (systematic risk) and firm-specific events (unsystematic risk);

3. Diversification cannot rid the security of risk, but is a strategy to minimize/eliminate the unsystematic component of risk; and

4. CAPM is a tool widely used to capture/isolate developments that influence the return of an individual firm (this is illustrated in the readings with the example focusing on the sale of a plant). Thus, in later readings, when reference is made to a firm's having higher or lower returns if they incorporate in Delaware, are the target of takeovers, or are the target of shareholder proposals, the tool used is the CAPM since there is a need to remove market-wide effects on the return and focus only on the phenomenon/event being studied.

Section 4.   Market Efficiency: The Hypothesis and Qualifications

An understandable way to begin teaching the Efficient Market Hypothesis (EMH) is how the hypothesis came to be formed. The long-ignored study of a statistician showed that stock prices were random. That is, one could not mathematically predict Thursday's stock price by the pattern, changes, etc. of stock prices in the days or weeks preceding Thursday. Thus, what could explain such a "random walk?" Random Walk was the first name given to the so-called weak-form of market efficiency (holding that one cannot extrapolate future stock prices from past stock prices).

The hypothesis for such a random relationship, namely that stock prices for any security were independent of each other over some observed period of time, was that 1) stock prices respond (change in response) to economically significant information and 2) that the response is rapid (otherwise we would observe price dependence not independence between Wednesday's price and Thursday's price). These are the joint tenants of the semi-strong form of market efficiency. Empiricists spent much of the late 60s and the entire 70s observing (via event studies built on the Capital Asset Pricing Model) stock prices to test these two components of market efficiency. They produced a wealth of information that prices of larger capitalization firms do respond to economically significant information, and that the stock prices embed the price change fairly rapidly, or at least quick enough that on average a trader obtaining such information could not on average earn an above market rate (risk-adjusted) rate of return by trading only on information that was publicly available.

There are, of course, degrees of efficiency. This all depends on the depth of the market, the presence of institutional investors, and most importantly how closely a particular security is followed by analysts or others who have the ear of big traders whose choices can move the security's price.

12

Students can be asked whether, in a world in which markets were efficient in the strong form, there would be wide-spread call to regulate inside trading? Not likely, as those trading on non-public information cannot be deemed to have earned any advantage by their knowledge and use of that information, since the stock price would have already reflected the information. No serious support exists for the proposition that markets are efficient in the strong form.

But the EMH stands substantially qualified by the fact that there is lots of evidence that trading is not always driven by rationality, but sometimes trading reflects simplifying heuristics, moods, fads, and the like. Thus, there is evidence that markets are noisy, meaning there are lots of imperfections in the pricing of securities. Thus, not all markets are sufficiently deep to attract institutional investors; hence, the trading by such large investor is not present to move rapidly a security's price. Their absence means the absence of analysts as well. Moreover, even in deep markets, arbitrage may not always be engaged in to the full extent necessary to correct a bubble; who would have wished to bet against Google, Apple, or (earlier) Netscape when their prices were in the stratosphere. Most importantly, whether retail or professional trader, the readings point out that human beings suffer from a number of cognitive biases (over confidence, conservative failure to update beliefs, and framing) that impede pure, or even functional, rationality.

We also need to observe that saying that a price is determined in an efficient market talks about the market price reflecting not homogeneous. but heterogeneous, expectations regarding its risk and return characteristics. This means that the security's price responds to information, and does so rapidly, but the result is not say that the price so reflected is the intrinsic value of the security. That is, evidence that a stock responds quickly to the release of financially significant information refers to the *informational* efficiency of the market. To go to the next step, which few economists do, and for which there is negligible support, and assert that the price of security reflects its intrinsic value is referred to as *fundamental* efficiency.

Errata:

At page 40 of Unabridged (page 35 of Concise) Edition, the denominator of the present value formula should be $(1 + .05)$ and $(1 + .08)^{20}$, respectively, and not $(1 + 1.05)$ and $1 = 1.08)^{20}$, respectively.

Chapter 3

Partnerships

Chapter Overview: Practices vary widely across professors regarding how much time to devote to the partnership sector of the study of business organizations. While LLC's are the entity of choice for small businesses, the casualness of the partnership, as well as professional limitations that exist in some states that foreclose professionals from forming other entities, support the view that partnerships are with us, if not ubiquitous. Thus, one can allocate as few as two and as many as 5 plus class periods to this sector of the material. Related to the time allocation and what material to cover is just how deeply you believe your class should press into the UPA and RUPA as well as the RULPA. Each of these forays demand time, given the challenges many students have with statutory materials. Among the cases in the materials a mild - to - strong preference among them are: *Lupien v. Malsbenden* (casual formation of partnership), *Summers v. Dooley* and/or *Sanchez v. Saylor* (management of partnership), *Northmon Investment Co. v. Milford Plaza Assoc.* (partner's authority), *Bauer v. Blomfield Co.*(rights of assignee of partner's interests), *Meinhard v. Salmon* (fiduciary duties among partners), *Creel v. Lilly* or *McCormick v. Brevig* (whether dissolution compels liquidation), *Page v. Page* (introduction to potential freeze out via dissolution), *Drashner v. Sorenson* and *Crutcher v. Smith* (wrongful dissolution), *Gateway Potato Sales v. G.B. Investment Co.*(limited partner who participate in business), *In re USACafes, L.P. Litigation*(responsibility of directors of corporate general partner), *Gotham Partners, LP v. Hallwood Realty Partners, LP.*(private ordering for fiduciary obligations) and *Ederer v. Gursky* (liability of limited liability partners).

Section 1.   What Constitutes a General Partnership

Hilco Property Services, Inc. v. United States

Why would it be good public policy that the parties' subjective intent should not matter in deciding whether they have formed a partnership? Just what does this statement in *Hilco Partners* mean? This is the one form of business organization studied in the course for which a filing with the state is not required for its existence. By comparison, the corporation or LLC is not, "whoops, you mean we're a corporation? A LLC?" Because the partnership lacks any required formalities or governmental filings for its creation, but nonetheless a body of principles and norms (some default, some not) accompany a partnership, the issues are bigger than the individual parties' intent. For example, one norm is that partners have liability for the debts of the enterprise. Thus, third-party interests are implicated by whether an organization is a partnership or not. As such, the issues are, as stated earlier, bigger than the individual parties' intentions. Note that the intent that is relevant is not whether they intend to be partners or participants in a partnership; rather it is the intent to do those things that qualify the organization as a partnership, e.g., carrying on as coowners for profit.

Martin v. Peyton

Before getting into the somewhat complicated facts, you might wish to address the easier part of the case; why is it important whether this is or is not a partnership, and, if it is a partnership, who are its partners? It appears the firm, K N and K failed and that Mr. Martin is seeking personal liability from Peyton on the grounds that Peyton was a partner of the firm.

Now the deal. K N & K was a brokerage and trading firm. Apparently it was not very good at trading. It experienced losses due to speculation. Peyton, Perkins and Freeman, lent $2.5 million in securities to K N & K (receiving as security more speculative securities which could not, as with the lent securities, be used for collateral for K N & K may advance for bank loans to keep itself afloat). Peyton et. al. annually were to receive 40 percent of the K N & K profits (but not less than $100,000 and not more than $500,000). They also had the option to join the firm. There were various protective covenants in the arrangement, including that securities could only be sold with the consent of Peyton and Freeman (labeled trustees) and that the firm would always maintain the securities separately and at a value that would support loans of $2 million). Up to this point the court sees all this as pure lending arrangement.

The court concluded it was still a lending arrangement with the provision designating that Hall would direct the management of K N & K and that he would be covered by a life insurance policy with the trustees as beneficiaries.

Also, not surprising that as a loan the trustees extracted the right to be kept advised of business and had the right to inspect the firm's books.

Most troubling was the trustees' power to veto activities deemed speculative or injurious. This too appears related to protecting the value of their loan.

Similarly, the limitations on draws made by each partner and the security interest the trustees had in each partner's share of the firm were also related to their status as a creditor and not as an owner.

Note that the real control over improvident behavior was the resignation that each partner was required to give; indirectly this was significant power over partners' conduct. But the court did not find this .

As we look back on this, these were protective provisions. That is, they appear to address the risks that K N & K would return to its old speculative ways. These do not appear provisions designed to increase profitability as much as to prevent loss due to speculation. As such, they are creditor based and not profit maximization based.

Lupien v. Malsbenden

How is Mr. Lupien like Mr. Martin? Each are unsatisfied creditors of a failed business. Lupien had advanced funds to Cragin, doing business as York Motor Mart, to have Cragin

16

assemble a kit car, a Bradley. Cragin disappears. Malsbenden had loaned Cragin $85,000 interest free to finance Cragin's assembly of Bradleys with the expectation he would be repaid from the sale of each Bradley.

Note here the contrast with *Martin*. There is no governor on the amount Malsbenden is to be paid or for that matter any minimum that was to be paid. The open-ended nature is more consistent with an investment than a loan. Note we don't see the protective provisions that we saw in *Martin*.

Moreover, the record supported court's conclusion that Malsbenden had not only the right to participate in control of the business but actually did participate in control i.e., Cragin skipped town. He opened the business, stayed there, and ordered parts. This is not how most creditors operate. Note also that there was a representation issue here as Lupien dealt with Malsbenden on several occasions.

Here you might wish to walk the students through both UPA § 6(a) and RUPA § 202 focusing on how the facts support each of the elements for defining a partnership.

Thus, the court concludes there was "co ownership" here via the evidence of control exhibited by Malsbenden.

Note on the Formation of Partnerships

The note makes the point that cases calling for the four elements-profit sharing, loss sharing, mutual right to control and community of interest may overstate what is required and that these are relevant areas of inquiry but not necessary elements to conclude there is a partnership. Thus, courts find a partnership even though management is delegated to a single person, reasoning that the delegation was evidence that the partner at least once had the authority but then delegated it

Section 2.   The Legal Nature of a Partnership

Note on the Legal Nature of a Partnership: Entity or Aggregate Status

To begin the discussion we might as why it matters in drafting a partnership statute whether a partnership enjoys entity or aggregate status? If it is not an entity, then the statute needs to address questions such as 1) how does the partnership hold property, 2) convey property it owns, 3) sue or be sued, and 4) enter into contracts. As a logical proposition, if it is not accorded entity-like features in the statute, then each of these would have to occur via the signatures of all the partners. With entity status, then those authorized to act on behalf of the partnership can enter into these transactions in the name of the partnership.

As the Note explains, the UPA has a good deal of awkwardness due to its somewhat schizophrenic history of changing reporters with two very different views of this question. The RUPA accords the partnership entity status and as the readings point out this simplified the drafting. It does still have some aggregate like qualities, such as its imposition of individual liability on partners (a result that is inconsistent with according the partnership an existence distinct from its owners).

Section 3.   The Ongoing Operation of Partnerships

A.   Management

Summers v. Dooley

With two equal partners, equal divisions of opinion are inevitable. But what makes this one reach a level that drives the party to sue, alleging breach of fiduciary duty? The decision was really whether to expand the work force from two to three. Each partner was to work in the trash collection business; Dooley became unable and per the written agreement provided at his expense a replacement. Summers believed they were still understaffed and hired a third person (after himself and Dooley's stand in) to work and then sued Dooley to recover his part of the sum paid to this third person.

How does the court resolve the matter? Would this be resolved differently under UPA § 18(h) or RUPA § 401(j)? No, each provide for ordinary business decisions this requires approval by a majority of the partners, unless the partnership agreement provides otherwise. What if one partner held 60 percent of the equity? It is by partner not partner's interest so you would still have an even division regardless of how insignificant the percentage ownership interest of the smaller partner. Thus, one lesson to draw is that in drafting a partnership agreement do the parties wish to have their management according to the default rule?

What would make this decision be one that required unanimity? Under RUPA it is one in contravention of the agreement? The Note on the Management of Partnerships points out that the "partnership agreement" at least under RUPA includes not just the initial partnership agreement entered into when it was organized but any explicit or implicit agreements after that time can be intended by the parties to supplement or even modify the partnership agreement.

Returning to the facts of *Summers*, what advice do we have for Summers since he lost this case (and gets stuck with the full cost of the newly hired employee)? His choices are likely not that good. He could just stay the course and deal with the work load that calls for a third person. Another option is to quit and proceed to dissolution discussed later in the materials.

Sanchez v. Saylor

Note the prior case focused on how decisions are made within the partnership. Here the dispute was how a partner, Sanchez, made a personal decision, namely refusing to provide personal financial statements in connection with a bank's condition for loaning money to the partnership. The court makes an analogy to *Covalt v. High* which is similar to *Summers* in that one equal partner refused to approve raising the rent charged to CSI, a firm in which he owned 75 percent.

First, we might question whether these are analogous situations? Saylor charged that Sanchez's refusal to provide the financial statements was a breach of his fiduciary duty. As mentioned earlier at the end of Note on the Legal Nature of Partnership: Entity or Aggregate

Status, partners owe fiduciary duties to their other partners. These are broadly duties of care and loyalty. We might possibly reason that there could be no breach of duty by Sanchez if he could easily have vetoed the loan as one of the firm's two partners. The case for him doing so is that he had personal reasons, likely, for not providing his personal financial statements. The personal stake was even stronger for High in *Covalt* since he opposed raising the rent to a firm that he had a 75 percent interest. This may well strike us as acting out of self interest, conduct that certainly is included within the duty of loyalty. But if acceptable there, it should at least be acceptable under the facts of *Sanchez.*

Both cases have some disquiet to themselves as each appear to support the position that decisions by partners can be made out of self interest even if that self interest harms the partnership. To be sure, decisions by partners will be guided by informed self interest; but should not they also be guided by that self interest not harming the partnership or its partners? To this end, the court may have just kicked that can down the road by suggesting, not too subtly, that Saylor's remedy is to seek the firm's dissolution rather than pursue a breach of fiduciary duty claim.

Note on the Management of Partnerships

Important points, made earlier in this section of the Teachers' Manual, are that the default rules governing partnership management can be changed by the partnership agreement. Note as well that the partnership agreement is something of an evergreen agreement in that it includes explicit and implicit understandings reached after the original partnership agreement was made. Thus, the partnership agreement can have implied agreements, not just those memorialized in the written agreement.

An important point is the role of UPA § 18(e) and RUPA § 401(f) in preventing rump sessions by, for example, three of the four partners to reach a decision. All partners, subject to the agreement providing to the contrary, are entitled to be consulted; this does not mean you have to accede to their opinion, but you can't just bypass the partner.

Note on What Law Governs the Internal Affairs of Partnerships

As will be seen in Chapter 4, Section 1, the internal affairs of corporations are governed by the law of the state of incorporation. Partnerships, because there is no filing, do not follow this internal affairs choice of law rule. RUPA § 106 provides the choice-of-law rule for internal affairs for a partnership is the law where its chief executive office is located.

B. Indemnification and Contribution

As the Note points out, partners who pay a partnership debt have a right to *indemnification* from the *partnership.* In contrast, a partner who pays more than his proportionate ownership share of a judgment or debt for which all partners are liable can obtain *contribution* from each of the *other partners* for their proportionate share.

C.   Distributions, Remuneration, and Capital Contributions

Absent a contrary provision in the partnership agreement, losses and gains are divided equally among the partners; their "share" is therefore not determined by their relative capital investments.

D.   Capital Accounts and Draws

For future lawyers, many expecting to join firms, it is important to know what a "draw" is. The materials in this excerpt also illustrate what it means to have an equity account, namely that gains and losses of the business flow to the residual claimant, the holder of equity. The illustration also makes clear the point discussed in Chapter 2, regarding accounting. Accounting is a means of assigning costs to revenues and is generally based on historical cost. Thus, value frequently does not align with accounting-generated numbers, as illustrated in the examples in the excerpt.

Klein, Coffee & Partnoy Excerpt

The excerpt is a very understandable discussion of the impact of gains and losses on the individual partner's capital accounts. You may be well advised to assign this excerpt in connection with *Farnsworth v. Deaver*, in Section 8, where the role of capital accounts plays a prominent result in resolving the issue before the court.

Section 4.   The Authority of a Partner

RNR Investments Limited Partnership v. Peoples First Community Bank

RNR involved a limited partnership in which the partnership agreement expressly limited the authority of the general partner to incur indebtedness to a certain percentage above the construction budget that was approved by the limited partners. The general partner borrowed $990,000, but the authorized amount was only about $650,000. The loan is unpaid and the bank is seeking foreclose. The limited partners, seeking to cut their losses on a project that apparently went south, argue that the general partner lacked authority so the bank cannot collect the full sum due, but only the amount for which the general partner had authority to borrow.

Students should understand that the limited partners are not fearing personal liability on this debt; they are, after all, limited which students can, even at this stage of the materials, understand they are different from Mr. Malsbenden in *Lupien*. The limited partners' simply wish to reduce the claim that the bank can make in foreclosing on the property, so that their remainder interest in the partnership is larger.

Why were the limited partners not successful? This issue invites review of the language of UPA § 9(1) vs. RUPA § 301. The following Note on the Authority of a Partner makes clear that the latter resolves the ambiguity of the former, by making it explicit that apparent authority is based on the ordinary business of *the* partnership as well as the ordinary business *of the kind* carried out by the partnership. Thus, the partnership is more at risk under RUPA for acts of its partners.

Why are we consulting UPA or RUPA for a limited partnership? This issue is addressed in footnote 7 of the case, which points out that the limited partnership act defers to partnership default rules except where there is a conflict.

Students may be asked what would be the relevance in litigating *RNR Investment* if the property to be developed was in Palm Beach versus the rural panhandle of Florida? The idea behind this question is what would support a factual determination that a loan of $990,000 negotiated by a general partner is more likely usual, i.e., ordinary business, where land values are higher than where they are lower.

Under RUPA what would prevent the bank from asserting that the full $990,000 was within the general partners' authority? RUPA § 301(1) requires that the bank either "knew" or had notification of the limits on the partner's authority. Knew and notice are in turn defined in RUPA § 102(1). The excerpt from the article by Weidner and Larson allows discussion of the public policy surrounding placing the burden of a partner acting outside the scope of her actual authority on the partnership. The practice RNR should have followed is that authorized by RUPA § 303 whereby at least for real estate transactions, such as that in *RNR Investment*, filing of a limitation of authority in the registry for land-title recordings is binding on the third party. In this case, the bank lacked such knowledge or notice and the opportunistic claims of the limited partners are defeated.

Northmon Investment Company v. Milford Plaza Associates

This case is different from *RNR Investment,* although each involve claims of a partner acting outside the scope of the partners' actual authority. In *Northmon* the claim is among partners (but could clearly impact the third party) namely that their partnership was for a term so that the 99-year lease, well in excess of the partnership's term, entered into by one of the partners was not binding on the others. This poses the interesting question whether the third party, if in the same position as the bank in *RNR Investment*, could still assert a right to a 99-year lease? We might read this opinion as holding that the third party, not before the court, could not succeed in arguing there was apparent authority since a 99-year lease cannot be deemed ordinary would this not assume that the third party would have reason to believe that the partnership was for a term less than 99 years? But this is not difficult to imagine given the fragility of partnerships. Does this mean that leasing, even for say 2 years, would not be ordinary since if it is a partnership at will it might be terminated at any time?

Section 5.   Liability for Partnership Obligations

Davis v. Loftus

So, what's it mean to make partner at the law firm? This may well depend, as this case points out, on the meaning of "partner," because it might not be the type of relationship covered by the UPA/RUPA. That is "income partners" or "non-equity" partners are not owners and, as illustrated in the case, are not bound on partnership debts. While having less upside, presumably such a status has no appreciable downside.

We might wonder how persuasive is the court's reasoning that in this firm "income partners" were not partners in the sense covered by the act? Their income was not apparently fixed to a significant extent, but also included a bonus which on the presumably varied somewhat not just with their performance but the performance of the firm. On the other hand, this type of compensation is often used for ordinary employees. To be sure, upon any winding up any surplus would not be shared with an income partner as it would with other partners. All this suggests limits on but these are also consistent with agreement among partners how to divide the pie. The court strikes pay dirt when it observes that at the firm the income partners had not voted whatever on the management and conduct of the business. This is compelling in concluding that they were not partners.

Note on Liability for Partnership Obligations

You might wish to begin generally by asking why does it matter whether a partner's liability is joint or joint and several. The answer is captured in the note material: where liability is only joint, then subject to special statutory procedures (e.g., Joint Debtor Statutes), the creditor needs to proceed after all those who are jointly liable and may not pursue only the most conveniently reached joint obligor.

Note also the exhaustion rule in RUPA § 307(a) for creditors pursuing a partner on a *partnership* liability.

Section 6. Partnership Interests and Partnership Property

Rapoport v. 55 Perry Co.

Both the UPA and RUPA provide, as a default rule, that consent of all the partners is necessary for the transferred to become a partner. Students may be asked why the default rule is that a transfer does not confer partnership status absent consent of all the other partners? The answer is that partnerships are consensual arrangements and their formation leads to mutual obligations among the partners. Moreover, because the default rules are that all partners are entitled to participate in management and that each partner has apparent authority with respect to partnership business, as a practical matter it matters to the partners who their partners are. In combination, it is not surprisingly that one cannot become a partner in an existing partnership merely by a transfer of an existing partnership interest.

That consent, however, can be in advance, such as authorizing a transfer to carry with it partnership status. That was the issue before the court in *Rapoport*, but a majority of the court concluded the partnership agreement was not ambiguous in providing that the transferee did not become a partner. Note here the language in their agreement: "No partner . . . shall . . . transfer . . . his . . . share in this firm, nor enter into any agreement as a result of which any person shall become interested with him in this firm." Query, could this language be read broadly enough to have proscribed even a transfer of a financial interest in the firm that did not rise to the level of partnership? This language does seem fairly broad prohibition. Note the transferee does succeed to economic rights, but has no managerial rights.

Bauer v. Blomfield Co.

Here we consider the rights of an assignee, not a person claiming to be a partner. The assignee, Bauer, held an interest in the partnership as a security interest for a loan he had made to two partners, the Holdens. Bauer now sues alleging bad faith in partnership paying an $877,000 commission to another partner, Blomfield, in connection with Blomfield arranging a lease by the state of property owned by the partnership. A companion settlement covered a variety of claims against the state that Blomfield had. The arrangement likely did benefit the partnership and some compensation to Blomfield was in order. As the dissent points out, the amount paid could be seen as being so excessive as to constitute intentional unfairness against Bauer.

What then separates the majority from the dissenters? This is the reasoning in footnote 2 of the majority, namely stating that the duty of good faith and fair dealing owed to partners does not extend to assignees. In contrast, the dissent makes the point that there are duties of good faith and fair dealing that flow from contractual relationships. This is not a fiduciary duty but the view in contract law that one party cannot use its powers under a contract to destroy an expressly contracted benefit of the other party. As pointed out in note 2 of the dissent, under the UPA (as well as RUPA) an assignee has a right to seek dissolution; this is a check on abuse by the majority. This right may weigh against a contract right of good faith; we might conclude this right supplants the good faith contract remedy. But apparently it was questionable whether an assignee could obtain dissolution under the Alaska statute which gives all the more reason to uphold the contract-based argument. The dissent also raises the question whether there was any persuasive evidence that 5% was an appropriate commission level: since the state was already a tenant it might not be reasonable to believe this was the level of commission a third-party broker would have extracted. And the dissent makes the point that Blomfield, not Bauer, had the burden of proof since Blomfield is the moving party seeking summary judgment.

Query, would the Holdens still be voting members in the partnership? Yes, per RUPA § 503(d).

Note on Partnership Property

Students can be asked why it matters to a creditor whether Blackacre is partnership property or a partner's property that is being used by the partnership. We might begin by asking who is a debtor to the creditor? This goes to the material in the next note related to the relative rights of creditors of partners and creditors of the partnership. But the point is that if Blackacre is partnership property, then control of Blackacre and claims to Blackacre must flow through the partnership. The issue also gets tied up in the entity – aggregate distinction and as the Note makes clear, RUPA by embracing the entity approach deals more cleanly with rights with respect to partnership property than does the "smoke and mirrors" approach taken in the UPA through the lens of "tenancy in partnership."

Note on Partnership Interests

There is a wealth of information in this Note. You may wish to observe that while "dual priorities" or "jingle" rule is dead under the Bankruptcy Act and RUPA, in a state with only the

UPA, the rule survives in state insolvency proceedings, so that creditors of a partnership may be disfavored as against the creditors of the partner.

Section 7.   The Partner's Duty of Loyalty

Meinhard v. Salmon

This is a classic case and allows a broad discussion of a range of questions related to fiduciary obligations. The factual setting is fairly straightforward. Gerry leased the Hotel Brisol to Salmon for twenty years. The vision was to convert the hotel to shops and office space. Meinhard then entered into an agreement with Salmon to provide half the funds needed for the project, and they agreed to how profits and losses were to be distributed - ultimately being fifty-fifty. Near the end of the lease, with less than 4 months remaining, Gerry approached Salmon with a deal where much of the property around the former Hotel Bristol site as well as that site would be razed and replaced with more modern structure, to cost $3 million. The existing buildings could remain unchanged for 7 years but then the rental would jump seven to eight fold. Salmon jumped on the deal, never told Meinhard about it, and now Meinhard wants in.

This case's prominence may be due Cardozo's classic and much-cited prose. It also can be due the somewhat problematic conclusions reached with that prose. But reasonable minds can differ, so apologies for some of the questions poked about the case in this analysis.

A place to begin is what makes the parties' arrangement a joint venture rather than a partnership? This is a point that underlies the difference in result reached by Andrews, who would not have dissented if this were a partnership. We might believe this is joint venture because Meinhard and Salmon were not looking for multiple projects, but only to co-venture in the conversion and management of the Bristol Hotel property for 20 years. But why is this not like a partnership for 20 year term? It may again be that it was the single-focus on the Bristol Hotel property.

Now, if the arrangement was a joint venture, then how do we reach the idea that Salmon misbehaved when his conduct extended to properties that, while including the former Bristol Hotel location, were in addition to the Bristol Hotel location?

Cardozo admits that if the prospect was, say, in Brooklyn or Queens, there would be no problem. So, why is this geography so important if the property is not the same identical property as the current one?

Also, why doesn't the twenty-year lease not also set the term for their partnership? That is, although the new deal was within the twenty-year term, it would begin only at the end of that term. Could we not conclude that the parties implicitly understood their relationship was limited to this deal during this term, and not to some future deal for this and other property for another term?

What is the relative skills of each of the parties? Does this question matter? Salmon appears to be a real estate mogul of sorts and Meinhard was a money guy. Do we really expect that if this arrangement were negotiated by Citibank that the same result would have been reached?

Hoe likely is it that the parties would have agreed to ex ante regarding future deals? This questions appears problematic in supporting the result reached by Cardozo.

So, what was the breach and how great a burden would it be to comply with what Cardozo thinks should have been done? The breach was Salmon's failure to disclose the offer to Meinhard; it does not appear that Cardozo is holding that they would then have a duty to form a partnership to exploit this together: what about the burden? Well, the burden of informing Meinhard of the proposed deal would not have been great, but could have led to competitive bidding between Meinhard and Salmon (each putting together their own teams of eager developers). But would this be so bad? We might believe it robs Salmon of the benefits of his entrepreneurial activity. But wait, this is not as if he believes there is gold in the Sierras and is obliged to announce it to the world. This is a case where Salmon had no search activity at all; rather the deal fell into his lap thanks to his on-going contract with Gerry. That said, would it not have been in Gerry's interest to see competitive bidding? But why should we care about him? If he can't figure out how to maximize his gains why should the law help him and disfavor Salmon?

In the end, it appears the outcome here does not lead to norms that incent productive behavior but in fact discourage the Salmons of the world to bring in passive investors.

That said, if you do have a fiduciary relationship, a basic requirement is that of candor, at least relative to issues connected to that relationship. What seems in doubt in *Meinhard* was whether the offer/deal with Gerry was connected to that relationship. None of the quibbles above are inconsistent with this statement so we can leave the case with beautiful prose, rarely seen in decisions today, and with an understanding that if we have a partnership partners have a duty of candor to each other on matters germane to that partnership.

Latta v. Kilbourn

The quote/dicta provides something of a laundry list of the fiduciary duties commonly associated with being a partner.

Enea v. Superior Court

You may wish to begin discussion of this case by first reviewing RUPA § 404 and particularly the limited areas for the "duty of loyalty" in subsection (b), along with the Hillman, Vestal and Weidner excerpt. To this end, note RUPA § 103(b)(3) authorizes private ordering and this would be particularly useful in addressing ex ante how to deal opportunities (a la *Meinhard*). Note in § 404(d) there is a non-fiduciary duty to act in good faith and fair dealing. This appears to mean that a claim based only on a breach of a duty of good faith or fair dealing, and nothing else, is foreclosed. But this may just mean it cannot be asserted as free standing fiduciary duty claim, but is a condition associated with the contractual relationship among partners and with partners to the firm so that when they do exercise their rights per the statute or partnership agreement and do not do so in good faith or fair dealing, then they have been in breach of that statutory or contractual provision. Note finally that § 103(b)(5) allows "good faith" and "fair dealing" to be defined but not eliminated. Students need to appreciate that states vary widely in their own approaches to § 404.

What is the claim in *Enea*? It is that the partnership is renting its sole assets to one of the partners, William Daniels, at below-market rates. Daniels apparently wants to camp out in this space until he retires and has argued that the understanding in the partnership was ultimate gain on disposition of the property and not income via rent prior to that time.

Note too that California is among the numerous states that modify RUPA by treating the three listed areas of duty of loyalty as illustrative, but not exclusive.

Note that the case actually helps us understand a bit about the scope of the enumerated statements of the duty of loyalty, as the court points to this conduct easily fitting into § 404(b)(1). You may wish to ask a student how this exactly fits within that set of facts, just to sharpen everyone's focus on what is proscribed.

Defendant then moves to invoke the provision that acting in one's self interest is not a breach. This issue is discussed in the Hillman, Vestal and Weidner excerpt. The court deals with this by sensibly concluding, and likely narrowing the provision, that, without more, there is no harm from acting in one's self interest. So read, it might be concluded that if this is indeed the intent of § 404(e) that it likely did not clarify anything since we normally expect partners to act to advance their own interest, as that is not inconsistent with the interests of the firm or its other partners.

Section 8.   Dissolution (I): Dissolution By Rightful Election

There are a lot of moving parts to partnership dissolution and several days could be devoted to the material in Sections 8 and 9. That likely is not a wise use of scarce time in the course. In Section 8 you may wish to give priority treatment to either *Creel* or *McCormick* (issue of whether to order buyout as opposed to liquidation), *Farnsworth* (settling up capital accounts on winding up), and *Page* (opportunistic use of dissolution), and adding all or most of the note material for background.

Girard Bank v. Haley

The case correctly interprets UPA §§31(1)(b) and 38(a), namely, that in a partnership at will a partner can withdraw, and with impunity, at any time. Hence, the meaning of "at will." Note that RUPA § 602 expressly provides that a partner can dissociate at any time. As will be seen, there are different consequences depending on whether the withdrawal is wrongful or rightful. But the bottom line is that partnerships are fragile. The partnership agreement can contract around this fragility, but as we've seen, many partnerships are casually entered into so that private ordering is not practicable. Thus, the default rules are important and ought to make sense. The focus of the first few cases tests that question.

Creel v. Lilly

The cause of dissolution was the death of Joseph Creel, the namesake of "Joe's Racing." UPA § 31(4). Similarly, RUPA §601(7)(I). Note, partnerships are consensual and with the aggregate view, the departure of a partner means that partnership is over, i.e., dissolved. Here Creel's two partners continued the business for a while, produced an inventory of the company's assets, mainly inventory (NASCAR memorabilia), and offered to pay the decedent's widow her fair share of that value based on an evaluation of an accountant. Mrs. Creel was invited to use her own accountant to value the partnership assets. Why was not this within the UPA?

Could the two remaining partners continue to run the store after Joe's death? Yes, this is provided for in UPA §33, which allows continuation for the purpose of winding up. Broader authority exists in the limited instance, set forth in UPA §34, in which the partners are unaware of the death of the partner. Note that UPA § 42 does not appear to apply here since the continuation was not pursuant to the authority covered in UPA § 41.

So what did the decedent's widow want? She wanted to have the firm sell its assets; she did not want to have the value of her interest determined by calculations. Why did they not sell the assets? Well, they are continuing the business under a new name and were fearful that a sale would be a "fire sale" and they would not realize the full value of the assets. But does that assume that the assets would be sold piecemeal and not as unit? Why not just have a sale, publish the event, and likely they would be the only bidders and bid the same price as the accountant determined. This reduces the law to a hollow ritual and likely introduces some transaction costs. The appeal of the liquidation sale is the market check on the insiders' calculation of the amount the withdrawing partner is entitled.

Note that the court is applying the UPA, but given that Maryland had recently adopted RUPA, makes a policy choice, apparently in conflict with the UPA per the above analysis, based on RUPA's provisions, which clearly allow continuation of the business and a buyout in this instance. This conclusion flows, somewhat backhandedly, by §801 identifies when there must be a winding up. There are many events identified there, but none is the death of a partner. Section §601(7)(I) identifies death as an event giving rise to dissociations. So we have a dissociation and under §701 the remaining partners can continue the business without liquidating it.

Was this an easy case, given that the two continuing parties made their offer within six or seven weeks of Joe's death? What if it were two years later? With the analogy to RUPA we would see that receipt of a demand for payment by the widow begins a 120 day period. Note there appears to be no time period within which payment must be made.

A final point in the case is the case is whether the profits made by the successor to Joe's Racing must be shared with the Joe's widow? The answer is no, because the court saw that as an entirely different business, having been persuaded that Joe's Racing ceased business when the lease on its location ended, August 31, six weeks after Joe's death.

Disotell v. Stiltner

At the introduction to the block quote reflects, the case presented the same issue as in *Creel* and the court came out at the same location. The case does contain some specifics missing in *Creel*, such as the party's estimate of the cost to liquidate and the additional reasoning that there may be no buyers. The obvious concern is that if there is a buyout do you want the courts to be available to referee the price in the likely event the parties disagree. That is, just what leverage does the withdrawing party have to make sure the continuing parties, who sit on the assets and gain little by transferring a bunch of cash to the withdrawing partner, will negotiate in good faith? Is the court prepared to police this? Or does its approach in both *Creel* and *Disotell* suggest benign neglect?

McCormick v. Brevig

This dissociation is different from the prior cases because it is a result of judicial order. Review of the possible bases for judicial dissolution in Section 801(5) would give the students a flavor of what is required for the court to take this extraordinary step. On the bare allegations of this case, one can speculate that any one of the three grounds set forth in the subsection were applicable.

The issue here is whether the disgruntled partner can compel a liquidation when the court has ordered dissolution of the partnership. This is broadly the same issue as in *Creel*, but it arises on a different ground for dissolution than *Creel*.

Thus, it is clear from the statute, Montana's version of RUPA, that when there is a judicial decree of dissolution the firm is to be wound up. RUPA § 801(5) is similarly worded. Thus, the statute answers the question and notice that *Creel* was somewhat different for another reason as the court was working with a partnership governed by the dead hand of the UPA, as the legislature had recently adopted RUPA and the language of the UPA on the issue was not nearly as definitive as the RUPA language is for the facts in *McCormick*.

Farnsworth v. Deaver

This case addresses the role of capital accounts on winding up. The broad rule in the case is that a partner with a positive balance in his/her capital account does not have to contribute anything to the partnership; however, one with a negative balance must make a contribution to eliminate that balance. A review of the earlier covered Klein, Coffee & Partnoy excerpt in Section D and the following Note on Distributions in Dissolution and "Services Partners" can be used in connection with this case.

First, what do the capital accounts represent? They represent the accounting statement's projection of the amount of each member's interest, in dollars, in the firm. They assume that if the company was liquidated, and the assets fetched their book/accounting entry and liabilities were paid for exactly their recorded amount that the amount in each partner's capital account would be what s/he was entitled to receive. Now, if that mythical situation arose, and partner X had a balance of $10 and partner Y a balance of -5, what does that mean? It means that essentially Y owes the firm $5. That is, the firm has apparently suffered reverses or not done sufficiently well to put all the partners in the black. Thus, as losses were recorded against the accounts of X and Y, we see that Y's account must not have been large enough to absorb the full charge and thus went into negative territory. But, X's claim is still $10, but the balance sheet would show assets of only $5. To get the $5 that he is due, it must come from Y.

The following note material makes the point that those who contribute valuable services may find they are like Y in that their services are never really valued and recorded as such. The answer would be to make sure that the services are recorded on the balance sheet as an intangible asset, offset by an increase in the service-contributing-partner's capital account.

Page v. Page

Here we have two brothers who might conveniently be identified as Plaintiff Page and Defendant Page. The ball can commence rolling by asking what relief Plaintiff Page seeks? It is declaratory judgment that the parties have only a partnership at will. What possible reply could there be? Defendant Page argues this was at least for a term, to pay off the sums invested (equity $43,000 each and loans). Note the partnership owed Plaintiff Page's corporation $47,000.

The court finds nothing explicit or implicit that supports the contention. It believed the facts were clearer in *Owen v. Cohen*, cited in the opinion. More generally, the court concludes that the goal of recouping one's investment does not make the partnership one for a term.

Now the fun part of this case. If we were told that one of the brothers was a dentist, which would it most likely be? It would be Defendant Page, because we are told that Plaintiff Page operates a corporation that provides linens and machinery for the linen business. Now, why is Plaintiff Page seeking to end the partnership? It appears that with the creation of Vandenberg Air Force base, their business picked up considerably. Thus, what emerges from these two data points is that the entrepreneur, Plaintiff Page, brought Defendant Page in at the early stage to share the risks of starting a new business, and when those risks diminished because of the good fortune of the Vandenberg base being established now wishes to rid himself of an unwanted appendage, his co-owner. If so, this poses the "freeze out" problem that Traynor discusses in the closing paragraphs of the opinion.

Traynor clearly was not going to countenance a freeze out, citing *In re Security Finance*, but he observes that if this were the case there would be liability for wrongful dissolution, a topic covered later in Section 9.

As an abstract proposition, we might wonder why we should protect Defendant Page from a freeze out? And, if there is to be protection, what would be the extent of that protection? Should not the entrepreneur have the right to minimize his risks by bringing in outside capital and then terminating those investors' interests when the entrepreneur finds it in his best interest to do so? What would be the reasonable expectation of Defendant Page? Is this not similar to the issues raised in *Meinhard v. Salmon*? Starting with that case, who most resembles Meinhard? It would be Defendant Page since Plaintiff Page, like Salmon, is the more experienced in the business. In *Meinhard* the breach was Salmon failing to give Meinhard fair notice of a chance to participate in a new lease. Is Traynor saying something more here? He seems to suggest that there is some continuing value in which Defendant Page should be able to participate. Does this mean they are joined at the hip forever? That would be hardly reasonable. Would we not like to encourage entrepreneurial activity to the extent of allowing the promoters to bring in outside investors but removing them when it is convenient? This provides a way for them to manage their risk. Isn't this similar to what startups do with venture capital firms. Everyone understands that the VC will depart at some point. But that departure is at a fair price or one determined by market conditions. Should Defendant Page be entitled to more than compensation for the fair value of his interest in the partnership? To be sure, he would be cheated if the business just had a fire sale (who would be the likely purchaser at that sale, most likely Plaintiff Page). Thus, rather than being awarded the liquidation value, he should be awarded his fifty percent share of the going concern value. This would reflect the future value of the upturn in profits.

Note on Partnership Breakup Under the UPA

This note makes a very good point that deduction should not drive the result; policy, morality and experience should drive results. Thus, we see in dissolution the problems that surround the aggregate approach taken in UPA. We might think the problems with this approach are neatly illustrated by *Fairway Development Co. v. Title Insurance Co.* where a change in the membership of a partnership caused it to lose coverage for title insurance. What principle was advanced by that outcome?

Note on Partnership Breakup Under RUPA

Note the two routes: liquidation versus buyout. One determinant for which route is whether the dissociation was wrongful. If the dissociation is wrongful this renders the wrongfully withdrawing partner liable for to damages

Hillman, Vestal & Weidner Excerpt

These two excerpts from the very helpful work remind us that a process of winding up merely continues the partnership relation through the process. Thus, we need to be aware that if there are divisions among the partners that prompted ending the partnership and, hence, winding up, those divisions are likely to continue during that winding up process, unless the court or parties provide otherwise.

Note also that the buyout price per Article 8 is a floor for what the withdrawing partner will receive. There is a safety valve of judicial review of the buyout price in the event the withdrawing partner is dissatisfied.

Section 9. Dissolution (II): Dissolution by Judicial Decree and Wrongful Dissolution

Drashner v. Sorenson

We might begin with why this was not a partnership at will? The parties seem to wish to rid themselves of the plaintiff, an apparently bar fly, among many alleged acts of misconduct. The court concludes that the intent of the parties was that the partnership would continue at least until the partners recouped their initial $7500 investment. Plaintiff and defendants seek dissolution, alleging 1) breaches of the partnership agreement and 2) conduct that renders it impracticable to carry on the business of the partnership. The relevance of these allegation is UPA § 32(1)(d) which sets forth both conditions as bases for judicial dissolution. See, as well, RUPA § 601(5), where we might add to the preceding items (i), "wrongful conduct that adversely and materially affected the partnership business."

The court refers to the trial evidence that "plaintiff neglected the business and spent too much time in a nearby bar during business hours." He had exceeded his draw and was demanding more funds, threatening to dissolve the firm if his demands were not met. Overall, the court concluded, as did the trial court, that his insistent conduct and continuing demands for cash "rendered it reasonably impracticable to carry on the business in partnership with him."

In the background, but actually emphasized in the closing passages is the role of reputation in this business. This bears on why the plaintiff's conduct rendered carrying on business of the partnership with him impracticable. But also note that under the UPA, one who wrongfully causes dissolution is not entitled, on winding up, to any share in the goodwill of the firm. Here there is a double win here for the continuing partners. First, under UPA § 38(2)(b) the partners who have not caused dissolution wrongfully can continue the firm subject to posting a bond for the value of the wrongfully withdrawing partner's interest. Second, the value of the wrongfully withdrawing partner's interest excludes the firm's good will. In this case, it appears, from the purchase price that most of the value of the firm is good will. This raises the insight in the Note on Wrongful Dissolution that the potential exclusion of much of the firm's value may well chasten individuals from asserting their rights in a partnership under the UPA out of fear they may, after the fact, be adjudged to have caused a situation that justifies the firm's dissolution.

Pursuant to RUPA § 801(5), a judicial order of dissolution, such as occurred in *Drascher*, leads to winding up. Hence the buyout procedures of Chapter 7 do not apply. See RUPA § 701. Rather than foreclosing participation in goodwill, as under the UPA, RUPA § 602(c) provides instead that the wrongfully dissociating partner is liable for damages. While there continues to be a price that might be paid by rattling one's saber, it is not nearly as great a price as Drascher paid.

Note on the Expulsion of a Partner

The facts and reasoning of *Winston & Strawn v. Nosal* is likely to stir a good deal of interest among the students, certainly those who aspire to firm practice. By way of background, review RUPA § 601(3) and (4) providing for expulsion via the provisions of the partnership agreement and by unanimous vote, respectively. Note that (3) lacks the "bona fide" qualification that is in UPA § 31(d). Under the UPA there is no provision for expulsion by unanimous vote. Arguably that could occur via the relevant partners just quitting and forming a new partnership, but that could, if wrongful, provide costly as we've seen earlier given the damages these partners would become subject to, and under the UPA, the loss of the right to participate in the firm's goodwill upon winding up.

Students may be asked to explore just what made Nosal's expulsion not bona fide? Was it that he was expelled for merely asserting his rights under the partnership agreement? Was it a vindictive act by one whose wrongdoing Nosal sought to identify, and perhaps address via leveling formal charges. There is language in the opinion to support both bases.

Levy v. Nassau Queens Medical Group

The reasoning regarding what constitutes "bona fide" appears akin to analysis we see later in the corporate area, namely the business judgment rule.

Crutcher v. Smith

In inquiring whether the expulsion was wrongful, the court appears to suggest the misbehavior here involved trivial amounts so that it could not be bona fide. This raises a question. If it is OK, as *Levy* concludes, to expel provided there is not "business or property advantage for the remaining partners," then can you expel if you just conclude that the targeted partner is disagreeable, out of step, or not on the same page as the other partners? It would appear you could, since, as *Levy* concludes, partnerships are personal and contractual. Should the partners in *Crutcher* have argued that they believed Debtor was harming their ability to run the business so that they are better without him?

Section 10. Limited Partnership

A.   The Uniform Limited Partnership Acts

The note material here is provides a thumbnail sketch of the history of these acts as well pointing out that there are a lot of limited partnerships.

B.   Formation of Limited Partnerships

One does not casually become a limited partners. Once we enter the realm of some owners enjoying limited liability is a state filing is required. Reviewing the formation process of RULPA § 201 and the definition in §101 are worth the time. The materials set forth in the remainder of this section address the issues that shape and define why parties opt for limited partnerships (at least in an era before LLC's became as popular as they are today).

C.   Liability of Limited Partners

Gateway Potato Sales v. GB Investment Co.

We might begin by asking how the parties sought to protect against the risk that the venture would fail? Sunworth Packing Limited Partnership had a general partner, a corporation, Sunworth Corporation, and a limited partner, G.B. Investment. Gateway is suing the latter for "seed potatoes" it sold on credit to Sunworth Packing. Why not sue Sunworth? The general partner? Probably because it had insufficient assets.

What is the difference in the wording between the 1976 and 1985 versions of the RULPA on this point? The more recent version, cited in the case, impose liability on the limited partner to third parties only where the third person transacts business with the limited partnership "reasonably believing, based on the limited partner's conduct, that the limited partner is a general partner." This is a much more demanding test for liability than providing that a limited partner is liable "to persons who transact business with the limited partnership with actual knowledge of this participation in control." As the court points out, the latter does not require, as does the former, that this knowledge must be based on the limited partner's conduct.

So, does the court impose liability? It held that Gateway's evidence should have allowed it to withstand G.B. Investment's motion for summary judgment. There are statements by Ellsworth, the president of Sunworth, that he was a partner with G.B. Investments and that they were actively involved in the operations. The evidence set forth in footnote 1 supports this, but there is no evidence in the footnote that any of these specifics were known to Gateway. In fact, the opinion states that Gateway relied only on Ellsworth's statements. Under the 1985 version this clearly would not be enough, but it appears well within the likely meaning of the 1976 version of the RULPA since that focuses on dealings with the partnership with actual knowledge (did Ellsworth statement communicated such knowledge?).

Instead, the court said in a review of the defendant's grant of summary judgment that, reading the facts most favorably to Gateway, the facts, likely those in footnote 1, raise the alternative ground for liability, namely powers being exercised by G.B. Investment that were substantially similar to those of a general partner.

More broadly, you may wish to explore with students why Gateway should have any cause of action against G.B. Investments in principle? If G.B. Investments really did exercise control, then it should be no different than any other partner. This is because allowing them to mask their investment as one bearing limited liability is a disguise for what is really happening. Ok, so why would allowing G.B. Investments to participate in control and enjoy limited liability at the same time be a bad idea? The owners of corporations or LLCs can participate in control and enjoy limited liability. But Sunworth was neither a corporation nor an LLC, and the general principle is that unless otherwise provide by statute ownership and control leads to liability.

D.   Corporate General Partners

As pointed out in the note, the revised acts for some time have expressly recognized that the general partner to a limited partnership can be a corporation, much like what occurred in *Gateway*.

In re USA Cafes, L.P. Litigation

To understand the issue addressed by Chancellor Allen it is essential that the students grasp the organizational structure. There is a limited partnership and 47 percent of the limited partnership interests are held by Sam and Charles Wyly. The Wylys also own all the stock of the general partner, USACafes General Partner, Inc. The defendants are the four individuals who are the directors of the corporate general partner. The suit is brought as a class action on behalf of the limited partners. The allegation is that there was a good deal of self-dealing through various forms of side payments to the Wylys and the general partner (as well as the two non-Wyly directors of the general partner) in connection with Metsa Acquisition Corporation's purchase of USACafes L.P. There are also allegations of misrepresentations in the 1986 offering of the limited partnership units related to the kind of approval that would accompany any future sale of USACafes. This latter allegation does not play a prominent part in this opinion. Metsa is joined as an aider and abettor to the alleged breaches of fiduciary duty.

So, what do we learn from this case? Well, that people, not entities, do bad things. If the complaint's allegations are accepted as truthful (which is the case for a motion to dismiss), the issue is whether individuals serving as directors and controlling stockholders for the corporate general partner, but who are not themselves general partners can be personally responsible to the limited partners, or is the recovery limited to the general partner.

Allen cites some precedent, and provides a lot of sound reasoning to support the conclusion that just as trustees cannot hide behind the veil of the trust, so it is that the directors and controlling stockholder of the corporate general partner cannot hide behind the corporate veil. This is not a matter of piercing the corporate veil but how Allen defines the duties of the directors of the corporate general partner so that the duties transcend the corporation and extend to the limited partners.

An interesting possibility to consider is what result if the corporate general partner was not closely held by the Wylys but rather itself a public company, and Metsa offered side payments that would benefit not the Wylys but a group of shareholders. This should not change the result; the holding and reasoning advanced by Allen is based on the fiduciary obligation that the general partner owes to the partnership and the limited partnership. This should be unaffected by who or how many actors own the general partner.

E. The Taxation of Unincorporated Business Organizations

Later you can more fully explore the benefits, usually anyway, of flow-through tax treatment versus entity taxation. Simply stated, owners are usually better off (but not always) if there is only one incidence of taxation and not two. Hence, we will see later that the corporate form of business customarily means that the entity is a taxpayer (not just a reporting entity, as in the case of unincorporated business organizations) and if there is a distribution, that distribution (to the extent there are earnings and profits in the business) is taxed to the recipient. (Note the popularity of the Subchapter Selection. But you might wish to defer further discussion of this issue until Chapter 9, where we see that the driving force behind the LLC is the quest to combine limited liability with partnership tax treatment.

F.   Fiduciary Obligations

Gotham Partners, L.P. v. Hallwood Realty Partners

   Gotham illustrates two important points in the area of partnership law. First, the case illustrates the role that private ordering can play in establishing ex ante the scope and content of fiduciary duties, most typically for the general partner(s). Second, the case illustrates, in the context of a restructuring, the entire fairness inquiry and particularly the twin components of that test - fair price and fair dealing. The case also raises a range of considerations for determining the remedy/sanction when the insider engineers a transaction to increase its ownership interest, i.e., essentially transfers control to itself.

   The dispute arose from a set of transactions that included a reverse stock split (thus reducing the number of shares outstanding, but making many holders the owners of fractional shares, not just odd lot holdings), coupled with a purchase of fractional shares. This step resulted in increasing the general partnership's ownership of partnership units from 5.1 to 11.4 percent of the partnership units. The big shift followed from a second-step tender offer to acquire the substantial odd lot holdings and reissue those shares to the general partner. This step boosted the general partner's ownership from 11.4 to 29.7 percent of the outstanding partnership units. Removal of the general partner required a two-thirds vote of the outstanding units. Although the general partner held less than the number of shares required to assure a veto of its removal, the realities of voting are that many votes are not cast and non cast votes were the equivalent of a vote against removal of the general partner. Thus, the general partners' maneuvers effectively assured that the general partner's control could never be seriously challenged.

   What is the defense? The general partners argued that Section 9.01 of the Agreement accorded the general partner a good deal of discretion in issuing partnership units.

   However, the court concluded that the transaction was not an issuance, but a reissuance. The court then refers to 7.05 (where the reference is to the price being "substantially equivalent" to what would be struck in an arms-length bargain which sounds like "fair price.") and Section 7.10 (which calls for self-dealing transactions, such as that involved here, to be reviewed and approved by the audit committee, steps that sounds like "fair dealing") of the agreement.. Allen concludes that there was no evidence about the price before the general partner and certainly no use of the audit committee. He therefore concludes the deal not only fails the smell test, but the "entire fairness" standard as well.

   Note the statement in footnote 21, which has a good deal of appeal. In the partnership setting, inquiry as to the content and scope of fiduciary duties should begin with the partnership agreement. The issue is whether it can move beyond that to general norms and societal expectations, etc.? The answer to that question is no, if the partnership agreement, consistent with the enabling language of the state statute, forecloses such further inquiry. On this point, observe that the Note on Gotham Partners v. Hallwood after the case which reports that following the dicta in the Supreme Court case under the Delaware statute the partnership agreement could not eliminate, but only modify or enhance fiduciary obligations. However, the safety valve is that the contractual oriented duty of good faith and fair dealing could not be eliminated. What does this mean? It at least carries forward law, much of it made by Chancellor Allen, that parties cannot act to destroy a benefit expressly contracted for by the other party. Thus, if the Hallwood partnership agreement had, for example, provided that the limited partners who were unaligned with the general partner would have the authority should they collectively believed it appropriate to change the general manager, the actions taken by the defendants could be seen as intentionally interfering with that contractual objective and would, arguably, be within the realm of a contractually-based claim of good faith and fair dealing.

It is interesting to consider the dual nature of the sanction. First, it is to require compensation to the extent less than fair value was paid for the resold partnership interests? Why would this price not just be extrapolated from the price the limited partners were willing to sell to the limited partnership their shares? Arguably they were duped and the market for these shares may not have reflected all available information bearing on their value. Second, there is requirement that there be some compensation for control. That is, as a consequence of the transaction, the general partner gained control; in an arms-length transactions when one acquires control, customarily a premium is paid for control. Later in Chapter 14, Section 1 the materials explore the issue of control premium and how their existence does not mean the firm has more value but that one cluster of ownership, the minority, now have less value after the control transaction. This may make the participation in the control premium appear more problematic, but we might conclude that if the parties were dealing at arms-length that we would expect a hard bargain to be driven by the selling unit holders who understanding that control, and its value, is something the general partner would quite likely pay extra to acquire.

Section 11   Limited Liability Partnerships

So, what is the difference between a limited partnership and an LLP? Recall that in the standard limited partnership that a limited partner runs the risk personal liability on partnership debts if he participates in the management of the limited partnership. In contrast, if the owners form an LLP, they can all be on the management committee of the law firm and still have limited liability. An LLLP allows the general partner of the limited partnership to manage, have limited partners, and still enjoy limited liability. But note, limited liability does not mean that your capital tied up in the partnership is free of creditor claims; limited liability refers to whether there is liability beyond the capital invested in the partnership.

Ederer v. Gursky

At the outset, it is wise to clarify for the students that the dispute centers on the LLP's and its member's obligations to Ederer, which was created from the earlier professional corporation (PC) with which earlier understandings likely carried forward. The issue is whether

36

the LLP provision which no one disputes eliminates personal liability to third parties also eliminated personal liability to other partners, except for their own torts.

We might believe this is resolved in Section 26(b) which provides "which are incurred, created or assume by such partnership." This would appear to support the majority in their conclusion that the limitation of personal liability applied only to third parties and not among the partners themselves. Here we had a partner who withdrew but agreed to perform services on a case after he withdrew. He now sues to be compensated for those services. Apparently the partnership has no assets (hence the capital accounts of each of the partners is wiped out) so he is now suing the remaining partners. This is analogous to the dissents illustration regarding the potential liability for the 2% owner.

Why might a legislature choose to distinguish between inside and outside creditors with respect to their personal liability? Is this not the issue that separates the majority from the dissent? As an owner, you might have greater ability to manage risk through self help or private ordering with respect to the risks posed by your fellow partners than you could manage risks with third parties. Thus, you might not know if your partner committed malpractice; but you should be able to introduce procedures within the firm to prevent pilferage of assets by a partner so that funds are there to pay Ederer. Similarly, in the 2% example, if the 49% partner withdraws and some money is owed to him, some steps can be undertaken internally to protect against that situation and, minimally you do have contribution rights against the other 49% owner so you ought to be vigilant with respect to your own rights.

Finally, are not limitations on liability to be interpreted narrowly which also supports the literal reading of the majority.

Bromberg & Ribstein Excerpt

The observation in § 3.02 heightens interest in the precise wording of the LLP statute because if the "misconduct" for which there is no vicarious liability is based solely in tort, the clever lawyer could argue, as Bromberg and Ribstein point out, that the malpractice claim against a professional is based on the contractual relationship and, thus, beyond the limitation. We see the earlier point made introduced in § 3.02, namely that a partner's capital remains at risk for misconduct of fellow partners in an LLP; it is only the personal liability that can be insulated by the entity choice that is made. Finally, §3.04 raises a very good point whether the wording ""or that of any person under his direct supervision" imposes vicarious liability on one who supervises. This is tricky because the employer presumably is the LLP so that respondeat superior applies to the LLP but respondeat superior does not apply to the individual partners in the LLP, it is a means for imposing liability on the employer organization. One far-fetched construction of this provision is to reason that, if the employee misbehaves so that the LLP is liable vicariously under respondeat superior, the supervising partner, but not the others, has personal liability. As the excerpt makes clear, the important qualifier is "shall not affect" which refers to the state of the law regarding a supervisor's or control person's responsibility before this provision was enacted. If there was none, then there would be no liability. If there was liability, then the legislature can be seen as carrying forward the public policy for such supervisoryor control person liability

Chapter 4

The Foundations of a Corporation

Chapter Overview: This chapter contains the bedrock for understanding how the corporation operates. You likely will allocate four class periods to the material. Class one will cover VantagePoint (and optionally Friese) as well as Selecting the Corporate Domicile. This material sets the stage for understanding not just entity choice, but more importantly choice of domicile and particularly the reasons Delaware is an important domicile. Class two can focus on formation issues, including the introductory materials on Basic Types of Financial Securities (and if you choose the Unabridged edition the materials on leverage) and Equitable Subordination. Class three gets into the weeds regarding board and shareholder votes and the issues surrounding the Election of Directors. With the final day you have much to choose from. However, given the importance of Dodge v. Ford Motor Company, that case should be a centerpiece of what you choose to wrap around it.

Section 1. The Characteristics of a Corporation

Students might be asked why each of these characteristics would be important to a promoter or investor in a new venture? Limited liability is a powerful social subsidy for undertaking risky ventures. Students might be asked what "limited liability" means. Continuity of existence is fairly important to those investing, because they would like some assurance that the capital committed by others will be "locked in," so that the operating assets can not only be acquired and stay employed in the venture so that the business has a chance to perform and develop customer patronage. Entity status has several functional benefits such as ease of acquiring and transferring title to various assets, and being able to sue and be sued. For most small businesses, the transferability of interests is not a desired feature; but, as the firm grows, the corporate form allows greater aggregation of capital because transferability enhances liquidity of the shares and adds to their attractiveness. With centralized problems of apparent authority are reduced vis-a-vis a partnership where each partner has the apparent authority to act within the scope of the partnership business.

Section 2. The Architecture of Corporate Law

Students can be reminded of the various sources of law that affects the operation of the corporation: the state of incorporation's general corporation law, common law, federal law (mainly in the form of various provisions of the federal securities law covered in the course), and private ordering. Throughout the materials we see illustrations of both traditional conflicts, such as self-dealing transactions by officers, directors and dominant stockholders, and positional conflicts particularly as managers seek to entrench their position.

Section 3.   Which State's Law Governs A Corporation's Personal Affairs

VantagePoint Venture Partners 1996 v. Examen, Inc.

Students might be asked what is the issue that is before the Delaware Courts and how did it get before the court. This began with a race to the court house by both the plaintiff and the defendant. VantagePoint got to the California courthouse five days *after* Examen filed its suit in Delaware for declaratory relief whether their dispute should be resolved according to California law. The California court laid back, letting the litigation move forward in the Delaware Chancery Court.

Who is VantagePoint. It is a venture capital firm and like most venture investors its investment was in the form of preferred stock. The issue was whether the preferred enjoyed a class vote on the proposed merger of Examen with Reed Elsevier. Because Examen was incorporated in Delaware, and the traditional choice of law rule, the internal affairs doctrine, holds that the law of incorporation resolves such issues. California has its own choice of law provision, Cal. Corp. Code Section 2115, which extends certain of its provisions to "pseudo foreign" corporations. This invites discussion of what is a "foreign" corporation, and what made Examen a pseudo-foreign corporation under Section 2115? Here more than half the Examen shareholders, and more than half its property, met the standard summarized in footnote 1 of the case so that select provisions of the Cal. Corp. Code apply. One of those provisions is that in a merger each class affected gets a class vote. Here the preferred got a vote, but their vote was lumped with the votes of the common, so that the much larger vote of the common would overcome any negative vote by the preferred.

Are we persuaded that the choice of law rule, the internal affairs doctrine, is enshrined in the Constitution, as the court reasons? This seems hard to believe. The court cites *CTS Corp. v. Dynamics Corp.,* but that was a case where the state lacked any substantial contact with the foreign corporation. This seems hardly persuasive in the face of the more than fifty percent factors that are a predicate for Section 2115's application. What arguments support rejecting the California approach? The court appears concerned that there may be conflicting demands so that the corporation's activities will be mired in regulatory uncertainty. But is this necessarily the case if complying with the most demanding standard is would occur in practice? Also, the multiplicity of directives seems less persuasive if all states took the approach of California and applied their local law only when *more than half* of the company's shareholders were located in the state other than the state of incorporation.

Why is it that California adopted a provision like Section 2115? It was to protect the California residents who invest in corporations that are formed in states that are less solicitous of shareholder interests than California. At the same time, it is difficult to believe that the Delaware

Supreme Court could have reached any different result since the franchise of Delaware depends so heavily on the internal affairs doctrine's longevity.

Friese v. Superior Court

It is best to start this case with students noting the distinctions from *VantagePoint*. Both were Delaware corporations; but note there is no reference in the facts to how significant were the California operations of Peregrine. California Civil Code Section 2116 embraces the internal affairs doctrine; thus if it controls, then Delaware, not the California Corporations Code sections, would control. The California Corporations Code sections cited here not only proscribe insider trading, but grant a remedy up to treble the insiders' profits which, among others, the trustee in bankruptcy could pursue. Indeed the California Corporations Code provisions speaks in terms of the total assets and number of shareholders of the company; but do not require that any of these two items be located in California. Thus, these California statutes seem to have an even broader reach than California Corporations Code Section 2115 that was the subject of *VantagePoint*.

As for the facts, the trustee alleged that the defendants collectively dumped over 5 million Peregrine shares on their secret knowledge that the company's financial statements overstated its revenues by 38 percent, i.e., more than $500 million. The lower court dismissed the suit, believing the internal affairs doctrine was mandated by section 2116. The Court of Appeals reversed for the reasons developed below.

Is this case inconsistent with *VantagePoint*? While reaching different results, it may be comparing apples to oranges. *Friese* reaches a different result by characterizing the underlying claim as a securities question, not an internal affairs issue. This essentially defines the issue out of *VantagePoint* and other cases. As seen in the references to the ALI Restatement of Conflicts, securities regulatory issues are territorial, so that local laws of the state where sales and offers to sale and trading occur are applied to securities issues. But this distinction works well if the question of what right California has if Peregrine was trying to sell its shares in a public or private offering to residents in California. But would California be able to apply its requirements for disclosure if the offering was only to Texans in Texas? Hardly. Thus, if Peregrine's shares were listed on the NYSE, just what conduct does California have with the trading by the defendants?

Western Air Lines Inc. v. Sobieski does not adequately answer the preceding question. That case can be seen closer to the public offering of shares *in* California example than to the example of offering of shares only in Texas. In *Sobieski*, the Commissioner of Corporations, Mr. Sobieski, correctly understood that amendment of the articles of incorporation changes the rights of the shareholders so that it is truly reflective of a new issuance of shares. Since many of the Western Air Line shareholders were residents of California, it was appropriate to view this as the offer to sell shares in California. In contrast, insider trading might be seen as involving the duties of directors, officers and controlling stockholders. These are matters within the historical realm of corporate internal affairs. To be sure, we might also believe that insider trading is an abuse of investors who are on the other side of the insider's trading. But if the trading occurred in New York, are the investors deemed to be there or where they reside? Thus, it is not totally within the realm of internal affairs but involves the protection of investors. But why would we think that

41

California, and not Texas and even Rhode Island, should have authority with respect to such misbehavior, if the physical trading occurred in New York? Thus, while characterizing the misconduct as involving securities does not totally answer the question, although superficially it did in this case.

Section 4. Selecting A State of Incorporation

We usually begin discussion of this section of the material, "Why Delaware?" The answer includes 1) a rich body of precedent that has surrounded a relatively stable statutory scheme, 2) that has been shaped by a judiciary that has much greater experience in corporate matters prior to moving to the bench than we find elsewhere, 3) there are the network effects captured by the Klausner (after all, the students in your BA class are learning a lot about the law of Delaware and nothing about the law of, well Paduka); and 4) a commitment by the legislature to keep its statute abreast with developments. Why has Delaware made these commitments? (You might raise this question by a sign on the overhead or whiteboard, "Law for Sale!" Asking, "Why do we find this when we cross the Delaware River?") The franchise tax from corporations and other business entities plays a significant role in the overall tax revenues of Delaware (contrast this with New York or California). You might wish to make the point, stated near the end of the material, that the differences between Delaware and many state provisions, including the Model Act, are slim, and in some instances, we will even see where the Model Act is more solicitous of managers' interests than of shareholder interests.

A review of the thesis of Cary in his classic article, as well as a consideration of Judge Winter's race-to-the-top position, are useful to frame the ultimate point, which is not just a rejoinder to Winter: the costs are at the margins with respect to the cost of capital so that swinging too far in the direction of the prerogatives of managers may not produce any change in managerial or shareholder behavior since the pricing of the change gives rise to minimal change in share price. The real point to draw from this are: 1) when does the choice of Delaware occur-not when the company is first incorporated, but later via reincorporation; 2) what is a reincorporation = merger of operating company into a shell created under the laws of Delaware; 3) if a student were asked to draft a proxy statement seeking shareholder approval for such a reincorporation, e.g., relocating from California to Delaware, what points would you raise =greater flexibility, certainty and speed in undertaking a range of wealth increasing transactions; 4) who gets this process rolling=the directors but more likely the senior officers, 5)why is it that the impetus for relocating to Delaware comes from management=all the benefits mean they have more discretion, less friction, more power, i.e., power is a double-edged sword, there is power to do good and power to serve yourself; and 6) what does the data by Daines and Subrahmanian suggest Delaware companies are valued on average more highly in the market. Why would Delaware companies trade at a premium? On the latter point, we should consider that there is a self selection bias among firms that are domiciled in Delaware. Those firms are attracted by the stability of its broadly permissive corporate statutes. This attraction likely is driven in most cases not by the self interest of managers; location in Delaware may likely reflect companies who seek the stability of engaging in mergers and other corporate transactions for which greater certainty, flexibility, and speed. These may more likely be growth firms and, hence, the premium captured in the data tells us something about the firms, on average.

Section 5.   Organizing A Corporation

This is an opportunity to review, if you've not already done so, the extremely minimal demands to complete the articles of incorporation. Students can be asked what provision is likely to consume the most time. The answer is the description of the type of shares to be issued, but only if you are going to have in addition to common a class of shares so that you need to consider the rights, privileges and preferences of that class. It is worth noting here that when you sit in your office in Paduka and are advising a group of entrepreneurs on creating their new business, little or no thought of forming a Delaware corporation will occur. You keep things cheap; why pay taxes in Delaware and also in the state which is your principal place of business. And, why create a foreign corporation in whose law you likely just dabble, if at all, when you have the choice to form an entity of the state in which you practice daily. And, startups have little, if any, need for the discrete provisions of Delaware law that provide certainty, flexibility, and stability. The startup just doesn't have transactions where these qualities are of measureable benefit. When that day arrives, you can then choose Delaware via a reincorporation.

Some review of the preincorporation stock subscription provision under the law of the state statute you use in the class. The key provision here is the provision, such as Delaware and the Model Act, referenced in the readings, that renders, subject to a contrary expression of intent, preincorporation subscriptions irrevocable for six months. What public policy supports this choice? The idea is that most startups require a critical mass of capital. Thus, shareholders expect that the commitments of others are firm and, thus, make their investment accordingly. To be sure, if explicitly understood, this would render their mutual understanding enforceable. But in many, if not most, cases the shareholders are subscribing independently and not collectively so that establishing mutual intent is problematic.

Section 6.   The Basic Types Of Financial Securities

The fine points of preferred stock and debt securities are traditionally covered in the Corporate Finance class. The materials in this section provide an overview of the distinction between common and various types of senior securities. You might consider getting the ball rolling by placing the material in the contemporary context of startups and the investment by a venture capital firm. Why is it that startups seek VC and not bank financing? Why is it that VC take a convertible preferred stock rather than common? Debt that is convertible?

Startups customarily do not have tangible assets that can secure the loan; also, their problematic cash flow, and need to reinvest what cash is created through operations, each weigh against bank financing. The risks of the loan would likely call for high interest which poses the fear that a missed payment would trigger not just default, but foreclosure or bankruptcy filing.

The VC wish to have some representation on the board, but want protection against default. Hence, they seek a liquidation preference. Where is this found? Any differences in rights, privileges and preferences must be set forth in the articles of incorporation. An exception to this statement arises in the case of a blank stock authorization which gives the board within the class so authorized in the articles to set these relative rights, etc.

The VC wish to have not just downside protection-liquidation preference over common- but upside potential. Hence, the convertibility feature. Note that the common is likely held by the promoters/insiders. VC negotiate for voting rights, usually set forth as certain number of positions on the board.

Students might be asked what is the difference between a cumulative and non cumulative dividend? How is cumulative preferred different from a bond? This goes to the mandatory nature of the interest and principal payment for the latter versus the former. That is, a missed dividend does not trigger a default. This is relevant to the material that follows in this section and the next.

Ayer, Guide to Finance for Lawyers

You might wish to go through the simple numerical example Professor Ayer has created in which Skeeter believes he has found the City of Gold. You might then ask whether the company's value, as compared to the value of its ownership represented by the common, has changed with the introduction of debt. The Note on the Tax Shield of Debt reflects that to the extent debt alters the timing or amount of free cash flow that it would change the value of the firm. That is, the tax shield effectively creates value. But the Note on Leverage and the Risk of Financial Distress provides a sobering qualification that the value added by debt (or more precisely, the tax shield) does not continue forever; at some point the cost of bankruptcy failure (the deadweight costs associated with a business' failure-e.g., trustee and lawyer costs, plus the increased likelihood of failure as the quantity of debt and its allied fixed payments increase) will mean that at some point the additional unit of debt reduces the value of the firm.

You might wish to ask whether, aside from the tax shield, what are some other good features of debt? One benefit of debt is the discipline debt imposes on managers. The amount of cash flow that managers have discretion is less with debt, so that they are less likely to pursue suboptimal or negative value opportunities. Second, managers can signal their confidence about the future by taking on more debt. Thus, leverage is frequently understood as a positive signal.

Section 8.   Equitable Subordination of Shareholder Claims

Students can be asked what is happening in *Gannett Co. v. Larry*, a case that, no pun intended, is viewed by most as the high water mark of the "Deep Rock" doctrine? Facts to learn about the doctrine's application, particularly in *Gannett,* are that Gannett converted Berwin's operations to fulfill its own business desires and not to necessarily make Berwin more profitable. The conversion was funded by loans by Gannett. The newsprint shortage never arose, causing Berwin to fail, i.e., enter an insolvency proceeding.

The Deep Rock doctrine applies only in an insolvency proceeding (state insolvency or federal bankruptcy); historically, it was created in equity but now is codified in the Bankruptcy Act. The basis for subordination is not dominance, but some "act of mismanagement." Most cases this is met by establishing the parent did not adequately capitalize the subsidiary. Note the link between poor capitalization and failure of the subsidiary. What makes *Gannett* so unique is that the "mismanagement" was the decision to change Berwin's operations. But why isn't this not in the same league as Ford's decision to produce a new car, the Edsel? Gannett changed Berwin's operations to meet Gannett's needs for newsprint if a feared shortage developed; Ford created the Edsel in the era of fins and gas gobbling monstrosities to make a profit. Also observe the causal link for *Gannett*: the conversion caused Berwin to cease being profitable and led to its failure; moreover, the conversion was financed via loans by Gannett. Hence, the equity placing Gannett at the end of the line of creditors. Would Gannett's position be improved if it had a security interest/mortgage? Usually the mortgage stands on no better footing than the debt it secures.

Arnold v. Phillips poses a different question: what is debt and what is capital. Students might be asked how the issue before the court in *Gannett* is different from that in *Arnold*? Why is it that the characterization is important in this case? If treated as debt, the incorporator/shareholder recovers part of his "investment" by being able to share pari passu with the outside creditors. If treated as equity, he receives no payment until all creditor claims are satisfied. With insolvency, this means non recognition as the holder of debt for that part of the investment results in non payment.

Are we persuaded the court's division of the baby was reasonable? Does the preceding material support the court's reasoning that the funds needed to make the firm viable should be deemed equity? As seen in the preceding material, particularly material regarding the tax shield, well-informed lawyers should recommend to their clients that some of the formative capital be represented by debt, provided the cash flow (recall the preceding discussion regarding startups and VC taking preferred stock). We might also believe that, when the business started to fail, advancements by insider then occurred because no one else would lend. Thus, was repayment reasonably anticipated or was this a last gasp effort to salvage the firm in with disguised debt? At the same time, why not encourage promoters and insiders to save the company by stepping forward with new funds that will, if failure results, share pari passu with outside creditors? It is hard to see in such a case how creditors have been harmed, save to pro long the life of the firm so that more assets are dissipated via losses. But is the chance for saving the firm a social benefit worth the risk of such dissipation?

Benjamin v. Diamond

The case emphasizes the three items that must be causally related for veil piercing. You might wish to assign this as background for your discussion of the facts and holding of *Gannett Co. v. Larry*.

Section 9.   Requisites for Valid Action by the Board

This section can be covered with a simple problem designed to force the students to apply the notice, quorum and voting requirements for valid board action within the statute used in your course. Thus, assume a regularly scheduled meeting attended by 4 of the 7 authorized directors. The vote to acquire Blackacre is 2 yes, 1 no and 1 abstention. Valid action turns on whether the statute, as most do, requires approval on a majority of those present (some base the outcome on those voting). Notice and quorum need to also be reviewed. Now, what if this is a special meeting, initiated by a phone call by the board chair who could only reach the 4 directors. This leads to reviewing the process by which notice can be waived under the statute.

Section 10. The Normal Requisites for Valid Shareholder Action

Corporations and Other Business Organizations

Assume a meeting where the resolution to approve a bylaw change is voted upon 300 yes, 200 no and 100 abstain. Assume further there are outstanding 1000 shares entitled to vote. In Delaware and the Model Act, the default rule is a majority of the shares present or represented (i.e., proxy) constitutes a quorum and the resolution is approved if a majority of the shares *voting* approve. Assuming a greater quorum or vote is not required, the resolution would be approved.

Note that in most states a change in shareholder quorum or voting must be in articles of incorporation; however, some states permit this deviations to be in the bylaws (most states permit deviations for director actions to be either in the articles of incorporation or bylaws). But note that for fundamental changes, e.g., amending the articles of incorporation or mergers, the statutes frequently call for a majority of the shares entitled to vote. Where this is required, the above resolution before the shareholders would not have passed.

Section 11. The Election of Directors

A. Staggered Boards

You likely will make the point what is a "staggered" board and why can it serve as an entrenchment device; each of these points is discussed in the introductory note.

Kahan & Rock, Embattled CEOs

What do we find happening among public companies? Staggered boards are becoming less common? Why? They are seen as entrenching management, particularly when coupled with a poison pill, discussed later in Chapter 15, where it makes it more difficult for a change in control. Why do shareholders dislike entrenchment devices? Why not favor continuity of leadership? While continuity is a virtue, stability among the directors is possible without a staggered board. The staggered board makes it difficult for outsiders to change control of the company rapidly. On this point, look at the Delaware General Corp. Law § 141(k)(1) where we see that unless the articles provide otherwise, staggered board directors can only be removed for cause.

B. Cumulative Voting

You can illustrate four features of voting in a single illustration: 1) straight voting, 2) plurality voting, 3) majority vote provisions, and 4) cumulative voting. To illustrate, assume Sally owns 700 shares and Bill owns 300. They are the only shareholders. Sally nominates M, N and O. Bill nominates X, Y, and Z. Under straight voting, the maximum votes each can cast is the number of shares owned multiplied by the number of directors standing for election. Hence, Sally = 2100 and Bill = 900. But, under straight voting, the maximum that can be cast for any single director is the number of shares owned. Thus, Sally will cast 700 for each of M, N and O and Bill's nominees will get 300 each. Plurality voting means the directors receiving the highest number of votes for the number of open positions win. Thus, the winners are M, N. and O. Shareholders of public companies have not as a normal matter been able to nominate directors, See Chapter 5, Section 1. They have organized withhold the vote campaigns and pushed for majority vote provisions. Absent the latter, we would find that their displeasure does not yield much. Thus, assume in Ajax Corporation that A, B and C are standing for election (per the

46

parties in control of the nominating process, which could be A, B and C) and a group of shareholders are unhappy with C. They encourage shareholders to not vote for C. Indeed, they recommend a vote against C. The result, A and B receive 10,000 votes, but C has 3 votes in support and 9,997 votes against. Who's elected? Under plurality voting, A, B and C are elected. Thus, as discussed by Vaaler, majority vote provisions have become increasingly common in public companies so that at a minimum C has to tender her resignation if receiving less than a majority of the cast shares. With cumulative voting, no longer is there a ceiling on the number of votes that can be cast for one director. Therefore, Bill can place 900 on X. Sally can counter with 901 on M and N each, but that leaves here with only 298 votes to place on O. The result, the directors elected are M, N and X.

You can then examine what was a foot with *eBay Domestic Holdings, Inc. v. Newmark*, where eBay's ability as a 28% owner to elect a representative was undercut by classifying the board with the result that only a single director would be elected each year to a three-year term. The court reasoned this was valid and beyond the entire fairness standard. You might later wish to return to this when you discuss *Schnell* and *Blasius* in Chapter 5, Section 1.

Also, the Delaware Supreme Court in *Airgas Co. v. AirProducts, Inc.* held that the terms for classified boards must be annual so that a resolution accelerating the next annual meeting (at which directors would be elected) was ineffective since it would substantially shorten the terms of the sitting directors.

C.   Plurality Voting

The mechanics of both plurality voting and majority vote are illustrated in the hypothetical discussed above. What you can further emphasize with this material is the increasing popularity of majority vote provisions and the various configurations of the provisions with respect to what happens if a director fails to secure a majority vote.

D.   Short Slates

To illustrate this device, consider that management's proxy materials seek the election of A, B, C, D and E. A group of investors wish either to alter the mix of the board without triggering any "change of control" provisions that are part of the firm's defensive mechanisms. They may find A, B and C unobjectionable so only wish to run three, N and O. Thus, they advance a short slate, N and O. As we will see later in Chapter 6, Section 2, with respect to the proxy rules authority for short slates.

Section 12.   Removal of Directors

A close review of the statutory provision used in your course addressing the procedure for removing directors. Cause, if required, is a pretty good barrier to removal since it requires proof of some conduct engaged in the director that was wrongful. Thus, directors have a good deal of insulation against removal. Why might we believe this is a good thing? We might believe it encourages directors to balance the interests of other constituencies, take the long view, and that shareholders lack sufficient information to second guess directors. At the same time, we might also believe that accountability not only matters, but matters a lot, so that insulating directors from the firm's owners is not an optimal choice.

Section 13. Requisites for Valid Action by Corporate Officers

This material introduces the officers typically found in business operations. We might not have a chief operating officer, and the treasurer may be subsumed within the CFO rubric. The general counsel may also double as the corporate secretary. What is relevant here is to understand that these positions carry certain understandings of authority such that the title emits apparent authority within those understood areas.

Section 14. The Classical Ultra Vires Doctrine

The topic of ultra vires is largely historical. To drive this point home, close review of the statute used in your course will show the multiple ways in which this topic has been marginalized. First, look at the constrained statement of purposes, namely that the articles of incorporation can provide that the company shall engage in *any* lawful business. Second, review the extensive list of powers all corporations have. Thus, the former days of prolix statements of purposes and powers are now obviated by the statute providing a company can simply say it can engage in any lawful business and conferring a laundry list of powers to carry out this broad purpose. Finally, consider how constrained the authority for anyone to prosecute an ultra vires act. Kent Greenfield interesting article, Ultra Vires Lives: A Stakeholder Analysis of Corporate Illegality, 87 Va. L. Rev. 1279 (2001), reasons that the "any lawful business" could be he means to redress unlawful acts.

Section 15. The Objective and Conduct of the Corporation

A.   The Maximization of Shareholder Wealth

What separates the two conceptions (traditional vs. competing) of the purpose of the corporation? It appears to be that today, rather than to reason that what is good for GM is good for its shareholders, it is to recognize that there are differences here. That decisions should be made based, not on whether this is best for the corporation, but rather increases shareholder welfare. But how can these be different? One is that if shareholders are diversified so that the risks that matter are those of the well-diversified shareholder and not the position of the non-diversified corporation. Also, earnings of the company are relevant only to the extent they are surrogates for value measurements to the shareholders. Thus, perhaps generating cash and distributing it as dividends is more important than reinvestment when the market does not value reinvestment. What should drive such a change where the milestone is shareholder and not corporate wealth? It might be, at least in part, the rising institutionalization of markets where large investors are making their voices heard. More on this topic in Chapter 5, Section 1.

B.   Interests Other Than Maximization of Shareholders' Wealth

Note on Dodge v. Ford Motor Co.

This classic case requires understanding the facts and Henry Ford's vision. We might ask how Ford could have won this case? One suggestion is not take the stand to defend his position for terminating the special dividends where his references to those "awful" profits most likely sunk his position. The holding is summarized nicely "A business corporation is organized and carried on primarily for the profit of the stockholders." While speaking of profit rather than share maximization, we can easily see these as synonyms. Accepting this as the standard, students might be asked how Ford should have answered questions put to him by the Dodge brothers' attorney regarding his reasons for cancelling the special yearly dividend? Ford could reiterate that there are three ways to fund expansion: issue equity, borrow, or reinvest profits. The latter is the most common because it has the lowest level of accountability by managers; it is a means that does not require the concurrence of a willing investor or lender. Reinvestment of profits is a way to broaden the production base and likely increase profits. Thus, Ford could have reasoned that his best estimate was that by increasing production, and hiring more individuals, that the per unit cost (i.e., economies of scale) would have declined and the automobile would have become a more commonly purchased item as the income of America rose (in the early 1950s one in six jobs in the U.S. economy could be linked to the automobile). That is, he needed to cast his decision as an astute business decision and not as a philanthropic one. As an aside, Ford never paid the dividend; he bought the Dodge brothers out and ran Ford as a private company until a very nervous Ford Foundation caused the company to go public in the 1950s.

A.P. Smith Mfg. Co. v. Barlow

We might begin the discussion here of how is A.P. Smith Manufacturing Company's contribution to Ol' Ivy (Princeton) any different from what Ford was scolded for doing in the preceding case? Two answers: first, there is quite a difference in scale and, second, there was an articulated business justification. But also, it appears the court also justified the contribution on the theory of the "responsible and enlightened citizen." This is further buttressed by the deductibility of the contribution, at least to some level. Observe that there is express authority in most statutes for corporations to make contributions to charitable organizations. What about, after *Citizens United,* direct contribution to political campaigns? These deductions are not deductible but are within the business judgment rule protections covered later in Chapter 10.

Note the case illustrates the importance of the "reserved power" clause in most corporate statutes. That is, the New Jersey statute authorized within certain limits charitable contributions. But the shareholder-appellants argued this provision was inapplicable, and likely unconstitutional, to company formed before the statute was formed. But the Darmouth College Case held that a reserve clause which subjected all corporation to changes introduced by subsequent amendments to the New Jersey statute meant there was no violation of the Contract Clause by a later amendment to the corporate statute authorizing acts that earlier were not permitted. Gotcha on the reserve clause.

What then is the possible abuse of corporate contributions, or for that matter political contributions. We all favor charitable contributions, but we disagree over the object of our munificence. Not everyone would revel in a contribution to: Planned Parenthood or the National Rifle Association. So, who makes the decision which charity receives the corporation's largesse? It likely is the senior management, or more particularly the CEO. Ah, always better to play with others' money isn't it? This then frames the on-going governance issue with charitable contributions and after *Citizens United* political contributions.

Note on Other Constituencies under Delaware Law

A review of a sample of "other constituency" statutes reveals quite differing approaches. Many apply only in the "change of control" setting. Others do not. We might then ask why the Model Act does not include another constituency provision? The explanation offered by the Committee of Corporate Laws (the body that drafts the Model Act) is that under such a statute it disconnects the objectives of the board of directors and senior management from any mooring. That is, if you are free to serve the interest of labor, consumers, creditors, stockholders then for any decision made how can we decide whether it was appropriate?

How does Delaware address the issues in *Ford* or tilting toward other constituencies? *Revlon* allows serving other constituencies when the decision also advances the interests of stockholders. The *eBay Domestic Holdings, Inc. v. Newmark* decision, summarized in the note material, does not waiver in holding that while community service is a great idea, when the founders of craigslist opted to be a for-profit corporation it became bound by duties and standards that apply to corporations generally; these duties include the duty to "promote the value of the corporation for the benefit of its stockholders."

Chapter 5

The Legal Structure of Publicly Held Corporations

Chapter Overview: This is the corporate governance chapter of the book. It covers questions about the relative roles of owners and managers, the scope of bylaw amendments, the potential potency of institutional shareholders, vote buying, the funding of proxy contests and the on-going developments of the monitoring board for public companies. Four or five class periods can easily be allocated to this chapter. The first class can examine *Charlestown Boot & Shoe*, *Schnell* and *Blasius Industries*. This material will likely spill over to the second class where you can add *CA Inc.* and the Thompson & Edelman excerpt. Day three can be devoted to qualifying Thompson & Edelman with the material on supervoting and empty voting as well as the note material on the rise of financial institutions. Day four can you can add *Portnoy* and any loose ends..

Section 1. The Legal Distribution of Power Between the Board and the Shareholders, and Equitable Limits on the Board's Legal Power

Charlestown Boot & Shoe Co. v. Dunsmore

Charlestown Boot & Shoe provides a great basis to introduce the "keystone" provision of any corporate statute, the over-arching authority of the board per, e.g., MBCA § 8.01(b); Del. Gen. Corp. L. § 141(a).

The students must understand the point made in the Note to the case that the opinion's reference to the "corporation" refers to a resolution approved by the shareholders. While many claims are raised about the directors, e.g., negligence, the focus of this case is whether the directors are responsible for the losses of continuing the business because they failed to follow the directive of the shareholders to listen to the counsel of Osgood.

The court reads the statute, indeed reads it literally, and concludes that the power over such matters is not in the shareholders, but the board. This remains the case today, albeit arguably the articles of incorporation may restrain the directors.

Students might be asked why so centralize management? Why not place authority among the owners as occurs in a partnership? One idea is that, if such disperse authority is requested, individuals should opt for a partnership. or better yet, a member-managed LLC. Another idea is that the corporate form can be seen as offering a set of default rules believed optimal for broad ownership, namely centralized management, so that passive owners can rely on the talents and expertise of others. In this way, each individual can be employed to his/her optimal attainments. Dentists can fill teeth and invest their disposable income in firms managed by individuals who have skills in design, production, marketing, etc. While the board may not have all these skills, the board can retain, as officers, those who have the right skills. It may be difficult for all the owners to supervise the officers; but a smaller body, charged with ultimate authority, can provide this oversight and the necessary set of experiences to carry out the oversight.

People ex rel Manice v. Powell

This case more clearly states the holding in *Charlestown Boot and Shoe,* holding that the board is not an agent of the shareholders, but instead the board as a body collectively possesses the original authority to act on behalf of the corporation.

B.   Equitable Limits on the Board's Legal Powers

Note on Condec Corp. v. Lunkenheimer Co.

Students may be asked what rendered the share issuance here invalid? Transparently, the shares were placed in the hands of a company supportive of Lunkenheimer's management and also by increasing the number of shares outstanding the board increased the number of shares that the unwanted suitor, Condec, had to acquire to gain control of Lunkenheimer. Note the court premises the reasoning on the harm to Condec, not the harm to Lunkenheimer (most likely the shares presumably were issued at their fair market value). Thus, the focus was on the *purpose* which the court concluded was to dilute the holdings of Condec. Hence, we see the equity powers of the court being invoked to preserve something of a fair or level playing field when control is at issue.

Later in the course you may wish to return to this case to consider whether this fact situation is covered only by *Unocal* or does it rise to the more demanding standard of *Blasius*? But at this point, not enough is known about either standard to allow this question to be thoughtfully engaged. Thus, best to use this as a case illustrating that courts look closely at the use of corporate resources (in this case, the issuance of unauthorized shares) to preserve control. *Schnell* adds further to this insight, but the true magnitude of the guiding standard does not arise until Chancellor Allen's opinion in *Blasius*.

Schnell v. Chris-Craft Industries, Inc.

Students may be drawn into the case by asking what is Schnell's complaint? The complaint is that the board amended the bylaws to advance the annual meeting date from January 11 to December 8. In the background is that Schnell had apparently requested a list of the stockholders which management has not produced. That request is not before the court, but nevertheless supports the view that management is not cooperating in having a fair election contest.

Why is advancing the meeting date harmful? It shortens the time which is important since the insurgent needs to persuade the shareholders, not only that the current management needs to be replaced, but also to make the shareholders comfortable with the slate supported by the insurgent. That is, inertia among current shareholders is on the side of the management. so that shortening the time necessarily benefits the incumbents.

The case allows you an opportunity to review who, under the corporate statute used in your course, has the authority to amend the bylaws. There is no dispute that the directors had the authority under Chris-Craft's bylaws to amend the bylaws. But, as we see, the court invoked its equitable powers. However, little insight is provided as to the governing standard guiding that exercise, save the rather empty expression the directors cannot use their power to adopt bylaws "for the purpose of obstructing the legitimate efforts of dissident stockholders in the exercise of their rights to undertake a proxy contest against management."

We might sharpen the students' analysis of these facts, asking how the above phrase can be used to explain the result reached in *Condec*? The Berle and Means excerpt is consistent with the result reached in both *Condec* and *Schnell*, namely that corporate powers are to be exercised for the benefit of all shareholders. But might we say that the board could, in both *Condec* and *Schnell*, have legitimately believed they were protecting the shareholders from the misguided management of Condec and Schnell, respectively? That is, Berle and Means by focusing on the shareholders, may just invite arguments by management that the insurgents are a menace to shareholder value. The next case more clearly puts this not on issues of good faith or corporate purpose. That is the significance of *Blasius*.

Blasius Industries, Inc. v. Atlas Corp.

You may wish to begin by making sure the students understand the two competing visions for the conducting the future operations of Atlas Corporation: stay the course vs. a leveraged recapitalization. Atlas had just gone through a process of changing its operations by identifying the extraction of gold as its core business. Blasius does not disagree with that decision, but wishes to see more debt included in Atlas' capital structure so that if their plan is adopted the shareholders would hold the following: cash (in the form of a special $35 million

53

dividend) which itself would be mostly funded by a loan secured by gold), debt (debentures) distributed pro rata in the amount of $125 million, and the shares they currently hold. Blasius's team reasons that if its approach is taken that there would be more value held by the Atlas shareholders than if the stay-the-course route is taken.

We might ask who is Blasius? This appears to be a hedge fund that is run by Lubin and Delano. Blasius owns 9.1% of Atlas.

How is the complaint that Blasius raises similar to that in *Condec* and *Schnell*? Steps were taken by Atlas that greatly prejudiced their effort to gain control of Atlas. How did they propose to wrest control from the incumbents? Atlas could have as many as 15 directors; before the board acted, there were 7 directors. Thus, Blasius had begun (this is important) the process of soliciting written consents (students need to know this is a procedure that can substitute for a shareholders meeting) to fill the vacant 8 seats with the nominees of Blasius.

At this point, you can introduce the provisions dealing with 1)flexible size of board, 2) the mechanics of written consents, 3) filling vacancies on the board, 4) staggered boards and 5) Del. Gen. Corp.L.§ 141(k) which provides that unless the articles provide otherwise directors serving staggered terms cannot be removed for cause. The latter adds to the angst of Blasius as not only would it, after the board's expansion and filling two newly created seats, have to amend the consents to seek removal of some of the directors (so as to have at least eight vacancies to fill with its nominees) but to accomplish such removal cause would have to be established).

As seen above, management responded by filling two seats on the board so that Blasius could not gain a majority of the board seats by the simple fiat of securing the consent of a majority of the shares to amend the bylaws to expand the board and to elect eight new directors to the newly created vacancies.

Students might be asked: did the court conclude that the Atlas directors acted in bad faith? For an improper purpose of perpetuating themselves in office? In Part III of the opinion the court states that the motive or purpose are not the issue. The question is the illegitimacy of interfering with the *ongoing* exercise of the shareholder franchise. That is, Allen sees this as a master-servant issue, and not a corporate powers issue. The management of Atlas, albeit well meaning, nevertheless engaged in acts that interfered with the shareholders' right to nominate and vote for directors. As he announces in this case, this subjects their acts to the "compelling justification" standard and management has the burden of proof.

You might backtrack here to both *Condec* and *Schnell* to illustrate just how those cases can be fit within the *Blasius* formulation.

Observe that had these changes occurred before consents were solicited, it is unlikely that *Blasius* would apply as later cases emphasize the need for the shareholders to be engaged in the exercise of their rights when management interdicts their efforts. Thus, in *Schnell*, if the meeting date had not been set, or if Schnell were not then seeking proxies, the conduct would not be reviewed under *Blasius*.

C.   The Role of Bylaws in the Allocation of Power between the Board and the Shareholders

If the topic of who has authority over bylaws and the content of bylaws was not covered earlier, e.g., in connection with *Schnell*, then this is the place to begin. If the authority and mechanics of amending the bylaws was earlier covered, then the topic of advance notice bylaws can be approached with the question: what is the purpose of such provisions and what do we see as the courts' approach to these provisions per the excerpt from Cox & Hazen? We see that this is minimally an early warning system to management and it also introduces a hurdle so that there is the possibility that shareholders will fail to act per the bylaw so that their actions must await another meeting since they failed to satisfy the bylaw requirement. Either of these is a plus for management. Since this obviously frustrates, or at least has a chilling effect, on shareholder governance rights, the approaches illustrated in the two cases summarized in the excerpt reflect the narrow, technical construction, at least before the Delaware courts, accorded advance notice bylaw provisions. For example, seeing the purpose of the bylaw to broadly assure due notice is given to the topic that will be raised at the meeting, in *Office Depot* the issuer's call of the meeting at which directors would be "elected" included the nomination of those to be elected.

CA, Inc. v. AFSCME Employees Pension Plan

It is worth taking the time to review how this case got to the Delaware Supreme Court. The conflict began with a proposal pursuant to Rule 14a-8 of the Exchange Act proxy rules. Management, as will be seen in Chapter 6, Section 3, can omit a proposal on certain narrow grounds. Management asserted that the proposal was not a proper subject for shareholder action. Historically and presently most such questions are resolved by the staff of the SEC, i.e., staff of the Division of Corporate Finance. Delaware had recently passed a statute authorizing its Supreme Court to entertain certified questions of law. Thus, the SEC invoked that procedure and the Delaware Supreme Court accepted the question.

Who is the proponent? This invites students to consider why a labor union pension plan cares about this issue? The questions lays the foundation for what is covered in Section B, the rise of the institutional investor, and the belief that improved governance can improve the performance of the portfolio company.

What is the proposal? In a sense, this proposal is like the second shoe dropping to the real issue, namely the power of shareholders to nominate directors. The instant proposal addresses the complementary issue, namely reimbursing the campaign costs of successful insurgents. The proposal provided for reimbursement of "reasonable expenses," and only applied when a minority of the seats were so elected. Thus, the proponents did not wish for this proposal to become a means for a change in control; that clearly would have been more threatening, perhaps even spooking the SEC or courts asked to consider the appropriateness of such a proposal.

What then is the tension that the Supreme Court is asked to resolve? It is between the broad grant of authority to shareholders to amend the bylaws and the keystone provision Section 141(a).

Why didn't the shareholders avoid this conflict by moving to amend the articles of incorporation to include this provision? This would likely have avoided the conflict, as even Section 141(a) carves out "except as may be otherwise provided . . . in its certificate of incorporation." Reference to the Delaware General Corporation Law Section 242 reveals that any amendment to the articles requires prior approval of the board of directors. This is common to U.S. corporate provisions, but not common to foreign company law where customarily shareholders can without board approval introduce amendments to the articles of incorporation. The U.S. approach has a significant impact in lodging power with the board vis-a-vis the shareholders.

The court resolves two important issues. The report to the proponent by their lawyer, "well, we got good news and bad news." The good news for the proponent is that the court views reimbursement and hence nomination as related to the process of electing directors. Hence, this is a proper subject for shareholder action. The bad news is the absence of a "fiduciary out" provision whereby the board could deny reimbursement when to do so would violate their duty of act in good faith and reasonably. The court point out that the proposal as written would require reimbursement if the newly elected director had sought board membership for personal (prestige, perquisites, access to information) and not corporate reasons.

Notwithstanding the outcome for the proponent in this case, the outcome was a big victory for activist shareholders, and shareholders generally, because it certainly clarified that proposals related to the process of nominating and electing directors was not precluded by Section 141(a).

Section 2.   Corporate Governance and the Rise of Institutional Shareholders

A.   Shareholder Voting

The trilogy-like materials here address in sequence the following: why have a shareholder vote, the introduction of supervoting shares and the distortions that might causes in the alignment of economic interests when it comes to voting, and empty voting which carries the preceding concern to its zenith. In sum, these three blocks of material makes raise important questions surrounding the benefits of voting as advanced by Thompson and Edelman. The response might be that law should seek ways, such as how record dates have been recently addressed, to reduce the incidence of empty voting. Nonetheless, we should leave this topic with a good deal of unease about the alignment of economic interests and voting power in a world of supervoting shares and derivatives that can so quickly and costlessly separate economic power from control. Isn't this what Berle and Means warned about nearly a century before?

Thompson & Edelman, Corporate Voting

The excerpt provides a succinct and accurate summary of the views regarding voting set forth by the major commentators on this topic: Bebchuk, Easterbrook/Fischel, and Bainbridge. To me, Thompson & Edelman build wisely and insightfully on the gap filling-incomplete contracts perspective by linking shareholder action to the principal signal of the firm's performance, the market price for its shares. They observe that giving owners a right to vote inherently aligns the corporation's interest with those of the shareholders such that the latter's wealth maximizing objectives will in turn lead to wealth maximization by the corporation.

We might believe this has relevance only for public companies and then only for those traded in an efficient market. Much is misunderstood about market efficiency and stock prices so that what Thompson and Edelman counsel is worthy of any corporation, whether publicly traded or not. Even in a private company, shareholders can discern whether income, revenues, book value, liability, etc. are up or down. That is, there are a variety of metrics available to inform owners that can be employed to assess the firm. Giving shareholders a vote on matters that are within their skill set, to assess whether directors/managers are doing a good job, whether the firm should dissolve, whether the company should merger, and the like, all play on the heuristics and skill set that first equipped the investor to become an owner in this firm. If we believe they lack these skills, then why do we let them invest in the first place. And, as Thompson & Edelman implicitly recognize, the owners have an economic interest to advance when they vote.

Note on Weighted Voting in Publicly Held Corporations

Stroh v. Blackhawk Holding Corp. illustrates the use of voting-only shares in the governance structure of a company. What is the legal basis for the attack on the Class B, voting only, shares? What does voting only mean? The basis of the attack is the inclusion in the Illinois statute, and see how this got carried forward even today in the MBCA, of "proprietary" in the definition of "shares." Hence, can you have a share without an economic interest? Why might we say that the legislature wanted shares to carry some economic interest? It would be to carry out the vision similar to that championed by Thompson & Edelman of linking voting to shareholder economic self interest to that of the corporation. Instead, the court in *Stroh* embraced private ordering.

What then happens in *Providence & Worcester*? This actually reduces the voting authority so that those with a large economic interest have a smaller vote. Why was this sought? Upheld? We do not know why the shareholders approved this amendment to the articles of incorporation, but having done so that appears to answer the legality of the arrangement; a nod to private ordering. We might surmise that the winner in this process is the managers who need not worry about large blockholders wielding influence within the company. Does this sound like a wise public policy?

You might take a minute to introduce the more modern, and converse situation, to *Providence & Worcester*, namely "tenure voting" whereby the articles of incorporation are amended (or this is included when the company is formed) so that each share has, for example, 10 votes. But upon a transfer the transferee enjoys only 1 vote per share, to be increased to 2 votes per share if held for 1 year, and increased to 3 votes per share if held for 2 years, and so forth to a maximum of 10 votes. Who wins by this process? Insiders who are less likely to transfer their shares ultimately hold a disproportionate share of the super voting shares. Hence, tenure voting can be seen as an entrenchment device.

Note on Empty Voting and Record Date(s)

The Hu and Black excerpt provides a nice summary of how empty voting can arise. The easiest means is via any one of several derivatives. Note what was happening, or was sought, in the much-publicized Mylan-King acquisition, which was believed a bad deal for Mylan shareholders and good deal for the King shareholders because Mylan was overpaying for King. We find a hedge fund held shares in both companies, but its holdings in Mylan were fully hedged so that it would take no economic hit if the deal was approved (but would gain mightily as a King shareholder. Truly the financial version of "you two guys go out and fight."

What is the problem with the record date customarily used by public companies? Share ownership on that date, but not the date of voting, determines who can vote on a transaction. Thus, changes in ownership post record date can result in individuals holding the shares who, unless they negotiated for a proxy, could not vote and those that no longer hold the shares voting. Note now the Delaware and Model Act authorize dual record dates so that companies can separate the record date for receiving notice of the meeting from the date for determining the shares entitled to vote.

B.   Financial Institutions and Their Advisors

Note on the Role of Shareholders under Modern Corporate Practice

When teaching this set of materials, we frequently open with the question, "so, who owns America?" (Most recently a studied answered, incorrectly, the Chinese, although once they foreclose on the national debt that might become a correct answer). The answer is that ownership is still about evenly divided between households and financial institutions. The relevance of who owns a company's shares can be illustrated by the following; the following illustration also backs into a discussion of the insights of Berle and Means regarding the separation of ownership from management.

Assume a company with 10,000 holders each owning 100 shares. The management is proposing a transaction of the type that there is a 1 in 10 chance this will cause for this company a $5 million loss in shareholder value. Assume further that by reading the 187 page proxy statement that any shareholder could determine whether this was a negative or positive value transaction (management supports the transaction as, in either case, it benefits them). Assume further that it would require 3 hours to read the proxy statement and that each shareholder places a $40/hour value on their time. What result? The illustration can be used to illustrate 1) rational apathy (why invest $140 of time for the expected value of doing so is $50 ($5 million x 10 percent/10,000); 2) the collective action problem related to the burdens of coordinating the actions of such a large number of holders (observe here also that if an aroused shareholder were to communicate to fellow shareholders this would still encounter their rational apathy?; and 3) the free rider problem that the shareholder who does step forward, turn things around, will only benefits proportionately while those that are passive in essence free ride on the diligence of another share proportionately as well.

Thus, in a world of dispersed ownership, as witnessed by Berle and Means, we see why it is true that management hires capital and that capital does not hire management. Now how has this changed in light of institutionalization (define that term) as captured in the material in this section and presented in the Conference Board data? It means that we are likely not dealing with actions by10,000 holders, but instead the actions of a score or slightly more so that the coordination costs are not that great. That is, the collective action problem is not as great. This then poses several issues.

First, the rise of institutions might be thought to change the calculus that supported the insights of Berle & Means. But note that most of the institutions are unlikely to challenge management. You might ask student which of these seem more likely to challenge management (public pension funds and labor pension funds) and which are less likely (all the rest-see later the discussion of hedge funds which are likely not aggregated here since they are not registered investment companies).

What do the readings say about the coordination costs? We see that not only are these costs lowered where there is concentration among institutions, but we find that their use of proxy advisors, such as Risk Metrics (ISS), the ease of voting, the recurring nature of the issues (so that overtime heuristics if not principles develop easily), and, as studied later, reforms to the proxy rules introduced in 1992 all facilitate greater activism among institutions.

You might wish to take time to explain who is a hedge fund and particularly who its investors are, since the readings devote some attention to their rising role. See the excerpt from Brav, et. al. later in this section.

The excerpted data from Choi, et. al. makes the point that ISS has a role, and it would seem like an important role, in affirming values among their institutional clients. It is hard to believe that ISS does not have an important role, since management takes ISS seriously and makes its pitch to ISS and then cries loudly when ISS says, "nope."

Note on Impact of Activism on Shareholder Value

The data captured in this note is not supportive of the social value of shareholder activism. Thus, CalPERS' efforts to shame managers by its annual list of the ten worst performing companies would not be supported by this data, as the data suggests no long-term residual benefits of such activism. But, as the next excerpt reflects, we likely need to disaggregate the data and we get a very different picture if we focus on the efforts of hedge funds.

Brav, Jiang, Partnoy & Thomas, Hedge Fund Activism, Corporate Governance, and Firm Performance

This study stands a lot or prior scholarship and beliefs on their head. First, note that the data collected does not support the view that hedge funds are short-term investors. The average holding period of hedge funds approaches 20 months.

And, why do managers clamor for restraint on hedge funds and activists? Look who are the targets of the activists. The Brav, et. al. data is consistent with the data summarized in the preceding note because it reflects that poor performing companies (e.g., low market value to book value) are the targets of such activism and note that Brav, et. al. point out that due to hedge fund activism agency costs are lowered (lower executive pay and increased dividend payouts) and CEO turnover increases, i.e., they're fired. It appears that more often than not that hedge funds are not confrontational. but cooperative with management. They also pick companies where they are likely to have allies, i.e., firms with a heavy institutional presence. Note here that the market reacts positively to the hedge fund's appearance, a favorable 7-8 percent abnormal returns associated with the announcement of the hedge fund acquiring a block of shares.

Section 3.   Vote Buying

Portnoy v. Cyro-Cell International, Inc.

Portnoy is a juicy set of facts that are well worth the time. There are four legal issues before Vice-Chancellor Strine. We have the sitting CEO worried about losing the election (and thus likely her job). She pulls out all the stops: 1) She co-opts an adversary, Filipowski, by offering to put him on management's slate if he supports that slate. She also approaches shareholders who have an interest in selling their shares to sell them to Filipowski. Consider that selling shareholders are likely individuals who wish to get out while the getting is good and, hence, are not likely to be supporters of management. 2) She makes a secret pact with Filipowski that if management's slate prevails, that the board will expand and appoint a nominee of Filipowski to the board. 3) Part of the votes secured for management's slate were cast by Saneron, a firm that used laboratory space in Cryo-Cell and Cryo-Cell owned 38% of Saneron; the support of Saneron followed Walton putting various unnamed pressures on Saneron (who before this happened was undecided how it would vote). 4) The CEO filibusters the shareholders meeting so that some arm twisting can continue and does not call the vote until she is assured that management's slate carried the day.

Items 1 and 2 pose vote buying issues. Students can be asked why it is that Portnoy's complaint fails in one instance, but succeeds in the second, on the vote buying issue. This goes to the standard that is applied to vote buying, which is linked to *Schreiber*. If the facts suggest vote buying, then the transaction is subject to heightened scrutiny under the entire fairness test with management bearing the burden of proof. What happened in this case was merely giving Filipowski a chance to be on management's slate. Moreover, this occurred more or less in the open, as Strine concludes that the shareholders must have deduced that Filipowski was on management's slate because he agreed to support the slate. Thus, with such an understanding this just kicks the issue to the shareholders, who with this knowledge, decide which slate to support. Note that if the decision went otherwise, it likely would open a good many matters up to the entire fairness standard since forming coalitions among voters will always involve such horse trading.

Item 2 does not have the same transparency. The shareholders did not know of the inducement to Filipowski of have his designee appointed to the board. Note the unsavory background of that designee - he had recently been the target of an SEC insider trading and tipping of inside information enforcement action, and as a result of those charges, forced to disgorge his gains and those of his tippees. Vice-Chancellor Strine observed that if this were disclosed, then we'd have a different set of facts. The reasoning emphasized that the shareholders were unaware of the promise. It is not clear whether the response here is premised on vote buying (the agreement with Filipowski) or failure to disclose important facts to the shareholders so that this violates the more basic duty of candor ala *Lynch v. Vickers Energy Co.* discussed later in Chapter 11, Section 5.

Item 3 is not vote buying. Rather it addresses misuse of a corporate resource, namely threatening the withdrawal of company business and offering rewards of company business depending on which way Saneron voted. What made this wrong is that the coercive conduct was being used to elect the Walton-management slate. Vice-Chancellor Strine speaks of coercion.

Notice that one of the factors that takes a defensive maneuver out of *Unocal's* protection is coercion. Thus, we will later see in defensive maneuvers that company resources can be used to defend (preserve) control. But such use is not permitted if the actual acts are deemed coercive.

Finally, the filibuster, carried out by the CEO appears driven by self interest, but it was self interest to retain control. Thus, under *Unocal*, not cited in the opinion, but likely shaping Strine's reasoning, the burden of showing good faith concern for the stockholders' interest was placed on Walton. What appears here is that Vice-Chancellor Strine reasoned this was way beyond acting for the firm but looked really like acting to close the polls only once Walton knew they had the last arm twisted and had secured the margin of victory.

Section 4.   Funding Proxy Contests

Rosenfeld v. Fairchild Engine and Airplane Corp.

This derivative suit seeks to recover sums paid to both the former incumbents and the successful insurgents for expenses incurred in connection with their recent proxy contest. As an opening matter, it is useful to broadly distinguish what separates the three opinions.

The majority opinion applies the rather broad rule that so long as the issues driving the contest are related to corporate policy, which presumably means divisions over how best to pursue the objective of profit/share value maximization, then the funds are reimbursable. Here we might recall the insight of *CA Inc.*, covered earlier in this chapter, namely that reimbursing expenses would be a violation of fiduciary duties if the contestant was seeking the position not to advance a particular view of what is best for the corporation and/or its shareholders, but rather for the personal interest of prestige, perquisites, and the like of being a director. Thus, the majority opinion in *Rosenfeld* lines up nicely with *CA Inc.* We might question, as does Desmond's concurring opinion, whether this is a distinction easily made, or simply, is it as a practical matter a distinction at all?

Desmond believes that the only expense that is reasonable for the corporation to absorb is that related to giving notice. We don't know what he means by notice, but broadly (and reasonably) interpreted this would be more than announcing a meeting, who the candidates are, and asking for a vote. It would include information disseminated related to the issues that separate the candidates as well as those issues on which they do no disagree. Any other expenses Desmond believe are problematic but ultimately resolves the matter by concluding that the plaintiff has failed to prove the expenses were unreasonable. Thus he concurs in the result but on the procedural basis of a failure of proof by the plaintiff.

Van Voorhis wisely points out the difficulty of applying the litmus of campaigning to advance corporate policy vs. personal interests. He expands on Desmond's point about the clear reasonableness of supporting reimbursement for costs related to imparting notice. But he believes expenses beyond that level are *ultra vires*. Note that he points out that the real policy issue is the employment contract and pension rights that the former board awarded a former officer, Ward. The insurgents reduced these sums and, as Van Voorhis points out, this may cause us to wonder whether the shareholders in rejecting the policy of the former incumbents should not be seen as their judgment that the disbursements to be made to Ward or that were made were not in the corporate interest. He suggests this would be in violation of their fiduciary duties; this seems a bit of an overstatement. The shareholder decision, throwing the old board out, merely means a change in policy, not that the former policy lacked a rational basis or constituted waste. Note finally that Van Voorhis believes that any sum spent beyond the level justified for giving reasonable notice would require shareholder ratification, and that the ratification would have to be by unanimous vote. This seems strange as well since could not shareholders ex ante have authorized reimbursement via a bylaw provision passed by a majority of the shareholders? If so, why would we demand a greater vote ex post?

The larger questions here is what would the world be like if incumbents were limited to using corporate funds only up to some minimal level deemed to constitute notice. This would mean that if they were locked in battle with an insurgent who was willing to spend mightily to rest control that the directors, largely outside directors, would either be outspent or have to spend their own sums. We might ask why the insurgent would be willing to spend so much if the insurgent was also limited? The insurgent may seek recovery by the rents it could extract once in control. We might also wonder about the willingness of outside directors to serve if they knew that they could face contests with limited funding to defend their prior policies and future vision.

As the note material following the case illustrates, there are few proxy contests in any year, and the expenses are large, but not out of sight. This may mean that while finding the right balance is problematic so that the open-ended test embraced by the majority provides very little regulation in this area, that the weakness in this norm is tolerable.

Section 5.   The Allocation of Power Between the Board and the CEO

Note on the Management of Publicly Held Corporations

There is a good deal of data here bearing on the following. Just why have we found that boards have moved from a management board to and outside board charged with monitoring management. The data reflects this shift, and partially it is that boards are poorly suited to manage since that requires more daily and hands-on conduct. But aside from the functional limitations on a board, we also find that the outside board continues to be seen as one means of addressing agency costs flowing from the separation of ownership and management. This is not to say that outside boards succeed; it is to say it is something that has a good deal of intuitive appeal.

Thus, notice that with an outside board that the time demands of being a director are great. That is, if the average director logs 140+ hours a year serving on the board of a public company. Where does that time come from when you consider that many of those that serve as directors are themselves captains of industry? Thus, the outcry when we see someone serving on five or six public boards. That is a whopping 800-900 hours of work in addition to what that individual normally does. Part of the answer is selecting retired individuals whose experience equips them to monitor the CEO.

What do Kahan and Rock tell us? It is that the board's functions in many respects have been balkanized across numerous committees. Listing requirements and even disclosure requirements of the SEC, compel companies to have not just audit committees, but compensation and governance committees. While these require some specialized skills, and have demanding assignments, we might also wonder whether those who serve really know how the company makes its money. That is, does balkanization and various compliance oriented agendas rob the board of the time and insight to be a reliable sounding board for business policies, practices and plans advanced by management. Jill Fisch's excerpt presents a very positive view of the multiple contributions of the movement toward outside boards. Not all data support this view; several studies reject the idea that a majority of the board versus a minority of the board changes the long-term performance of the company. An obvious issue hard to calculate in such studies is the degree of director independence as well as time committed by the outside directors. Intuitively we would expect widely differing levels of independence and commitment across "outside" directors so that any empirical result looking at the firm's performance, etc. in the aggregate is just too lumpy for concluding that independence does not matter.

Chapter 6

Shareholder Informational Rights & Proxy Voting

Chapter Overview: This chapter can easily merit four to five class periods. The first class could focus on *Saito* and the accompanying note material. The second class would include the SEC excerpt on the Proxy System and the balance of the material in Section 1. The third class can be devoted to the mechanics surrounding proxy voting under the federal proxy rules, the material in Section 2 and you might include some overview of the shareholder proposal rule or Rule 14a-8 itself. If you cover the shareholder proposal rule you likely will want to include the empirical review by Thomas and Cotter. The Rule 14a-9 materials in Section 4 can be easily divided over two days. If you feel time is short, you might omit *Virginia Bankshares.*

Section 1.   Shareholder Information Rights under State and Federal Law

A. Inspection of Books and Records
Saito v. McKesson HBOC, Inc.

You might find it helpful to begin this area by orienting the students to the inspection rights set forth in the statute used in your course. For example, if that statute is the Model Act, contrasting the shareholder rights under section 16.02(a) to inspect and copy items such as bylaws and minutes with their somewhat more circumscribed rights under section 16.02(b) with respect to accounting records and shareholder lists. This contrast should invite some discussion of what exactly is the difference in requirement for these two contrasting provisions and why the difference. The former are items more germane to activities or matters pertaining to shareholders (notice that section 16.01(e) covers not all board minutes but only those dealing with fleshing out rights, privileges or preferences of any shares issued pursuant to a blank stock authorization). The latter are more sensitive material such as accounting records (as an aside, the Official Comment to section 16.01 indicates that accounting records may not be just the trial balance or journal but could extent to "vouchers and receipts.").

It is worth considering whether the inspection right extends to only a shareholder of record, thus excluding a beneficial owner, or to a beneficial owner as well (see later discussion in this chapter regarding shares held in street name).

Once the distinction is noted, section 16.02(b) requires a "proper purpose" to inspect most company records and to access the list of stockholders. You can therefore move to *Saito*'s connection to the provisions just examined. The case provides several points to emphasize that the core feature of the inspection right is that of an ownership interest in the company so that we will see that Saito's rights to certain documents are linked to his status vis-a-vis McKesson, not to the other defendants, such as HBOC or the advisors on the acquisition.

What does Saito want, or more particularly, why? He earlier was one of the plaintiffs in a suit alleging the McKesson directors breached their duty of care in handling Mckesson's acquisition of HBOC. The suggestion here is that McKesson overpaid or just engaged in a bad acquisition by not discovering a series of accounting irregularities at HBOC. That suit was dismissed on a motion to dismiss, but without prejudice. Saito now seeks more information to flesh out his complaint so as to overcome whatever weaknesses were alleged in the earlier complaint. His stated purpose is set forth in a block quote in the opinion.

As a preliminary matter, Saito cannot launch an inspection request to carry out a fishing expedition to uncover wrongdoing. As the court points out, he needs to set forth in his request "credible evidence of wrongdoing" to support his request.

His next problem is whether he can access records that precede him becoming a stockholder, October, 20, 1998. Note that the board's agreed to the acquisition three days earlier and the deal was consummated in January 1999. The court grants access to records prior to the date he became a shareholder, because gaps in due diligence regarding McKesson's board and management failure to learn of HBOC's accounting irregularities, created on-going failures. It concluded that alleged earlier failures were "reasonably related" to the purpose for which access was sought.

A more ticklish subject is the ability of Saito to gain access to records of its financial and accounting advisors on the acquisition. Ah, that could be where the real money is in any suit, not the McKesson directors. After all, why else would God have created accountants but to be sued? To be sure, Saito's rights cannot extend to records not in the corporation's possession. This point should be emphasized as the inspection right flows from the shareholders' ownership status in the corporation. The Court of Chancery denied access to these documents, apparently construing Saito's request narrowly to seek documents related to a claim against the McKesson directors (and not McKesson's claim against its advisors). Even under this narrow view, the reasoning is not persuasive, since what the McKesson directors received from their advisors would be relevant in assessing whether they had acted reasonably and, therefore, would inform a shareholder whether suit should be initiated. The Supreme Court appears to read Saito's request broadly to include whether the corporation has a cause of action against the advisors. As such, the documents are more clearly necessary and essential to both whether the McKesson board, and managers, acted reasonably and whether McKesson has a claim against its advisors.

Finally, returning to the basis of the right, we find that Saito cannot gain access to books and records of the wholly owned subsidiary, HBOC. His rights are only as to the parent, McKesson, as the court holds that the separate identify must be recognized so that the shareholder entitled to records in HBOC's custody is McKesson. But, any HBOC generated records that are in the possession of McKesson can be accessed by Saito.

Note on Shareholders' Inspection Rights

Note 1 emphasizes the point made in *Saito* that a precondition to gaining access to support a law suit, i.e., using the inspection right as a substitute for discovery, there needs to be a showing by the preponderance of the evidence of a "credible basis" of mismanagement. Note the role that shareholder inspection rights can play in light of the PSLRA's constraint on discovery in securities fraud suits.

Note 2 offers several insights, and perhaps the most important is that absent clear statutory preclusion, courts have fairly consistently held that common law inspection rights continue to supplement legislative provisions, so that a statute's coverage of only some types of records allows other records to be accessed pursuant to the common law right.

Pillsbury is worth the time devoted to the issue raised in that case, even though it is likely is not binding precedent. As background, you might find it interesting reading the entire case to discover that Pillsbury muddled around for some time trying to gain standing. The shares were first held in a trust, then in street name, and finally he satisfied the "shareholder" status by buying shares in his own name. What exactly was his purpose and what records did he seek to obtain? He wanted a list of stockholders, but also accounting records to inquire whether Honeywell as making money, and how much, from its manufacture of munitions (fragmentation grenades). While applying Delaware law, the Minnesota court's reasoning does not make sense. We might well conclude that given the increasing revulsion with the Vietnam War that the public relations hit suffered by Honeywell was a sufficient corporate interest. At the same time, might not we see Pillsbury akin to Henry Ford, proceeding ahead regardless of the profitability of making more cars for less? We might wonder, therefore, whether the repudiation of *Pillsbury* in *Credit Bureau* is as sweeping as it is or should that decision be confined to the shareholder list, provided the request is anchored in a quest for profit maximization? Note 6 emphasizes as well that requests for stockholder lists elicit a more favorable response from courts than do requests for accounting records.

B. The Stockholder List in a Dematerialized World

Concept Release on the U.S. Proxy System

A threshold question is why don't retail investors have paper certificates to reflect their ownership in public companies? "T+3," the requirement that settlement must occur within three days of the trade, is part of the reason; if there were certificates, the shareholder selling GE shares would have to deliver the indorsed certificates to the company secretary (or most likely an external intermediary) for transfer on the company's books to the purchaser. This would add immensely to the carbon footprint for trading securities but importantly it would risk not occurring within three days of the trade..

The excerpt presents an understandable description of the hierarchy that exists among DTC, in which most banks and brokerage houses are participants, holding shares on behalf of their customers through DTC's nominee, Cede & Co. Thus, on GE's stockholders list, we find, Cede & Co., not Hazel Smith. Corporate notices go through DTC to the banks and brokerage firms that are its participants. This can be bypassed in the case of NOBOs. Note as well the "omnibus proxy" executed by DTC passes voting rights on to the same group of participants. The proxy rules do require issuers to engage in a search process by sending a 'search card" to identified participants. This is the means by which the issuer learns whether they hold for beneficial owners and the number of proxy statements/ballots needed by each participant to forward to the beneficial owners. Beneficial owners instruct the bank/brokerage firm via the VIF form how to vote their shares. Note that without instructions, the broker can vote the shares in uncontested matters (director elections, whether or not there are competing nominees, are deemed contested matters, so that brokers cannot vote uninstructed shares in director elections). Note in the release that retail investors are heavily oriented to being NOBOs and of all outstanding shares that are held in street name slightly more than half are OBOs, i.e., the institutions prefer being OBOs. We might ask why they like this anonymity. One idea is that this enables institutions to conceal their trading so as not to telescope to the market their strategies. They may also prefer the anonymity to avoid public pressure, or even pressure from the issuers. In any case, this is where proxy soliciting firms make their money; they greatly assist issuers in identifying who the large block holders are within any public company.

Note on Consents and Who's a Record Holder

This is a fairly technical case, but it shows how outcomes to proxy contests can go down to the wire and turn on fine legal points. The case does illustrate in dramatic fashion both the provision by which shareholders can act without a meeting and also the mechanics of voting/consent when shares are held in street name. Action by consent is an important provision. The Delaware provision is covered in the Note. The legal issue in *Kurz* can arise in other provisions as well. First, reviewing Delaware section 228, we notice that action by written consent is the default provision; you can avoid this route, and many companies see section 228 as a menace as it is something that unwanted insurgents can use (recall *Blasius*). Under MBCA § 7.04(b), the default rule is there is no action without a meeting (except per 100 percent ala § 7.04(a)), unless the articles of incorporation authorize action by consent. The issue in *Kurz* was the inconsistency between the use of "holder" for the consent provision in section 228(a) and then in subsection (c) providing that the expression of such consent had to be by "the stockholder." In the EMAK proxy contest, DTC never executed the omnibus proxy to the participating brokers. Thus, the brokers had been instructed by their respective beneficial owners who to vote for, and in particular to this dispute, whether or not to execute a consent per section 228. Instead, one of the contestants, Crown, had DTC execute the consents (in the name of Cede & Co.). Crown argued that DTC/Cede & Co. is the "holder" as that expression is used in the statute. It supported its position by the provision in section 219(c) which calls for the issuer to prepare a list of those entitled to vote. On the other side of this is TBE (Take Back EMAK), who had their consents executed by the participants (not Cede & Co). The Vice-Chancellor ruled in favor of TBE, concluding that the brokerage firms were the "stockholders entitled to vote." This position was extrapolated from the long-held position in Delaware that a shareholder could get the Cede breakdown (list of brokers holding in street name for their clients) so that this is the list referred to in section 219(c) and, therefore, defines who is a stockholder for consent purposes. The Supreme Court refused to budge from practice and its prior reasoning, holding that it is Cede & Co. who is the record holder, not those on the breakdown list. Thus it is Cede & Co. who had the authority, absent the grant of an omnibus proxy, to execute the consents, and not the firms listed on the breakdown list.

Balotti & Finkelstein Excerpt

This makes the point that corporations are not required to request and hold the NOBO list. Moreover, the inspection rights and the rights of shareholders generally do not include mandating the company to obtain a NOBO list. Thus, if a proxy contestant or other stockholder wishes a list of the stockholders, that list is likely to be pretty redundant in listing Cede & Co. and not very helpful. The company may at some earlier date, or at some later date, have obtained from the Cede Breakdown list the identity of stockholders, and from that process obtained the identities of NOBOs by contacting the participants. But if that list was subsequently shredded. and the stockholder made a request for the list, too bad for the shareholder, since as seen earlier the inspection rights go to records in the company's possession.

C. Reporting under State Law

This brief section sets the stage for why, in part, there are federal reporting requirements for public companies. State corporate law historically has made minimal demands on the company to provide information. Note that the Model Act and Delaware are at opposite ends of the state law disclosure spectrum.

D.   An Overview of the SEC and the Securities Exchange Act

Students likely have heard of the SEC. They need to be reminded about its multiple hats: rulemaking, enforcement and adjudicatory. Not all enforcement occurs before the federal courts. The agency has a broad panoply of enforcement powers and sanctions. Administratively it can compel disgorgement of ill-gotten gains, impose fines on broker-dealers, and issue cease and desist orders. In the courts it can also seek disgorgement, fines and injunctions. Officer and director bars are also possible as against public companies. An important prophylactic function is by the staff's review of compelled filings as well as inspections of broker-dealers.

Its independence comes from the term of office for each of the five commissioners who are appointed by the President and sit after confirmation by the Senate. Funding, however, is on a yearly basis so that the power of the purse, not to mention political persuasion, can have its impact.

You may want to point out that the SEC juggles two objectives that are sometimes in conflict: protecting investors and promoting capital markets.

E.   Periodic Disclosure under the Securities Exchange Act

What is important here is identifying the three ways a company becomes a reporting company: 1) per section 15(d) by engaging in a registered public offering, 2) per section 12(a) by having a class of its security (note it could even be debt) listed on a national securities exchange (Nasdaq is now such an exchange), or 3) per section 12(g) engaging in interstate commerce, having assets greater than $10 million and a class of securities held by 500 or more holders.

It is worth the time to review what the periodic reporting requirements entail, i.e., annual reporting per Form 10-K, quarterly reporting per Form 10-Q and disclosure on Form 8-K within two to four days of certain events set forth in that form.

F.   Disclosure under Stock Exchange Rules

There is a broad requirement for NYSE and Nasdaq listed securities for prompt disclosure of financially significant information. Each however is qualified the need for disclosure by a company purpose advanced by nondisclosure.

Section 2.   The Proxy Rules: An Introduction

Students likely need some assistance in understanding what a proxy is and why they are a necessity in public companies and even common outside of public companies. Simply put, if the annual meeting is in Topeka, just how many people really want to travel there, particularly if the meeting is in January. The reality is that few holders actually attend meetings, so for shareholder business to occur, proxies must be used. Thus, the real meeting is the proxy solicitation. And, if there is a matter that requires not just a majority of the votes cast, but a majority of the outstanding shares, shares not at the meeting are effectively no votes. Hence, management has an interest in turning out the vote which means soliciting proxies.

Next it likely is worth the time to review section 14(a), noting is jurisdictional reach and that it is an enabling statute.

The notes cover a series of important issues related to proxies. Notes 2-5 lay the foundation for why it is important whether a communication is a "proxy solicitation." If it is a proxy, there are a variety of concerns such as format (Note 2), anti-bundling (Note 3), meeting the minimal disclosure requirements that must accompany a proxy solicitation (Note 4), and whether that communication needs to be filed with the SEC (Note 5).

Hence coverage is important. Here we might want to consider a hypothetical that ultimately leads to an exemption. Suppose that Ajax (or call it ISS or Glass Lewis) intends to recommend to a group of financial institutions that they vote against three of management's nominees to the board of directors of Publico, Inc, a NYSE listed company. Must this communication be filed with the SEC and comply with the format etc. requirements.

The short answer is there is an exemption, but to get there we must start with why this is a proxy solicitation. See Rule 14a-1(f)(l). We can see this as "dissent" and that it is a solicitation as a "request to execute. . . a proxy". If it is to a number larger than 10, it is beyond the exemption in Rule 14a-2(b)(2). The exemption that likely applies would be Rule 14a-2(b)(1), assuming that Ajax does not seek for itself a proxy, and that it is not within any of the ten enumerated exceptions to the exemption of that rule.

Now what happens if CalPERS, one of the institutions receiving Ajax's recommendation, announces it intends to follow Ajax's recommendation and vote against the three directors? This would be within Rule 14a-1(l)(2)(iv)(A).

What then happens if CalPERS takes its announcement and mails it to 20 other financial institutions? This would be a proxy solicitation, being outside Rule 14a-1(l)(2)(iv)-it is not within (B) of that provision because CalPERS presumably has no fiduciary duty to the other funds. But note it would fit within Rule 14a-2)(b)(1), so long as CalPERS is not asking or seeking on another's behalf a proxy.

So what happens if you have a communication that falls outside these safe harbors? This leads into a discussion of the *SEC v. Okin/Studebaker v. Gitlin* standard. Note that context is everything so that in *Long Island Lighting* stands in contrast to *Brown*, being perhaps distinguished by the communication's proximity to the shareholder voting process. This is a ticklish area and we can see that if communications are subject to the proxy rules that we raise the price of communicating. This exacerbates the collective action problem. It is this reasoning that led to some market liberalization of the SEC's rules in 1992, which created the exemptions now found in Rule 14a-1(l)(2) and Rule 14a-2(b)(1). The latter facilitate institutions communicating among themselves and with proxy advisors such as ISS.

Section 3.   The Proxy Rules: Shareholder Access

A.   The Dissident's Access Provision: Rule 14a-7

So, in light of Rule 14a-7, why would anyone every resort to state law to gain a list of the stockholders? First, not all companies are subject to the reporting rules and, hence, subject to this rule. Second, there is a strategic advantage of timing your communication to shareholders, even reaching them before management, as well as following up on an earlier communication. These advantages can disappear under Rule 14a-7 since under the rule management has the option to send the dissident's materials with its own rather than to provide the list of shareholders.

B.   Shareholder Proposals under Rule 14a-8

It is possible to cover this material without resort to the *Standard Pacific Corp.* no-action letter. Indeed, the rule is fairly straightforward and this is not one of the complex topics of the course. It is an uncertain area, to be sure, given the gradations that surround the lore the SEC has created around Rule 14a-8. However, this is not an area where much clarity is likely to be provided to the morass of no action letters and the shifting sands that those letters stand.

A logical place to begin is with Rule 14a-8 itself. The format of the rule is user friendly. You may wish to outline the process, using the provisions of Rule 14a-8 to mark the way. It begins with a proposal that the proponent wishes included on management's proxy statement. Why not use Rule14a-7? Because that rule requires the proponent to pay the costs related to the solicitation; Rule 14a-8 allows the proponent's proposal to free ride on management's proxy materials. Thus Rule 14a-8 only applies is management will engage in a proxy solicitation.

Next standing/eligibility can be reviewed per paragraph (b). What then is happening in (i)? This is the battleground, namely the basis on which management can omit a proposal. What do we see in (j)? The heading answers this. Recall our experience earlier with this issue involving the question certified to the Delaware Supreme Court in *CA Inc.*

The work horse provisions for omission are (i)(1) and (i) (7).

Standard Pacific Corp.

This case illustrates the art form of the no-action letter. Note that the procedure set forth in Rule 14a-8 calls for the company to file with the SEC its reasons for omitting the proposal. That is what is happening with the January 18th letter. Management's grounds are that the proposal deals with "ordinary business operations" because it calls for a "risk assessment." The "R" word never appears in the proposal, which calls for goals to be adopted for addressing greenhouse gas emissions related to the company's products. Management argues the proposal invites micromanaging the company. Of interest to the art form is the authorities relied on are other no-action letters. Hard to see why this is not parallel to the facts the cited in the *Ace Ltd.* proposal asking for report on strategy and actions related to climate change. Note the proponents increasingly provide their own response to management's letter, and that occurs with their February 12th letter. That letter recognizes that heretofore the SEC staff had with fair consistently upheld omitting proposals that called for a risk assessment. Specifically, the proponent points out that its proposal does not call for any disclosure how greenhouse gas emissions will affect the company. To do so would clearly be calling for a risk assessment. It points out that the proposal merely asks for goals to be identified with respect to greenhouse gas emissions; it leaves to management what those goals are so there is no intrusion on their management.

The SEC staff was ultimately persuaded by the proponent and concludes the proposal is not covered by the exemption.

The following Note underscores the hopelessness of the distinction between assessments of risk and developing policies to address risks. The SEC's staff, therefore, adjusts its course so that the topic of the proposal is what will guide whether it might be omitted, and not whether achievement of that topic involves some assessment of risk. Thus, the proposal may be omitted if the underlying subject matter of the proposal is one that involves ordinary business. Even here we should observe that some topics transcend ordinary business. Where the gravity of the subject matter "raises policy issues so significant that it would be appropriate for a shareholder vote, the proposal generally will not be excludable..." We might well conclude that global warming is likely such a topic just as two decades earlier it was employment practices with respect to women, minority and gays.

Thomas & Cotter, Shareholder Proposals in the New Millennium: Shareholder Support, Board Response, and Market Reaction

The excerpt provides a contemporary analysis of characteristics of firms that become the target of shareholder proposals, who the proposers are, and the outcome of different types of proposals. Not surprisingly the targets are firms with relatively high institutional ownership; proposals need to attract support so going where the institutions roam is where one is more likely to find that support. Many types of proposals garner substantial shareholder support; for example those focused on elimination of poison pills garner 56.7% support. We might be surprised that it is individuals who submit about 70% of the corporate governance proposals. We might have thought this would be something dear to the institutions. We find the institutions propose about one half of the social responsibility proposals, the category of proposal that receives the least support (10.75%) among the categories studied. Suggesting class warfare around the rule, we see that unions proposed 56.6% of the proposals focused on executive compensation. Of note is that roughly one fourth (23.5% of the) of all proposals receive more than 50% support and this rises to 32.2% when we just look at corporate governance proposals. Thus, we might conclude that the shareholder proposal rule is more successful than commonly thought, with success being defined solely in terms of majority approval. Note however, that when the governance proposal does receive majority support, the boards implement the proposal in at most half the cases. We might also believe that success can be even greater if we believe that even unsuccessful proposals at least establish a medium for discussing issues with management.

C.   Shareholder Access to the Nominating Process

In July, just after this edition of the casebook was published, the D.C. Circuit, in *Business Roundtable and Chamber of Commerce v. SEC*, __ F.3d __ (D.C. Cir. 2011), held that the SEC failed to adequately consider the costs and benefits of Rule 14a-11. Thus, the multi-year odyssey continues for the institutions that wish to see the rule available and the SEC which continues to suffer mightily by the demands of the DC Circuit in its review of SEC rulemaking. This is an area where the benefits are likely very difficult to quantify, but the costs are fairly clear. What concerned the DC Circuit was the rather low frequency in which the SEC estimated that the Rue 14a-11 would be used. Again, this seems like a difficult issue to marshal hard evidence without resorting to a lot of assumptions. What is of interest in the decision is that the DC Circuit never referenced *Chevron*'s call for deference, even slight deference at that.

Section 4.   Materiality of Misleading Proxies and Rule 14a-9

Note on J.I. Case Co. v. Borak

We that the Warren Court clearly embraced the role of the private attorney general as a necessary concomitant to SEC enforcement. *Wyandotte* anchors this more with the Restatement of Torts's perspective related to the role that a statute can play in say negligence cases. The lofty rhetoric of both these Warren Court decisions is missing in more recent Supreme Court decisions studied in Chapter 12 where the antifraud provision is covered. Note when the balance in the Court began to shift in the mid-1970s, so did the approach toward private rights of action a la *Cort v. Ash* which sets today's template for a more restrained approach to determining whether future implied private rights of action exist.

Mills v. Electric Auto-Lite Co.

It is likely best to begin by reviewing the language of Rule 14a-9. It says nothing about private suits. It says nothing about a remedy. It does prohibit misrepresentations in proxies that are of reporting companies.

You might begin by laying out the facts of the case by having a student identify whether this was an omission or misstatement case? What was omitted? What is the issue of this case? It is not materiality, that was decided by Judge Parker and not appealed. It was rather whether causation was established by the plaintiff. Does "causation" appear in Rule 14a-9? No, the

Corporations and Other Business Organizations

Supreme Court and lower courts are creating this cause of action and doing so by analogy. What is the likely analogy? The common law action for deceit or misrepresentation each had causation as an element so why not include here.

How did the Seventh Circuit decide causation? It reasoned that if the acquisition's terms were fair, that it could conclude that the failure to disclose that all the Electric Auto-Lite directors were the nominees of its merger partner (so, what kind of voting = straight voting), Mergenthaler (the owner of 54 percent of the shares and hence vote), would not have a causal relation to the transaction's approval, i.e., no causation.

What was wrong with this? Court says this is based on the dubious assumption that shareholders would approve a merger just because it is fair. Why wouldn't they? Well, fairness is not a point but a range, so it might well be that the shareholder would disapprove if they believe the terms were on the low end of the range or that another bidder with a better offer would be forthcoming.

So what does the court do? Its language is fairly mysterious: "proves that the proxy solicitation itself, rather than the particular defect in the solicitation materials, was an *essential link* in the accomplishment of the transaction." What does this mean? Well, look at what Judge Parker did at the trial level. The vote required two-third's approval of the 1,160,000 outstanding shares. Thus, two thirds would be 773,337 votes. Since Mergenthaler held 54 percent of the votes, or 626,400 votes/shares, it was short 146,937. Judge Parker therefore concluded that causation was met.

But why not just ask Mrs. Mills how she voted? Do we even know if she voted? The short answer is that she is irrelevant since this is an aggregate decision. Thus, causation in the common law action of deceit or misrepresentation is customarily addressed via the element of reliance, i.e., did the plaintiff rely on the omission or misstatement. Those are one-off transactions, e.g., buying a used car represented to have been owned by a deacon but in fact was a refugee of Katrina and owned by a weekend NASCAR hellion. Thus, causation under Rule 14a-9 is an aggregate decision so that the reliance, if any, of the individual plaintiff is usually not relevant. (It would be relevant if there was an appraisal remedy and the issue was whether the misrepresentation duped the investor to vote for the transaction and therefore foreclose herself from the appraisal remedy)

Note that the court punts on what the appropriate remedy. We don't see rescission being awarded in these cases. If you move quick enough, the plaintiff can seek either a TRO or preliminary injunction. If the deal is unfair and consummated, damages would be awarded. Note here that Judge Parker awarded damages, but this is reversed, surprise surprise, by the Seventh Circuit.

Finally, Part IV of the opinion, not included in the edited case, upheld the award of attorney fees to the plaintiff's counsel for work done through the Supreme Court decision. *Mills* is a significant decision on this point alone given that it was a very early Supreme Court decision to not base the award of fees on the salvage value approach that required the creation of a fund of money.

Note on Materiality: TSC Industries, Inc. v. Northway

It is worth exploring the wide reach of materiality. As the block quote reflects, materiality does not depend on proving that the fact reaches such a level of significance that it causes the shareholder to changer her vote, e.g., yes to no. Rather it is sufficient that the fact is of the order that it would achieve actual significance in her deliberations. Sort of, "hmmm, let me think about that for a minute. Ok, good to have known that, but does not change my vote."

Note here that materiality is contextual as the court refers to the "total mix" of information. This has wide significance but most aspects of the "total mix" issues are beyond the introductory course. What can be said is that there is no magic list of facts that are material, but that these are customarily seen as a combined question of law and fact so that in most instances the judge resolves these on pretrial motions to dismiss.

The block quote from *Texas Gulf Sulphur* suggests that the materiality standard is wider yet, with the objectively qualified shareholder not being like the cautions objective person in tort law, but includes speculators as well. You might try to bring this home by asking the students whether they'd rather have a date with the reasonable person in tort law or the reasonable investors as captured in the quote.

Virginia Bankshares, Inc. v. Sandberg

We kick off the case by asking what does this add to our understanding of Rule 14a-9? It addresses, or rather qualifies, the causation issue, where the outcome of the vote if foreordained because the defendants control enough votes to assure approval. It also addresses when a misstatement of opinion can be a fact.

The facts involve the cash out merger of the Bank minority holders by VBI, the owner of 85 percent of the Bank's shares. For some reason, a proxy was circulated and the Bank director's said in the proxy statement that the transaction was being accomplished at a "high price" and was "fair." The price was $42 cash, which was above the then book value and market. Sandberg sued alleging these statements were false. To support the claim of misrepresentation was evidence that 1) the board had before it evidence that the going concern value was $60, 2) that the book value did not reflect the appreciation in the Bank's real estate holdings, and 3) that the market price was thin according to the investment banker's report.

The causation issue is the easier to deal with and you might wish to begin the analysis of the case following the factual development with Part III. Also, this puts the case closer to the topic addressed in *Mills*. The court concludes that we cannot say that the proxy solicitation was an "essential link," since. unlike *Mills*. the votes of the minority were not needed as only a majority vote was required and VBI owned enough shares to assure approval. What if there was an appraisal remedy? This relates to *Wilson v. Great American Industries, Inc.,* which wisely holds that the presence of an appraisal remedy moves the inquiry from an *aggregate* to an *individual* one. To have an appraisal remedy requires the shareholder not vote in favor of the merger; thus, it is the impact of the misrepresentation on the individual that is relevant not the impact on the group. In that inquiry, the over whelming voting power of VBI is irrelevant to the defect preventing a shareholder from taking the steps needed to preserve her appraisal remedy.

On the materiality issue, it is first important to address what the court concludes in part IIA, namely that the directors' opinion is material. But the rest of this section addresses whether, or in what instances, such an opinion statement can be a "fact." This gets into the distinction between what has become known as objective and subjective falseness. The issue of subjective falseness is the claim that the directors misrepresented their opinion because to state otherwise would jeopardize their relationship with VBI and its parent company, FABI. This type of falseness is not actionable. What is required is a statement of opinion that is objectively inconsistent with the evidence/facts known to the directors. Thus, in this case such objective falseness was present with respect to the assertions the price was "high" and "fair" vis-a-vis the book value and market price information that was before the board when it uttered these statements. As seen with the three items listed earlier, each of these facts were counter to the assertion. Hence we have objective evidence of falseness, so that the statement of opinion became a misrepresentation of a "material *fact.*" Thus, you can't successful survive in your suit by baldly charging, "you did not really believe what you said." You can survive on that if you support your allegation with facts that were known by the speaker of the opinion statement that were materially inconsistent with the opinion statement.

Note on Causation, Reliance, and Standing in Private Actions Under the Proxy Rules

This makes the point, made earlier in *Mills* and *Virginia Bankshares,* that we need to determine whether the issue involves an aggregate or individual decision. *Cowin* even holds that the non-voting shareholder should have standing to sue under Rule 14a-9.

Note on the Standard of Fault In Private Actions Under the Proxy Rules

There continues to be uncertainty regarding what level of fault gives rise to a violation. The cases do not require fault if the relief sought is a TRO or preliminary injunction. But when we move to rescission or damages, or some other retrospective relief, we see divisions among the circuits on whether mere negligence or some consciousness of the violation, e.g., recklessness or knowledge that a misrepresentation has been committed.

Chapter 7

Personal Liability In A Corporate Context

Overview: The materials in this chapter address pre-incorporation contracts, defective incorporation, and veil piercing. About two class periods can be allocated to the discussion, with the bulk of that time devoted to veil piercing questions. We've found that *Walkovsky, Minton* and *Sea-Land* provoke a good deal of discussion.

Section 1.   Preincorporation Transactions by Promoters

To begin the discussion, students might be asked what issue is raised in this section and what appears to separate the approach taken in *Goodman* from *Company Stores Dev. Corp.*? Each involved the promoter entering the contract before the corporation was formed; it is not clear why the intent for the contract to become binding at the moment the contract was entered into was stronger in the former than the latter case. We might believe *Goodman* was unquestionably the right result, if the facts reflected that Goodman had begun work on the renovations before November 1st, the date the articles of incorporation were filed. But the facts did not reflect that. Even the manner in which the first payment was made by DDS is not all that persuasive since a "–" is very different from a "&" in suggesting that Goodman was believed by DDS to be a party to the renovation contract. Bottom line, the outcome of these cases turn on intent and that is not always clear. Students may be asked how you would have advised Goodman? There are several easy options: 1) take an option on behalf of the corporation yet to be formed; 2) provide expressly for a novation discharging upon the corporation's adoption of the contract Goodman of any possible liability he may have; or 3) providing expressly that the only duty Goodman assumed was to use his best efforts to form a corporation and secure adoption of the contract.

Section 2.   Consequences of Defective Incorporation

This is an area now largely controlled by statute. You might wish to begin by reviewing the corporation code that you use in your course with respect to its treatment of this topic. We regularly find two provisions: conclusive presumption of corporate formation against all but the state upon filing, and provision regarding liability for those who purport to act on behalf of the corporation before it is formed. Does the latter have a knowledge of the defective formation?

What could the Attorney General complain about if the articles are filed? The importance of the statutory provisions in this section is to ask how much of the doctrine related to de facto corporations and corporation by estoppel remains. You might wish to use the facts of *Cranson* to illustrate the issue. Note here that during the nearly six month hiatus between Cranson entering into the contract with Big Blue to acquire office machines and the corporation's formation (the hiatus being caused by an oversight by the attorney and being something Cranson was unaware of), several machines were delivered and invoiced to the Real Estate Service Bureau for which Cranson was president. We might ask is this the kind of estoppel studied in the first-year contracts course? No, estoppel in its customary form is invoked to estop the person making the representation from claiming something else later. Here it is the *relying* party who is being estopped! We might ask why this is so? One thought is to prevent IBM from obtaining a windfall, the personal liability of Cranson. We might ask whether the defect in any way caused the firm to fail? Altered the risks of the contract that IBM had entered into? These questions sharpen an understanding of why the legislatures have taken such a relaxed view toward this area.

We might wonder how we resolve the issues in Section 1 with those in Section 2? One easy answer is that in the preincorporation contract cases covered in Section 1 the parties know that there is no corporation. This would appear to still invite the analysis illustrated in Section 1, namely, what was the intent of the parties. If they intended a binding contract to be formed prior to incorporation, then someone must be bound on that contract, and the logical choice is the promoter (save when one of the three steps set forth above, e.g., novation, are taken).

Section 3.   Limited Liability and Its Exceptions

Fletcher v. Atex, Inc.

To get the ball rolling, students can be asked what the Fletcher is attempting to do and why? We don't know much from the case but it appears that Fletcher is asserting a product liability claim related to the design of the "Atex" keyboard which repeated use caused the plaintiff to suffer "stress injuries." He is seeking to hold Kodak as the sole shareholder of Atex.

You should consider assigning the Berle excerpt, "The Theory of Enterprise Entity," since the court's reasoning is consistent with much of what Berle suggests, namely the litmus that would persuade *Fletcher* to pierce the veil is that Kodak and Atex (later 805 Middlesex Corp.) operated as a "single economic entity."

The court considers five factors raised by the plaintiff to justify piercing. You can review each of these five factors. In the end, the veil was not pierced. Question for the students is would it have been easier and less costly to Kodak to have carried out these operations as a division rather than a subsidiary? Hard to believe it would not have been easier. After all, with a division it would have eliminated a board and decisional hierarchy that would occur if this occurred through a subsidiary. That said, why didn't they? It likely is because of the quest for limited liability.

Students might be asked if this is a triumph of formalism over substance? If so, why? This invites a discussion of why there is limited liability. It is a fairly powerful subsidy for commerce, or at least undertaking risky ventures.

Walkovsky v. Carlton

I usually begin the discussion with an overview of the ten cab companies, each with two cabs, and a central dispatcher. I then ask why the decision, cited in the case, *Mangan v. Terminal Transportation System*, is not determinative of the outcome of this case? *Mangan* is consistent with the Berle excerpt, "The Theory of Enterprise Entity," as it held an affiliate corporation liable for the tort committed by another affiliate. Here the quest is to reach the sole shareholder of all ten, not to treat all ten as responsible for the tort (presumably because none of the ten had any significant asset). Note here the most valuable asset, the "medallion", or permit to operate a cab, could not be foreclosed on by Walkovsky, so the best he can likely find within the ten companies is the small non-mortgaged interest in the 20 cabs, all bright yellow.

What then is the plaintiff's argument? What are the social welfare implications of the argument? This, in part, overlaps with the "Note on Limited Liability Against Tort Claimants" where we see Hansmann & Kraakman conclude that the present system of limited liability encourages overinvestment in risky industries. That is, if there were personal liability in all tort cases (why just tort and not other cases?) this would encourage owners (i.e., shareholders) to insist on greater insurance. But note as well the practical problems pointed out in the Note regarding how this would be enforced, namely against larger holders (pension funds for retired school teachers no less). Should insurance be a substitute for inadequate capitalization? What exactly do we mean by inadequate capitalization? If this is determined at the moment of incorporation, is it not likely that for most businesses there never will be enough capital to meet its prospective risks (since most newly formed businesses fail)? Would this not have a harmful chilling effect on entrepreneurial activity? While the prevailing view is that products and activities should internalize the full costs of their operations for resources are to be allocated efficiently, are the costs of doing, this in terms of the dampening incentives for new ventures, too great? What appears compelling are the numerous practical issues raised toward the end of the Note which appear to support that limited liability is convenient, if not efficient.

What happens in *Walkovsky* in the amended complaint? The entire case arose in the context of a motion to dismiss so that the amended complaint provided the allegation that Carlton was operating the ten companies in Carlton's "individual capacity." This suggests that perhaps the idea set forth in footnote 2 was within the amended language, namely that Carlton prevented the companies from ever having sufficient capital by siphoning funds to himself, perhaps even in violation of dividend restrictions.

Minton v. Cavney

How is this case different from *Walkovsky*? One big distinction is the deciding judge, Roger Traynor who was a great fan of enterprise liability and causing enterprises to absorb, and not externalize, the costs of their activities. But factually this was a company that this company had ZERO capital. Indeed, it never really completed its formation, as after the Commissioner of Corporations denied a permit for the issuance of shares the company gave up on issuing shares, but nevertheless commenced business in the leased swimming pool. Unfortunately the plaintiff's child drowned in the pool, for which this wrongful death action is brought against Cavney, who was temporarily the firm's secretary, most likely as an accommodation to the client. Nonetheless, the court pierced the veil, holding that on these facts this was sufficient to disregard the corporate veil. Might we just say that the corporation was in this case just a sham, having never issued any shares? We could, but that is not what Traynor said. Later cases in California, following the trend outside of California, hold that inadequate capitalization is one, but not a sole, consideration in veil piercing. As we see later, this may have to be qualified where the question is whether the parent and the inadequately capitalized subsidiary are treated as one and the same.

We might ask how much capital would have been adequate? Note students need help in understanding that capital does not, in this context, mean assets but rather equity invested by owners in the business. Query, what result if the company carried $5000 insurance? With the judgment of $10,000 this might not appear sufficient and, unlike *Walkovsky*, there was not a legislatively determined minimum amount of insurance that was required. These are all speculative questions, as going forward when the issue is piercing the veil to reach an individual shareholder, if there is some payment for the shares, then lack of adequate capitalization is may not be alone sufficient for piercing the veil.

Radaszewski v. Telecom Corp.

Why wasn't the $11 million insurance policy sufficient in this case? The carrier went bankrupt two years after the accident. *Radaszewski* sees insurance and "capital" as interchangeable ways to assure financial responsibility. It therefore focuses on a broader, but perhaps more reasonable, approach for evaluating whether under the facts the veil should be pierced to hold the parent corporation for the torts committed by its inadequately capitalized subsidiary. We might ask whether this masks yet another question: what is the right amount of financial responsibility? That is, just how much insurance is enough? And, what if a company could no longer afford an $11 million policy? Is it to raise more capital? (hardly likely if it could not afford the premiums for the former policy). Is it to cease operations? If operations are continued, then as Hannsman and Kraakman argue the presence of limited liability encourages the conduct of risky ventures, or at least ventures that, if they fail, externalize their costs.

Sea-Land Services, Inc. v. Pepper Source

How are the arguments for piercing the veil different in *Sea-Land Services*? The students may be directed to the two-part test set forth in the opinion and focus initially on the factors raised in the complaint as to why the first prong of the test is met. Why would we pierce the veil for such factors as 1) poor record keeping, 2) breakdowns in corporate formalities (what did that mean here - no paper trail or approval process surrounding the transactions among the companies controlled by Marchese or for that matter transactions with Marchese?), and 3) commingling of funds? We might well justify veil piercing as a prophylaxis for possible fraud on creditors. That is, the factors raised in the complaint, and the court's examination of the facts, in combination point to a serious likelihood that money was moved from borrowing corporations to another corporation and ultimately to Marchese so as the "hinder, delay or defraud" creditors. As covered in Chapter 16, assets can be transferred from the corporation to its owners only in strict compliance with statutory limitations, e.g., that assets are not reduced below liabilities. These restrictions exist for the protection of creditors. We also know that fraudulent transfer/conveyance laws prohibit a transfer for insufficient consideration when companies are insolvent. And those same laws prohibit a transfer designed to "hinder, delay or defraud creditors" regardless of whether the company is insolvent. The point is that Sea-Land Services raised several facts supporting its efforts to pierce the veil; the acts by Marchese can be seen as indicia, or badges, of fraud. Thus, without having to prove actual intent to "hinder, delay or defraud," or that the transfer was made in exchange for insufficient consideration and while insolvent, the creditor(s) can sue the dominant stockholder to recover the funds owed them (this is more liberal than fraudulent conveyance or fraudulent transfer acts since under those provisions only the transferred item can be reached.

How then was the second prong of the two-part (i.e., fraud or injustice if veil not pierced) test met? The dominated companies were experiencing financial distress, in part exacerbated by Marchese "milking" funds from the controlled companies. His deflection of company funds to personal uses necessarily meant there were fewer funds available for the controlled companies' creditors.

Kinney Shoe Corp. v. Polan

If *Sea-Board Services* has been covered, you might begin the discussion by asking what is new in *Kinney Shoe Corp.*? The facts appear consistent with veil piercing under what we have seen before: poorly capitalized subsidiary (never issued any stock), no formalities in its operations, and no assets. Industrial, the subsidiary, was essentially an empty shell controlled by Polan. We see the court begins with the two-prong test applied in *Sea-Board Services*. However, West Virginia law adds a third test in contract cases and Polan was saved by this third test. The third test the third party, the contract creditor, will be deemed to have knowledge of what a reasonable investigation would have uncovered and assume the risks of those circumstance, assuming this is reasonable for the type of creditor the third party is. Thus, widows, widowers and orphans are not to be held to the same standard as say General Electric. Kinney was believed sophisticated, and could be held to have assumed the risk of Industrial's inadequate capitalization. But what of the other factors: no minutes, no officers? Presumably this too could have been discovered, quite likely as easily as the failure to issue shares (and hence inadequate capitalization). However the Fourth Circuit reasons that the third prong is "permissive" and thus reasons it is equitable not to apply the third prong where the shareholder has never made the effort to form anything other than an empty shell. That is, as interpreted by the Fourth Circuit, the third prong is available for the dominant stockholder if the formalities for maintaining the corporation are satisfied. We might well wonder whether this essentially eviscerates the third prong since the court states "maintaining," not "forming," the corporation so that this would seem include not just providing adequate capitalization but also formalities for its operations. Thus, what risk is left for the sophisticated or nearly sophisticated contract creditor to have discovered via reasonable investigation?

There are not many states that apply the third prong to the common two-prong test.

Eisenberg, Corporate Groups & Berkey v. Third Avenue Railway Co.

Eisenberg makes the point that subsidiaries, rather than divisions within a single company, are preferred because it is a risk-management strategy. Cardozo remind us that they may well be separate entities, but at some point it is perverse to view the parts as separate. That perversion would appear to exist in the eyes of the beholder, as the empirical evidence, later reviewed, and the frequent attempts to pierce the veil, each support the view that this is an area of ad hoc determinations guided by fairly fuzzy standards.

Note on An Empirical Analysis of Piercing Cases

Bob Thompson's classic study has now been expanded and as the data summarized here reflects the pot has been duly stirred. One common link is that misrepresentation makes piercing more likely. A surprising finding is that veil piercing is not more common in the parent-subsidiary setting than the individual-corporation setting.

Note on Direct Liability

This Note sets forth the very important area of vicarious liability under CERCLA, that of the "operator." *United States v. Bestfoods* illustrates that control and dominance alone are not sufficient to render the parent an operator of the subsidiary. Thus, the existence of overlapping boards is not enough to render the parent an operator. This conclusion is reached because "operator" suggests some action on the parent's part and action with respect to the environmental event for which liability is to be imposed. As the court reasons, "[t]he government would have to show that . . .the officers and directors were acting in their capacities as CPC [the controlling stockholder]officers and directors, and not as Ott II[the subsidiary] officers and directors, when they committed those acts." There was such evidence in the conduct of Williams, a CPC employee who was in charge of CPC's governmental and environmental affairs and was heavily involved in environmental decisions at Ott II.

Section 4. The Corporate Entity and the Interpretation of Statutes and Contracts

The Note in this section reviews how veil-piercing issues can arise in the context of determining whether statutory directives or policies are being circumvented by a party creating a controlled company to engage in an action that the parent could not engage in under the statute or regulation.

Chapter 8

The Special Problems Of Shareholders in Close Corporations

Overview: There is a lot of material in this chapter. The subject of small business enterprises is an important one and this is one of two chapters (the other is Chapter 9 dealing with LLCs) where the dissolution of such enterprises is addressed. You can comfortably allocate 4 – 5 class periods to this material. This necessarily means that not every section can be covered and within sections some cases and materials will have to be omitted. That is the nature of a comprehensive set of materials. The following are some ideas how to prioritize the material.

The introductory note material sets the stage and from there we can turn to the very interesting story behind the facts in *Ringling Bros.-Barnum & Bailey Combined Shows* which also sets the table for the chapter, where we see a range of objectives and problems common to small businesses: the wish to maximize control, the importance of exit, and most importantly that one always has to be aware that past is not prologue so that harmonious relations today can become acrimonious tomorrow. The case also sets the stage for understanding irrevocable proxies; hence the importance of *Haft v. Haft*. Here you can work in the statutes you use in your class dealing with voting trusts and voting agreements among shareholders. In the area of directors' agreements, you might choose to economize by assigning only *McQuade* and *Clark*, perhaps as background for considering MBCA § 7.32 and discussing as well super voting and super quorum requirements (*Sutton* is excellent background for these issues). These issues can consume two classes.

Coverage of fiduciary duties can include the important decisions of *Donahue, Blackwell* and *Wilkes*. You might consider advancing the dissolution cases, particularly *Kemp & Beatley* and some of the note cases (e.g., *Measelman* and *Mullenberg)* since the oppression concept is complementary to the topics covered in the fiduciary duty area. Of likely lesser importance are *Smith* and *Merola.*

The valuation materials in Section 6 are interesting but can be covered later in the discussion of the appraisal remedy material in Chapter 12 (or there you can just rely on the descriptive note material). The valuation materials also overlap with material contained in Section 3 of Chapter 2. Frankly, in the next edition we will do a better job of consolidating this material into two locations, but not in three as is currently the case.

Transfer-restriction material is a bit like watching paint dry; in both cases it is not exciting but necessary. The two key cases to choose between are *FBI Farms Inc.* and *Gallagher*. There are more data points in terms of legal buttons covered in the former, but the facts of the latter make that case an easier and less complicate set of facts to teach. It is unlikely would wish to assign both.

Jordan is a wonderful set of facts that invite a rich discussion of the duty of employer to employee in the context of a mandatory buyback of shares. This case and *Nemec* are worth the time if your course syllabus permit.

If dissolution is not covered after the fiduciary duty cases, then the key cases to assign are likely *Wollman, Kemp & Beatley, Meiselman* and *Muellenberg* along with the excerpts from the Hetherington & Dooley plus Haynsworth articles. The material in Section 9 dealing with custodians, provisional directors, and arbitrators is pretty compact and should be assigned with perhaps a half a class period to their coverage.

Section 1.   Introduction

By way of a reminder of the material covered earlier, students might be asked why don't small groups of investors prefer the partnership form over the corporate form? Since they have this preference for the corporate form, what do the students see from the introductory material regarding what appears to be the underlying policy statutory "close corporation" provisions regardless of the particular legislative approach? The short answer is to provide the private ordering flexibility that is the hallmark of partnership law in the corporate context.

Do the statistics in Note on Legislative Strategies Toward the Close Corporation tell us there are not many close corporations? No, it merely tells us that few small business opt to be within the specialized close corporation provisions; though a small business may not opt into the close corporation regime it still confronts an array of problems covered in this chapter. Hence, the fewness of numbers captured here do not document that the problems are not substantially pervasive.

Note on Non-Electing Corporations

So how do *Ramos v. Estrada* and *Nixon v. Blackwell* appear to embody contrasting approaches? In *Ramos* the question was whether an agreement entered into among stockholders in which they would vote as a block according to the will of a majority of them would be enforceable when the California statutes expressly authorized such an arrangement for corporations opting in as a statutory close corporation. The opt in required a statement in the articles of incorporation that the corporation is a "close corporation" and that its shares will be owned by not more than a stated number. What precipitated the dispute? Some of the group that was a party to the agreement wished to vote their shares in a way contrary to the will of a majority. The California court upheld the agreement, believing that the statutory close-corporation provisions were not the exclusive means by which such an agreement could be entered into and be valid. We might also find this case somewhat unremarkable since why shouldn't shareholders be free to enter into voting agreements (discussed in Section 2). The holding therefore may be a victory for corporate law only in the sense of saying that the overriding principle of a corporate statute is facilitative so that an expressly facilitative provision, such as section 706 of the California Corporations Code, is not a sword to impale agreements and arrangements entered outside that provision if they do not independently violate a non-facilitative principle or provision of the state's corporate law.

Nixon v. Blackwell is not dealing with an agreement among owners, as was the dispute in *Ramos*. The issue is whether stronger fiduciary obligations exists in close corporations, and in ruling the court in a backhanded manner suggests that there is separate treatment for corporations (on some items) that expressly opt into the Delaware close corporation provisions. Nonetheless, there is a rigidity in the tone of *Nixon* that is disquieting.

Section 2. Voting Arrangements At The Shareholder Level

A. Shareholder Voting Agreements

Ringling Bros.-Barnum & Bailey Combine Shows v. Ringling

A place to begin the case is understanding why Edith and Aubrey entered into the vote pooling agreement: to maximize their voting power so that under cumulative voting they would be able to elect five directors. The history of this is that North, with the support of the banks that stepped in during the Great Depression to keep the circus alive, had run the circus for years. When the loans were paid off, and the voting trust (into which all the parties had transferred their shares as collateral for the loans) terminated, Edith and Aubrey said, enough of the abrasive North. Aubrey had married the firm's auditor, James Haley, for whom Aubrey wished a more managerial position, and Edith's son Robert needed a position of stature too. Hence, it was time to push North aside, install themselves, and better yet, get some real work for James and Robert.

But in 1946, the wheels came off the cart. A great Hartford fire occurred during a matinee performance of the circus, causing 147 fatalities, with about two-thirds being school-age children. There were cries of recrimination, and ultimately James was prosecuted successfully for criminal negligence in overseeing the circus being set up that day. There ensued a hue and cry about whether the circus, then in ashes, would, like the Phoenix, be able to rise from its ashes. After all, what could be more American than the Ringling Brothers Barnum & Bailey Circus? It doesn't get any better. At a special hearing to see if James's sentence should be suspended, Robert testified essentially that James services were not essential to rebuild the circus. This did not set well with James, and worse for his bride, Aubrey. So, the two sisters decided to go their separate ways.

Students can be asked did the agreement deal with the event of a disagreement among its signatories, Edith and Aubrey? How?

With the mechanics of the agreement behind us, now on to analyze the opinion.

How do the approaches of Chancellor Seitz (one of the great Delaware Chancellors) and the Supreme Court differ? The latter issued an injunction canceling votes (or rather future votes). Aubrey might cast in violation of the recommendation of the arbitrator, Loos. The Chancellor specifically enforced the agreement, essentially having Aubrey's shares voted in accordance with the guidance provided by Loos.

What is the practical consequence of each of these two approaches? With Seitz, the Edith-Aubrey axis elects 5 directors. With the Supreme Court (assuming Aubrey remained uncooperative, and what else would we expect under the circumstances, since James went to the slammer because of Robert's lukewarm support), it means that North will obtain control (he owns 370 shares and Edith 315). What then is perverse about the Supreme Court's result? It means that the very objective of the agreement, i.e., removal of North from the helm, is defeated by the Supreme Court's approach.

What separates each of these approaches? Seitz justifies his result by "implying" a proxy in the cooperative person, Edith, to vote the shares of the person, Aubrey, who does not cooperate with the arbitrator. With the implied proxies, Seitz then has construed an agreement that is sufficiently specific so that he can grant the extraordinary remedy of specific performance. In contrast, the Supreme Court believed there was no basis for implying such cross proxies, relying on the circumstantial evidence of their probable intent based on the fact that Edith never tried to vote Aubrey's shares.

Standing back, what are some lessons here? First, agreements to act in concert are great if the parties are of one mind. But over the long haul, particularly in the business environment, parties seldom are of one mind at all times. And, when the divisions are deep and most likely irreconcilable, as in the Edith-Aubrey case, the pooling agreement is unlikely to achieve its objective. A second question is which opinion achieved the right result? That is, is the Supreme Court really wrong in restoring North to the helm if the choice is two sisters whose antagonism would just spill over to the boardroom if Seitz's order carried the day? Third, why not another remedy, namely declare the agreement terminated by frustration of purpose. This gets into an area of contract law but it is not likely to carry the day because the objective of voting in agreement was neither a legal or practical impossibility in the sense that usually supports this defense. Fourth, why is the remedy at law not adequate? This case was brought in the Chancery Court which is only an equity court and thus lacked jurisdiction to award damages. A somewhat different question is what justifies invoking the historical jurisdiction of equity in these facts. That is, to obtain either specific performance or an injunction the jurisdiction of equity requires proof that the remedy at law was not adequate. Another way of phrasing this inquiry is that if Seitz is correct and there was proxy in Edith to vote Aubrey's shares, why couldn't Aubrey just terminate the power like any agency power? The short answer is that a proxy is irrevocable when it is "coupled with an interest." The interest here is the power to share in the control of the company for which money damages would not be adequate. Much like the *Haft* case discussed in the notes, the voting agreement was a means to obtain a position for Robert and James. This is recognized as a sufficient interest to make the proxy irrevocable. Fifth, at the time this case was decided, the only effective way for separating voting rights from share ownership was a voting trust. That is, with Seitz's interpretation there is a direct inconsistency with the case law invalidating "secret voting" trusts. Thus, *Abercrombie v. Davies*, discussed in Part B, would probably hold the agreement constructed by Seitz to be an illegal voting trust. This may well have tilted the Supreme Court's decision.

Note the effects of Delaware Corporation Law § 218(c) which clearly implores the courts to carry out the parties' intentions with respect to such agreements. Most believe this eviscerates the holding of *Ringling*, although it remains a great teaching laboratory on the practical limits of locking in shared expectations, if not affection.

Note on Shareholder Voting Agreements and Irrevocable Proxies

Palmbaum v. Magulsky is an interesting example of a proxy being deemed invalid, although the dispute did not arise over the enforceability of the right to vote the shares, but rather whether the agreement itself was void as against public policy. We might recharacterize the public policy as being vote buying, a subject covered earlier in the materials.

On the availability of an extraordinary remedy of equity because the remedy at law is not adequate, see *Weill v. Beresth*, which is consistent with the earlier analysis in this Manual regarding access to equitable remedies vs. damages in *Ringling*.

In this regard, you may wish to demystify the expression "power coupled with an interest" captured in subpart (c) of the Note by explaining that the ultimate question is whether the 'agency" can be revoked, and this really asks whether the breach should be addressed via damages or one of the extraordinary remedies of equity. Each of the cases set forth in this part of the Note can be so explained.

Haft v. Haft

What then is new about *Haft v. Haft*? We suggest you review the grant of the proxy, but more important why Herbert requested a proxy for the shares sold to Ronald. First, we might believe this was for security purposes since Ronald like most Americans, did not pay cash but a note for the shares (which represented 57% of the voting power). But security does not explain why the proxy was the duration of Herbert's life. What then would be the basis for Ronald to argue that the proxy is invalid? It is that there was not a valid interest to which the voting power was coupled. Chancellor Allen points out that the apparent purpose of the power to vote the shares was to enable Herbert to continue as CEO. This, much to Allen's apparent chagrin, was authorized under the then recently amended Delaware statute that included "an interest in the corporation." This may be an unnecessary conclusion, since employment appears not to be an interest in the corporation but an interest in your own income, power, etc. It is not the same as having made a loan to the corporation or a licensing arrangement with the corporation. But Allen still sees the position as CEO as being the type of interest in the corporation.

B. Voting Trusts

The mechanics of establishing a voting trust is set forth in most state statutes. This could be briefly reviewed, particularly requirements as to duration and how public the trust agreement has to be. The Note material captures the former rigidity of the cases striking down voting agreements where 1) the title to the shares was not transferred to the person empowered to vote the shares and 2) there was a failure to file the voting agreement with the corporation. This was the failure in *Abercrombie v. Davies*, the last notable secret-voting-trust decision in Delaware. Since then the world has become more tolerant and such tolerance is illustrated in Del. Gen. Corp. L. § 218(c) and MBCA § 7.31.

C. Classified Stock

One device that can be used by all forms of corporations is to issue classes of stock that differ from one another in the number of directors each is permitted to elect. Such an arrangement raises a question, not addressed here, of the duty of a constituent director to represent the class that elected him or to represent all the shareholders. The focus here is the validity of such a class of stock when, as occurred in *Lehrman v. Cohen,* the class had no other right except to elect a director. The attack here was that this was an illegal voting trust. The court saw no separation of voting rights from share ownership. Another attack could have been that these are not shares because absent some financial claims on the firm they are devoid of a "proprietary" interest. Recall earlier in Chapter 5 we discussed whether a share could exist if it had no "proprietary" interest. There, we saw that *Stroh v. Blackhawk Holding Co.* held such shares were valid under the precursor to the MBCA.

Section 3.   Agreements Controlling Decisions That Are Within the Board's Discretion

McQuade v. Stoneham and *Galler v. Galler* are historically significant but long cases. If you wish to tee up the issue, show the modern response, and move on to the statutes or other material, you can omit both these factually rich cases and rely on the brief Note on Clark v. Dodge.

McQuade v. Stoneham

McGraw, McQuade, and Stoneham were all stockholders of the corporation that owned the Giants (then in NY). Stoneham was the controlling stockholder. The three entered into an agreement that among other things provided that each would act to continue McQuade as treasurer of the company. McQuade apparently earned the ire of Stoneham by opposing what McQuade believed were improvident financial acts sought to be undertaken by Stoneham. As a result, at the May 1928 meeting, McQaude lost his position because he lost the support of Stoneham and McGraw. He sued to enforce the agreement, and lost. The court broadly holds that directors cannot enter into a contract that would preclude them from changing officers, their compensation, or appointing others as officers. Along the way the court observes that as directors

McGraw and Stoneham owed a duty to the corporation and stockholders to be exercised in an unrestricted manner.

Should the result here have changed if the three parties owned all the company's stock? That is, is the principle of unfettered discretion of board members justified by the expectations and needs of non-parties to the agreement? Or, is a condition of corporateness that the directors are free of external contractual constraints? If the latter, what would be the purpose of such a rule?

Note on Clark v. Dodge

We might begin by asking why did Clark, the inventor of tooth paste, demand not only that he get 25% of the net income but that he would be the company's manager? Why not just take a contract where he would receive 25% of the net income in exchange for disclosing his "secret process"? One idea is that 25% as a manager accords him influence over what the income of the firm would be, i.e., he would have some control over the fruits of his secret process, whereas with a contract lacking such control he is at risk of the management of the secret process by others.

The dispensation from *McQuade* was premised on the narrowness of the agreement to a few items and that there was a condition about payments of dividends and salary to be reasonable which included the concerns for creditors. Note also all the stockholders were signatories to this agreement unlike *McQuade*.

Galler v. Galler

This agreement, signed by the owners of 94 percent of the stock, was upheld. The terms of the agreement included agreements to cast their votes for certain individuals as directors and, more to the point of this topic, as directors to pursue a set dividend policy and to pay death benefits upon the death of Benjamin or Isadore Galler. Here the court premised its relaxation on the special needs of the close corporation. There was a question raised about the duration of the agreement; the agreement had no sunset or term. The court read the agreement to say it ended upon the death of the last survivor between Benjamin and Isadore. And, like cases reviewed above, the agreement survived a challenge as a voting trust, since the parties voted their own shares. Importantly, the court was persuaded that the agreement provided sufficient protection for creditors against impermissibly high dividends and that the salary continuation agreement was a natural feature of small business enterprises.

As an aside, the case also ordered an accounting by Isadore and Aaron to assure that they received reasonable compensation post the 1955 Agreement but any sums in excess of the 1955 agreement had to be accounted for by them.

Wasserman v. Rosengarden is consistent with *Galler v. Galler* so that a directors' agreement between two 40 percent holders was upheld.

Alder v.Svingos is consistent with the flexible approach taken in *Ramos v. Estrada*, discussed earlier, as we see the court upholding an agreement that did not comply with the formal requirements of the N.Y.B. Corp. L. § 620, which required an agreement restricting director discretion to be in the articles of incorporation. In *Adler* the agreement was in a contract between the three sole owners of the firm. Note the agreement gave each party a veto power, and when two sought to sell the business, the third invoked the unanimity requirement. Citing the earlier New York precedent, *Zion v. Kurtz*, the court, like *Zion* reaches a sensible conclusion, much like *Adler*, that these provisions are enabling and facilitative and should not interfere with private ordering in another form if there is no apparent threat of harm to third parties.

What we might say from the preceding cases is that the trend line was in the right direction, namely away from empty formalism (empty in the sense of not appearing to protect any identifiable interest by the requirement, e.g., that the agreement had to be in the articles).

You likely will want to look at the statutory materials at this point to see what kinds of agreements restricting director discretion is authorized. For example, MBCA § 7.32 clearly authorizes a wide range of agreements, well beyond those of the type covered by *Clark or Galler*. Clearly the breadth of 7.32(a)(8) covers such arrangements. As to dividends, see (a)(4) under which board powers can even be placed in an individual. See (a)(6). Note the conditions for this occurring are set forth in (b) but has a ten year life. Note also there is an implicit unanimity requirement for these matters given the operation of the (b) and (c). More limited are the Delaware provisions, Del. Gen. Corp. L. §§ 350, 351 and 354. Note the gateway to these provisions, as seen in the introductory material, is opting into the close corporation chapter which requires a statement in the articles that the company is a close corporation, the holders are not to exceed a specified level, and the shares must be subject to a restriction on transfer. The point here is that statutes introduce a means for greater certainty, should the parties wish to pursue it.

Section 4.   Sutton v. Sutton

What kind of family reunions do you suppose the Suttons have? This lays the ground work for the case. Solomon Sutton and his mother, Yvette hold 70 percent of the company shares. David Sutton, brother of Solomon, holds the other 30 shares. The issue is whether the charter provision calling for any amendment to occur only by a 100% vote can be amended by a two-thirds vote. This goes turns on the construction to be placed on the corporate statute that was amended in 1962 to "clarify" the ability of less than a unanimous vote to amend a provision requiring a unanimous vote. Apparently the lawyers representing Solomon and Yvette didn't get the memo about clarification. Thus, the suit is initiated with the parties contending positions on the meaning of this arcane provision being well set out in the 6th paragraph of the opinion. Bottom line, fairly clear, is that the statutes reference that a provision calling for unanimous vote can be amended by a two-thirds vote "or of such greater proportion of shares . . . as my be provided specifically in the certificate of incorporation" means that a charter provision, such as that of the instant company" that says "any business" must be by unanimous shareholder consent, means including the business of amending the unanimous vote provision. It is worth pausing here about the social costs and benefits of a unanimous vote provision (or giving anyone a veto, e.g., if this called only for a 75% approval). The fear of course is deadlock. But at the same time, these are traded off for self protection. Thus, deadlock is terrible and gives rise to the tyranny of the holdout; but the minority also fears the tyranny of the majority. With a veto, the parties have to act in their informed self interest. In the small corporation we might find this acceptable since the externalities are not the same given the norm of these firms having smaller assets and, hence, a smaller footprint on society.

Now, you likely wish to orient the students to the how the statutes you've chosen to focus on in your course dealing with super vote and super quorum requirements. For example, MBCA § 7.27(b) essentially parallels the decision in *Sutton* by providing that a super voting or super quorum requirement can be amended but only the same vote or quorum then in effect. Note also that (a) talks about these being in the articles of incorporation as to voting and quorum requirement for shareholders. With respect to super voting or quorum for director actions MBCA § 8.24(a) & (c) provides that this may be in the bylaws as well as the articles.

Section 5.   Fiduciary Obligations of Shareholders in Close Corporations

Donahue v. Rodd Electrotype Co.

The facts of the case are relatively straightforward. It might be thought that the kids wanted to get their aging father's hand off the corporate tiller and thus engineered a plan for the corporation, whose board they dominated, to purchase most of his shares. Note there was never an allegation that the purchase price was unreasonably high, i.e., unfair. The complaint from minority Donahue family is they were deprived of an equal opportunity to sell their shares at the same price. This brings to light one crucial attribute of ownership in a close corporation, illiquidity.

The decision is the granddaddy of Massachusetts' path breaking decisions on close corporation fiduciary duty. While the case is clear in calling for heightened duties in the close corporations (vis-à-vis non close corporation disputes), students can be pressed to see determine just what is new here since if the book's order is followed it is in later chapters where the contours of fiduciary duties is more closely examined. What appears unique here is that the court sees that the relationship among owners of a close corporation is a fiduciary relationship. We do not find in the typical non-close corporation a fiduciary relationship exists between stockholders, save when we have a controlling stockholder whose duty has been extended not just to the controlled corporation but also the corporation's minority holders.

What then is the implication of this view? The court holds that the duty owed among close corporation shareholders includes a duty of equal opportunity in being able to sell their shares to the corporation (on terms equal to those received by Harry Rodd). What would have been the result here if the buyout served a corporate purpose (note here none was asserted). For example, what if buying out his shares was the only way to get the crazy old man out of the executive offices? That is, is there a qualification to what the court holds here, namely can a demonstrated business purpose for the action between the corporation and the dominant stockholder excuse the need to share this opportunity with the minority? On this point, see *Zimmerman v. Bogoff,* infra. And is this case also qualified by its facts, namely this was a complaint by a minority holder against the majority, so that more is at play here than simply a close corporation; the case involves the majority holders treating themselves differently than the minority. Thus, we might puzzle just how unique the holding is of this case. That is, we can characterize this as a self dealing case where the burden traditionally is on the self dealing (Harry Rodd) party. There was no independent approval of the transaction, unless you're willing to believe family members are independent of each other. This sort of showing normally places the burden of proof on the interested party who must show fairness. Does this mean more than fair price? In any case, the court states it is blazing new ground and that ground is one anchored in equal treatment of all holders within the close corporation. We might pause to ask students why there should be such a heightened duty? Illiquidity is one explanation- the Donahues had no means to exit. Also, in the close corporation we might think given the proximity of ever owner to the other owners that conflicts can be personal and not just about business as such. This suggests an additional edge to interactions among owners and adds to the friction that can occur in a business setting.

Note on Nixon v. Blackwell

The bottom line here is that Delaware refuses to embrace an equal opportunity approach to how E.C. Barton & Co. discriminated between Class A and Class B common shares. The court found there was a business purpose for extending benefits to the holders of the Class B stock since the holders were employees (good for morale and, hence, business). The corporation upon an employee's retirement offered the option to the employee to receive either Class B stock (prior to retirement the Class B was held in an ESOP) or cash. The latter provided liquidity which is something the plaintiff, Class A, holder sought. Moreover, if the employee or retired employee died holding Class B shares, the corporation would repurchase the shares from the decedent's estate. The repurchase was frequently funded by key man insurance for which the corporation paid the premium. Thus, we find employees had benefits that non-employees did not have. The court refused to impose a duty of equal treatment across holders of the same class. The

94

court accepted the discriminatory treatment was justified by business reasons (see earlier query about this for *Donahue v. Rodd Electrotype*). Note that a key feature of the court's reasoning is not just that there was a business purpose for the discrimination but that the differing treatment of stockholders (whereas rights within a class of stock must be the same).

Rosenthal v. Rosenthal

Students might be asked how *Rosenthal* is consistent with *Donahue*? The consistency appears in duty (4) providing that no member of a close corporation can gain a special privilege or advantage over another. Note also that the formulation imposes a duty of care as well on close corporation shareholders. Just what this entails remains to be seen as no case thus far has involved whether a shareholder in voting or some other conduct acted without due diligence under the circumstances. Note there is a duty here of candor so that apparently in Maine shareholders within a close corporation cannot deal with each other at arm's length.

Wilkes v. Springside Nursing Home, Inc.

Interesting enough this groundbreaking case was a pro bono case undertaken by a Boston law firm whose associate had met Mr. Wilkes at a weekend cookout at a mutual friend's house.

Students might be drawn into the case by asking why we might say Mr. Wilkes is the victim of a freeze out and how the freeze out occurred? We might also ask why it happened (note the bad blood that developed after Wilkes opposed the initial price of property that was ultimately sold to Quinn). The latter question reflects the reality that in the close corporation setting there are ample opportunities for personal animosities to arise.

One reason for exploring how Wilkes was frozen out is to ask how Wilkes could have prevented the freeze out via careful planning when the close corporation was created. He was frozen out by not being elected to the board, and the board did not thereafter appoint him to a position as an officer, for which a salary was paid (and it appears this was the sole source economic return to holders –initially $35 then later $100 per week). If Wilkes had demanded 1) cumulative voting and 2) unanimity vote among directors on any change in officers or pay it likely would have protected him against a freezeout in the manner that it occurred.

What then is novel about this case? The court expressly backs off from an unqualified requirement of equal treatment embraced *Donahue*. Instead the court embraces a three-step fiduciary duty formulation where after the last step (after first placing a duty on the majority to articulate why the disparate treatment was imposed on Wilkes – e.g., Wilkes could not handle electronic record keeping demanded to run the business, and giving Wilkes an opportunity to state how the articulated business objective could have been accomplished in a less harmful manner – e.g., send Wilkes to night school to receive the training necessary) the court exercises its independent judgment what the result should be. The latter is not clothed in any presumption to either side nor does it provide that the defendant's should win if they show some substantial or compelling justification. The statement of the opinion is that the trial court after hearing both sides makes the call with no deference to either side. The holding in *Wilkes* is the most sweeping authority we will see in the course in terms of the prerogatives of the court.

To be noted is the role that reasonable expectations plays in the court's formulation. The court observed "the majority effectively frustrate the minority stockholder's purposes in entering on the corporate venture and also deny him an equal return on his investment."

Zimmerman v. Bogoff

Clarifies that *Donahue's* equal opportunity language is qualified by the defense that there was a legitimate corporate purpose underlying the challenged transaction, e.g., Harry Rodd was a menace to the corporation and needed to be removed.

Smith v. Atlantic Properties, Inc.

Students might be asked how the parties in this closely held corporation sought to protect their interests in the corporation? There was a high vote (80%) provision so that each of the four equal owners effectively had a veto. So what was the dispute? Three of the owners wished for dividends to be paid; Dr. Wolfson opposed the dividends. Is there any reason why he opposed the dividends? His stated reasons were he wished funds to be devoted to maintenance and improvements on the property. We might wonder whether the good doctor was in a high tax bracket (this case occurred when dividends were taxed at the tax payer's ordinary income rates and the tax rates at the time of this case were very high (before the famous Reagan tax cuts). Money reinvested in the business could later be harvested at much lower tax rate (half the ordinary rate at the time of this case) if the business were sold and gain were recognized.

This is something of the converse of what we have seen before as in *Smith* we are grappling with the tyranny of the minority, not the tyranny of the majority. How then is this matter resolved? The trial judge relied on *Donahue*. The holdout caused the corporation to incur the excess retained earnings tax penalty (an IRC provision that imposes a significant excise tax when the company has not only unduly accumulated earnings and profits, but cash and other liquid assets that are not deployed in the operations of the business). The Appellate Court held that Wolfson was "reckless" in his holding out, so that the trial court was correct in holding him liable for the penalty taxes incurred. The court also affirmed the trial court's order calling for "reasonable dividend' to be paid and retaining jurisdiction to supervise compliance with the order.

We might see the trilogy of cases – *Donahue-Wilkes-Smith* – as reflecting the sensible approach for courts to embrace broad doctrines of fairness as a means for a neutral tribunal to address impasses. Certainly this seems to be one permissible result of the three-step fiduciary formulation in *Wilkes* and the operational effect of *Smith.*

Sletteland v. Roberts

Here we have the filing of a law suit, with apparent intent of disrupting refinancing efforts by the majority that had ousted the plaintiff, Slettland, as an officer. On a finding that the suit was initiated as retribution against those who had ousted Slettland, the court held he acted negligently and in breach of his fiduciary duty by filing suit. Again this illustrates the view that in the close corporation setting, shareholders owe fiduciary obligations to one another.

Merola v. Exergen Corp.

How is this case like *Wilkes?* This case too deals with the termination of a minority stockholder as an officer. The case poses a possible conflict between the "employment at will" doctrine act and the Massachusetts' courts protective attitude toward the minority. Crucial to the outcome in *Merola* is that while the plaintiff was a minority holder, stock ownership was not an expectation of his recruitment but rather something that he undertook on his own. That is, unlike *Wilkes*, the facts here do not support a finding of mutual expectation of continued employment and as the court points out there was no arrangement, as there was in *Wilkes*, whereby owners received an economic return on their investment in the form of salaries. Thus, the arrangement was not that of a co-founder but rather an employee who along the way purchased an interest in his employer. So, as Donald Trump famously says, "you're fired!" We therefore see further tempering of the broad swap of *Donahue* and *Wilkes.*

Section 6.   Valuation

The materials in this section can be covered as a means to illustrate buyout procedures and more importantly the determination of value in such an undertaking or can be skipped to be covered later with the appraisal remedy in Chapter 15.

Piemonte v. New Boston Garden Corp.

Piemonte is a thoughtful illustration of the Delaware Block Method. A comment on the weaknesses of this process is set forth in the Teacher's Manual in Chapter 15. The method continues to be popular. As the materials in Chapter 15 set forth, Professor Campbell's study reports that an average of 2.4 valuation methods are used in the appraisal process. The image of throwing arguments up on the ceiling to find what sticks is apropos here.

To begin, students could be asked what is happening at footnote 3 of the case. This was the trial judge's application of the Delaware Block Method. Review with the students just what do we mean by "market value," "earnings value," and "net asset value." Next, what does the weighting illustrate? Here the answer is twofold: the degree of likelihood that the firm's value would be harvested in this manner, e.g., liquidation = net asset value, and the level of trustworthiness of the number. Thus, why might we say that the market value is both trustworthy and not trustworthy? Trustworthiness of market value would arise because we can observe it, unlike the other two items; untrustworthiness may arise there due to there being a thin float so that little trading occurred, such that the market for the shares is unlikely to have been an efficient one. That said, why should any weight be assigned to this item? Note here that by assigning any weight to the market price typically brings down the ultimate number since market price typically is the lowest of the three numbers.

What about the statement that "a judge might undertake to "reconstruct" market value"? Isn't this the whole point of the appraisal process? If so, how might this best occur? This really moves us to the next two items on the block method.

Students might be asked what is involved with the Earnings Valuation process? If you earlier covered the introductory Chapter 2 regarding present value and stock valuation materials you might ask if we've seen this material before? We might also ask just what is the relevance of a "average earnings . . . for the past five years?" The relevance of such an average is its predictive quality for the future as it is future free cash flow that is being evaluated. Note here the multiplier, also known as the capitalization rate (discount of a finite stream of cash) reflects the relative risk/uncertainty with the future cash flow. How was this chosen here? What about the inclusion of the "expansion income?" Well, if you thought this new money would repeat then this sum should be included. However, these are one-shot affairs, not a perpetuity, so they should be treated as a present value of a future sum to be receive, not included in the yearly free cash flow. We might wonder how saturated the league was, i.e., would more franchises really be granted by the NHL?

How then does the Net Asset value differ from the Earnings Value? This appears to be valuing each asset owned by the firm individually. Would we not want to subtract from an asset's value the sum owed to creditors? The Net Asset Value can be thought of as what amount the firm would be liquidated for and available to owners if it sold its assets individually rather than as a unit (if a unit, then the value would be the Earnings Value). The court here dealt with book value of assets, which means just what the owners/stockholders would receive if the firm were liquidated. What's wrong with this picture? If this firm's liquidation value is, as the trial court concluded, greater than its earnings value, then why would not this firm liquidate? Note the per share Net Asset Value is twice as great as the Earnings Value per the trial court. Hmmmm.

What about the defendants argument that there is double counting by including the concession income in the calculation of Earnings Value and then attributing a separate value to the concessions in the Net Asset Value calculation? The court is correct in saying these are different measures of valuing the company, and that what is entailed with Net Asset Value is placing a number on each asset owned by the firm. The concession right is one such asset, separate from the NHL franchise and separate from the real estate owned by the company. Thus, putting a number on the concessions looks like the discounted cash flow analysis, but in this case it is to determine the value of that asset to a willing purchaser in a piecemeal sale.

This is not science, but rather a means for combat among warring sides to serve their client's interest.

Baauman, Palmiter and Partnoy, The Old Man and the Tree: A Parable of Valuation

This is a very straightforward description of the process for valuing assets and a business. It duplicates material in Chapter 2. The excerpt begins by covering the distinction between liquidation value and going concern value and introduces the concept of present value. The mechanics for determining present value are not presented in this excerpt but are very much the focus of the material in Chapter 2. The excerpt discusses what gets discounted, namely real cash flow, and also introduces the need to recognize that assets depreciate so some cash likely needs to be taken off the calculation table to replace the assets that are being consumed by depreciation, obsolescence and the like. It also talks about matching costs and revenues. The excerpt raises a consciousness with students about the valuation process and its beauty is its simplicity. To actually be comfortable with the mechanics of the valuation process requires resort to the material in Chapter 2.

Le Beau v. M.G. Bancorporation, Inc.

This is a fairly advanced problem on the valuation of a business. It can be easily skipped and likely can cause a good deal of angst with some of the students less familiar with business and uncomfortable with numbers. If taught, then doing so at a pretty general level is likely to be the safest approach, but it also is one that does not leave on the sidelines the important points illustrated by *Le Beau*.

The first issue to confront in the case is that MGB is the owner of two operating companies. It owns all their shares. Note that the appraiser determined the fair value for each of the two subsidiaries and then added a control premium to that number. The questionable inclusion of a control premium is discussed in the text material in Chapter 15. If the multiple (capitalization rate) for each subsidiary is determined by reference to market data for comparable companies, as done here, and the referred-to companies did not include a control stockholder (whose presence could depress the market value of the shares), then it makes no sense at all to gross up (here it was 35%) the derived value by the fact MGB owned all the shares of the subsidiaries.

Students might be asked what the Discounted Cash Flow analysis is comparable to in *Piemont*? It is comparable to the Net Earnings Value approach. Where did the court locate the discount rate? It was comparative data relying on a common source, Ibbotson. Note here again the court added a 35% premium for control.

What is the Comparative Acquisition Approach? It is an analysis of what multiples (of earnings and book value) recent acquisitions were effected at in recent months. This was then applied to the earnings and book value of the two subsidiaries. Why not gross up for a control premium? This would have already been imbedded in the acquisition price.

Note that other assets were owned by MGB; they were separately valued and added to the above numbers.

Section 7.   Restrictions on the Transferability of Shares, and Mandatory-Sale Provisions

A reasonable place to begin discussing transfer restrictions is the treatment by statute used in your course. The statutes customarily address three issues related to transfer restrictions: their authorization, what kinds of shares are subject to the restriction, what restrictions are authorized, and the impact of a restriction on a third party.

Using the MBCA § 6.27 to illustrate. Subsection (d) sets forth specific types of restrictions that are authorized (the "may" suggests this is a non-exclusive list). Reviewing these we might ask the student what would be a practical reason the corporation and/or its owners may seek each type of restriction:

(1)= *right of first refusal*: To maintain proportionate interest among existing holders vis a vis each other and also to control membership;

(2)=*mandatory purchase/sale*: To provide liquidity for an estate upon death of an owner or to provide liquidity for a withdrawing member (recall one of the issues in *Donahue* was the lack of liquidity in close corporations;

(3)=*consent restraint*: This type of restriction more clearly protects continuing owners against admitting someone who is seen not desirable; and

(4)=*prohibition restraint*: We might find that shares were issued pursuant to an exemption in the securities laws conditioned on purchasers meeting certain qualifications (e.g., all residents of state of company's incorporation principal place of business).

Which of these is the most draconian for the would be transferor? Likely it is the consent ,s this has effect (as could the prohibition restraint) of barring any transfer. This points out why all the other restrictions have been upheld at common law but not the consent restraint, which in all but Massachusetts was void as against public policy at common law. On this point, see the Note case, *Rafe v. Hindin.*

What is that public policy, and why have legislatures now broadly authorized in their statutes stock transfer restrictions? This reflects the awareness of the partner-like qualities of the close corporation. Under partnership law, unless otherwise agreed, new partners can be admitted only with the consent of all the existing partners.

Next, what shares are subject to the restriction? This is covered in subparagraph (a)'s second sentence. Notice the restriction can be imposed after the shares are issued. This would be by an amendment of the bylaws or articles of incorporation. If so, note that if three equal owners, A, B and C vote for the amendment and two other equal owners, M and N, do not, that the shares of M and N are not bound by the restriction.

Thus, if A and M transfer their shares to X and Z, respectively, Z's transfer is beyond the adopted restriction whereas A's shares sold to X are not. However, whether X is bound depends on the outcome of the determination in paragraph (b)(i.e., notice via the legend or actual knowledge).

You likely should choose between *F.B.I. Farms, Inc. v. Moore* and *Gallagher v. Lamber.* The former deals with several different types of transfer restrictions and the public policy issue of whether a transfer can apply to involuntary transfers, such as a foreclose per a sheriff's sale. The latter deals with the opportunistic exercise of a mandatory sale restriction and invites consideration whether fiduciary obligations or an implied covenant of good faith qualifies such a provision. We include both cases believing they are both instructive and it is possible for both can be covered in a single class.

F.B.I. Farms, Inc. v. Moore

Linda and Birchell (Moore) divorced, and their fourteen percent interest in FBI was awarded to Linda. Birchell (hereinafter Moore per the practice of the court) got in return a money judgment which Linda did not pay, resulting in Moore suing and executing via a sheriff's sale of the shares. FBI retaliated (being in the control of Linda's family members) by seeking to cancel the shares held by Moore. Moore filed an action for declaratory judgment that the cancellation was invalid and he was the owner of the shares.

Students might be asked to link each of the restrictions in the case with the MBCA (which was adopted and applied in this case) or with the statute that you are using in your course. The point of the exercise is to enable the students to characterize the restriction by linking it to the authorization in the statute. Here the first restriction is the consent type of restriction. The next two provisions in the FBI restriction are right of first refusal restrictions. The fourth restriction is a prohibition against transfer to non-family members.

The court concludes that Moore holds the shares, but takes them subject to the restriction. How did it get to this point? If the restrictions are valid, why then does he hold title validly to the shares?

As to the right of first refusal restriction, the court concludes that the board and shareholders were aware of the sheriff's sale, but did not act. Thus, they waived their right to claim the shares in that transfer; this waiver only affects, however, that transfer and does not itself remove the restriction from the shares.

As to the consent restraint, the trial court believed the restriction was unreasonable due to the lengthy and difficult history that Moore had with the other family members. But the court disagreed, concluding that the restriction's reasonableness should be judged when the restriction is imposed and not by subsequent developments. We might ponder whether the parties did not have an implied condition of "good faith" when they contracted. That is, do we really think it would be appropriate to withhold consent to the transfer out of animus and not genuine concern for the corporation's or shareholders' welfare?

What about the restriction against transfers to non-family members? This too was found valid.

Thus, how then does Moore end up holding the shares? Because the court reads "transfer" narrowly to not apply to "involuntary restrictions." What is an illustration of an involuntary restriction? Well, a sheriff's sale and also court-ordered transfers, such as a divorce settlement or intestate transfers. So, Moore gets the shares, but takes them subject to the restrictions.

Evangelista v. Holland

How does this case link to MBCA § 6.27(a)? The agreement to sell the shares at book value or some other referenced price/algorithm that later turns out to be a bad price for the seller, well, that's the bargain that was struck. That is, by seeing restrictions as private ordering, being binding only against "consenting" shareholders, this shoves the issue out of corporate fiduciary law and fair-dealing issues and toward contract law which is less focused on the equities of the particular case.

Note on Restrictions on Transferability and Mandatory Sales of Stock

This Note contains a good deal of background that would have been useful for the introductory discussion about transfer restrictions and *F.B.I.* If you prefer not to assign *F.B.I.* you might just assign the statute and this Note.

The material here covers a good deal of terrain in this area. The types of restrictions are covered as well as the policy arguments against the consent restriction are captured in *Rafe v. Hindin.* Another interesting case is the mandatory sale where good can occur by providing liquidity to the estate of a deceased employee; but also not in *St. Louis Union Trust* the estate resisted the purchase because it was on the eve of Merrill Lynch going public after which its market value soared and book value was just a pittance. But as seen in *Palmer*, a contract is a contract is a contract, so that agreeing to sell at book value is not unconscionable just because it is grossly out of line with the fair value of the shares. Restraints on alienation do call for narrow construction of their scope, a point made in part 3 of the Note. But fairness can be implied which is illustrated by *Helms v. Duckworth* where the party allegedly purposely forbore making the annual revision of the buyout price. The court held his forbearance was purposeful and in breach of his fiduciary duty.

Gallagher v. Lambert

To kick off the discussion, students can be asked what is the plaintiff's argument in this case? Or, would this suit have been filed if the redemption per the mandatory repurchase provision was exercised a few weeks later than it was?

Gallagher was fired on January 10th, three weeks before the buy-back price would have been based on the company's earnings and the length of the shareholder's employment rather than its book value. Was this important? The difference to Gallagher was $89,000 versus $3 million. Hmmmm, worth complaining over?

What triggered the corporation's right to buy Gallagher's shares? The provision enabled the corporation to repurchase the shares "if the employment ended for any reason prior to January 31, 1985." Note that Gallagher had worked with the company since 1976 (about 9 years) and had risen to the position of president and CEO. It was a position "at will," the standard relationship for most employment relationships (save law professors, whew).

What positions separates the diametrically opposed positions of the majority and the dissent? The majority sees this as contractual (recall the contractual nature of restrictions is embedded in provisions such as MBCA § 6.26(a) discussed earlier). Thus, this was the deal that was struck, so Gallagher has to live with the consequences. Note the excellent point made by in the dissent that if Gallagher were not an employee the ability to terminate the employee at will drops out of the analysis so that we would then focus on not just the express terms of the contract but likely their intent in entering into the arrangement and more broadly the fiduciary relations among stockholders (note here the earlier discussions in *Donahue*. However, it is nonetheless hard to imagine what such a mandatory buyback provision would look like and how it might not always be seen as something that could be exercised by the holder to the holder's advantage. But should this nonetheless trump the dissent's argument that engineering Gallagher's termination and timing of the buyback transparently was driven by opportunism by the majority and not for a corporate purpose? The dissent reasons that there is an implied covenant in such arrangements "that neither party will do anything which will have the effect of destroying or injuring the right of the other party to receive the fruits of the contract." Query, if the dissent prevailed, would this mean fairness challenges to restrictions, most certainly the mandatory sale variety, would become commonplace? Note the earlier text material that shows that complaints that the buyback price was too low customarily are, consistent with the majority's position, dismissed. What we have to distinguish this case is the quickly approaching reset date for the price which sharpens the inference that this is not just about unfair price, but calculated opportunistic behavior. If there are in fact fiduciary duties among the shareholders in close corporations then it would seem not a large step to proscribe such opportunism, and do so without premising the result solely on the disparity in the buyback price.

We don't know whether the result in *Gallagher* would have been different if he had complained his firing was also driven by a desire to confiscate his shares. He did not question his firing. It is hard to think this would have moved the needle for the majority.

Jensen v. Christensent & Lee Ins.

On a pretrial motion, the court reaches a result consistent with the result recommended in the dissent in *Gallagher.*

Jordan v.Duff & Phelps, Inc.

Students may be asked why it was important for Jordan to establish that his relationship with the firm was a fiduciary relationship? Jordan, for personal reasons, decided to relocate to Texas, quitting his job as an analysts. If he stayed through the end of the year, he would have the benefit of a higher book value to which the buyback provision was tied. He was never informed that his employer was in negotiations to sell the company. Had he just waited until January 10th, when the acquisition was announced, he would have received $452,000 (and a possible additional workout sum of $194,000) instead of the $23,225 book value.

This case is note worthy because two mavens of the University of Chicago argued persuasively to draw opposing views whether a close corporation has a fiduciary relationship to its employee-stockholders. Easterbrook states, rather boldly, that the fundamental purpose of contract law is to prevent individuals from acting opportunistically. Easterbrook states that the firm could not have opportunistically fired Jordan so as to confiscate the value of his shares. This, Easterbrook concludes, would have violated an "implied pledge to avoid opportunistic conduct." And, he further reasons that even if Jordan could have been fired, it did not follow that his shares could be have cashed out on the eve of the acquisition. Posner's dissent does not see the relationship as anything other than contractual and, therefore, would find no duty of candor here.

Nemec v. Shrader

Here the option was exercised by the board, transparently to advance the interests of the shareholders. Delaware, in a closely divided case reaches, a very different result than Easterbrook counsels in *Jordan*. Justice Jacob's dissent relies on the implied covenant analysis, namely that the exercise of the option to buy the shares must be in the corporation's interest. In this regard, his approach is consistent with that of Easterbrook. On the other hand, the majority view the arrangement as not requiring a narrowly defined corporate purpose but rather as one that serves the interests of its owners. We might wonder whether ex ante the stockholders would have agreed to this result, particularly if none of them knew whether they would have been the object of the repurchase. We might ask what other corporate purpose could there be for allowing the corporation to redeem the shares of a retired employee? First, this might be seen as employee friendly in the sense of providing liquidity to the employee should the employee wish it. This makes for happy employees while they are still working, knowing upon retirement they can cash in their shares if that is what they wish to do and the corporation is willing (its cooperation informs present employees they too can expect the same treatment). Related to this, liquidity could also be necessary if the employee dies and estate taxes are to be paid. Second, the corporation has a means to maintain a tight ownership group rather than having its shares held by the heirs, etc. of former employees. Third, redemption can be a defensive means should the company fear that shares held by former employees may fall into the hands of an unwanted suitor (assuming there are a lot of ex employee shares lying around). Fourth, it might be that the company is fearful that it would become a reporting company if the number of its holders rises above 500. These are just a few of the nonopportunistic corporate reasons for a repurchase exercisable two years after an employee's retirement.

Section 8.   Dissolution and Associated Remedies

A preliminary issue is to review the dichotomy that exists in most involuntary dissolution statutes, namely deadlock versus fraud/oppression. Students might be asked why these statutes are used by close corporations but not public firms? The answer is exit. That is, we don't find deadlock in the public firms, in part because the proxy machinery is dominated by management and all that is needed to win is a plurality. Thus divisions don't often occur and if individuals feel oppressed or defrauded they sell their shares. In the close corporation the concern frequently is to withdraw an owner's investment. This can only occur via dissolution since there is no market for the shares. To be sure, litigation can compensate for the harm done and bring it to a end (via an injunction). But litigation outside the dissolution statute does not return the investor's interest in the firm.

A. Dissolution for Deadlock

Wollman v. Littman

Likely best to begin with the facts. Students can be asked who probably knows more about the business in which both the Nierenbergs and Littmans are engaged? It likely is Nierenberg. They were vendors of fabrics. Nierenbergs began to compete with the business by selling directly to the business's customers. This prompted the Littmans to file a suit alleging the Nierenbergs were acting improperly by competing with the business. What was the Nierenbergs' response? The instant action , in which they sought to have the company dissolved. Here you might consider the students identifying either in the NY statute (it was a NY case) or the one used in the course what provision likely would come closest matching up with the grounds invoked by the Nierenbergs?

What relief and why? While there clearly was a deadlock, the case points out that dissolution, like the law generally, is not an unthinking process where merely lining up the facts with the statute leads to a predictable result. Dissolution invokes the equity jurisdiction of courts and although most corporate statutes set forth the grounds for invoking the jurisdiction of the court to obtain dissolution, that does not mean that dissolution will be granted. Was it here? No, the court instead appointed a receiver. Why not order dissolution? To have dissolved the company would have essentially meant that the Nierenbergs would never be held accountable for their wrongful competition with the firm. Moreover, it would then have allowed them to continue unrestrained in appropriating the patronage that formerly was that of the firm jointly owned by the two families.

The issues here are much like those studied earlier in Chapter 3 with the partnership case, *Page v. Page*. Namely, is it appropriate to link the greater experience, perhaps wisdom, of the more experienced owners, in this case the Nierenbergs, with the less experienced, perhaps passive investors, in this case the Littmans, to infinity? This court does not address this but appoints a neutral party, a receiver, to run the business. What is the likely ultimate solution here? Might it be a buyout? In which case, who is most likely to buy out the other party? That likely would be the party who can put the assets to their highest and best use: the Nierenbergs.

Note on Hetherington and Dooley

This classic study makes the point raised above, namely close corporation disputes are frequently focused on dissolution as a means for exit. Their study pointed out that dissolution orders lead to buyouts and not bust-ups of the firm. Why might we think this is reassuring? It is because the dismemberment of the firm, i.e., the bust-up, would destroy the social benefits of the firm's goodwill where the firm's going concern value is greater than its liquidation value. Their study showed that in about half the cases in which the court denied dissolution, there was nonetheless a buyout and in about half the other cases the business was sold to a third party. And, even when dissolution was ordered, the firm was not liquidated except in a distinct minority of the cases. Bottom line, the petition to dissolve is a means to an end, regardless of who wins, and the end usually is a buyout. Hence, courts and legislatures may well focus their attention on the inevitability of a buyout and not think that dissolution necessarily leads to value-destructive results.

Matter of Kemp & Beatley, Inc.

This is a leading case embracing the reasonable expectations formula for determining whether there has been "oppression" as proscribed in most dissolution statutes, *see e.g.*, the statute in the case- N.Y. Bus. Corp. L. § 1104-a; MBCA § 14.30(a)(2)(ii).

To begin the case, students might be asked why it was necessary for both Gardstein and Dissin to join in the suit? [for the grounds alleged the statute required a petition by at least at 20 percent holder or holders] Next, what provision of the N.Y. statute are they proceeding under? [that the majority had acted oppressively] If you are using the Model Act (or a statute based on the Model Act) you might ask what are the implications of this case's holding for practice under these other provisions? [oppression is a common provision and is found in the Model Act §14.30(a)(2)(ii).]

What was the approach the court took to determine whether the majority had acted oppressively toward Messrs. Gardstein and Dissin? The court begins with identifying the "objectively viewed" reasonable expectations of the petitioners and whether the majority had engaged in conduct that "substantially defeats expectations." Here there was a long-standing practice of awarding compensation, a bonus of sorts, that was linked to stock ownership. Once the petitioners left the firm this was discontinued and the bonuses were based on services rendered, which meant that Gardstein and Dissin were cut out of this portion of the profits that were distributed. Here we may probe the uniqueness of the facts. For example, what result if there had not been a prior history of bonuses? What if the bonuses that previously were paid were terminated so that funds that previously were distributed to owners were reinvested in the business? Each of these are quite different and we may see that what the court is engaged in is a lighter form of fiduciary-duty inquiry and not so much an unwavering commitment to the notion that past is prologue. The point is that we might not have here, as we also did not have in *Donahue* , a valid business purpose asserted for the change. The facts in the case can be seen as a thinly veiled grab for assets by the majority, which the court addresses through the lens of dissolution on the grounds of "oppression." After all, oppression should at least reach opportunistic behavior by the majority.

What then is the remedy? The court's holding that oppression is present merely kicks the can down the road. The court modifies the trial court order to allow extended time for the buyout process, which is covered by the NYBCL § 1118. Here we might note that not only does a liberal interpretation of the grounds for judicial dissolution provide a counterbalance to the majority's opportunistic grab for assets, but it provides a mechanism for an independent assessment of the buyout price. That is, the earlier-reviewed Hetherington and Dooley article points out that in an earlier legal era in most cases a buyout results regardless of the judicial outcome; what the modern liberalization might be seen as doing is making that buyout process a more refereed one than heretofore.

Meiselman v. Meiselman

So, two brothers, "Meeselman" and "Miselman" who could not agree on anything, even how to pronounce their names, find their way into corporate law history because the North Carolina Supreme Court, embraced the reasonable expectations approach even in a case where the petitioner inherited his shares. We might question whether it is reasonable to so extend the doctrine? Certainly all the reasons advanced in *Kemp* and for that matter all the other cases in this chapter where the courts have accorded special attention or protection to the minority in close corporations, are equally applicable whether one purchased their shares as one of the original shareholders or subsequently acquired the shares (e.g., lack of liquidity, dependence on the business for livelihood, close involvement in the business). Justice Frye, in this case, reasons that reasonable expectations can evolve over time , with perhaps the only significant limitation beyond "reasonableness" being that the expectations "must be known to or be assumed by the other shareholders and concurred in by them."

Haynsworth, The Effectiveness of Involuntary Dissolution Suits as a Remedy for Close Corporation Dissension

The excerpt provides a thoughtful and crisp statement of the three faces of oppression (departure from fair dealing, violation of strict duty of good faith, and loyalty found in partnership and defeating reasonable expectations), each having a fiduciary ring to itself. Students might be asked should it matter which of these approaches apply? That is, there likely is a good deal, if not perfect overlap, among them, so that it might be impossible to identify a set of facts that, for example, would constitute a departure from fair dealing that did not also appear to defeat reasonable expectations. It may be reasonable for cases invoking one way to verbalize the justification for a conclusion there was oppression not to apply in a jurisdiction that employs a different approach to verbalizing what is oppression.

Note on the Duties of Care and Loyalty in Close Corporations

The note raises the question whether a rational business purpose, long the major bulwark in corporate law for protecting discretionary decisions by directors and officers, is less of a force in the close corporation setting. We don't find in cases such as *Donahue* and *Kemp* any disposition on the courts' part to weigh a bona fide business purpose. The court in *Wilkes* did invite the majority to state its business reason for terminating Wilkes, but accorded Wilkes the benefit of attaining the majority's objective could have been accomplished in a less harmful manner. The note emphasizes that an overarching concern here is the unfairness of treating shareholders unequally and more fundamentally, what would the shareholders ex ante have expected to be fair treatment.

McCallum v. Rosen's Diversified, Inc.

The former CEO brought suit after discussions for the repurchase of his shares showed the parties had widely differing views on the fair value of his shares. He alleged various misconduct on the part of the majority.

Students might be asked just what is new about this case over prior cases, e.g., *Kemp*? One is the statute's wording, unique to Minnesota, that authorizes a buyout when those in control have "acted in a manner unfairly prejudicial" to the petitioner. How did the court interpret this phrase? In a way very similar to the reasonable expectations approach in *Kemp*.

What result? The expectations were defeated by 1) firing the CEO and 2) that the shares were granted to him as an inducement to join the firm and contribute to its growth. Compare this reasoning with the earlier *Merola v. Exergen Corp.*, where a vice president was unsuccessful in questioning his firing and the Massachusetts court held he was an employee at will. But there was no real complaint in *Merola* about the price of the shares. In *McCallum* the effect of the court's holding is to provide a neutral process for determining what is the fair price for his shares, and not to return him to the position of being CEO. Thus, the result here poses much less intrusion on the corporation's operation than was sought in either *Merola* or for that matter *Wilkes*.

Muellenberg v. Bikon Corp.

Students might be asked what is new in this case? One answer is that the court decides that the remedy is not dissolution but rather ordering a buyout. Thus, New Jersey is among the states that provide that once the grounds for judicial dissolution are successfully established, the court has a full panoply of remedies, short of dissolution, that can be granted. A buyout is one of those remedies. Second, it is distinctive because the court's order provides it is the petitioning minority holder who has the buyout option. Students may be asked why this would be so and is likely appropriate. Burg knew the business and may appropriately be seen as the business. And, the court may have been doing simply what would have happened in any event: placing the option in the hands of the party who most likely could place the assets to their highest and best use, Burg, since he was the one who knew the business.

Haynsworth, The Effectiveness of Involuntary Dissolution Suits as a Remedy for Close Corporation Dissension

Makes the point that the remedy most likely to flow from a dissolution proceeding is a buyout. What differentiates this piece from Heatherington and Dooley is that courts in that earlier study were less willing to entertain dissolution (but a buyout occurred as matter of private ordering). What we see today is willingness to find that the grounds for dissolution have been established, but not order dissolution but instead go right to a buyout.

Note on Dissolution

The material in this note sets for the evolution of dissolution cases over time to reach the point that is essentially captured in the preceding Haynsworth excerpt.

Note on Valuation of the Minority Shares

While we might believe that the best assurance of a accurate valuation of a departing member's shares is to just liquidate the business, the excerpt from Professor Bahls' article sets forth the issues that can prevent the sale of the business itself yielding a fair price for that business. Accepting this, not to mention the dislocation that might occur by the sale of the business, means the vagaries of the valuation process for the minority shares poses its own challenges and biases. This is the subject of the next case.

Chartland v. Country View Golf Club, Inc.

The Rhode Island statute provided the court could order a buyout of a petitioning shareholder "at a price equal to their fair value" when the court finds a ground for dissolution had been established. The appraiser was appointed and submitted two estimates. The students might be asked what distinguished the two bids aside from one being lower than the other? The answer is the lower bid reflected a discount for the petitioner's minority position (footnote 4 reflects this could also have been in part attributable to a discount for the shares marketability). Other materials in Section 6 of Chapter 8 as well as Section 1 of Chapter 15 address both forms of discount. The note material in Chapter 15 explores in some detail the notion of a minority discount and how this is unlikely to be very persuasive if the task is to measure a shareholder's interest in the firm. However, courts are more willing to apply both a marketability and minority discount if the statute focuses instead on the value of the shares rather the value of the interest in the firm.

What was the court's response to either discount applying in this proceeding? The court said the discount made no sense when it was the corporation is the purchaser. Moreover, if the court had instead ordered dissolution so that the firm would be liquidated, all shares would be treated equally in sharing the liquidating distribution. When liquidation is avoided due to a buyout, there should be no different treatment by the shareholders. Indeed, to permit such different treatment would essentially allow the majority-continuing shareholders to game the system by seeking a buyout over a dissolution so as to reduce the amount that would have to be paid.

We might question whether the result reached by the court, while very sensible, is consistent with the language of the statute. What is the "fair value" of the shares owned by the petitioner? Would not those shares trade in the market at a price discounted by the risk of majority opportunism? Nonetheless, the court's reasoning is perfectly sensible because if the grounds for dissolution are established – in this case the majority was alleged, and presumably the court found, to have engaged in illegal conduct – why should the majority be able to benefit by forcing the minority to sell their shares to the majority at a price reflective of their misconduct? This is a bit like the story of the boy who murders his parents and then pleads for mercy since he is an orphan.

The Note on Minority and Marketability Discounts makes the point that when the purchaser is the majority (or the corporation controlled by the majority), the threat of majority oppression is absent so that transaction would not be subject to such a discount (as would a sale to a third party).

Note on Matter of Pace Photographers

The case poses the intriguing question whether in a buyout sought by the majority as an alternative to dissolution, the fair value should be reduced by any discounts the parties had agreed would apply if any party voluntarily withdrew from the company. Students may be asked how the basis for the discount sought by the majority in *Pace* is different from that in *Charland*. In *Pace* the majority argued that their shareholders agreement provided for a fifty percent discount if any person withdrew from the firm within five years of the company's formation. Why would they have this arrangement? Obviously this was to balance a quest for liquidity against the need for capital to be committed for some reasonable period of time.

Three years after the company was formed, dissolution was sought on grounds of oppression and wrongdoing. The majority exercised their right to seek a buyout, but with fair value discounted by fifty percent as provided in their shareholders agreement.

How did the court resolve this? The court essentially reads the provisions of the shareholder agreement narrowly, or at least strictly, so that it applies only to voluntary sales. The sell here was pursuant to the majority's statutory right to buyout the petitioner. This is consistent with the approach taken earlier in the *F.B.I.* stock-restriction case which held that stock sale restrictions do not apply to certain types of transfers, namely those by intestate succession or foreclosure.

Note the majority in *Pace* then sought to revoke their election to repurchase. This was denied, finding that the "just and equitable" statutory basis for revocation did not apply. Students might be asked why this language was not satisfied?

Friedman v. Beway Realty Corp.

The case embraces two reasons for refusing to impose a minority discount. First, it is inconsistent with valuing the petitioner's interest in the firm (as distinct from the value of the petitioner's shares). Second, doing so would violate the principle that shares of the same class enjoy identical rights. The court also points out that a minority discount would erode the remedial nature of the dissolution-buyout statutes. Finally, any discounting would provide an incentive to the majority to act opportunistically.

Section 9. Custodians and Provisional Directors

Delaware has no analog to the dissolution statutes of the states covered in the cases in the preceding section, e.g., the New York or Model Act regimes. What Delaware does provide is the authority for the appointment of a custodian in deadlock situations. Many other states provide that among the remedies available when grounds for judicial dissolution are established is the appointment of a custodian, provisional director, or receiver.

Giuricich v. Emtrol Corp.

This is the leading Delaware decision on the scope of the custodian's powers. Note this was a deadlock. Students might be asked what appears to be the authority of the custodian? In one sense, very circumscribed, namely to break the deadlock by voting on the matter that has caused the parties to disagree. After that, the custodian is no longer needed. In another sense, however, a custodian may have very significant authority because she may break a deadlock on an extremely important matter.

Note on Custodians and Provisional Directors

Is there any real difference between a custodian and a provisional director? None seems to come sharply into focus. What separates the *In re Jamison Steel Corp.* and Hetherington & Dooley? It is whether the provisional director should have the power to expand the board to include a nominee that likely would side with the one faction over the other. But if the legislature has authorized a provisional director to overcome an impasse, should not this be seen as just

112

avoiding a repeat situation? It likely points to an obvious limitation for the provisional director: it is a panacea for a very limited problem, namely where a single item separates the two or more factions but the parties otherwise can work together. Where the differences are deeper, the provisional director is not likely to be useful and relief such as liquidation or buyout would be more efficacious.

Section 10. Arbitration

Application of Vogel

What is the legal issue before the court? It is whether an agreement to arbitrate disagreements among directors violated the statutory provision that commended business decisions to the board of directors. How does the court square arbitration with the statute that provided that the board of directors managed the corporate business? It was seeing arbitration as a one-shot matter, sort of along the lines of *Clark v. Dodge* studied earlier in Section 3. Note the case also was decided before New York had a more liberal approach toward judicial dissolution; hence, arbitration could be seen as a way of addressing an impasse short of ordering dissolution, or more consistent with the mid-1960s cases not ordering any relief whatever if the company was a profitable one.

Where was the authority for disputes to be arbitrated? It was in their shareholders agreement.

Students might be asked what prompted a division among the parties? It was whether to exercise the option to purchase the land on which all the company's operations (warehouse) was located. Vogel, a fifty percent owner of the company, was one of the principals that owned the property. Thus, he was hardly neutral, but at the same time it is not clear he was acting inappropriately either.

Lane v. Abel-Bey

While some of the complaints could only be asserted by or on behalf of the corporation, as a derivative suit brought by a shareholder, the court recognized these issues could also be set before an arbitrator.

Shell, Arbitration and Corporate Governance

This excerpt provides some fairly dramatic data on the prevalence of arbitration within close corporations.

Chapter 9

Limited Liability Companies

Overview: It is possible to cover most of the material in this chapter in two class sessions. The first class session can be devoted initially to reviewing the key portions of the LLC statute that is the focus of your class. Coverage would include quick overview of the formative documents, consideration of a manager-managed or member-managed board including the authority of members/managers, the provision dealing with transfer of interests, and any provision deal with the content of fiduciary obligations. Dissolution issues can be covered later in the context of dissolution cases. The balance of the first class and the beginning of second class can focus on the cases. *Kaycee Land and Live Stock* and *Tzolis* each introduce how the LLC is a form of incorporated partnership, so entity concerns abound. Equally important are the lacunae that persist across LLC statutes, so courts have to fill the gaps. If time is tight so that you feel you must choose between these two cases, the former has more to discuss than the latter. The fiduciary duty cases, *Salm, VGS, Inc.* and *Solar Cells* are filled with insights about the nature of the LLC, and particularly the importance of the operating agreement; nonetheless, they can be covered fairly quickly, as their facts do have some features in common to each. The two dissolution cases are each strong cases, although we might find the result reached in *Haley* the most problematic, since then Vice-Chancellor Strine reached a result that essentially ignores the private ordering that the parties had agreed to address any fundamental disagreement. This lets the chapter end on a big question: whether LLC statutes are to be seen as embracing unrestrained private ordering or is it appropriate for the court, as occurred in *Haley*, to protect the parties from their own deal.

Section 1.   Introduction

The opening material provides a good overview of the legal features of LLCs. Students may be asked initially why this entity came into existence? The answer is the blending of desirable features of corporate law - limited liability - with the contractual freedom and tax treatment of partnership law. What the latter means is that as the LLC has morphed over time it has become more the domain of private ordering with minimal default rules.

To emphasize the contractual freedom present in an LLC, students may be asked what are some of the items for which you have a choice for an LLC. A classic choice to be made is whether to be member or manager managed. Another point is whether votes among members is by interest or by member. A further area is the ability to contract around fiduciary duties. And abig area to consider is the freedom by which members can transfer their interest (and governance rights). In the corporate setting, many of these items have default rules which need to be opted out of, and sometimes only if in the articles. But with many LLC statutes, the bent of the statute is toward drafting around these provisions. Thus, the corporation is more an off-the-rack entity than is an LLC.

Section 2.   Piercing the Veil and Derivative Action

Kaycee Land and Livestock v. Flahive

The issue certified to the Wyoming Supreme Court from the federal district court is whether "absent fraud" the veil can be pierced in an LLC? Thus, the facts are not before the court and need not be the focus of classroom discussion on this issue.

The students might be asked what would prompt a court to believe the veil would NOT be pierced for LLC. The absence of legislative imprimatur for veil piercing arguably would foreclose veil piercing; but veil piercing occurs in all states for corporations even though there is no authority in general corporate statutes for piercing. But perhaps this just suggests that with the doctrine so well established for corporations that the absence of legislative recognition for LLCs laid the foundation for believing the legislature meant to exclude veil piercing. But what would be the public policy for not applying veil piercing to LLCs? It would be that the LLC is intended to be a less formal business entity, so that the absence of certain formalities is part of the legislative formulation. As we review the list of factors supporting veil piercing in the corporate setting that are set forth in the opinion many of those factors relate to formal matters. But the legislature was embracing with the LLC a means for operations to be carried out with less formality. However, we have seen that veil piercing is driven by concerns for fraud on creditors, where the factors for veil piercing are indicia of possible fraud on creditors. Thus, it is hard to believe that the legislature would wish to condone such opportunistic behavior; although likely the legislature would not wish purely formalistic requirements such as minutes, meetings, authorization of transactions through a managerial hierarchy, etc. to be considered, the legislature would not have authorized conduct rife with abuse of creditor interests. Students might be asked whether the analogy should be made to veil piercing in the partnership setting? But this is a red herring, as if a general partnership the issue does not come up due to unlimited liability; in the limited partnership context the inquiry historically has been whether the limited partners participated in ordinary management decisions (not weakened under the RULPA).

Note the opinion does state that the same factors that are considered in the corporate veil piercing context are not likely to apply to LLCs; thus, the formal operating requirements, discussed above, are likely to play no role.

Also observe the court, wisely, concludes that it is unlikely the legislature paid any attention to this topic whatever, in part because it was in the vanguard of LLC legislation so that later statutes which did address the topic for their state were not available to the Wyoming legislature when it paved the way toward LLC statutes.

Tzolis v. Wolff

How is this case similar to the preceding one? It addresses whether there is a derivative cause of action that LLC members can bring to address misconduct harming the LLC. Like *Kaycee Land and Livestock*, the LLC statute was silent on whether derivative suits were available to members of LLCs.

What reasoning did the court use to conclude the suits do exist? First, it made the analogy to limited partnerships where such suits exist. Second, it points to the need to address self-enriching breaches of fiduciary duty. Third, it noted some courts address the topic by treating a fiduciary's misconduct as giving rise to a direct cause of action; but concluding this approach is unacceptable as it raises practical problems (possible multiplicity of suits (why wouldn't class action procedures address this?)). We might add here whether it would be strange to recognize that violation of the corporation's rights had been incurred, but there was no independent actor who could initiate a suit to address the misconduct and obtain redress for the injured party?

Section 3.   Fiduciary Duties

Salm v. Feldstein

What was the alleged breach of fiduciary duty here? The defendant negotiated the purchase of the plaintiff's interest in the LLC, representing the fair value of the dealership to be $5-6 million. The plaintiff alleges that the interest's value was much higher? What supports the plaintiff's claim that the defendant knew when dealing with the plaintiff that the interest had a much higher value? The defendant's resale, at $16 million of the entire dealership, two days after closing the purchase of the plaintiff's interest supports the inference that defendant knew the true facts.

What then is the nature of the relationship between members and what does that call for? The court holds the relationship between members is that of fiduciaries so that this required the defendant "keep the plaintiff informed of all communications with the nonparty purchaser" and that this was not excused by a disclaimer in the contract of purchase.

Thus, we find a duty of candor among LLC members. Query, would there have been a breach if there was only negotiations taking place with the third party when the defendant purchased the plaintiff's shares? How much was known to the defendant then would be important, but we might also believe that the potential sale of the firm is so fundamental and

117

significant that it would be swept into the duty of candor. The facts are analogous to the close corporation case, *Jordan v. Duff & Phelps*, covered in Section 7 of Chapter 8.

VGS, Inc. v. Castiel

What is Mr. Castiel's complaint? How has he been harmed? He was, through two companies, Holdings and Ellipso, the owner of 63.46 percent of Virtual Geosatellite LLC (LLC). As such, he was entitled by the operating agreement to nominate, elect, and remove two of its three managers. He appointed himself and Quinn. But be careful who your friends are, or were. Quinn defected to the other side, to join forces with the third manager, Sahagen, who owned 25 percent of the LLC. In combination, Quinn and Sahagen approved the merger of LLC into a newly created LLC with the effect that Castiel's interest declined to 37.5 percent and Sahagen's interest was the remainder.

How were they able to accomplish this? The LLC statute (subject to opt out by the operating agreement) expressly authorized action by managers by written consent of a majority of the managers and the operating agreement empowered the managers to merge, etc. the LLC without a vote of the members. Note this is very different from corporate statutes which expressly condition any merger on approval of the shareholders. Hence, it is worth emphasizing here the greater flexibility that we can expect to find in many, if not most, LLC statutes.

What then was the breach by Quinn and Sahagen? It was they acted without giving notice to Castiel? Did the operating agreement require notice? This is the fiduciary gloss the court applied to the statute. While first reasoning that the broad statutory grant to act by consent was intended to apply when action was needed to be taken quickly and efficiently, what the court appears to ultimately hold is that the other managers owed a duty to their co-manager "to give him prior notice." They obviously did not wish to do this, knowing that with full notice Castiel would have swiftly exercised his right under the operating agreement to remove Quinn and appoint a true loyalist.

Students might be asked whether this was the best result for the LLC? This goes to the observation about why Quinn deserted Castiel. The court said the issue is not who is the better manager but the rules of the game require fair play.

Solar Cells, Inc. v. True North Partners, LLC

To get the ball rolling on the facts, students might be asked how this case is similar to the facts of the preceding case? Both involved the dilutive effects of a merger and the merger was approved by written consent of the three managers controlled by the defendant. In this case, the former 50 percent owner, Solar Cells, was reduced to a 5 percent owner. It should be noted here that Solar Cells' holdings of the voting Class A units was diluted slightly below the 50 percent level when the other holder exercised its option to convert some of the outstanding loan into Class A units, thus obtaining just a bare majority of the voting power so as to effect the merger.

We might ask why would Solar Cells have placed itself in a position to have its voting power diluted by the exercise of the convertible feature in the loan arrangement with True North? First Solar was desperate for cash and this was the deal driven by the lender, True North.

What is the argument that Solar Cells makes? It is that this is a conflict of interest transaction and subject to the "entire fairness" standard that Delaware has developed in the corporate arena for self-dealing transactions.

What is the defense? The first line of defense is the interesting provision, authorized in Delaware and common to LLC statutes, that is set forth in Section 4.18 of the Operating Agreement. This is an exculpation provision for self dealing transactions.

Why was this defense not successful? First, it deals with liability and the suit here was for a TRO. Second, the clause was not a blanket protection for conflict of interest, but subjected such transactions to a "good faith" belief test. The court reasoned the approval did not appear to be in good faith, mainly focusing on procedural considerations (i.e., the three managers approved the merger by written consent just one day after the full contingent of managers formal met at a meeting and no mention was made at that meeting of a merger).

Hence, the court believed the facts would likely support an entire fairness inquiry inviting consideration of both fair dealing and fair price. On these points, the court believed there as a substantial likelihood of success on the merits so that a TRO would be appropriate.

What were the issues examined on fair dealing? It was the absence of notice, absence of an independent bargaining mechanism regarding the price and structure of the merger. But doesn't the authority to act by written consent trump each of these considerations? No, the court believed the authority to act by written consent is not a license for the majority to act opportunistically.

What about fair price? There was an investment banker retained, but the banker shot the fairness opinion in the foot by characterizing it as "quick and dirty." Also, it went unexplained why a year-earlier valuation was substantially higher than the present valuation advanced by the banker. Related to this was the unexplained pessimism for the "multiple" i.e., high discount rate. The expert also included a marketability discount, much abhorred in Delaware, and the investment banker had no expertise in the industry. Thus, with the defendant's expert appearing to be discredited, the court concludes there is substantial likelihood of success on the merits.

What is the defendant's last argument: that there was no irreparable harm suffered since the plaintiff was already a minority holder and could not thus be harmed from going from a just barely minority holder to a really minority holder. Hard to believe that this is an argument made with a straight face.

Thus, what do we learn from the case. There are lots of opportunities for private ordering with LLC's, but these provisions are construed narrowly. It is also likely that courts will be careful that no contract provision will become a license for opportunistic wealth transfers from the majority to the minority. In this case, it occurred via the court's view of the meaning of good faith so that when this was drawn into question it was a naked self dealing transaction to which the classic entire fairness inquiry was applied.

Section 4.   Dissolution

In the Matter of 1545 Ocean Avenue, LLC.

This case illustrates the limited authority for judicial dissolution under the New York Limited Liability Company Law. Why might the legislature provide a more limited basis for dissolution? Recall the earlier close corporation cases and the liberal construction of "oppression" so that it includes substantial interference with the stockholder's reasonable expectations. The LLC statute encourages private ordering; therefore, we might well conclude on this topic fewer default rules, deferring to the parties to craft their own mechanism to deal with dissension.

So what was the dissension here? We really don't know what the cause for their repeated disagreement, but here we have two equal owners of the LLC. How did they contract for dissolution? Article 7.4 of their operating agreement provided dissolution would be according to the statute, which provided that the court should consider the operating agreement, but also provides that dissolution shall be ordered "whenever it is not reasonably practicable to carry on the business in conformity with the articles of organization or operating agreement."

Why was that not the case here? The operating agreement authorized each member to act on behalf of the company.. Note also that the court emphasized that unlike the Business Corporation Law, the New York LLCL act does not authorize dissolution for deadlock. Moreover, the operating agreement, by authorizing each member to act for the company, not only addresses the petitioner's complaint that there were no meetings, but also removes the possibility of deadlock. Indeed, the petitioner's complaint appears to be that Van Houten was a "cowboy" in the sense he just acted on behalf of the company and never consulted King. But this is exactly what we might expect when the operating agreement broadly empowers each member who is a manager.

There is a quote from a Delaware case admonishing that courts should not be eager to order dissolution, i.e., hair trigger dissolution orders. Why be so cautious? One explanation is the parties can contract to provide dissolution on demand or some other exit. Another is that dissolution may lead to liquidation and the loss of the going concern value of the firm. But this is true in business corporations as well, so it must be that the LLC is seen as bundle of private ordering arrangements with limited judicial or statutory interference.

Was King being abused here? He complains in part that Van Houten has performed work at a greater cost than would occur if there was true independent contracting. If this is case, perhaps King should assert this claim in a derivative suit. This is the suggestion in the closing paragraph of the case. And in the preceding paragraphs, the court said that this is the better approach to deal with the essence of King's complaints than to order dissolution.

Haley v. Talcott

Students might be asked initially what the law of Delaware cited in this case has that is identical to that of the preceding case? Each have the same statutory language for dissolution: "whenever it is not reasonably practicable to carry on the business in conformity with the articles of organization or operating agreement."

Who was seeking dissolution? What was the business of the LLC that was sought to be dissolved? Note the focus here is Matt & Greg Real Estate LLC, which owned the parcel of land on which the Redfin Seafood Grill operated. Greg Talcott had terminated Matt Haley as the restaurant's manager. The lease payments were just enough to pay the mortgage on the land and provide a very small monthly return. Haley seeks to dissolve the real estate business? Presumably this would result in the sale of the property to a third party who would raise the rent. It was not possible now to raise the rent since Talcott would oppose this.

Why then don't these facts establish the basis for dissolving the LLC? It would seem that the reason for the LLC would be to not just acquire the land, but also to rent it at its fair market value to provide a fair return to the members of the LLC. Note the court states that, if this were a corporation, dissolution would be ordered. But the Vice Chancellor reasoned that there was an exit provision here: Section 18 of the operating agreement provided that if any member wished to withdraw, the remaining member could elect to purchase the withdrawing member's interest at fair value. Did this did not occur so that the business would then be liquidated?

With this provision before us, why didn't Haley pursue this option? Could it be that he was fearful that Talcott would buy his shares and that what Haley really wanted was to see some third party buy the land and raise the rent to the restaurant? Was this all about spite?

The Vice Chancellor muses that this provision may suggest that the LLC could in fact continue to operate practically despite the inertial standoff between Haley and Talcott over raising the rent. But the court appears unwilling to enforce the provision? Why? That is, why not see the facts justifying the court enforcing Section 18, so that Talcott will buyout Haley? It reasons it would not enforce the parties' contractual provision because to do so would mean that Haley would continue to have liability as a cosigner on the mortgage. Haley can, in the Vice-Chancellor's eyes, protect himself against an uncertain future only if the LLC is dissolved, its assets liquidated (i.e., the mortgage paid off), and the residue distributed to its members. Note, the result here is not what the parties agreed; their approach was that Talcott would first have an option to buy Haley's interest at fair value.

Thus, what authority does the court have to abrogate the approach taken in their contract? Does this run counter to the repeated rhetoric of this chapter about the flexibility and private ordering that is the hallmark of the LLC? Was this the right decision?

Chapter 10

The Duty Of Care And The Duty To Act In Good Faith

Overview: Chapter 10 covers a significant area of the business organization field, the duty of care. The material in this chapter, while focused on corporations and arising from litigated cases, is far more pervasive, as the holdings shape what is believed to be good practices for business organizations generally. You likely will devote a minimum of three classes to this material, and to cover the key cases closely you will likely need 4 or 5 class periods. The key cases are *Francis*, *Kamin*, *Smith*, *Caremark*, *Stone* and *Miller*. To be added here are the note materials focused on immunity shields and the responsible corporate officer doctrine.

Section 1.   The Duty of Care

A. The Basic Standard of Care

Francis v. United Jersey Bank

The facts of the case are fairly straightforward. To get the ball rolling in class, you might ask who was suing and why? This may well clarify that creditors do not have standing to sue for a breach of fiduciary duty. The creditors representative is suing, but on the rights of the corporation as the successor to its interest. Thus, we emphasize the duty of care, which is the focus of this suit, is owed to the corporation. Later we will see that there are instances in which this duty extends to the shareholders (*Van Gorkom* was a direct not a derivative suit).

The why is that Lillian just stayed in bed, literally. During which the "boys" stole her blind. Don't miss the line, perhaps on Charles' senior's death bed, "steal the shirt off your back."Getting the students used to the facts in all these fiduciary duty cases is important. Thus, what is the relevance of the table comparing "working capital," "shareholder loans" and "net brokerage income"? If Lillian had not been in an alcoholic haze and attended the board meetings, then what would be the likely question to ask? What about these "loans", when will they be repaid, and who authorized these?

What then do we take away from the case; is it that Lillian was to manage the company as the statutes of that day suggest or what? The court reflects the thinking behind the monitoring duty of the outside director. Thus, while this is not a public company, it nonetheless reflects the view that the role of directors who are not engaged in the daily operations of the company are nonetheless to serve as watchdogs for the shareholders' interests and monitor the performance of the firm.

What then does this require? What did it require in the Note case, *Barnes v. Andrews.* The latter's facts are worth reviewing, see below. Lillian should have attended meetings, at least regularly (what does that mean in light of *Barnes* where only one of two meetings was missed). And, when her suspicions were aroused, she needed to pursue the points that piqued her interest, the rising level of unpaid loans. Then, as the court stated, she needed to object? What then if the boys' reply is, "gee Mom!" She should engage a lawyer, or other third party to assist her in getting at the bottom of the matter.

We might consider just how great a burden this places on the outside director? It would appear not to be a great burden. In the end, we will see that the duty of care does not demand much. Note the breach here costs Lillian's estate about $10 million. So the consequences of a breach can be great. Does this lead to over deterrence? Does it lead to the "deterrence trap" whereby the consequences of a momentary breach are disproportionate so that courts will be unwilling to conclude there was a breach? These are significant public policy questions that are unanswered by the fact that the burdens the duty imposes are not great.

In re Emerging Comm. Inc. Shareholders Litigation

How is the breach different in this case than *Francis*? The issues are similar because the allegation is inaction. But with *Francis,* it was perpetual absence; in this case the breach was remaining silent when the director Muoio had a duty to speak. Where did this duty come from? It is the duty of care; given his background and familiarity with the company, and apparent admission in the deposition/trial that the company could be sold for much more, he had a duty the court said to share his insights with others and to vote against the merger.

What about the other directors? The duty is applied on an individual case according to the circumstances of that director's actions or inaction. Thus, he had much less reason to rely. A reference to the MBCA reflects that directors are entitled to rely on third party providers, such as investment bankers, unless aware of facts indicating the reliance is unjustified. That appears to be the case here.

Note on Causation

Four points worth making here. First, facts in *Barnes* are not nearly as egregious as Lillian since Andrews missed only one of two meetings in his brief tenure. Second, except in Delaware the burden of proving both the breach and proximate cause are on the plaintiff. Third, Delaware in *Cede & Co.* imposes on the breaching defendant the burden of proving "entire fairness" once the breach is established. Students can be asked why the Delaware court concludes that causation should not be on the plaintiff? And, what exactly would entire fairness mean in a case like *Francis*? Fourth, what explains why the plaintiff prevailed on causation in *Francis* but failed in *Barnes*?

B.   The Business Judgment Rule

Kamin v. American Express Co.

To start discussion, students can be asked how the issue in this case is different from that in *Francis*? *Barnes*? Here the challenge is to an *action/decision* by the board. What was the decision and why the complaint?

The corporation held a losing investment in its portfolio. The holdings of DLJ were distributed pro rata to the shareholders as a dividend in kind. The plaintiff complained that this resulted in the company failing to harvest a loss on its tax return which would have reduced its taxes by $8 million. By way of background, students should be aware that under the IRC the receiving shareholders acquire the DLJ shares at the fair market value on the date of the distribution; hence, Uncle Sam never is burdened by the loss on the value of the DLJ shares.

Why did the plaintiff lose? The plaintiff lost because there was a rational basis for the board's decision. What was it? This is a good case to illustrate some of the thinking about the efficient market hypothesis. Hence, if not covered previously, the readings in Section 4 of Chapter 2 could be assigned. The point is that the board believed that, if the DLJ shares were sold, this would result in recording on the Income Statement a net loss of $17 million (($29.9 -4) - $8 million) and this would depress the value of the shares. Did they argue that it would never have to disclose the disposition of the DLJ shares? No, their expert said any disclosure/accounting entry would appear only on the balance sheet as a direct charge to equity. What then could be counter to this? It is that the market is efficient, so that it does not matter where financially significant information is reported, whether on the firm's balance sheet or income statement, it will not interdict the efficiency of pricing of the firm's shares, if the information is financially significant. Thus, we have two contending views of how American Express' shares are priced? The rational basis required for the business judgment rule does not require that the reasoning be either correct or compelling. It need only be rational. This likely

125

means that there is at least one reasonably based school of thought that supports the reason advanced for the decision. There is a good deal of dispute about whether markets are efficient, when they are efficient and efficient with respect to what kinds of announcements.

What was the argument that the decision was arrived at out of self interest? Why was this argument raised? Why was it unsuccessful? If a majority of the board had a financial interest served by not recording a loss on the income statement, e.g., bonuses were based on reported net income, the decision would be judged by the duty of loyalty issues studied later in this chapter. Under the duty of loyalty the board would face the burden of proving entire fairness. But this was not to be in *Kamin* since a majority of the board members were outsiders. This is the first instance where we see the impact on review standards and outcomes that flows when a majority of directors are independent.

Note on the Divergence of Standards of Conduct and Standards of Review in Corporate Law, and on the Business Judgment Rule

The note raises range of excellent discussion questions surrounding the burdens and meaning of the business judgment rule. As to perhaps the most fundamental, students may be asked what is the difference between a standard of conduct and a standard of review? On this point, you may follow by asking how MBCA §§ 8.30 & 8.31 link to this question? The latter is a standard of review, or at least identifying the bases on which a director is liable. The former is a standard of conduct, aspirational even.

Smith v. Van Gorkom

To begin the ball rolling, students might be asked why Van Gorkom decided to sell the firm? This is not developed in the facts, but there are at least two factors: the inability to harvest the economic benefits of the accumulated investment tax credits and the lack of an heir apparent (successor) for Van Gorkom who was long in the tooth. The former allows a chance to explain why this company had a tax problem that we wish would happen to us. Namely, for every railcar Transunion purchased (its business was rapidly expanding) it received a tax credit as well as rapid depreciation. In combination, they meant it never paid any taxes and in fact had carryover losses and tax credits that a purchasing company could apply, retroactively, and prospectively. You might wish to put dollar sign on this, just to illustrate, the magnitude of this underutilized company asset, say $90 million.

This is, of course, a classic case. It may be best for the students to be totally familiar with the facts, at least to what Romans did calculate and did not calculate. He was asked to determine if it would be feasible at prevailing interest rates to engage in a classic LBO at $55 per share assuming a five-year time horizon and an equity investment of $200 million. This needs to be explained further to the class, demonstrating that all that Romans calculated was whether the five-year loan (principal and interest) could be paid from the free cash flow of Transunion. What is left out of this equation? The calculation obviously does not assign a value of the cash flow beyond 5 years and does not value the accumulated investment tax credits.

The case has two time periods: the initial board meeting, September 20, and the post September 20 activities. While some might disagree about whether the board's post September 20th actions were reasonable and cured the missteps in the September 20 meeting, most agree that the board was indeed not engaged sufficiently at the September 20 meeting. So what were these events?

Students can be asked whether they wished Van Gorkom to represent them in trying to sell a trusted asset? This goes to how Pritzker and Van Gorkom arrived at the $55 price. It is the number that Van Gorkom suggested, not some higher number that was later reduced to get to $55.

Why did the board have to consider this at a special board meeting? Because Pritzker put a 72 hour clock on his offer. Does this justify the board's actions? No, but it is a circumstance for determining whether the board acted reasonable in light of the 72 hour limit. One point worth consideration is whether they were unreasonable by not asking for more time? They never did. They just took the hand that was dealt.

If they had more time, what would they have done differently? One idea is get an investment bank in place and also get a valuation from the investment bank. Why didn't they get a banker in anyway? Did they try? No.

What then informed them that the price was fair? The price represented nearly a 50% premium over market. Was the market inefficient? (If not already covered, you may assign in connection with the case Section 4 of Chapter 2 dealing with the efficient market hypothesis). But the market was valuing Transunion on the basis of what it knew about Transunion. What would have happened to the $38 market price if Transunion had announced it had retained Goldman Sachs to shop the firm? The market would have gone up, reflecting a likely buyer for Transunion. But why would such a buyer pay more than $38 if the shares are traded/price efficiently? The new owner could harvest the accumulated investment tax credits and losses; that unused asset now would have a user who would pay for the opportunity to receive the benefits of the tax loss carryovers and accumulated credits.

Why was Roman's appearance not a report that the board could rely on? Court says this was not a report on the *value* of the firm (see earlier discussion of what is in the LBO calculation). We also might wonder if their reliance is unreasonable, since Roman said he believed that $55 was fair, but at the low end of fairness. If someone said that to you what would you ask? What is the range and what could drive the deal toward the upper reaches of that range.

What is the significance that the court stated the meeting last two hours? Selling the company was a pretty significance decision, so why was there not more questions about the deal; two hours seems a pretty short time for such a fundamental decision to be resolved.

Why does it matter that no advance notice of the topic of the September 20 meeting, or about the deal was circulated and nothing was circulated at the meeting itself such as a term sheet? This indicates a lack of casualness toward the director's responsibility. Moreover, having materials at hand, and certainly at the meeting, stimulates reflection, inquiry and dialogue.

What's a market check? With this question students can be prompted to discuss the post September 20 events. For example, why didn't the overwhelming stockholder approval absolve the directors? The court held their approval was on incomplete information; they were not told enough facts about how the $55 price was determined for their approval to be ratification of the errant steps of the board.

What about the market check? What is a market check? This refers to the post September 20 window the board had to seek other bidders. It had two, but they dropped out. Why was this not circumstantial evidence that the Pritzker offer was a fair one? The court believed there was not sufficient time for competing bidders to formulate and execute an offer. We might wonder whether this is not a triable issue, especially since there appears to be no testimony the court relied on that this was insufficient time. We might consider this aspect of the opinion the weakest link to holding that the directors acted with gross negligence.

And, why didn't the overwhelming stockholder approval cure the board's deficiencies? The short answer is that the shareholders did not have before them all the facts, namely that the board never had a substantive fairness opinion.

What result? The court merely holds that there was a breach of a duty of care, i.e., the board acted with gross negligence. How is this different from *Francis*? *Kamin*? *Van Gorkom* is pretty much the entire content of the duty of care today, as the duty of care is a process and not a substantive requirement. Thus, the Transunion board had a rational basis for their action: they believed $55 was a fair price. They simply did not arrive at that rational basis through reasonable investigation and reflection.

The court remanded the case. What was to happen on remand? The court only resolves that there was a breach and the business judgment rule did not apply. Thus, there needed to be a hearing pursuit to the "entire fairness" inquiry, recall *Cede & Co., supra*, to determine the damages to the shareholders proximately caused by the breach.

Why did Pritzker, who was not a defendant in the suit, contribute toward its settlement. He obviously thought even with the extra payment this was a still a very good deal and this suggests the weaknesses in the settlement process where the litigants are more interested in putting the suit behind them (and their paychecks in the bank) than pushing the matter to the limits so that a meaningful competitive bidding process would follow and we could find out just what was the fair price for Transunion.

C.   The Duty to Monitor, Compliance Programs, and Internal Controls

In re Caremark International Inc. Derivative Litigation

Students might be asked at the outset why it might be that *Caremark* can be seen as one of the most important fiduciary duty cases we study? The question should lead to a general discussion of what this case says; its holding actually is quite narrow, being merely approval of a very weak settlement of a derivative suit claim.

Caremark's impact is that it greatly stimulated awareness of companies, particularly public companies, to maintain compliance programs. Students might be asked what we mean by compliance programs and how their wide use was stimulated by *Caremark*? Students might also be asked what would be examples of a compliance program? How might a compliance program for a professional baseball team (steroid use?, presumably to discourage) differ from one for a chemical company(environmental compliance).

This leads to what Allen says regarding the misunderstanding/no longer applicable rigid holding of *Graham v. Allis-Chalmers*. What has changed so that Allen can say, "In light of these developments . . . it would . . .be a mistake to conclude that our Supreme Court's statement in *Graham* . . . means that boards may satisfy their obligation to be reasonably informed concerning the corporation, without assuring themselves that information and reporting systems exist in the organization that are reasonably designed to provide to senior management and to the board itself timely, accurate information sufficient to allow management and the board, each within its scope to reach informed judgments concerning both the corporation's compliance with law and its business performance."

Allen points out is the role that compliance systems play under the Sentencing Guidelines, discussed in the note material following the case. Another is that the shift in thinking about the role of the board of directors from the days of *Graham* so that the view today is the monitoring role (recall the language in *Francis* on this point).

So all this said, what does it have to do with the task before Allen in the case? He approved the settlement, which he characterizes as not accomplishing a lot. Why would we say this? You might wish to review the settlement and ask what was new that was not already mandated by the law? It is likely the items in 3, 5 and 6 are not something that the company was already required to perform. Moreover, what is the relevance in this process of all the verbiage Allen devotes to the necessity of compliance programs, etc. The facts indicate that the board was actually responsive, perhaps not aggressive, to developments, so that there was some actions initiated by the company to address potential problems. While their steps were not successful - see the huge fine the government was able to impose - they suggest that the corporation and likely the board was not docile or unengaged with the topic of law compliance. Thus, it is not likely that the board mistook its obligations or did not monitor so that a weak settlement is about all that could be expected. They needed some governance issues to be imposed so that the suit could be dropped with the support of the plaintiffs' attorney.

Note on Corporate Criminal Liability, The Sentencing Guidelines, and Compliance Programs

Students might be asked what they recall is the purpose behind the Sentencing Guidelines and the impact of *Booker*? While the Supreme Court holds that the Sentencing Guidelines are not mandatory, they certainly are guidance to be considered. Thus, the Guidelines continue to impact courts. What is the relevance to this to the business entity? Well, the corporation, LLC and partnership can all be a defendant in a government prosecution so awareness of the guidance in the Sentencing Guidelines lays the foundation for arguing for a lesser sanction. Some discussion of the mechanics of the Sentencing Guidelines for business organizations can ensue with the ultimate question focusing on the role that a reasonably designed and maintained compliance program has under the Sentencing Guidelines.

Eisenberg, The Board of Directors and Internal Control

Internal control is an amorphous topic and, hence, one that the students can see as something of a black box or any discussion of it being akin to "inside baseball." As focused on in this excerpt, internal controls relates to a process designed to provide assurance that the information flowing to management and the board is trustworthy. That is, the board and senior management, as well as middle management, each depend on reports as indicative of not just how the firm is doing and what its financial position is, but those reports also are the means by which senior management and the board can evaluate whether their strategies, policies, etc. are being implemented. You would think there would be natural incentives for mandated internal controls and their evaluation so that this would not have had to be required by the Sarbanes Oxley Act of 2002.

Note on Civil Liability of Directors and Officers to Third Persons

The Thompson excerpt quoted here states one of the cardinal rules that middle managers, officers and directors are not themselves vicariously liable (as is the firm) but they are individually liable for their tortuous acts.

D.   Liability Shields

To kick off the topics, you may wish to review of the immunity shield statute for the corporate statute(s) used in your course. They entail a charter provision, most cover only directors, most apply only to damage actions so that injunctive actions are untouched (does this lead to the unintended consequence of more, not less, litigation since the deterrence trap is less present?), and most do not include the "good faith" exception that was central to the post-*Caremark* developments whether there was a third fiduciary duty, one of good faith.

Policy question here is if you were asking shareholders to approve amendment of the articles to include an immunity shield, what justifications would you advance? What downside to having such a provision would you have to disclose? Finally, you might wish to point out that the first immunity shield provision was in Delaware, and was enacted in a special session of the legislature in the shadow of *Smith v. Van Gorkom* (and to boot, the author of the majority opinion was not reappointed)

Emerald Partners v. Berlin

Fairly straightforward holding: if the company has an immunity shield, normally this comes up as an affirmative defense, so that the defendant must allege that the conduct that is the gravamen of the suit fell within the immunity shield. However, if facially the complaint alleges only a care violation the suit for damages can be dismissed. The actual operation of this is illustrated in the next case.

Malpiede v. Townson

What is the substantive complaint raised by the plaintiff? It is that the board acted in breach of its fiduciary duties in how it sold Frederick's of Hollywood. Note the facts indicated that the directors seemed to favor Knightsbridge, and that bidding was cut off somewhat abruptly by a "no-talk" provision pushed by Knightsbridge. Subsequently the competing bidder raised its bid substantially above the amount of the Knightsbridge, and even above the amount that Knightsbridge paid in the open market to acquire control which was about a dollar higher than the merger price.

Why is this not a loyalty case? If so, it would clearly be beyond the immunity shield. Court concluded that only one director was alleged to have a financial link to the transaction, so that there was otherwise independent action by the board. It thus saw the complaint being focused on a claim of gross negligence. The court believes the complaint failed to clearly set forth facts alleging a breach of the duty of loyalty or a lack of good faith. This was fatal to the suit. So, to survive, what did the plaintiff have to plead to survive a motion to dismiss? The plaintiff must plead enough facts to make this other than a gross negligence case.

Corporations and Other Business Organizations

What then can the plaintiff do if the facts are not sufficient? One idea is to move earlier, for a TRO, so that the remedy is beyond that protected by the immunity shield provision. This would require allegations of facts to support the finding that the plaintiff would have substantial likelihood of success on the merits in its ultimate pursuit to require the bidding to be reopened and the board to consider Veritas' offer or that of others. Note that in this approach, there plaintiff's attorneys would still be compensated as a monetary fund is not necessary to justify the award of attorneys fees (discussed in Section 11, Chapter 14).

E. Directors' and Officers' Liability Insurance

Note on Directors" and Officers' Liability Insurance

The note provides an important overview of the standard D&O policy. This is an important item because corporate litigation, whether direct, class or derivative, is shaped in so many ways by the shadow of the D&O policy.

The following are the points that can be emphasized in the material:

1. The policy is typically a claims made policy.

2. A good deal of litigation ensues between the insured and the insurer whether coverage can be denied because of misleading information provided when the coverage application was completed.

3. Exclusions are important to the plaintiff, because settlement needs to be within the boundaries of the policy, i.e., in the non-excluded area. Hence, allegations of fraud or knowing fraud, or even willfulness can remove the carrier from the settlement process.

4. The policy is a wasting asset, paying for litigation costs incurred monthly through the life of the suit. Thus, if the plaintiffs want to dip their hands into the insurance bowl of money, you don't want to drag the process out too long.

Section 2. The Duty to Act in Good Faith

In re Walt Disney Company Derivative Litigation

This was a much-watched case that shows just how sloppy and stupid boards can be in making an important decision, hiring and then firing Ovitz, and still be within the protection of the immunity shield. The facts are titillating, but in the Supreme Court decision, the facts remarkably seemed not to move the needle. Justice Jacobs' opinion, while thoughtful and clear, pays hardly lip service to the facts. This was the Supreme Court's moment to reflect, what it later in *Stone v. Ritter* made definitive, that there is no third fiduciary rail, i.e., a duty of good faith independent of a duty of care or loyalty.

132

Thus, the focus can be on what made this a care case. There was no consciousness of fault on the part of the bumbling seemingly disengaged Disney directors. It is worth time reviewing the two categories Jacobs clearly describes.

Stone v. Ritter

This builds on *Disney*, but we might ask what is left of *Caremark*? The court in the closing passage adopts all that Allen stated in *Caremark*, making clear that good faith is to be contrasted with a lack of care, because the absence of good faith involves directors who "fail to act in the face of a known duty to act, thereby demonstrating a conscious disregard for their responsibilities . . . ." *Ritter* does clarify that the "sustained or systematic failure of the board to exercise oversight" to fit within the "good faith" exclusion of the Delaware immunity shield not only has to be characterized as a subpart of the duty of loyalty but in doing so has to "deliberate" quality to the failure. If directors were just chronically missing in action, e.g., Lillian Pritchard in *Francis*, this would not appear to reach the level of deliberateness embraced in *Ritter*.

Section 3.   The Duty To Act Lawfully

Miller v. American Telephone & Telegraph Co.

To kick things off, students can be asked what new is added to the duty of care formulation by this case? The plaintiff alleged that AT&T's directors engaged in an knowing violation of the federal statute prohibiting companies from directly contributing to political campaigns when they approved forgiving the $1.5 million phone bill the DNC had encountered in connection with the 1968 convention.

What is new here is that establishing a knowing violation of a criminal statute removes the rational basis defenses (recall *Kamin*).

Does this mean the plaintiff wins? If so what? Note the plaintiff here is prosecuting a derivative suit. *Miller* is the first case in the book to illustrate the overriding view that derivative suits are compensatory. Thus, we see in note 5 the so called "net loss" requirement, i.e., that for the suit to prevail the plaintiff must prove that the effects of the violation was to produce an overall/net loss to the company. For example, if a corporation consciously forbears on installing mandated antipollution devices on its power plant and by the delay saves $500,000 each year for three years, only to be prosecuted and then required to comply, the fact that it was fined and incurred legal costs of $1 million would mean that "crime paid" such that no derivative suit could be maintained for the $1 million (the benefits of illegal conduct dwarfed the costs).

Note that the ALI project suggests that this need not be the result if the derivative suit court believes the benefits of the principle being established justify the suit's continuance.

The larger message here is that shareholder litigation, and particularly the derivative suit, is not seen as driven by deterrence. We might wonder whether as both a practical matter and public policy matter this is a sensible view of the derivative suit. That is, the complaints leveled against the derivative suit is that most suits, because they involve single-shot abuses, usually self dealing, they recover small amounts compared to the market capitalization of the firm (we are talking here about complaints in the public company; these complaints seem not to have much traction in the non public company). But if we see the suits as premised on deterrence, the small recovery per shareholder is offset by the disciplining threat that wrongdoing will be redressed.

Students might be asked what AT&T will do after this decision? Is the company likely to step forward and justify its action by saying forgiveness of the phone bill resulted in certain rents being collected from a grateful Democratic Party? As a practical matter, it is best to settle this case.

Note On Criminal Liabilities of Directors and Officers

Students can be asked what appears to be going on in *Dotterweich* and *Park* versus the more recent approach in *Meyer*?

The responsible corporate officer doctrine remains alive and well under federal and state statutes. It applies only to statutes that do not contain a mens rea requirement. In the federal courts *Meyer* tells us that some intent by Congress must now guide the result. This restrained view was not present in the earlier Supreme Court jurisprudence.

It is worth reviewing with the students just what Park knew and did not know. Also, worth reviewing just what made him a responsible officer versus those in the Baltimore and Philadelphia warehouses.

While he was aware of FDA notices, he also had a good faith belief this was being addressed. The fine here was a few hundred dollars per violation, not jail, but nonetheless since he was the responsible party he was liable. Students must understand that if a customer were somehow harmed as a result of the adulteration, in this case rodent hair, that under respondeat superior that Park would not be vicariously liable. Thus, the responsible corporate officer doctrine is broader in its scope than the respondeat superior doctrine.

Chapter 11

The Duty Of Loyalty

Chapter Overview: Five to seven class periods can easily be allocated to the material in this chapter. You may believe, as do we, that the core cases within the following areas are those set forth in brackets: self-interest [*Gantler*], self-dealing [Marsh and *Lewis*], compensation [either the *Tyson* or *Ryan* plus Aggarwal excerpt], usurpation of corporate opportunity [*Harris* and *Broz*], secret profits [either *Hawaiian* or *eBay*], duties among classes of stockholder [*Zahn* and *Nemec*, and *Trados* can easily be moved into this group to form a nice trilogy] duty of controlling stockholder [*Sinclair*, *Jones* and *Trados*], sale of control [*Perlman*] and sale of corporate office [*Essex*]. This is an area where the facts matter, and matter a lot. Thus, while the legal principle or norm can be easily stated, the vacuousness of that standard requires that some significant time must be devoted in class to the facts likely pivotal to the court's holding. Material in addition to the above cases should be selected depending on your own preference for where you believe more time should be allotted.

Section 1.   Self-Interested Transactions

We might puzzle over the meaning of *self-interested transaction*. It most clearly covers self-dealing transactions in which the fiduciary, usually an officer or director, but it could also be a controlling stockholder enter into a transaction with the corporation. It also can refer to the motive, or a circumstantially derived conclusion regarding the motive, for why a fiduciary acted as she did. *Gantler* illustrates the latter; the balance of the material in this section illustrates the former.

Gantler v. Stephens

The facts of the case are a bit involved. This is a shareholders derivative suit brought on behalf of First Niles Financial Inc, whose sole asset was Home Federal (the Bank). The complaint focused on the 4 to 1 vote to reject the offer by Cortland Bancorp to acquire the Bank. Later the board voted 3 to 1 to proceed with a privatization plan supported by Stephens, the chairman of the board. The lower court granted the defendants' motion to dismiss.

Students can be asked how the approach in this case is different from *Kamin*? From *Van Gorkom*? This is a duty of loyalty case. Hence, if sufficient facts are alleged, a damage action can proceed even though the defendants or some of them had an immunity shield against duty of care liability.

The court held that the business judgment rule did not apply and subject the transaction (rejection of the Cortland offer as well as the resulting recapitalization plan) to the entire fairness standard. What argument supported removing the board's decisions from the business judgment rule? The board believed sufficient facts were alleged to support the allegation that a majority of the directors acted "to preserve personal benefits, including retaining their positions and pay as directors, as well as valuable outside business opportunities." The court emphasized:

Stephens was not just chairman of the board, but the president and CEO of First Niles and the Bank. He also demonstrated hostility to the deal by conduct the plaintiff alleged amounted to sabotage and supported by evidence that Stephens did not provide due diligence material requested by Cortland (and the other bidder, First Place). Moreover, he did not disclose to the board his lack of cooperation.

Kramer was president of an HVAC company, the Bank was a major client, and Kramer's firm was highly leveraged.

Zuzolo was the firm's outside counsel and also the owner of a real estate title company that derived business from the Bank, doing most of the Bank's title work.

The above three were believed for purposes of a motion to dismiss to have reached a decision out of personal interest and not with a view toward serving the corporation's interest. Query, how would you prepare to establish entire fairness at a trial if you were representing each of these three defendants? One obvious method would be to introduce evidence that the recapitalization plan provided greater value to shareholders than was offered by the competing acquisition offers. Another approach is to demonstrate that the HVAC, legal, and title businesses were not in jeopardy if there was a change of control (no other local HVAC provider or title company or local attorney with banking experience). Would there be evidence that there are reasons other than the defendants' conflicts of interest why the suitors for First Niles withdrew? The delay in providing due diligence materials might be explained by externalities, such as changing computer systems, etc. The point of this question is that having lost on its motion to dismiss, the litigants' next move is to assess the relative strengths of the case.

The case provides important clarification that officers owe a fiduciary duty identical to that of directors. This was not previously a holding of a Delaware Supreme Court. Note that the court then concludes enough facts were alleged to deny dismissal of the charge that as an officer Stephens sabotaged the acquisition by Cortland (and First Place) and was assisted in doing so by First Niles' vice-president and treasurer Safarek.

What defense is discussed and rejected in Part III? The bare majority 50.28% by the independent shareholders was argued by the defendants to constitute ratification. On the subject of ratification, there is later note material in the chapter on ratification of self-dealing transactions. But the development in *Gantler* is its holding that shareholder approval does not constitute ratification of alleged self-interested behavior unless the approval is separate from a vote that is required by law. The stockholders were asked to approve the recapitalization and their vote was required because this involved amending the articles of incorporation. The Supreme Court reasons that ratification must be understood as interjecting an independent layer of shareholder approval only in circumstances where shareholder approval is not required. Moreover, the court also held that sufficient facts were alleged regarding material defects in the proxy statement so that the consent/approval could not be seen as an informed act of the independent stockholders.

Marsh. Are Directors Trustees? – Conflicts of Interest and Corporate Morality

This classic excerpt provides a crisp description of the fairly rapid movement in most jurisdictions from automatic avoidance to fairness as the judicial approach to self-dealing transactions.

The excerpt can, therefore, be seen as providing excellent background to examining the content of the conflict of interest provision of the corporate statute used in your class. There are really three broad areas of inquiry under the typical statute: 1) what transactions or contracts fall within its coverage; 2) assuming you have a transaction or contract that falls within the statute, what steps does the statute provide for addressing the conflict of interest; and 3) what is the effect of compliance with the steps set forth in the statute. You can then use next case to apply the same drill under the statute used in your class, after first examining the Second Circuit's handling of the facts before it.

Lewis v. S.L. & E., Inc.

The case illustrates a classic conflict of interest transaction. SLE leased its sole asset to LgT, a retailer of tires. The lease expired in 1966, but the parties never renegotiated the annual rent of $14,400 even though since 1966 taxes, payable by SLE, had increased from $7,800 to $11,000. SLE was owned equally by six siblings but only two of the siblings owned LGT, Richard (71%) and Leon, Jr. (39%). In the background is a shareholders agreement that required non-owners of LGT shares to sell their shares to LGT at book value on June 1, 1972. One of the siblings, Donald, initiated a derivative suit, arguing that the defendant directors of SLE (who included Richard and Leon Jr.) had wasted SLE's assets by maintaining the rent at too low a rate. There were no SLE directors who were not also directors of LGT.

One approach to teaching this case is to simply apply the conflict of interest provision that is in the corporate statute used in your class. Another approach is to follow the reasoning of the court's decision and then return to how this would be examined under the statute used in your class. In either case, we doubt that the approach taken under your statutory provision would be different from that taken by Judge Kearse in the case.

As openers, who had the burden of proof regarding waste? The district court placed this on the plaintiff, but the Second Circuit holds it should be on the defendants. Why? Because this is a patently self dealing transaction, so that we draw adverse inferences of self interest from the financial interest the fiduciary had in the transaction.

Were any of the provisions of the state conflict of interest statute satisfied? The New York conflict of interest statute is not quoted in the opinion but it parallels that of Delaware. There was no disinterested director approval (see above regarding overlap of directors) and no shareholder approval. Thus, the ultimate question is fairness of the transaction.

We have few cases that illustrate what we mean by fairness. One question is what does fairness require in this context? How will we know if a transaction is fair? What standard should we apply to satisfy these questions? One idea is what we would expect in a truly arms-length setting. A surrogate for this is likely prevailing rental rates for comparable property. That is what we would expect two strangers' bargaining to produce. Here the court reviewed a good deal of evidence at the eight day trial to conclude, not that the rent was too low or what the rent ought to have been, but simply that the defendants had failed to meet their burden of proof.

We might wonder what good all this does regarding the book value of SLE's shares. The cash recovered as a result of this litigation would likely be distributed, not adding to the book value of the firm.

Note on Remedies for Violation of the Duty of Loyalty

The note raises some inherent problems that can flow from the remedy for breaches of the duty of loyalty. The standard remedy is rescission and restitution. Sometimes there is collateral relief in the form of making the fiduciary disgorge any salary during the period of his misbehavior. The ALI tries to increase the sting of the sanction by imposing on the breaching fiduciary the obligation to pay the corporation's litigation costs incurred to redress the wrongdoing.

Talbot v. James

This is a fairly complicated dispute between two equal owners of a business to develop an apartment complex. Talbot contributed land and the agreement with James was that he was to contribute various undertakings. The complex was constructed and operated profitably for a while, then failed. Talbot then brought suit alleging that James paid sums to himself in violation of their agreement and in breach of his fiduciary duty. The case turns much on the facts, in which the majority were more disposed to follow the findings of the Master who favored Talbot and the dissent appears much more inclined to follow his own interpretation of the facts. The essence of the dispute was whether the "overhead" payments to James were subsumed within the undertakings he was to contribute for his fifty percent interest or were these payments in the form of additional compensation for his additional services. Along the way we do see some disquieting facts that do not support the dissent's disposition toward James: the minutes of the board meeting never identify that it was James's company that was the contractor retained to build the complex, Talbot was denied access to company records. There was an overall lack of independent voice in the company's various dealings with Talbot.

Note on the Duty of Loyalty

The note case reflects that the fairness inquiry can include not just price and what would have been expected in an arms-length transaction, but whether the company should have entered into the transaction or contract at all. In this case, the company was experiencing financial distress so that expansion, even at a fair price, arguably was not the wise course of action.

Note on Associates of Directors and Senior Executives

The Note raises some interesting questions, and demonstrates the sweep of the restitutionary remedy, regarding the scope of any remedy for self dealing and breaches of the duty of loyalty generally. If the breaching fiduciary garners only part of the gains should the remedy be focused only on the gains garnered personally or the entire wrongful gains? What if all the gains go to the employing entity? Should the misbehaving employee be liable for those gains?

Section 2.   Statutory Approaches

If the conflict of interest provision of the statute used in your class was not already reviewed, you likely will do so here. As stated above, the provisions can be broken down into three distinct questions: 1) what transactions or contracts fall within its coverage; 2) assuming you have a transaction or contract that falls within the statute, what steps does the statute provide for addressing the conflict of interest; and 3) what is the effect of compliance with the steps set forth in the statute.

Cookies Food Products v. Lakes Warehouse

This is something of a "rags to riches" story for a company whose initial product was barbecue sauce and later expanded to taco sauce. Cookies floundered until it engaged the auto parts dealer, Herrig, to take over its marketing. Soon Cookies sales skyrocketed and ultimately

139

Herrig became the 53 percent owner of its shares. Under his wise and tireless leadership the firm continued to grow and with that growth Herrig took on more responsibilities and activities for which the ever grateful board approved increases in his compensation, frequently in royalty arrangements. The minority, however, grew restless about sharing in the gains. The company was a close corporation and the shareholders' illiquidity was exacerbated by the fact Cookies paid no dividends. A derivative suit was initiated, challenging the various compensation arrangements with Herrig on the ground they grossly exceeded the value of the services.

After getting the facts before the class, students might be asked how this contract fits within the introductory paragraph of Iowa's conflict of interest statute which is quoted in the case? You might also ask them to opine on whether the same result would occur under the statute you regularly use in the class?

You might ask why it is that Herrig had the burden of proof? Does the statute compel this? The short answer is that once facts are alleged with sufficient particularity to demonstrate an adverse inference of self-dealing or self-interested transaction, the common law removed the presumption of the business judgment rule (see earlier excerpt by Marsh). Thus, while not explicit in the statute, it is embedded in the common law. This means that the interested party has to establish compliance with one of the three subparts of the statute.

What then is the role of this statute in the case? Frankly, it does not seem like much. Did the court consider who were the outside directors? Their probable independence? Degree of diligence and probing of the contracts? Did it consider whether there was ever shareholder approval and particularly approval by the non-Herrig holders? What appears is a broad inquiry into fairness. And is this the kind of fairness inquiry that is consistent with the "entire fairness" inquiry that we have seen in some of the earlier covered Delaware cases? In Delaware fairness includes not just fair price, but fair dealing. What might that include here? As the dissent points out, the majority believed Herrig was a valuable person to the company. But is that the focus for whether that valuable servant is ripping off the company? Would it not be whether those services could be independently procured and if so for what price? Would this approach by the board have "spooked" Herrig and drove him away from the company? This might well be an area where the real focus should have been on whether the board functioned independently and with due process and less on whether the outcome of their various decisions was at a price the court believed justified by the market.

Note on the Effect of Approval of Self-Interested Transactions by Disinterested Directors

The Note points out a good deal of variance among jurisdictions regarding the effect of director approval and likely what is meant when the statute refers to "good faith" approval (see Judge Friendly's guidance here that this needs to include some objective rationality). Worth reviewing is the large divide between whether such director approval merely removes the adverse inference (and hence is only a burden shifting provision) versus the *Marciano* approach which appears to do more by limiting future inquiry to whether the transaction was a gift or waste, i.e., lacked any rational basis. See here the description of the more explicit standard embraced by the ALI.

Sutherland v. Sutherland

This case illustrates the limits of private ordering in this area (note that most LLC statutes invite such private ordering on self-dealing transactions).

Prior to the 1967 sweeping amendment to the Delaware General Corporation Law, interested directors did not count toward a quorum. Many corporations addressed this problem by expressly authorizing such directors to be included in the quorum determination. Such a provision was in the articles of this company. Students can then be asked why this issue is being litigated? It goes to the burden of proof, as the defendants appear a bit vulnerable in defending their perquisites (the company jet) and salaries if they had the burden of proof. Thus, this arcane provision can well determine the outcome of the suit.

The court concludes first that it is unlikely that the provision was intended to cover more than the quorum issue – now moot under DGCL § 144. Second, that even if the provision was intended to treat all directors as independent regardless of the substance of a transaction that would not be permissible for a corporation (but is for the more contractually-based LLC and limited partnership). Thus, it would be void as against public policy. Query, why should there be such a more limited ability in the corporate setting for private ordering?

Note on Waste and Shareholder Ratification

The note provides a very helpful definition of waste. This is important, certainly under the Delaware scheme, since disinterested good faith shareholder or director approval of a self-dealing transaction can only be challenged for waste. Allen's thoughtful review of the four approaches regarding the consequences of ratification are valuable and worth reviewing. You might ask by way of review how this is changed by the *Gantler* examined earlier in Section 1. Query, how likely is it that fully informed, shareholder ratification by disinterested holders would ever occur in a transaction lacking a rational basis or adequate consideration?

Section 3.   Compensation

Aggarwal, Executive Compensation and Corporate Controversy

Restricted stock has come more into vogue after the Credit Crisis so spending some time discussing the mechanics of restricted stock versus the mechanics of more classic stock option would be useful. What might be a restriction on shares that would tie the officer to a goal of long-term sustainable growth? It could be that the officer must hold the shares 3-5 years after their grant.

In re Tyson Foods, Inc. [Tyson I]

The case can be used to illustrate the mechanics of stock options generally including the tax consequences. Students can be asked why stockholders may wish an option's exercise price to be equal or greater than the stock's price on the day of the grant? Those that have had a tax class could be asked what the tax consequences are for the corporation and the recipient of the option if the exercise price is the same price as the stock's price on the date of the grant? What if the exercise price is lower than the price on the date of the grant? These tax consequences are summarized in the Aggarwal article just before II.2.c. of that excerpt. Footnote 78 provides a nice summary of IRC § 162(m) which many believe is one of the culprits behind the unqualified use of stock options. Students might be asked, to make sure they understand both the mechanics of the option and how "spring loading" the option yielded a gain, how the corporation was injured by granting these options; the injury arises because the recipient received the optioned shares at a lower price than if the options were granted after the announcement of the market-moving information.

What is the relevance of the factual scenarios set forth in Part II of the opinion? The allegation is that the options were "spring loaded," providing their recipient a running start on gain by awarding the options and setting their exercise price on a date just preceding the release of good news that was known would increase the value of the options.

What is the basis on which Chandler sustains the complaint against seven of the recipients? Why the others were dismissed? They were not directors, and hence there was a view they were not self dealing (but would not the approving directors be responsible here for the excessive compensation lavished on those dismissed; this seems to be the point raised in footnote 72 of the case).

Critical to the court's approach is that the approving directors knowingly acted with the intent to circumvent the shareholder-approved plan's restrictions regarding the exercise price. Chandler states, "[a] director who intentionally uses inside knowledge not available to shareholders in order to enrich employees while avoiding shareholder-imposed requirements cannot, in my opinion, be said to be acting loyally and in good faith as a fiduciary." Note in footnote 15 the incentive options were not to be exercised for a price less than fair market value but the non-qualified could be at less than fair market value.

Tyson Foods, Inc. [Tyson II]

Why is this back before Chancellor Chandler? As seen above, the non-qualified options (those outside the "Incentive Stock Option" plan) could be granted for less than fair market value. See footnote 15 of the prior opinion. This causes some refinement of the reasoning to sustain the complaint in the face of the motion to dismiss.

The Chancellor focuses on disclosure. He reasons that had the stockholders never been asked to approve the non-qualified options, the directors would still have been required by their fiduciary relationship to disclose, on the announcement of any option's grant, their spring loading, as this is material information. He further states that purposefully withholding material information with the effect of covering up earlier actions is itself an act of disloyalty. Thus, the holding here is actually broader than the prior holding. The earlier holding is based the directors' failure to disclose they were acting contrary to the fair-price limit of the shareholder approved plan. Tyson II's holding is that the directors had a disclosure duty when granting the option to say that the shares were being granted at other than fair value, and that their failure to do so was purposeful and not the corporate interest.

Ryan v. Gifford

How is the abuse here different from that in *Tyson*? Here the market-moving information was released before the options were granted, but the date of the grant was backdated so that the option recipient received the optioned shares at their fair market value as determined at some earlier date. How is the abuse the same, just to make sure the students understand the option? If the recipient has not sold the optioned shares, how has she benefited? (this goes to the last portion of the case, related to whether the backdating of Gifford's shares produced any "unjust enrichment") The employee still has shares at a lower price than if the backdating had not occurred; it would seem that the "bargain purchase" would always be present and would unjustly enrich the recipient regardless of whether the shares were sold.

What evidence supported the backdating charge? This question allows you to get into the facts that surrounded the backdating scandal, as well as the facts in this particular case including the study by Merrill Lynch as well as the 243% return executives harvested on options versus the overall 29% return for the company during the same time period. How can these two returns differ so widely? The stock was volatile, so granting options in the valley and measuring their benefit at the later peak would explain this, whereas the overall return of the company does not take into account the intervening valleys.

How is the reasoning here different from that in *Tyson*. Like *Tyson*, this was in response to a motion to dismiss. Since derivative suit procedures comes later in the casebook, that portion of the case dealing with the excuse of demand has been heavily edited and essentially duplicates much of the reasoning in denying the defendants' motion to dismiss for failure to state a cause of action. We suggest focusing mostly on II B 1 of the opinion. *Ryan* focuses on the content of "bad faith" coupling the failure to abide by the rules established by the shareholders for the grant of options (at their "fair market value") and allegedly deliberately concealing the departure as disloyal conduct. This is consistent with *Tyson* but stated much more clearly.

Note on Challenges to Compensation

The Note emphasizes that few successful challenges to executive compensation exist in public companies. The facts of *Disney*, set forth earlier in this chapter, illustrate that significant breakdowns in corporate governance of a public company can be present but the compensation arrangement can nevertheless survive a challenge by shareholders. The spring-loaded and option backdating cases are exceptions here. In private companies we find compensation challenges more successful due to the lack of independent approval and the relative magnitude of the compensation to the company's earnings/revenues. Moreover, many of the challenges occur not in shareholder suits but rather by the IRS, a point illustrated in the note.

Wilderman v. Wilderman

This case lists multiple factors to be taken into consideration regarding the reasonableness of the compensation received by an executive. This is that this becomes something of a check list or playbook for those approving executive compensation, and consideration of these factors, by independent directors, e.g., a compensation committee, aided by compensation consultants, will likely make the ultimate decision bullet proof.

Note on CEO Compensation

This Note captures the points that are part of the national debate not just about increasing executive compensation, it increased 28 percent in 2010 for S&P 500 firms, but the malaise is further fed further by statistics reflecting growing income disparity within the U.S.

Note on the Effect of Federal Income Tax Rules and Accounting Principles of the Forms of Executive Compensation

The standard business organizations course is neither a tax nor an accounting class. However, knowledge of how these two fields shape compensation is central to this topic. It is no coincidence that the expensing of stock options occurred post Sarbanes-Oxley which not only removed the super-voting requirement that had long prevented the FASB from grappling with sensitive issues such as expensing options, but also made the funding of FASB independent of the auditing firms and their clients. When options were not expensed, the failure of boards to report the burdens of their grant underscored the observation that "you manage what gets measured." Therefore, if options were not accounted for in terms of their actual cost to the firm then they were not managed. At the same time, IRC § 162(m) mightily fed the cause of options as the currency of the realm.

Note on the Compensation of Nonexecutive Directors

This Note sets forth more about the background and the sordid practices that have surrounded compensation, this time on directors. The message here is that if everyone partakes in the "warm bath" no one is likely to worry about consuming too much water out of fear there won't be enough left for others to enjoy.

Section 4.   Use of Corporate Assets: The Corporate Opportunity Doctrine

So that students understand how the facts and hence issues raised in this set of cases differ from the preceding conflict of interest cases, it is a good idea to ask why, even though this case illustrates the duty of loyalty, its facts do not lend themselves to analysis under the state conflict of interest statute.

Hawaiian International Finances, Inc. v. Pablo

This is not a "conflict of interest" transaction because Pablo is not dealing with Hawaiian Int'l Finances, of which he was president and a director. He received a side payment from the real estate brokers representing the sellers of real estate. Pablo never disclosed this in connection with either his recommendation, or deliberation/voting as a director, to acquire the property.

What was the remedy here? Why not damages? This appears to be a fairly straightforward application of the restitution principle that the fiduciary cannot make a secret profit. The gains are required to be disgorged as a disincentive. Why? As the court emphasizes in its analysis, knowledge by the other directors that Pablo would gain if the property was acquired would prompt the other directors to be less deferential to his recommendation and engage in more independent scrutiny.

So what was Pablo to do? Disclose his interest, allow the independent directors to consider the option independently of his recommendation and participation, and seek approval of his receipt of the side payment.

What if he received the payment only after approval? Would this still seen as payment received because of his position? While it would not influence the board decision, there could still be the belief he received the payment due to his position, akin to the decision in *Reading v. Attorney General,* Section 2 of Chapter 1.

Forkin v. Cole

The case illustrates that fiduciaries are accountable if they use corporate assets even though this produced no tangible or out of pocket harm to the asset or corporation. Here it was reasoned that subjecting the company's asset to a personal mortgage deprived the company of an opportunity to use that asset.

Northeast Harbor Golf Club, Inc. v. Harris

This case has a very clean and interesting set of facts and a nice illustration of not just the corporate opportunity doctrine but the greater clarity in the doctrine's application that occurs under the approach embraced by the ALI, as opposed to the fuzzier approaches captured in the later note material that follows.

To get the facts before the students, you might ask what appears to be Mrs. Harris's passions. One answer is golf and another is purchasing real estate. She likely played many rounds of golf but she at least had three rounds of real estate purchases then subdivision of lots and gifting lots. She was a woman of unsurpassed energy. You might wish to discuss the history of her real estate purchases and the proximity to the golf course. Related to this, just what piqued the interest of the other club, members in proceeding against her in this action? Was it the fear that the bucolic setting would be disrupted by development (was Wal-Mart coming?) or was it the odor of money for the club given the significant increase in the value of the land? Does any of this matter to the approach taken by the court? No, the inquiry does not focus at all on the motivations of the plaintiff, or for that matter the motivations of Mrs. Harris. The focus is somewhat more neutral.

To begin the analysis, you might wish to point out that so much of fiduciary duty is common law and, being judge-made law, can be reformed by the court. That is what is happening here, with the Maine Supreme Court adopting the approach of the ALI, as have several other states. Thus, to unpack the result reached in the case you might wish to examine closely this provision of the ALI, linking it with the overarching theme of the ALI, namely the embrace of independent director approval, consistent with the monitoring role of directors embraced in Chapter 3 of the ALI.

To begin, why is it important to define, as subsection (b) does, what is a "corporate opportunity?" Absent a corporate opportunity, there is no need to resort to the approval/cleansing procedures in subsection (a). Students might be asked what is the distinction between(b)(1) and (b)(2): which test appears to include more opportunities within its reach and why? This goes to the reasoning first advanced in the Brudney & Clark article cited in the opinion, namely that senior executives, in contrast to outside directors, sit in very different situations, so that the former should be subject to a more demanding line-of-business standard than the latter, who

146

should be subject to a narrower use or abuse of corporate asset standard. Thus, what result here if Mrs. Harris were not the club president? As to the Gilpin property, we might easily conclude that she would fall within the (b)(1)(A), since the listing agent testified that he approached Mrs. Harris because she was the club's president (this is made clear in the post remand trial, where she so admitted that she had learned of the opportunity in her capacity as an officer). We don't have this showing in the other properties, but we might wonder if, at least circumstantially, the same would not have been true. As the Note material following the opinion reflects, the court concluded that all parcels fit within the (b)(2) test.

It is then important to review what happens if the property is indeed a "corporate opportunity." This is set forth in subsection (a) and is reviewed in the closing paragraphs of the excerpt, in the Note, from the Superior Court opinion on remand. Had Mrs. Harris presented the opportunity to the board or shareholders, then she would have a defense by showing their rejection of the opportunity was fair. But her failure to present the opportunity at all and she did not avail herself to the late approval process proscribed in subsection (e) which is not available if approval has not occurred before suit is filed.

Under the ALI formulation what role is there for the argument that the corporation lacked the financial capacity to acquire the property? This would come in only for showing that the rejection by the board or shareholders was reasonable. Why so limit this defense? One idea is that if it is a good opportunity then the corporation can find the resources to embrace the opportunity; whether this in fact would have been the case is problematic, but the ALI embraces a cleaner disposition, one that dumps the question into the independent decision-makers' hands to sort out.

Broz v. Cellular Information Systems, Inc.

This is a leading Delaware case and illustrates a more diffuse, and hence less predictable, approach. Broz was the president and sole stockholder of his own cellular phone company and also served the board of CIS, a competitor of his company. Broz learned of an opportunity to acquire an license to provide cellular service adjacent to Broz's current area; he was approached, not CIS, because the seller believed CIS's financial ability to acquire the license was impaired by its ability in its post-bankruptcy life to incur new debt.

The evidence before the court reflected that Broz approached CIS's CEO and also spoke with two CIS directors about the likely interest of CIS acquiring the license. Also, the record reflected that all the CIS sitting directors at that time expressed the view that CIS would not be interested in the license. CIS then sued. What changed? CIS had been acquired by PriCellular nine days after Broz closed on the license purchase. PriCellular had been in negotiations to acquire CIS during the time that Broz was considering the purchase of the license. Thus, there was indeed a new sheriff in town.

What test does the court apply? What are the crucial considerations under this test? How would this matter have been resolved under the ALI? These are fair areas of inquiry to the students.

Note the block quote from the Supreme Court's opinion summarizing the approach by *Guth v. Loft* and its progeny. The lengthy list of considerations pretty much cover the waterfront on what could be considered; note this includes a line-of-business test as well as multiple equitable considerations.

It is interesting that the court first considers that CIS lacked the financial ability to acquire the opportunity. It later takes the possible interest of PriCellular off the list of considerations, reasoning that Broz was not a fiduciary as to PriCellular. But would not any value associated with the cellular license weigh in the deal being negotiated between CIS and PriCellular?

Note the approach here to the "interest or expectancy" test, which historically is narrower than the line-of-business inquiry. The narrower approach of this test is to require that the plaintiff company have some legal or equitable interest in the opportunity from which an expectancy could spring. In *Broz* the court takes a different approach and slips back to the line-of-business framework and then reasons this was not within that test since CIS was actively unwinding its license holdings. Really, then what was it doing negotiating the sale of the company to PriCellular?

Perhaps the strongest portion of the reasoning is that akin to waiver; namely, CIS sought Broz on its board being fully aware that he was a competitor. Certainly it appears that Broz did not conceal anything here – he first discussed it with the CEO and then a couple of directors; their reaction is consistent with the idea that they did not view his service on the CIS board as circumscribing his own personal competitive interest. At the same time, Broz seeking their approval, or some of the directors' approval, suggests that he did not believe he had a "pass" on taking opportunities in the same line of business. What his sin may have been is failure to formally present this to the full board. But is that enough to cause him to give up the opportunity now that there is a new owner?

As for the ALI, the result is cleaner and more predictable. Hard to see this as a corporate opportunity which would be under (b)(1) of the ALI provision. The seller of the license clearly presented this to Broz as owner of his own cellular phone franchise.

Note on the Corporate Opportunity Doctrine

The Note provides an overview of the multiple approaches and considerations for the doctrine. It can serve as background to the two principal cases, *Northeast Harbor Golf Club* and *Broz*. Where you can draw into the discussion some of the points set forth in this Note.

In re eBay Inc. Shareholder Litigation

Students can be asked how this case is different from *Northeast Harbor Golf Club* and *Broz*? This is a secret profit case premised on the prevalent 1990's practice of investment banks sharing high-demand allocations of underwritings with senior executives of attractive startups and even established companies whose business investment banks wanted (Bernie Ebbers of WorldCom harvested millions of dollars in gains from such allocations). These are the modern day "Christmas Goose" given to purchasing agents by vendors. Are these corrupting bribes? Was it necessary for the suit to go forward to show that Whitman and Skoll directed business to Goldman Sachs because of the allocations? That Golman Sachs was unworthy of eBay's business? This is not part of the formulation for a secret profit approach. Much like the abuses in *Hawaiian International Finances*, the duty and the outcome turns on full disclosure and related approval and not actual adverse consequences as a result of the breach.

Section 5.   Zahn v. Transamerica Corporation

This classic case retains its pedagogical attraction because of its facts; the holding is not only eclipsed by subsequent decision in *Speed v. Transamerica Corp.* set forth in the Note following *Zahn*, but by the many years of maturing of the case law surrounding inter-class conflicts and the duties of the controlling stockholder. But there are few other cases that so clearly allow the professor to pull the rabbit from the hat in exploring where we might begin in determining in inter-class conflicts what duties the directors and the controlling stockholder owe the holders of the other class of security.

You can begin by reviewing the relative rights, privileges and preferences of the Class A and Class B common. This is an excellent location for the students to learn something about very common provisions of the preferred stock contract. The following are some questions that can be raised:

1. Which class is more like preferred?

2. What does it mean for the shares to be cumulative?

3. Why would Class A wish to have a conversion right?

4. Why have they not yet converted?

5. Under what conditions does the Class A have the right to vote for directors?

6. What is the purpose of this kind of contingent voting provision?

7. Why are the Class A being paid $80.80 for their shares and not $60? Why do the dividends in arrears "feed" the redemption price?

8. For whose benefit, Class A or B, is the redemption right?

9. When would the Class B like to see the Class A redeemed?

Thus if the right to redeem is intended for the benefit of the Class B, then how can there possibly be a breach of fiduciary duty in carrying out the very purpose that underpins this provision? The answer is the key to this case. That is, we should begin to analyze the duties that the "common" and board of directors owe the senior security holders in light of their contract. There is a large body of law that holds that the common, board of directors, and even a controlling stockholder do not owe a fiduciary duty to the senior security holders; their rights are set forth in their contract. After all, is there any reason why preferred holders should be treated differently than bondholders. While the latter have stronger rights, those rights are in their contract. The preferred holders bought a security with lesser rights than bondholders, but does that mean they should enjoy rights equal to common holders?

This case can best be understood as holding that the parties would not expect that one of them could act opportunistically to destroy or eviscerate an expressly agreed upon provision of their contract. What the board is seeking to do is to deprive the Class A of their right to convert into the Class B when it was in the Class A's interest to do so by fostering an enriching liquidation in which only the Class B would participate. Thus, the missing term being provided, so as to avoid frustration or evisceration of the express conversion provision is that of reasonable notice. This is the essence of the *Speed* holding in the Note. But what about the 2-to-1 preference on liquidation that the Class A enjoyed? That term must also be interpreted in light of the express terms of the agreement, namely the right of the Class B to act opportunistically in redeeming the Class A. Thus, the liquidation preference can be read as designed for those instances in which repurchase before a liquidation could not occur, namely when the company could not meet the restrictions for repurchase. This would be the instance in which the liquidation is involuntary (insolvency proceeding) and not, as here, voluntary. Hence the measure of relief here is the difference between what the Class A would have received on liquidation if they had converted and received Class B shares (and as such participated in the liquidation as Class B holder) less any redemption payment already made to the class members.

Compare the reasoning above with that covered earlier in *Nemec v. Shrader*, in Chapter 8. The distinction is that there is no showing on the facts in *Nemec* that an agreed upon express provision would be frustrated or eviscerated if the majority exercised its right, as it did, to redeem the retired employee's shares.

Note on the Duty of Disclosure by Controlling Stockholders Under Delaware Law

The facts of *Lynch* introduce how a less than 50% owner can be a controlling stockholder. This concept may be developed here or later in *Kahn,* where a 43% holder was concluded to be a controlling stockholder.

In any case, what was the breaching behavior here and why is *Lynch* an important case? This is the leading case for the principle that officers, directors, and controlling stockholders have a duty of candor to stockholders, at least when the transaction entails some form of stockholder action. Here the transaction was a tender offer; more frequently it is a acquisition that needs the approval of the stockholders. The breach of this duty was the dominant stockholder's failure to disclose estimates of the firm's book value which were significantly above the tender offer price. Note the information withheld was speculative, subject, as most value estimates, to wide ranging assumptions. But the court said this did not prevent the withheld information from being "germane" to the decision whether to accept the tender offer.

What we see in the remaining cases is that the law morphed from a test of "germane" to materiality standards that are the mirror image of what we saw earlier in *TSC Industries* dealing with omissions and misstatements in proxy solicitations.

But the real significance of *Lynch* is the duty and that it extends to the controlling stockholder.

Note on the Target of Suits by Minority Shareholders

This brief note makes clear that as a matter of practice the focus of the suits in this section is directly on the controlling stockholder, the person with more than a positional conflict of interest, because it is just easier for the trier of fact and law to see the conflict, and as a practical matter that is where the money is.

Sinclair Oil Corporation v. Levien

There are two transactions in this case and you might find it best to focus first on why the plaintiff lost as to the former, then review the second from the insights gained about the benefit-and-detriment test as applied in the first transaction.

One way to begin the discussion is to ask why this transaction is not within the Delaware conflict of interest transaction, section 144? There are two possible answers. First, the directors of Sinven, while employees and officers and directors of other companies controlled by Sinclair were not themselves on the Sinclair board of directors. Hence, technically they are not within the scope of the introductory paragraph of the conflict of interest statute. Secondly, this court appears to be saying we don't have a "contract" or "transaction" unless the matter is one that meets the exclusive benefit and exclusive detriment test.

How was this case resolved below? The Chancellor held this was a conflict of interest transaction so that the presumption of the business judgment rule did not apply; this would then require Sinclair to show that there was no opportunity it took that was an opportunity that Sinven, but for the extraordinary dividends, would have acquired. The Supreme Court reversed, holding that whatever benefit and whatever detriment was felt proportionally across the Sinven shareholders.

How does this work through with respect to the contract binding Sinclair to purchase set quantities of oil from Sinven? Here there was no proportional sharing of benefits, the breach of the purchase and timely payment requirements were to the exclusive benefit of Sinclair and the harm likewise was felt by the minority (since they did not recoup, as did Sinclair, the benefits of the breach).

We might ask is this a test that merely allocates the burden of proof on fairness or is it a test of fairness itself such that once the *Sinclair* test removes the transaction or contract from the protection of the business judgment rule it means that the defendant loses the case? The entire fairness standard is surmountable so that perhaps we might think that Sinclair could have introduced evidence that as a quid pro quo for the breach it provided funds or some other benefits to Sinven equal to the gains the subsidiary would have made had the contract been honored.

David J. Greene and Co. v. Dunhill Int'l, Inc.

What was the breach here? It was alleged that Dunhill usurped a corporate opportunity that would have gone to its 80.3% owned subsidiary. Thus, in the context of this material, the duty of the controlling stockholder includes obligations respecting corporate opportunities. Note the problems this likely introduces for the controlling stockholder with respect to whether an opportunity rejected by the subsidiary and acquired by the parent was a "good faith" and independent rejection. The students might be asked how the parent can proceed to acquire such an opportunity? The answer is installing an independent body of directors to pass on whether the subsidiary wishes to acquire the opportunity. The next case illustrates how even an independent committee can fail to provide the insulation sought.

Kahn v. Lynch Communications Systems, Inc.

An initial area to focus is what persuaded the court that Alcatel, the owner of 43.3% of Lynch's shares could nonetheless be deemed a controlling stockholder. Alcatel appointed 5 of the 11 directors, 2 of 3 of the members of the executive committee (may wish to review with students why this is significant in light of the likely authority of that committee), was by far the largest holder, and in the face of the classic collective action problem within public companies likely to be the voice that is most often heard. Add to this the charter provision that conditioned any acquisition on an 80 percent vote and it is not hard to conclude that Alcatel was likely deferred to by the board. Finally, the facts reviewed under "Alcatel Dominated Lynch" certainly bears out a few former instances in which its views were deferred to by the full board.

How did Lynch deal with the decision whether to acquire Celwave, a company controlled by Alcatel? The court was satisfied here that the independent committee did act independently when it ejected the Celwave acquisition. What other evidence do we have that the board acted independently in exercising its rejection (as if confronting the largest shareholder was not itself enough)? The committee retained outside investment bankers (two).

How does this change with respect to Alcatel's bid to acquire Lynch at $15.50? The committee appeared to cave, while first showing great independence, rejecting bids of $15, $15.25 and even $15.50, before ultimately approving a $15.50 bid. What changed their heart on the $15.50 bid? Was it the threat of Alcatel that it would proceed with a tender offer at an even lower price? Why should this cause the independent committee to waiver?

First note that creating an independent committee can shift the burden of proof, but the litmus, regardless of who has the burden of proof, remains "entire fairness." But did the burden shift? Court states that more than the presence or appearance of an body of independent directors is needed to shift the burden: the majority must not dictate the terms and there must be real bargaining.

While demonstrating independence in the Celware rejection and later in rejecting three initial bids by Alcatel, the facts are unclear whether there was independence with respect to the merger proposal. The court sets forth their contending positions, emphasizes that the heavy handed threat to launch a lower offer if the offered price were not accepted, raise important factual issues, as expressed in footnote 57, whether by doing so the controlling stockholder had hemmed the committee's options so narrowly that they did not have the power to negotiate. These are issues to be dealt with on remand so that what we are left with is very little guidance as to just how strong a negotiating strategy a dominant stockholder can take.

Levco Alternative Fund v. The Reader's Digest Ass'n, Inc.

How did the board, clearly under the guidance of voting Class B shares 50 percent holders, two funds, seek to address scrutiny under *Sinclair*? They had an independent committee and it relied on a fairness opinion with respect to the recapitalization plan. However, Goldman Sachs's fairness opinion failed to address the fair price issue? Why? It was an opinion on the fairness to the entity, Reader's Digest, and not as to the fair division between the Class A and Class B shares. Moreover, there is reason to believe here that the court is also saying the overall plan was not reasonable, i.e., fair, since it involved requiring borrowing to provide the cash payment to the two funds for their Class B shares at a time when the company was in "tenuous" financial shape. This was on a pretrial motion for an injunction so all that was required was a showing of reasonable probability of success; nonetheless, the case illustrates the fair price and fair dealing each turn on the handiwork of the investment banker's fairness opinion.

Jones v. H.F. Ahmanson & Co.

Here and under the ALI approach that is followed in a minority of the states, the benefit/detriment inquiry is in the disjunctive. You might wish to illustrate the contrast by the simple illustration of P who owns 80 percent of S. They file a consolidated tax return and the result is that the $10 million profit that S had is offset totally by the much larger losses of P. The result is that the $2.5 million in taxes that S would have had to pay do not have to be paid. Can P consistent with its fiduciary duty as a controlling stockholder require S to issue to P a check for $2.5 million? Under the Delaware approach the answer is yes; there is no detriment to S since absent consolidation this amount would have had to be paid to the IRS. *See Case v. New York Central RR*, 204 N.E.2d 643 (N.Y. 1965). Under *Jones*/ALI the check would have to be limited to $2 million, 80 percent of the tax savings. But note here there would still be a benefit of sorts not enjoyed by the minority, since shareholder P does get the cash but the minority in S only see their funds remain in the subsidiary which would, of course, be under the control of P.

In re Trados Inc. Shareholder Litigation

Similar to *Zahn* and *Levco*, this deals with the allocation of assets between two competing classes. The triggering event is the sale of Trados to SDL for $60 million. The plan allocates the bulk of the consideration to the preferred, with nearly $8 million to the company's officers as part of their bonus. The common, plaintiffs in the case, receive nothing, the reason for their suing.

Of interest here is that the preferred stakeholders are the venture firms who see this transaction as their long overdue exit from Trados. What is the plaintiff's complaint?

The drill here is why this is a fiduciary duty case and not just a contractual dispute? What we see is that the liquidation preference of the preferred was triggered if there was a merger, not just dissolution and winding up. Thus, if this case were seen purely as a contractual matter, the preferred easily prevails since their liquidation preference is $57.9 million, and the only question then is whether the allocation to the officers was fair. This may be the essence of the case, since when we look at the court's reasoning, the court's emphasis is on the self-interest of some of the approving officers. That self interest comes from where? It is the bonus payments, and for some, the continuing relationship with the successor firm that was enjoyed by Cambell and Hummel, two of the directors, and that four others were tied closely to he preferred holders . Thus, they garner some pretty hefty payments if this deal goes through, such that it appears that four, a majority, of the Trados board suffered from conflicts of interest. This was enough to survive the motion to dismiss. Moreover, the fact question whether their self interest, and perhaps dominance by the preferred who had voting control, drove the entire decision, since the plaintiff alleged the firm was performing reasonably well, with Cambell's hire, was not longer losing money, and hence could have patiently awaited a better deal. Overall, the decision to sell the company and the allocation of the consideration do not appear, at the motion to dismiss stage, protected by the business judgment rule.

What then could Trados have done? Well, it would need some independent directors and, with these in place, take steps to arm a negotiating committee with all the weapons to act independently. It might have tried a plebiscite of the minority holders but not without something for the common. Lacking these steps, the preferred will just have to slug it out in court.

Section 6.   Sale of Control

Zetlin v. Hanson Holdings, Inc.

What is the allegation here? That control was sold for a premium, by the present controlling stockholders, and the opportunity to share in the third party's interest in acquiring control was a "corporate opportunity" that required proportionate sharing, i.e., and equal opportunity for everyone.

As a preliminary matter students may be asked why Flintkote Co. was willing to pay a premium for the defendants' shares? What would have been required had it instead made a bid to all the shareholders to obtain the same number of shares? These questions get into the view that all publicly traded shares trade at a discount; the quoted price merely reflects the last sale (perhaps the low hanging fruit) and not what the holders of a majority of the shares, or rather the person who holds the last share needed to make one a holder of a majority of the shares, would wish to sell those shares for. That, we are talking of a supply curve which is upward sloping.

Thus, as a practical matter, a premium, i.e., price above the last quoted price, will always be needed to acquire a majority of the shares. And what result if Flintkote had sought to make a bid for a majority of the Gable shares? The opposition of the 44.4% holders would make such an acquisition nearly impossible because it would require that of the remaining holders, more than 95 percent of those shares would have to be tendered. This sort of success would require a price well out on the supply curve.

In any case, if a price above the neutrally determined majority price on the supply curve is to be paid, what justifies this payment? It might well be the chance for the majority holder to act opportunistically in garnering disproportionate gains. Hence, we see the risk of majority opportunism and its impact on the minority's share price and therefore a minority discount.

Andrews, The Stockholder's Right to Equal Opportunity in the Sale of Shares

Justice Traynor in *Jones v. H.F. Ahmanson* and the Massachusetts Supreme Court in *Donahue* each embraced a view of equal opportunity for minority holders. What is the major justification for Professor Andrews calling for equal opportunity? It is that if the former controlling stockholder could only sell a part of his shares (in proportion to the number that the third party wished to acquire). This would incentivize the existing controlling stockholder to engage in meaningful due diligence to reduce the likelihood that the new controlling stockholder would harm the corporation or its minority, since now the former controlling stockholder would be among the minority holders.

Javaras, Equal Opportunity in the Sale of Controlling Shares: A Reply to Professor Andrews

The rejoinder in part is that transfers of control are to be encouraged. An equal opportunity approach would drive up the cost of acquisitions since it would effectively mean that the third party would be forced to acquire 100 percent of the shares, since the former controlling holder would never wish to sell less than 100 percent of its holdings.

Note, many countries around the world, including the U.K. do have mandatory bid rules that embrace the view of Andrews, namely that upon acquiring a certain percentage, which sometimes is as low as 30 percent, an offer must be made to acquire the remaining shares at the same price. What justifies this rule? Fear of oppression of the minority so that an exit is provided for the minority.

Gerdes v. Reynolds

This is an early case addressing the sale of control. Students might be asked what harm suffered allegedly was by the transfer of control? The company, an investment trust, had highly liquid assets, mainly securities of public companies. The new controlling stockholder misappropriated the assets soon after acquiring control. This came at the expense of the other stakeholders in the firm; note that the firm was highly leveraged so that the common represented a relatively small portion of the right-side of the balance sheet.

Who are the defendants? The suit here was against the officers and directors (who also were also majority holders of the common). The court's focus is on their obligations in that capacity and not any duty they had as majority shareholders.

What then is the duty the court embraces for the directors/officers in this situation (of resigning their office and securing the appointment of the new controlling stockholder's nominees)? While recognizing they likely had no knowledge that harm would occur, the court nonetheless said their duty would be breached if they are 'chargeable with notice" of possible harm. Hence the now fairly well established knew or have reason to know standard.

It is worth reviewing what imparted the notice: most importantly the wide differential $2 paid per share versus the probable book value $0.06 and estimates of fair market value $0.25 - $0.75. Moreover, the liquid nature of the company's assets made it ripe for looting. Third, the court noted the lack of distinction in the assets-why would someone pay such a premium to the controlling stockholders if you could easily assemble a portfolio of comparable investments. Finally, the sellers were aware that not all the purchase price had been paid, they were about $600,000 short, without making any effort to learn where that amount would come from.

Thus, the case reflects an easy illustration of how harm can flow to the corporation and its minority holders at the hands of a new controlling stockholder. Hence, some duty is appropriate to protect the corporation in transfers of control.

Perlman v. Feldman

This classic case illustrates the prophylactic approach to sale of control. The plaintiff's theory was that control was a "corporate asset" such that any disposition for any consideration means that the consideration belonged to the corporation and all its shareholders. This theory may be illustrated as little more than metaphor if we ask, "ok, so what happens on the second disposition or third disposition of control?" Would there continue to be the right of the corporation and its shareholders to share in the premium paid for control? If so, is it really the payment for something that was transferred because if so, would not the first transfer trigger sharing but thereafter the owner of what was transferred would have the right to the premium?

How many times can the minority be paid for control? Well, in any case, Father Bayne notwithstanding, the notion that control is a corporate asset has never found its way into the case law.

What then is the approach taken in this case? It is that the controlling stockholder has a duty when disposing of control not to sell control to one who the former controlling stockholder knows or has reason to know will harm the company. This is part of the fiduciary duties that attach to a controlling stockholder.

How then did that occur here? This invites discussion of both the "Feldman Plan" and the opportunity to establish customer patronage with geographically remote users of steel during the Korean conflict. Do we know that the Feldman Plan would have worked as it had during WWII? Do we know that the customer goodwill with remote users of steel would have occurred and continued after the steel shortages abated? The answer is no. Another way to approach these questions is to ask what the remedy here was and why disgorgement and not damages?

Indeed, in the very lengthy proceeding referred to in the Note following the case where the object was to determine the fair value of Newport shares the evidence revealed that Newport flourished under the control of Wilport. Should this have caused the court to reverse course and dismiss the case?

The answer is that there was a technical breach of the duty by Feldman; he sold control to a purchaser who he had reason to believe would not be vigilant for the long-term benefits of Newport. Thus, the remedy is to provide a disincentive for breaching conduct, regardless of whether there was actual harm.

As an aside, later in the materials, Chapter 12, Section 3, we encounter the purchaser-seller requirement for standing in Rule 10b-5 private suits. The leading case, *Birnbaum v. Newport Steel, Inc.*, involved allegations that holders of Newport were defrauded when Feldman broke off merger negotiations with Follansbee Inc. so as to garner all the control premium for himself by selling his shares (and the friends of Feldman) to Wilport. Note this would more clearly show a breach under state law; under Rule 10b-5 the suit failed because the holders of Newport shares were not sellers or purchasers in connection with the alleged fraud (which the Second Circuit in *Birnbaum* characterized as not fraud but an "act of mismanagement").

Breacher v. Gregg

How is this case different from *Perlman*. While neither case demonstrated any actual provable harm to the corporation or its minority stockholder, the difference is that *Perlman* posed a threat of such harm, thus giving rise to a technical breach by Feldmann, whereas the issue in *Breacher* is the sale of a corporate office. What makes this not a sale of control but a sale of a corporate office? It is because Gregg was the owner of only 4 percent of the shares and did not persuade the court that his transfer of shares represented control. Hence, this is an easier configuration to apply the sale of corporate office doctrine than the next case.

But does this make sense in light of the fact that Gregg did engineer the transfer of control to SEPCO? What do we make of the fact that a few weeks after Gregg pulled off the change that there was a revolt and SEPCO's nominees were thrown out? This reflects that the power to persuade directors to resign, and with whom to fill the seats, resided in Gregg himself and not quantum of shares that he owned.

What remedy? It is the disgorgement approach designed to remove the ill-gotten gains.

Essex Universal Corp. v. Yates

To get the facts rolling, students may be asked what is at the heart of the dispute? Essex sued for specific performance of the contract with Yates to purchase his 28.3% ownership in Republic Pictures, a publicly traded firm. Why does Yates have seller's remorse? The shares have skyrocketed (largely due to the box office success of the movie Ben Hur). Yates agreed to dispose of his shares at $8/share when the market was about $6. But at the time of the suit, the non-controlling shares were trading at $12.75. What defense is raised? That the provision calling for Yates to deliver a majority of the board was illegal because it constituted the sale of a corporate office/directorship.

Reviewing the mechanics of seriatim resignations and appointments, with reference to the provision of the statute used in your course that authorizes vacancies to be filled by the board introduces those frequently used provisions of the code.

What is Henry Friendly's suggested approach in his concurring opinion? It is to leave the parties where they are namely Yates is a weasel trying to get out of his deal to make more money, likely to enter into the same contract with another buyer, and not try to second guess this difficult question of state law.

What makes this a difficult question? It is that 28.3% is less than 51%, so how do we know that Yates was a controlling person? But why should it matter whether he is in control? This opens up the topic for discussion whether and why it is good public policy to facilitate quick changes in control. But for the doctrine announced in this case, i.e., that seriatim resignations and appointments are not the sale of corporate office if accompanying the transfer of a control block of stock, what options would be open to the new controlling stockholder? Call a special meeting, likely solicit proxies if you don't have enough votes and are uncertain what others might do, and see what the results are. But this has some non trivial costs and time would be likely about 45-60 days.

How practical is the approach suggested by Judge Lumbard? As Judge Friendly points out ascertaining the result assuming absolute neutrality on the part of the board is a very unreal set of circumstances. Note that Judge Lumbard would place the burden on Yates to prove that Essex could not elect a majority of the directors assuming neutrality on the part of the board.

So, what evidence do we look to for determining whether a person is a controlling stockholder? As this case illustrates, the ability to secure the nomination and election of a majority of the board. As seen earlier in *Kahn*, control can be demonstrated as well by evidence that the board lacked independence with respect to prior actions where the will of the largest stockholder was followed by the board.

Chapter 12

The Antifraud Provision: Section 10(b) and Rule 10b-5

Chapter Overview: In the Tenth Edition, we placed issues related to insider trading in a separate chapter, Chapter 13. Because the materials are modular, if you prefer, that chapter can be taught first before moving to the more plaintiff-oriented cases in Chapter 12, as contrasted to the government enforcement orientation of insider trading cases.

A reasonable place to begin is with the text of Rule 10b-5 and Section 10(b). This is important because, since the mid-1970s, the Supreme Court has repeatedly began, and in some instances completed, its interpretation of the scope of the antifraud provision by resort to the text of the enabling statute and Rule 10b-5 itself. While the actual text of the provisions is not particularly specific and helpful when read alone, it is important to pick out the jurisdictional reach of the provisions as well as the specific language of the enabling statute and the broad sweep of Rule 10b-5. Nonetheless, many of the elements studied in this chapter, e.g., scienter and causation, are not expressly referenced in the statute or rule.

Because of the opacity of the statutes, the rich case law that has accreted over time is where guidance is to be found. What is clear, and can be emphasized in a review of Section 10(b), is the broad jurisdictional reach of the provision. Hence, a purely intrastate phone call, mailing of a letter for delivery across town, or likely driving a few blocks on the cross-town interstate, would each appear to meet the jurisdictional requirement. Moreover, the direct or indirect language has been held to mean that the fraudulent representation need not occur via an instrumentality of interstate commerce. Hence, a face-to-face misrepresentation followed up by mailing the securities that were sold via the earlier fraudulent representation meets the jurisdictional requirement.

With respect to coverage, professors vary widely in how deeply they press into the intricacies of the antifraud provision. In four class periods, you can actually cover quite a bit a ground in this chapter. If you were to allocate four days, you would open with the material in Sections 1 – 3 (likely omitting forward looking statements). This material would take well into the second class period. For the balance of the second class you would add either *Pacific Investment Management* or *Pugh.* Class three could include *Affiliated Ute* and *Basic Inc,* along with the introductory note material to Section 6. You would then conclude with *Metzler Investment* and *Santa Fe Ind.*

Section 1.   An Introduction to Section 10(b) and Rule 10b-5

The Wharf (Holdings) Limited v. United International Holdings, Inc.

This case provides something of an anchor for much of the discussion that occurs in the next few sections because it does review some of the central elements of the private or government suit. It refers expressly to 1) deceptive practice, 2) in connection with a security, 3) the jurisdictional scope, 4) scienter, 5) the materiality of the deceptive practice and 6) damages. Left off this list are standing and causation.

The facts are fairly straightforward. Wharf sold United International an option to buy stock in a new cable system, but secretly never intended to honor that option. This arrangement flowed from United agreeing to assist Wharf to prepare a bid for the cable TV system in Hong Kong. Wharf won the contract, but refused to honor the option. Internal documents supported United's claim that Wharf never intended to fulfill its promise to allow United to acquire 10 percent of the venture.

The Supreme Court reasoned, in part, that "even were it the case that the Act covers only misrepresentations likely to affect the value of securities, Wharf's secret reservation was such a misrepresentation. To sell an option while secretly intending not to permit the option's exercise is misleading, because a buyer normally presumes good faith. … [T]he secret reservation misled United about the option's value [since the option was actually valueless due to Wharf's intention not to honor it]."

The case serves several introductory purposes.

1. Students can be asked to fit the facts expressly into the language of Rule 10b-5; the easiest would be subsection 2 dealing with the omission of a material fact. A second question here is the jurisdictional element. Finally, where does the court get the other elements it mentions. This allows you to raise the introductory observations above, namely the vacuousness of Section 10(b) and Rule 10b-5 and the heavy borrowing here of elements from the tort of misrepresentation.

2. What makes us think that this was material? Was relied upon? This strikes us as a pretty easy case for materiality and reliance because United International would never have entered into the arrangement with Wharf on the terms agreed to if the option was known in advance to be valueless. That is, we might conclude here that the statement that an intent not to honor the option did not relate to the value of the option is nonsensical.

3. An important observation is that this is a federal statute, but one that does not require broad injury. This was a commercial dispute that wound up in federal court because the misrepresentation was in connection with the purchase and sale of a security, the option. This illustrates again the breadth, if not the ubiquity, of Rule 10b-5.

4. We might make the side observation that this seems like a strange case for the court to have granted cert. The right decision was reached in the Tenth Circuit, no new principle was really established, and the stakes were not all that high.

5. The case leads to the following note material on the source of the implied cause of action and the types of cases that prompted the PSLRA.

Section 2.   Private Securities Litigation Reform Act and Securities Litigation Uniform Standards Act

There are multiple components of the PSLRA, and SLUSA is itself complicated by its definitions of what is a covered security and what is a covered class action. So much of securities litigation practice surrounds these two acts that some coverage in the basic business organizations class is desirable. But it is hard to believe in the basic business organization class that issues dealing with contribution, proportionate liability, and the like are necessary. Thus, the introductory note material stresses three important features of the PSLRA: the lead plaintiff, the discovery bar, and the heightened pleading requirement. The importance of the latter two is that the plaintiffs wishing to bring a securities suit (note that the pleading requirement and discovery bar are not limited to class actions) need to find sources of information to meet not just the particularity requirement, but also be sufficient to establish a strong inference the defendant committed a violation. Some of this can come from press reports. Some can come from government actions if the government suit moves quickly enough. Some will come from whistleblowers. With SLUSA, the material is focused on applying to class actions, defined as 50 or more members. There is a carve out for fiduciary duty claims premised on state law, such as those discussed in Chapter 11, Section 5.

An historical aside: the PSLRA was the only Clinton veto, and recall there were many post the 1994 election reversal for the Democrats, that was overridden.

Section 3.   The Elements of Standing, "In Connection With," and Scienter

As noted above, there are five (or perhaps six) elements to a successful private securities fraud lawsuit: (1) materiality, (2) "in connection with," (3) reliance, (4) loss causation, and (5) scienter. (As noted, a sixth element would be damages.)

Note on Standing and "In Connection With"

A. Purchaser-Seller: In Blue Chip Stamps v. Manor Drug Stores, 421 U.S. 723, 95 S.Ct. 1917, 44 L.Ed.2d 539 (1975), the Supreme Court held that the "in connection with" language in § 10(b) precluded recovery by a plaintiff who had *neither* bought nor sold securities, but, rather, who had allegedly been induced by fraud to do neither. You might wish to ask the class why the Ninth Circuit felt the facts before it justified an exception to the long-recognized purchaser-seller standing requirement. Note that the antitrust enforcement order identified not just who could be a purchaser, but how many shares, and at what price. Thus, this is not exactly open-ended in terms of who could have standing to sue. Nonetheless, the Supreme Court based its holding largely on policy, noting that: "There has been widespread recognition that litigation under Rule 10b–5 presents a danger of vexatiousness different in degree and in kind from that which accompanies litigation in general....[I]n the field of federal securities laws governing disclosure of information even a complaint which by objective standards may have very little chance of success at trial has a settlement value to the plaintiff out of any proportion to its prospect of success at trial so long as he may prevent the suit from being resolved against him by dismissal or summary judgment. The very pendency of the lawsuit may frustrate or delay normal business activity of the defendant which is totally unrelated to the lawsuit...."

Some notable exceptions to the purchaser-seller requirement: Clearly the requirement does not apply to SEC enforcement actions and most courts that have ruled on the subject allow a non-purchasing, non-selling shareholder to seek injunctive relief..

Note 4 illustrates the effect of SLUSA on non-selling investors duped into holding their shares in *Merrill Lynch, Pierce, Fenner & Smith v. Dabit*, 547 U.S. 71 (2006). The plaintiffs in *Dabit*, suing as a class, found themselves removed, via SLUSA, to federal courts. There the court found the policy of the act was not mere circumvention of the procedural and substantive hurdles of the PSLRA, but the quest for uniformity in substantive standards. Thus, once removed to the federal court, the securities claim then must be judged by the federal securities laws and not the state-based misrepresentation claim (which did not have a purchaser-seller requirement). How can removal have been avoided? By not having a class action, suit by fewer than 50 investors. This means that the investors could have a remedy, but if each had small claims that remedy may not be an effective one because without substantial aggregation there would be not be a sufficiently large recovery to attract counsel.

B. In Connection With: With respect to the "in connection with the purchase or sale" of securities element, there are actually two issues at play: First, there is the *Wharf* issue of whether the fraud was one sufficiently tied to a security (which was an issue also addressed as noted in the casebook in *SEC v. Zandford*), and, second, there is the issue – discussed below – of whether the private plaintiff who is suing is a purchaser or seller of a security such that she has standing under Section 10(b) to sue. In *Zandford*, the sale clearly would be present if the offending broker sold shares from the unsuspecting customer's account so as to have the funds that could then be embezzled. This seems to be the reasoning of the court. Accepting this sequence, then assuming (which appears to be the clear import of *Green v. Santa Fe Ind., Inc., infra,* that the sine qua non for a Rule 10b-5 violation is a material omission or misstatement), where would such a misrepresentation be found in the facts of *Zandford*? The Court emphasized that there was something of a continuing representation by the broker that his services would be provided to assure safe conservative investments. Stealing was inconsistent with this representation, thus rendering the representation false. Ok, you want a misrepresentation, we'll find one for you! Compare this with *Gavin* where the broker failed to disclose some less costly means by which shareholders in a merged company could receive consideration for their shares. The court held this was not "in connection with" the purchase or sale of shares. How come? It did not relate to the sum that the investors would receive for their shares, but rather to the costs of their realization of any consideration. In *Zandford* the deception, much like *The Wharf (Holdings)*, related to the value of the security itself.

It bears reminding students that *Blue Chip* does not impact the ability of the SEC to bring suit even though the SEC is never a purchaser or a seller. As will be seen later, the SEC is not required to prove reliance or loss causation; as will be seen these can be burdensome requirements in private suits.

Note on the Scienter Requirement and Its Pleading

In *Ernst & Ernst v. Hochfelder*, 425 U.S. 185 (1976), the Supreme Court held that a private plaintiff who is seeking damages under Rule 10b–5 must establish that the defendant acted with the requisite scienter, to wit, the "intent to deceive, manipulate, or defraud." In footnote 12 of the *Ernst & Ernst v. Hochfelder* opinion, the Court declined to confirm whether reckless behavior was sufficient to satisfy the standard of "intent to deceive, manipulate, or defraud," but federal appellate court opinions since *Ernst & Ernst* have held that recklessness does indeed satisfy the scienter parameters.[1] Students may be asked to verbalize what is recklessness. For Rule 10b-5 purposes, it is not just an extreme departure from a standard of care, but a departure with a conscious awareness that the representation made has a significant chance of being false (although not known to be false), e.g., stating that you expect next quarter to be as good as this quarter, but you are aware that your largest client has just defected to another vendor.

As seen earlier, the standard for pleading the requisite level of scienter was made more stringent in the PSLRA, which requires that a plaintiff state with particularity facts that gave rise to a "strong inference" of scienter. It is unclear, however, what is required to satisfy this "strong inference" standard. The Second Circuit, even before the PSLRA, developed the "motive and opportunity" test,[2] but Congress made clear when adopting the PSLRA that it was not necessarily adopting the Second Circuit's test. The materials in the Unabridged edition sets forth broad standards embraced in the three apparently distinct approaches taken across the various circuits. It is not clear what would be gained by studying closely the three approaches, particularly in the business organizations class. This is a factually-laden area and has the excitement of watching paint dry.

In Sundstrand Corp. v. Sun Chemical Corp., 553 F.2d 1033, 1045 (7th Cir.1977), cert. denied 434 U.S. 875, the court said:

[R]eckless conduct may be defined as [highly unreasonable conduct], involving not merely simple, or even inexcusable negligence, but an extreme departure from the standards of ordinary care, and which presents a danger of misleading buyers or sellers that is either known to the defendant or is so obvious that the actor must have been aware of it.

[2] The "motive and opportunity" test requires something more than a plaintiff simply alleging that the defendant had a motive of a sort that all insiders have, such as the desire to sustain the appearance of corporate profitability. The plaintiff must allege something more concrete and personal, such as a defendant's desire to inflate the price of stock so that he can sell at a higher price.

The only Supreme Court decision to date interpreting the PSLRA's pleading requirement is *Tellabs, Inc. v. Makor Issues & Rights, Ltd.*, 551 U.S. 308, 322-323 (2007), in which the Court noted:

[I]n determining whether the pleaded facts give rise to a "strong" inference of scienter, the court must take into account plausible opposing inferences.... The inquiry is inherently comparative: How likely is it that one conclusion, as compared to others, follows from the underlying facts? To determine whether the plaintiff has alleged facts that give rise to the requisite "strong inference" of scienter, a court must consider plausible, nonculpable explanations for the defendant's conduct, as well as inferences favoring the plaintiff. . . . A complaint will survive, we hold, only if a reasonable person would deem the inference of scienter cogent and at least as compelling as any opposing inference one could draw from the facts alleged.

To be noted, if there is a tie, i.e., equally strong inferences, then the plaintiff's allegation survives the motion to dismiss. Without discovery, the class might be asked where the plaintiff can be expected to find facts to support an inference that someone acted with knowledge. The question is not what facts would support such an inference, but where can the plaintiff's attorney can expect to locate such facts. One easy source could be what comes available via 1) investigative journalists, 2) government enforcement actions (need to pay attention here to the statute of limitations), 3) disgruntled (ex) employees who are whistleblowers, 4) chat rooms are cruised by the plaintiff's bar for tipsters, and 5) circumstantial facts (e.g., Tuesday the company issued buoyant forecast, sold options Wednesday, and Thursday issued a whoops correction). Trolling for disgruntled employees and whistleblowers in part explains the steeper costs plaintiffs' counsel face post PSLRA to initiate suits.

Note on Scienter and the Forward Looking Statement

You might introduce this subject by asking why the Congress and the courts have developed special defenses (the statutory safe harbor and bespeaks caution doctrine, respectively) for forward looking statements? Why not for all representations, even historical facts? One easy explanation for the statutory safe harbor for forward looking statements is that, in the years leading up the PSLRA, there was an epidemic of such suits, particularly against high tech companies. They were difficult for the defendants to prevail in a motion to dismiss in such suits. The statutory safe harbor and the heightened pleading standards have greatly reduced the frequency of the suits. Another explanation for the safe harbor is just the nature of forward looking statements. To wit: when you talk about the future, you are most likely not to predict the future with perfect accuracy. Thus, you begin with a statement that with hindsight is not correct. From there, just how do we determine whether there should be culpability for the statement? Thus, the safe harbor can be seen as weighing in on this: is it not material, was it accompanied by meaningful cautionary language, or was it not made with knowledge of its falsity.

Legislation: Section 21E of the Securities Exchange Act provides a safe harbor with respect to forward-looking statements under three different circumstances (we might really think of this as only two, since if something is not material then it is not actionable; hence, the meaningful cautionary language or no knowledge of falsity are the workhorse defenses). A threshold issue is that the students understanding what is and is not a forward looking statement. Note the implication of the disjunctive in the defenses. If the forward statement is not accompanied by "meaningful cautionary" statements, liability still does not arise if the plaintiff cannot prove that the forward-looking statement was made with *actual knowledge* that the statement was false or misleading. Hence, the statutory safe harbor embraces a somewhat more demanding scienter level since recklessly made forward looking statement falling within the category of forward looking statements covered by the statute is not actionable, even though recklessness, as seen earlier, is included within scienter in other contexts.

Common Law: *"Bespeaks Caution."* Apart from the above-mentioned legislative protection, the judicially created "bespeaks caution" doctrine coexists so that in those instances where the safe harbor does not apply, e.g., the forward looking statement was in connection with an initial public offering, tender offer, or going private transaction, the forward looking statement, even though erroneous and committed recklessly is protected if accompanied by meaningful cautionary language. To be meaningfully cautionary requires more than boilerplate, e.g., "forecasting in these troubled times is always fraught with uncertainty." But there is no requirement that the cautionary statement itself be prescient in identifying the particular event or force that caused the forecast to vary from what actually resulted. This is a factually intensive area.

Section 4.   "Duty to Speak"

Students likely will believe that, if there if information is material, that there is a duty to disclose it. Duty and materiality are two very different items and one does not ipso facto lead to the other. As seen in the note material, there is a duty to disclose material information in certain limited contexts (e.g., duty to update, duty to correct, and the half truth).

As seen earlier in Chapter 6, Section 1, under the federal securities laws large publicly-held corporations have periodic disclosure obligations (e.g., annual and quarterly reports as well as Form 8-K for certain events, e.g., (change of auditors). There is a duty to correct or update an earlier released statement that is subsequently discovered to have become materially misleading; albeit this duty is qualified by the need for that statement to continue to be influencing investor behavior. Adding to the complexity is the prerogative of companies to time the release of new information. Consider here the observation of SEC v. Texas Gulf Sulphur (2d Cir. 1969), that "the timing of the disclosure [of material facts] is a matter for the business judgment of the corporate officers entrusted with the management of the corporation within the affirmative disclosure requirements promulgated by the exchanges and by the SEC." However, the business judgment of the corporation does not justify the release of misleading information and does not relieve the corporation of its duty to correct or update an earlier statement that is now known to be misleading. Hence, the quote refers to the release of material new information. But what if this new information would alert investors that the earlier released information is no longer reliable? This is the subject of the *Gallagher v. Abbott Laboratories.*

Gallagher v. Abbott Laboratories

Investors who had purchased Abbott Labs shares when the company had not disclosed that it was experiencing serious operating problems, and as a result of those operating problems, was likely to incur significant fines by the FDA sued Abbot for its failure to disclose these problems and the prospect of fines and other costs (tens of millions of dollars of inventory was ultimately discarded as a result of the FDA enforcement action) flowing from the problems. The Seventh Circuit was asked to determine whether Abbot had a disclosure duty.

The thrust of the suits is that the prior Abbott reports accurately, at the time, revealed that all was well with the company. These were quarterly and annual SEC reports. When internal problems arose they were not disclosed. A key here is that Easterbrook concludes that the plaintiffs had not identified either an affirmative obligation under SEC rules or a specific prior statement that needed to be "corrected." As the court observed.

"What sinks plaintiffs' position is their inability to identify any false statement—or for that matter any truthful statement made misleading by the omission of news about the FDA's demands.... We do not have a system of continuous disclosure. Instead firms are entitled to keep silent (about good news as well as bad news) unless positive law creates a duty to disclose.... [A] statement may be "corrected" only if it was incorrect when made, and nothing said as of March 9 was incorrect. In order to maintain the difference between periodic-disclosure and continuous-disclosure systems, it is essential to draw a sharp line between duties to correct and duties to update. . . ."

Bad or good news may not be bottled up for long, at least for a reporting company. This is because the quarantined information may have to be disclosed to avoid engaging in a half truth.

We might question what result if in early March 1999, Abbot had stated it was in "regulatory compliance" with FDA requirements or had stated affirmatively in response to an analyst's question, "there were no significant contingencies that were on the horizon." Each of these appears to be the kind of statement that would be misleading under the half truth doctrine. Now, what if these statements had been made earlier, say in January or February? Here we might think that developments on March 17, 1999, with the threatening letter from the FDA, could well be the basis for updating the earlier "no worries" statement. These two illustrations point out the crucial point missing in the plaintiff's complaint: an affirmative statement that needed either correcting, updating or qualification (the latter to avoid a half truth).

Section 5.   Primary Participants After *Central Bank of Denver*

Central Bank of Denver dramatically changed the landscape of litigation under the antifraud provision. For many years, courts allowed private plaintiffs to bring claims against persons who aided and abetted violations of Section 10(b) and Rule 10b-5. An aider and abettor is one who with knowledge of another's violation lends substantial assistance in the commission of that violation or the transactions at the heart of the violation. In 1994, however, the Supreme Court rejected aiding and abetting liability in suits brought by private plaintiffs in *Central Bank of Denver v. First Interstate Bank of Denver,* 511 U.S. 164, 114 S. Ct. 1439, 128 L. Ed.2d 119 (1994). In the PSLRA, Congress granted the SEC specific authority to pursue aiding and abetting cases, but private plaintiffs could only bring actions for "primary violations" of Section 10(b) (as opposed to aiding and abetting violations). The 2010 Dodd-Frank legislation expanded this to permit the SEC to pursue reckless aiders and abettors. However, neither enactment restored aiding and abetting to private suits.

In the years after *Central Denver,* the lower courts have set forth two competing approaches, the substantial participant and the "bright-line" test. The latter is the view embraced in the PIMCO case that follows and appears most consistent with the *Janus Capital Group Inc. v. First Derivative Traders,* 131 S. Ct. 2296 (2011) where Justice Thomas Observed:

> One who prepares or publishes a statement on behalf of another is not its maker. And in the ordinary case, attribution within a statement or implicit from surrounding circumstances is strong evidence that a state was made by – and only by – the party whom it is attributed. This rule might best be exemplified by the relationship between a speechwriter and a speaker. Even when a speechwriter drafts a speech, the content is entirely within the control of the person who delivers it. And it is the speaker who takes credit – or blame – for what is ultimately said.

With this quote students may be asked whether the "speechwriter" illustration is analogous to the corporation issuing fraudulent financial reports prepared by its CFO. While the CFO may be seen as the speechwriter, is not the situation different from the politician giving the speech in that the corporation, unlike the politician, only operates through people. Can we ever really say that only the corporation gives the speech? Is this what investors assume? In any case, it appears after *Janus Capital Group* that the bright-line test, requiring attribution is likely the only test that is available.

The Supreme Court, in *Stoneridge Investment Partners v. Scientific-Atlanta, Inc.,* 552 U.S. 148 (2008), rejected the plaintiff's creative use of "scheme" in Rule 10b-5 to reach third parties who cooperated in the company's fraudulent scheme. Motorola and Scientific-Atlanta at the cable company's insistence submitted false documents supporting a series of "roundtrip" transactions that inflated the cable company's purchases of set boxes from each of the vendors; in return, the vendor purchased advertising with the cable company, thus inflating its revenue growth. The court saw this as just a disguised attempt to resurrect aiding and abetting.

This section contains two cases. You can choose between the more doctrinally oriented, but less factually interesting, *PIMCO* or opt for *Pugh* which reflects the full impact of the "bright-line" standard for primary participant liability. Both cases read well, complement each other, and do not overlap in their treatment of doctrine so you can proceed as Cox does and assign both. After all, this and causation are the battle grounds for Rule 10b-5 litigation these days so the areas merits close attention.

Pacific Investment Management Co. v. Mayer Brown

Refco provided brokerage and clearing services. It suffered massive losses when many Refco customers defaulted on their margin loans. Refco concealed its losses through a series of elaborate "sham" transactions with the substantial assistance and guidance of Collins, a partner in Mayer Brown's Chicago office. Refco, during this period, carried out several offerings of securities ((1) an Offering Memorandum for an unregistered bond offering, (2) a Registration Statement for a subsequent registered bond offering, and (3) a Registration Statement for Refco's IPO) each of which described these transactions but also identified Collins and Mayer Brown as counsel on the matters. However, as would prove fatal, none of the documents specifically attributed any of the information contained therein to Mayer Brown or Collins. Plaintiffs, attempting to tack as close to the *Central Bank* winds, alleged that the law firm penned false statements and with full knowledge of their falsity, thus had made a false statement.

This case illustrates the bright-line test. The court rejects the substantial participant test. As observed earlier, the most recent pronouncement on this subject, *Janus Capital Group* appears to embrace the attribution requirement and, hence, the bright-line test. The standard to use when assessing liability in a private action against secondary actors is the "attribution" standard, not the "creator" standard (which is very similar to the substantial participant standard, but appears to be a tad more demanding than that test by requiring the defendant to be an active part of the transaction beyond just assisting in drafting, editing, etc.).

Students may be asked what would be the purpose served if the court had reached the opposite conclusion. Well, there would likely be a deep pocket on the other side, Mayer Brown. We might also think that the personal assets of Collins would also be at stake. We might also believe that deterrence would be enhanced by at least holding Collins liable. There is a fierce debate whether respondeat superior liability leads to more compliance or less. On this point, we might ask the students what would be their position as future partners in a firm if a different result were reached in *Pacific Investment*. It is not clear just how law firms can police their partners' behavior, nonetheless one wonders whether the associates working on the deal ever had suspicions so that if there were whistle blower procedures or an anonymous complaint mechanism this may have made Collins a bit more wary.

What we find in this case is that a plaintiff must show, among other things, (a) that a defendant MADE a material misstatement or omission and (b) that the statement is one that can be attributed to the defendant. Attribution means that a third party reading the statement could identify the defendant as being responsible for the representation. While reliance underlies the reasoning of the attribution requirement; the cases adopting the bright-line test do not alter the case law surrounding the fraud on the market theory for causation i.e., where reliance on a particular statement is not required so long as the security is established to have traded in an efficient market and there is a general allegation of reliance on the integrity of the market's pricing mechanism and not the particularly statement. .

Pugh v. Tribune Company

This is a great set of facts to illustrate that the bright-line test fails to reach the party responsible for the lie and, as a result, that person's employer is not liable either. The Seventh Circuit adopts the bright-line test with the result that in the consolidated financial statements it is not possible to attribute the false inflated revenue (and hence income) numbers to the party with scienter, Sito. Thus, no one has liability for the knowingly made false statement. Would the result have been different if Sito had acted in complicity with the CFO of the parent company, Tribune? Hard to imagine why the result should change just because we kick the culprit up higher in the organization, since under the bright-line test the issue is whether the statement can be attributed to that person. But perhaps we could argue that we surmise the CFO prepared the statement, and hence can thereby attribute, that the CFO of the parent prepared or was involved in the preparation of the financial statements, so that if they act with scienter they are primary participants. This is the reasoning taken earlier in the Second Circuit. See the discussion in footnote 1 of *Pacific Investment Management, Co.*, supra. Note the other wrinkle here is that there is no vicarious liability on the part of Tribune for the misdeeds of Sito; the court reasoned that Sito was not acting in furtherance of Tribune by inflating the subscriptions, revenues and income of the subsidiaries, but rather to advance his own interest. Thus, the plaintiffs are without a primary participant. We might ask, was justice well served here by the attribution requirement? How great an incentive to monitor the reporting practices of presidents of subsidiaries by the court's standard for determining whether Sito acted within the scope of his employment when inflating the subscriber numbers?

Section 6. Causal Relationship: Loss Causation and Transaction Causation.

Two elements in a successful private lawsuit under Section 10(b) are transaction causation (frequently handled via reliance) and loss causation. In order to establish transaction causation, the plaintiff must show that the misrepresentation induced the plaintiff's trade. This most commonly occurs, but not always, as we'll see later in *Affiliated Ute* by alleging reliance on the omission or misstatement. Loosely speaking, she must show that the defendant "caused" the plaintiff to engage in her securities transaction.

To prove loss causation, the plaintiff must prove that the economic loss she suffered is due to the material omission or misstatement (that of course the defendant committed with scienter).   More specifically, to prove loss causation (which is sometimes equated with proximate causation), the plaintiff must prove that the defendant's misrepresentation affected the price at which the plaintiff purchased or sold the security: "The loss causation inquiry typically examines how directly the subject of the [violation] caused the loss, and whether the resulting loss was a foreseeable outcome of the [violation]." *Suez Equity v. Toronto* (2d Cir. 2001).

As a policy matter, loss causation addresses fortuitous recoveries. Thus, a national calamity may cause all stocks to sharply decline, losing much of their market value. Without loss causation, a firm that knowingly committed a material misrepresentation would be liable for all the decline in its shares. Loss causation is something of a governor on liability, permitting recovery only for the harm proximately caused by the misrepresentation. But, as we will see, this poses huge problems to the private litigant because, for example in the national calamity situation, just how do you separate the harm caused by the misrepresentation from the market-wide forces for which the defendant is not responsible.

Caremark, Inc. v. Coram Healthcare Corp. (7th Cir. 1997), provides a helpful summation of the difference between loss and transaction causation: "To plead transaction causation, the plaintiff must allege that it would not have invested in the instrument if the defendant had stated truthfully the material facts at the time of the sale. To plead loss causation, the plaintiff must allege that [it] was the very facts about which the plaintiff lied which caused its injuries."

As a prelude to *Affiliated Ute Citizens,* you might wish to ask why it might be easier to show actual reliance on a misstatement than on an omission. That is, reliance on an is problematic because it is difficult to say that a plaintiff affirmatively *relied* on a statement that was never made.

Affiliated Ute Citizens v. United States

As part of a settlement of historic claims, members of the Ute tribe were awarded shares in UDC; the shares were held by First Security Bank of Utah. When the plaintiffs, members of the Ute tribe, sold their UDC shares through Bank's employees (Gale and Haslam), the employees did not disclose to them that non-tribal members were then-trading the shares at much higher prices than the defendants were offering the selling tribal members. Thereafter, the employees were able to sell the shares that the tribal members wanted to liquidate to ready purchasers who paid higher prices, and Gale and Haslam bought some shares themselves. When suit was later brought under Section 10(b), the 10th Circuit Court of Appeals ruled against the plaintiffs because the record did not disclose evidence of the plaintiffs relying on "material fact misrepresentations" by Gale and Haslam.

To get the ball rolling, you might ask what is the issue before the court? Why isn't materiality in question? This brings out what was not said. This was an omission case and whether sophisticated or not, anyone would find it important that the price they were getting for their shares was substantially below what third parties where then paying for these shares. Thus, on materiality, there should be no issue. Then why did they lose below? What then does the court say about transaction causations?

"Under the circumstances of this case, involving primarily a failure to disclose, positive proof of reliance is not a prerequisite to recovery. All that is necessary is that the facts withheld be material in the sense that a reasonable investor might have considered them important in the making of this decision..... This obligation to disclose and this withholding of a material fact establish the requisite element of causation in fact."

We can ponder the full scope of *Affiliated Ute.* One view is that *Affiliated Ute* seems to eliminate the "reliance" element for *pure* omission case. This is somewhat qualified by subsequent appellate court cases that hold *Affiliated Ute* merely establishes a presumption in favor of the plaintiff, and a defendant can rebut the presumption by showing that the plaintiff would have sold or purchased his securities even if he had known the full and complete truth. Under this view, reliance is part of the case, if it is a combination of omissions and misstatements. An even more restrictive interpretation of *Affiliated Ute* is that more than an omission was present to support the Court's relaxation of an affirmative showing of reliance: a position of trust and confidence between the plaintiffs and Gale and Haslam, the lack of sophistication by the plaintiffs, and the undisputable conclusion that if the plaintiffs were aware that a substantially higher price was available for their shares they would not have sold at the price they did. Moreover, in a mixture of material omissions and material misstatements, reliance is not relaxed.

Affiliated Ute deals with the difficulty in proving reliance in an omissions case in a face-to-face context. The next case, *Basic v. Levinson,* also deals with the establishing transaction causation, but in the context of securities that are traded in an efficient market   Specifically, *Basic v. Levinson* establishes parameters for use of the "fraud on the market" theory   While it may well be that each investor could in fact prove reliance on an alleged omission or misstatement, the real issue is that such a requirement renders the aggregation of their claims into a class action inappropriate under FRCP 23, since common questions of law and fact would not predominate. Individual inquiries into reliance instead would predominate. And, given the fact that typically open market frauds, i.e., misrepresentations committed by publicly traded firms impact large numbers of holders, but few of them have suffered a loss sufficient to merit retaining their own attorney, aggregation through the class action procedure is the only route by which most of the injured investors can obtain meaningful relief.

Basic Inc. v. Levinson

A reasonable place to begin the analysis is to ask the students whether this, like *Affiliated Ute*, is an omission case? It is a misstatement case- on three occasions the company denied there were merger negotiations underway. Next, who is included in the class: the class is made up of those who sold after the first false denial of merger negotiations and the announcement of a deal being reached with Combustion Engineering. From here you can ask if this is an omission or misstatement case. Thus, what justifies not requiring the class members to allege they had read and relied upon any of the three false denials? This moves the analysis to causation?

Along the way, you might wish to ask why it is that the court does not just apply the earlier studied, Chapter 6, *TSC Industries* test for determining whether a fact is material? This goes to the Court's adoption of the *TGS* probability-magnitude test, a test reaffirmed in 2011 in the *Matrixx Initiatives, Inc. v. Siracusano,* 131 S. Ct. 1309 (2011). In *Matrix Initiatives,* the company maintained its forecast of a rising sales despite the fact that it was receiving numerous reports that its principal product caused the permanent loss of smell. None of the reports was a broad statistically conceived study. But the reports were numerous and the company was named in several product liability suits. The district court had held that absent a "statistically significant correlation" the reports were not material so that the on-going buoyant reports by the company were not materially misleading by failing to disclose the reports. The Supreme Court held that the probability-magnitude test is not so bounded.

Now for the factual background of *Basic*. Plaintiffs are former Basic shareholders who sold their Basic stock at prices that allegedly (and quite likely true) would have been higher had Basic announced on Oct. 21, 1977, (the date of the first denial of merger negotiations) that it was then engaged in active merger negotiations.. The shareholders sought class certification in order to bring suit against Basic for securities fraud. The district court certified the class in part by adopting a presumption of reliance that allowed the court to conclude that the requisite common questions of fact or law needed to certify predominated, but the district court granted summary judgment for the defendants on the merits, holding that any misstatements were immaterial since, although negotiations were taking place, the negotiations were not "'destined, with reasonable certainty, to become a merger agreement in principle.'" The Sixth Circuit Court of Appeals affirmed the class certification but reversed the materiality determination.

With respect to materiality, the court observed:

"The Court ... explicitly has defined a standard of materiality under the securities laws, ... concluding in the proxy-solicitation context that '[a]n omitted fact is material if there is a substantial likelihood that a reasonable shareholder would consider it important in deciding how to vote.'" However, the application of this standard of materiality to things that are uncertain to bear fruit – such as preliminary merger discussions – is not "self-evident." Therefore, when an event is contingent or speculative, its materiality "will depend at any given time upon a balancing of both the indicated probability that the event will occur and the anticipated magnitude of the event in light of the totality of the company activity."

An initial question for the students is what is there about the facts of *Basic* that introduces the probability-magnitude analysis where we did not see this earlier in *TSC Industries*? Note that this is not a duty to disclose case, but a case of an alleged material misstatement. Thus, this is not a case where we are concerned that premature disclosure of negotiations will kill the deal. They can negotiate in secret. Nothing in *Basic* changes that. What they can't do is lie about it. That said, what made the magnitude so large here? Why is a large magnitude significant in this case to concluding that the denial was material? This is something of the law of big numbers. That is, a huge premium paid by Combustion for Basic means that even if the negotiations have a small chance of resulting in a takeover Basic at that premium of will under the jointness of the probability-magnitude test be material. Observe the court rejected the price-and-structure approach then common among many of the circuits. It thus embraced a less fixed test for determining the materiality of negotiations.

The Court's contribution to the lore on reliance is summed up as follows:

The Court concluded that it was proper for the fraud on the market theory to be applied as a rebuttable presumption of reliance: "The fraud on the market theory is based on the hypothesis that, in an open and developed securities market, the price of a company's stock is determined by the available material information regarding the company and its business.... Misleading statements will therefore defraud purchasers of stock even if the purchasers do not directly rely on the misstatements.... The causal connection between the defendants' fraud and the plaintiffs' purchase of stock in such a case is no less significant than in a case of direct reliance on misrepresentations.

The Court does observe that the FOTM presumption is rebuttable, however: "Any showing that severs the link between the alleged misrepresentation and either the price received (or paid) by the plaintiff, or his decision to trade at a fair market price, will be sufficient to rebut the presumption of reliance."

It bears repeating what the result would have been if the FOTM approach had been rejected by the court, i.e., common questions of law and fact would not then predominate so that class certification would have been inappropriate. Thus, individual, not aggregate actions, would have to be brought. This is not what the small or medium sized investors wish and certainly not their attorneys who wish aggregation whereby the recoverable amount is larger and can justify a larger fee.

Students should be asked to identify what cases FOTM is appropriate? Would it apply in *Affiliated Ute*? Would it apply if a fraud occurred in the sale of an IPO? Would it apply if a company issued a false annual report to its 300 stockholders? Answer in each of these cases is no, because the sine qua non is that the security trade in an efficient market. That is, the court premised its reasoning on the price of the security being fairly determined "in an open and developed securities market, the price of a company's stock is determined by the available material information regarding the company and its business...." This succinctly describes a market that is efficient in the semi strong form. See the note on the *Crammer* decision regarding some features courts consider in determining whether the subject security traded in a market so that the FOTM theory would apply.

Metzler Investment GMBH v. Corinthian Colleges, Inc.

Metzler Inv. Illustrates the effects of the loss causation requirement that has assumed new vigor post the Supreme Court's decision in *Dura Pharmaceuticals Inc. v. Broudo.* The case also illustrates the perverse effects of requiring, in FOTM cases, evidence that the securities price adjusted following disclosure of the truth.

You may begin by asking what is new about this case? What appears to be the significance of *Dura Pharmaceuticals Inc. v Broudo*, cited in the beginning of part III of the opinion? *Dura* broadly held that the plaintiff must allege both transaction and loss causation and the latter is not met by merely asserting that the misrepresentation inflated the stock's price, i.e., had there been no lie the investors would have acquired the shares at a lower price. *Dura* was quite clear in requiring allegations that when the truth was publicly disclosed that there must be allegations that the market price corrected itself. Hence, we see in *Metzler Investment* the plaintiff alleging the negative market response to two announcements. As the *Metzler Investment* states, to plead loss causation, "the complaint must allege that the defendant's 'share price fell significantly after the truth became known.'"

Plaintiff Metzler sued Corinthian Colleges ("CC") for securities fraud, alleging that CC's colleges were "pervaded by fraudulent practices designed to maximize the amount of federal Title IV funding--a major source of Corinthian's revenue--that those schools receive," and CC's failure to disclose such made CC's financial status disclosures materially misleading.

To meet Dura Pharmaceutical's requirement of pleading loss causation the Plaintiff alleged the negative reaction of the market price of the company' shares to two different publications:

(1) June 24 *Financial Times* story revealing a DOE investigation of the Bryman campus and the DOE's decision to place that campus on "reimbursement status" (other CC schools were not implicated in the story).The story was accompanied by a drop of $ 2.55 (10%) on June 24. However the stock bounced back to roughly 6 cents higher than its pre-June 24 price by June 29), and

(2) August 2 CC issued a press release disclosing that the company was cutting its revenue and earnings projections due to factors including adverse publicity related to the DOE matter, delays in opening new branches, and "higher than anticipated attrition." The announcement also disclosed that the company had met with the Calif. Att'y Gen. regarding CC's business practices. This prompted the stock to decline 45% to $ 10.29.

The district court granted the defendant's motion to dismiss, and the Ninth Circuit Court of Appeals affirmed, finding that "loss causation" had not been adequately pled. Invoking *Dura Pharmaceuticals Inc. v. Broudo*, the Ninth Circuit panel concluded that the plaintiff failed to allege that the press releases that were alleged to trigger the stock price drop actually disclosed "or even suggested" to the market that CC was engaging in the sort of fraud that the plaintiff suggested. First, because the Financial Times story related only to one of the company's campuses. Second, the August 2 press release identified problems that were not the same issues that were in the TAC filed by the plaintiff. This shows the pernicious aspects of *Broudo's* holding. The true facts of the defendants' chicanery, if couched in points quite different from those set forth in the complaint, will not be seen as an admission or truthful release of the facts alleged earlier to have been false. Another strategy is that if the true facts are to be released, the defendants can bundle that with other bad news about the company so to the plaintiff's have a difficult time identifying what part of the stock price correction is attributable to the alleged misrepresentations and what part is due to facts released that are not part of the plaintiff's complaint.

It is worth noting that *Metzler Investment* and *Dura Pharmaceutical* were each fraud on the market cases. Thus we can see the courts' focus in such cases in the market price to an alleged "truthful" or "corrective" disclosure. What should be the result if the case is a face-to-face transaction involving the shares of a close corporation? Or, what if the shares were purchased in a market, but not an efficient market? In the former, an allegation of loss causation could likely be supported by expert testimony. In the latter, we don't have a lot of cases, but presumably the same skepticism about the efficiency of pricing securities would cause the court in such a non fraud on the market case to accord less obeisance to stock price changes and perhaps accepting of other evidence regarding allegations of loss. But the question still remains whether whatever alleged inflation was created by the lie had been removed by subsequent events.

Section 7. The Junction of Breaches of Fiduciary Duty and Rule 10b-5

Santa Fe Industries, Inc. v. Green

A threshold matter is to review some of the elements for the case, returning perhaps to *The Wharf) Holdings* limited. How was jurisdiction and purchase or sale satisfied? This lets the students see how mergers and cash out mergers each involve the disposition of shares and hence constitute a sale. From there you can ask the students whether this is an omission or misstatement case? It is neither, and that is the problem the plaintiff incurred in the Supreme Court. Note what the Second Circuit held: a claim exists under Rule 10b-5 when "the majority has committed a breach of its fiduciary duty to deal fairly with the minority shareholders by effecting the merger without any justifiable business purpose." What was the alleged unfairness here? Note the plaintiff is alleging their shares had a value greater than the $150 that Santa Fe was to pay.

Bottom line of the case is that absent deception, there is no cause of action under the antifraud provision. Or, as the court crisply states, "The transaction, if carried out as alleged in the complaint, was neither deceptive nor manipulative and therefore did not violate either § 10(b) of the Act or Rule 10b–5."

We might wish to return to the language of Rule 10b-5. After *Santa Fe Industries*, what is the import of provisions (a) and (c)? It would appear clear that what *Santa Fe Industries* requires is some misstatement or omission. Bad behavior not involving a material omission or misstatement does not sustain a Rule 10b-5 cause of action. The Court even states that actionable manipulation requires some form of omission or misstatement.

You may tease out what would be the result here if Kirby Lumber had omitted that the appraised value of its assets equaled $640 per share? This likely would be material to a shareholder. But what option did the shareholder have? Well, if there were an appraisal remedy, then one option would be to "sell" shares through the appraisal process. Hence non-disclosure of the appraised value of the assets would be material to that decision and that decision is very much like an investment decision, i.e., accept what is offered by the company, $150/share, or pursue appraisal and dispose of your shares through that process. Now, what result if there were no appraisal and the firm did not disclose the share's appraised value. Presumably, with this information, the plaintiff could retain a lawyer and initiate a suit for breach of fiduciary duty. But what does the court say about that in this case. It states at the end of part III of the opinion that this is not a likely purpose of the antifraud provision and at the end of the first paragraph of part IV it states "we are reluctant to recognize a cause of action here to serve what is "at best a subsidiary purpose" of the federal legislation. Note the result reached here is very similar to that reached earlier in *Virginia Bankshares, Inc. v. Sandberg* in Chapter 6. Section 4, holding that there is no proxy violation if the defendant controls enough shares to assure approval of the transaction (note that in that case there was no available appraisal remedy). Moreover, in *Santa*

Corporations and Other Business Organizations

Fe Industries, the Court further justifies the result in part by reference to fiduciary duties being the subject of another regime, state law.

Note on Goldberg v. Meridor:

In the early life of Rule 10b-5, circa the happy 1960s, there was the view that Rule 10b-5 proscribed breaches of fiduciary duty connected to securities transactions (the buzz words "acts of mismanagement" were tossed about by courts and commentators). A leading case for this view was *Schoenbaum* which spoke of controlling influence that caused the corporation's board to issue shares at a grossly understated price. Post *Santa Fe Industries,* any action under Rule 10b-5 need to be premised on a material omission or misstatement. Thus questions abounded whether a majority of the board or just some board members needed to be duped by the defendant. *Goldberg v. Meridor* reflected the permissive view that lying to some of the directors was enough, even though the majority knew the correct facts. We might wonder whether this survives the more restrictive view of causation that we saw earlier in *Virginia Bankshares,* Chapter 6, supra. Where the board or even a minority of the board is not duped, the focus is on whether there was a failure to disclose "sue facts" which would have enabled the stockholders to initiate suit to enjoin the harmful securities transaction. This is the reasoning in *Kidwell* and *Healey,* each of which seem to violate the spirit of *Santa Fe Industries* (recall here the language that Rule 10b-5 is not to advance a "subsidiary purpose" and also seem to confront the narrow causation approach taken in *Virginia Bankshares.* Students might ask why, in the face of these questions, anyone would launch a Rule 10b-5 suit based on the board knowingly selling shares at too low a price instead of proceeding on a state law breach of fiduciary claim. Note here that if the corporation is the issuer, each would have to be maintained as a derivative suit, discussed later in Chapter 14. One possible reason for a Rule 10b-5 action is that it may be forensically easier to plead "sue facts" than to make out that the "sue facts" violate the entire fairness standard.

Section 8. Remedies in Private Actions Under Rule 10b-5

Few Rule 10b-5 suits are injunctive actions. Most seek damages for which the predominant measure is the out of pocket measure of damages. Very rarely do plaintiff recover rescission and rarer yet if the benefit of the bargain measure. The real action in this area is the liability among wrongdoers, which after the PSLRA is proportionate based on degree of fault. The major exception is that those who violate the antifraud provision with knowledge have joint and several liability. Thus, if one of the defendants is wealthy, good to make the case against that s/he acted with knowledge. Plaintiffs always like deep pockets.

Chapter 13

Insider Trading

Chapter Overview: Future lawyers will have a lot of client secrets shared with them. Some may find the information of the type that trading on the information will produce great wealth. Thus, the material in this section invites a good deal of role playing and more generally may remind the students of additional reasons why we should preserve the confidential information of our clients. In any case, the material always elicits a good deal of discussion, and is rich with historical development. To cover all the materials in this chapter, you will likely require 5 class periods. You may well find that 3 or most of 4 is the maximum you can allot. If fewer classes are to be covered, then the three Supreme Court decisions (*Chiarella, O'Hagan* and *Dirks*) should at a minimum be covered. With more hours you would like wish to add *Texas Gulf Sulphur,* because of the richness of its facts and chance to play with concepts like materiality, how materiality is proven, in possession, and when information becomes public. After those four cases are covered, you likely will wish to cover Regulation FD, and some introduction to Section 16. If time permits you can add the material in Sections 1 and 4.

Section 1.   The Common Law Background

The common law background helps us understand why the federal courts entered this area through the antifraud provision. Students might be asked what separates the result reached in *Goodwin v. Agassiz* from say *Strong v. Repide*? The answer is that no duty was owed among anonymous traders in an open marke,t whereas in we see some exception, albeit initially quite narrow, for face-to-face traders. In *Strong,* the duty was owed to an existing stockholder and only by a true corporate insider, and only if that insider was acting on the basis of "special facts." What were the special facts in *Strong*? It was that Repide, a director, knew (he was in charge of negotiations) the state of negotiations with the government to sell the company; absent that sale, the company shares were worthless. This truly is an unusual set of facts and significant beyond the common standard for what is deemed material. It is difficult to say what the common law is today, i.e., whether *Goodwin* remains the norm for open market trading, because the antifraud rule has essentially dominated the legal landscape. We should also observe that outside the face-to-face setting, private suits are extremely rare for insider trading. This is explored later in the context of the limited private recoveries available to private litigants.

Section 2.   The Federal Disclose or Abstain Requirement

We suspect that most adopters will likely go from Chapter 12 straight to Chapter 13; the materials are modular and could be as easily reversed. The orientation of disclosure violations, the subject of Chapter 12, is very different from the orientation to insider trading. For example,in the federal area, the cases are government enforcement cases. Messy issues of causation, reliance, standing, and the like are not implicated. Essentially, the cases in Chapter 13 raise duty issues. With very few exceptions, the language of section 10(b) and Rule 10b-5 does not play a role in the courts' grappling with the scope of the prohibition. Whereas, as seen in Chapter 12, in cases such as *Ernst & Ernst*, *Blue Chip Stamps* and *Central Bank of Denver*, the language of the enabling provision as well as the rule itself plays an important role in determining the scope of the statute and rule.

In the Matter of Cady, Roberts & Co.

The beginning point in the development of the SEC's role in proscribing and prosecuting insider trading is *In the Matter of Cady, Roberts & Co.* Student's might be asked how this matter would have been handled under the common law? The broker was selling shares for his client on his secret knowledge that the company would soon cut its dividend. The SEC disciplined him on the ground he had violated the antifraud provision. Because these sales were in open market, for which *Goodwin* holds there is no duty for the broker, acting on behalf of his clients, to disclose his secret knowledge, the common law provided no basis for the broker's duty to disclose. Hence there would be no violation. What was the basis for the Commission holding that the broker had violated the rule? One is the broker using his privileged access to information to trade on information that was only available for a corporate but not personal purpose. Second, is the view it is unfair to the investors of a person using his privileged access to information to trade at their expense. We might label the latter as a quest for "parity of information" across investors in public markets. We might question after the Supreme Court decisions, later examined whether either of these two grounds exist (hint, we might think the first is akin to the thinking underlying the misappropriation theory and clearly *Chiarella* buries the unfairness argument).

Securities and Exchange Commission v. Texas Gulf Sulphur Co.

While there are a good many facts and characters in the case, we might think that what are most relevant are just a few of these: K-55-1, the two press releases, what the defendants (listed in the first footnote to appear in the edited case) did between K-55-1 and the second press release, when the second press release was deemed to have made public disclosure of the results of TGS's activities in Timmins Ontario.

The following is a list of questions that can be raised from the facts of the case that flow from the language in IA: "Thus, anyone in possession of material inside information must either disclose it to the investing public, or, if he is disable from disclosing it in order to protect a corporate confidence, or he chooses not to do so, must abstain from trading in or recommending the securities concerned . . . ."

1. When and why was the information material?

2. How did the court support its finding that K-55-1 was material?

3. Why didn't the court instead look at the market's response to the April 16th press release (this goes to the greater certainty attached to the April 16th announcement because of a dozen additional core drillings whereas K-55-1 could well have been an anomaly (note the probability-magnitude test here, namely while maybe a high likelihood K-55-1 was an anomaly, if true, the magnitude was gigantic).

4. Does the opinion support the statement that truly "anyone" is under the disclose or abstain rule? What did all the defendants have in common? To the latter, they all got a pay check from TGS, i.e., they were clearly inside TGS.

5. What does it mean to be "in possession"? In this regard, consider the attorney Huntington (who did not know about K-55-1, but deduced something big was happening from processing deeds in the Timmins Ontario area. And, add here what prompted the SEC to promulgate Rule 10b5-1, see Note On The "Use" Test Under Rule 10b-5, infra.

6. When can the insiders trade? (Note here some, e.g., Coates, instructed their brokers after the release, but before it was circulated over the medium of widest circulation, the Dow Jones tape).

7. What philosophy underlies the court's application of the disclose or abstain rule? Note this is consistent with Cady Roberts' second justification, parity of information.

8. The last question can provide the foundation for a discussion of the pros and cons of proscribing trading by insiders such as the cast of characters in *TGS*.

The following elaborates on some of the above questions.

In broad overview, the SEC's action against TGS and certain of its directors, officers, and employees was focused on the misleading press release plus the trading and tipping by the dirctors, officers, and employees.

1. Materiality: Note the probability-magnitude test for determining materiality?

"[W]hether facts are material within Rule 10b-5... will depend at any given time upon a balancing of both the indicated probability that the event will occur and the anticipated magnitude of the event in light of the totality of the company activity."

Note, this is the test approved and applied later by the Supreme Court in *Basic Inc. v. Levinson*, Chapter 12, surpa, and confirmed more recently in *Matrix Initiatives, Inc. v. Siracusano*, 131 S. Ct. 1309 (2011).

What was the fact that was determined to be material? Why not use the *TSC Industries'* standard that we examined in Chapter 6, Section 4? We don't know the outcome of all the core drillings. Even with 11 or 12 core drillings, it is hard to say as a factual matter just how much silver, copper and zinc in fact existed beneath the Timmins property. Moreover, what was the fact that was deemed material? It was the *first* core drilling, K-55-1, this was truly speculative in quality as its results could have been an anomaly. What was there about K-55-1 that removed it from the orthodox materiality standard to the standard established in *TGS*? The first core drilling could have been a complete anomaly. Thus, it might have had a very low probability for predicting that commercially feasible extraction would result on the Timmons property. But the magnitude of K-55-1, if an accurate predictor, was immense. Hence, a low probability with a high magnitude, rendered K-55-1 material. Thus, the probability-magnitude approach is used when the matter to be assessed for its materiality is a speculative event, e.g., is there a large supply of silver, copper and zinc beneath the Timmons property.

You might ask your students to consider how they would persuade the trial court that K-55-1 or some other speculative act or event is material? How did they do it in this case? They brought in experts, the news reporters, who cover mineral discoveries. They also hoisted the defendants by their own petard by showing how the defendants treated the information once in possession of it. Why not just look at how the TGS market price responded once the information was disclosed? By the time mid-April arrived we were no longer dealing with just K-55-1 as there had been an additional dozen other core drillings so that by the time of the press release much more certainty surrounded the discovery.

2. When Can Insiders Trade? You might want to return to the court's statement of the disclose or abstain rule. Ask, so does this mean insiders can never trade once they are in possession of material inside information? No, the full prohibition is when the information is "non public." So, when does the information become public, and when was that? It was when disclosure took place by the medium of widest circulation, the Dow Jones Ticker Tape, which was at 10:54 a.m. on April 16th. Was this just dicta? No, the court reasoned that Coates should not have been absolved by the district court for his order that was given to his broker before the 10:20 a.m., which was after the release of the information to the American press at 10 a.m. See also the points made by the court in footnote 17 of the case. Note how this treatment of this question supports the "parity of information" aspirations of insider trading regulation set forth in *Cady Roberts*.

3. What do the *TGS* Defendants Have in Common? All the defendants were true insiders as every defendant was drawing a paycheck from TGS. They were all employees, clear insiders, and the obtained knowledge about K-55-1 as a result of their employment positions with *TGS*.

4. Receipt of Stock Options. What was the issue related to the stock options? They received stock options from TGS without disclosing to the committee that administered the options their knowledge of K-55-1. So, who's the victim? With this question, students can then acquire some understanding that corporations can be duped too. That is, if the committee administering the stock option plan had known about K-55-1, would it have awarded more or fewer options to the Stephens, Fogarty, Mollison, Holyk and Kline? Would it have cut back on options to other recipients who did not know of K-55-1. The options had a lot more value because of K-55-1 than without it. If we think the purpose of the options is to award compensation and the committee believes X options is adequate award, and then learns that shares have a value twice a great as first thought, would the committee still award X shares? Not if its thinking correctly. Note that the district court held only the directors had a disclosure duty.

On appeal, the Second Circuit held Kline, the General Counsel, should have disclosed to the committee. Since the SEC did not appeal the dismissal of Mollison and Holyk, the court did not weigh in on whether they had a disclosure duty or could depend on the judgment of the senior managers, Stephens, Fogarty and Kline, regarding whether disclosure should be made. Does this make sense? One idea is that we may wish to think practically and junior people practice the rule of "those who go along get along." From a deterrence standpoint, imposing this duty on everyone regardless of position would appeal. But do Mollison and Holyk believe that Fogarty, Stephens and Kline may believe that those on the committee may leak the information about Timmins and thus jeopardize the interest of TGS in acquiring the property from all the dumb Ontario farmers? Not an easy question.

Insider Trading and Policy

The readings in the casebook ("How pervasive is insider trading" and "Why Prohibit") provide the basis for a policy discussion about the evils or value of insider trading and the differing viewpoints. Insider trading is uniformly condemned around the world, but a lively debate nonetheless continues regarding its harms. And, as the note material points out, there is a good deal of empirical evidence that insider trading is pervasive. Does this mean that regulators are not doing enough, should give up the battle, or that it is an insolvable problem? Students may find it useful to understand that the investor on the other side of the trade from the insider enjoy something of a fortuity if they have a private suit against the insider. That is, since the investor would have sold, regardless of the insider's trading, and may well have benefitted slightly by the insider's own trading driving the price higher (if the investor was selling, and vice versa), we might believe there is no causal relationship between the insider trading and the alleged harm suffered by the investor. The injury to the investor is caused by the insider failing to disclose her secret information before trading; but we have that duty to disclose only to curb the trading. So, if we allow insiders to trade when they do not have confidential inside information, why not allow them trade when the do. The readings put forth arguments on both sides of this divide. We might believe that insider trading is a means to protect the issuer's property rights in the information itself. That is, does not TGS have a business purpose served by maintaining the confidentiality of its discovery of minerals in Timmins Ontario? Why did we allow TGS to conceal its identity and not disclose its secret knowledge when buying property from all the dumb farmers? Would the reward for its search and discovery be jeopardized if its employees could freely trade and tip others? If these questions are persuasive on why insider trading is bad for TGS, then why do we make it a "federal offense?" Don't we in other areas use state resources to protect private property rights when it is believed in the public interest?

Note on the "Use" Test Under Rule 10b-5

At this point you might wish to return to *TGS* and consider the facts surround defendant Huntington. What distinguishes Huntington from Darke or Fogarty? Huntington did not know about the visual or laboratory assay of K-55-1. He deduced something was up from processing the multiple acquisitions of parcels of land in Timmins Ontario? So, this reflects the so-called mosaic theory that occurs in many insider trading cases, where the government is able to establish a violation because the defendant had a piece of the puzzle from which she was able to deduce the rest of the puzzle. As the Note reflects, in the 1990's, some court opinions drew a distinction between "use" and "possession" of material, non-public information – an insider was not engaging in unlawful insider trading even though the government established that she possessed material, non-public information when making trades if the government did not also prove that she made her trades on the basis of that inside information, i.e., overcome the defense that the defendant traded for reasons unrelated to that material, non-public information, (for example, a CEO has a standing order with his broker to sell $40,000 worth of stock at the beginning of each quarter over the course of the next two years to meet the mortgage on the weekend estate in the Hamptons). In 2000, the SEC deftly addressed the "possession" vs. "use" distinction with Rule 10b5-1(b) by providing that "on the basis" means the person making the trade "was aware of the material nonpublic information" when s/he traded. Hmmmm, clever! A second innovation of Rule 10b5-1 is set forth in paragraph (c) covering trading per a written plan, entered into before the insider became aware of material information

Chiarella v. United States

Chiarella worked for a financial printer, handling documents such as announcement of merger and acquisitions. In these documents, the names of the parties were concealed by a code until the night of the final printing. The printer employees could usually deduce the company names, and Chiarella often did. By breaking the employer's code, he made roughly $30,000 purchasing stock in target companies prior to several acquisitions being announced, and then selling the stock immediately after the public announcement. He was first confronted by the SEC and breathed a sigh of relief by settling that action by giving up his ill-gotten gains. The, next knock at his door was the U.S. attorney. In 1978, he was indicted on 17 counts of violating Section 10(b), and, after a trial, he was convicted, with the jury instructions indicating that he was convicted "because of his failure to disclose material, nonpublic information to sellers from whom he bought the stock of target corporations." While the Second Circuit affirmed the conviction, the Supreme Court reversed, finding that:

> When an allegation of fraud is based upon nondisclosure, there can be no fraud absent a duty to speak.... [A] duty to disclose under § 10(b) does not arise from the mere possession of nonpublic market information.

The court went on to observe;

> [A]dministrative and judicial interpretations have established that silence in connection with the purchase or sale of securities may operate as a fraud action under § 10(b) . . . . But such liability is premised upon a duty to disclose arising from a relationship of trust and confidence between the parties to the transaction. . . .

> No duty could arise from petitioner's relationship with the sellers of the target company's securities, for the petitioner had no prior dealings with them. He was not their agent, he was not a fiduciary, he was not a person in whom the sellers had placed their trust and confidence. He was, in fact, a complete stranger who dealt with the sellers only through impersonal market transactions.

Thus, we see the first qualification to *TGS*. The disclose or abstain rule does not apply to "anyone," but, per the majority in *Chiarella,* requires as a prerequisite a fiduciary relationship. But to whom? Stay tuned to *O'Hagan.* What is the difference between Chiarella and say Darke in TGS. Each traded on material nonpublic information. But Darke got the information by virtue of his employment relationship with the company he traded in. In contrast, Chiarella got the information by virtue of his employment position (and his employer's clients) but used that information to trade in the shares of company with whom he had NO relationship. Why should this matter in the scheme of things? Well it does, if you believe that parity of information is not a very workable approach and is mischievous because it is overly broad. This may well be the motive for Powell to persuade his colleagues to put some brakes on the disclose or abstain rule.

Burger's dissent also raises the interesting issue of whether Chiarella, because he had stolen the information on which he was trading, had a duty to disclose because he stole the inside information.. While unsuccessful in winning a majority of his fellow justices to this view, Burger's dissent provided an important impetus for the "misappropriation theory" for insider trading regulation, covered in the next case.

As an aside, we might wonder where Powell found authority for the proposition that the sine qua non for insider trading is a fiduciary relationship. This seems out of step for the federal securities laws, and particularly the Exchange Act, which are not about relationships, but rather largely disclosure duties among unrelated parties for which the duties were designed to supplement state law duties. One could do worse than simply conclude that Powell made it up and sold it to a enough colleagues to reverse the conviction of Chiarella. We then are entreated to the next couple of cases, *O'Hagan* and *Dirks* which have their own artificial qualities.

United States v. O'Hagan

This case addresses the opening created in Burger's dissent in *Chiarella,* embracing the "misappropriation" theory as a basis for an insider trading violation. Under this theory, a person who trades in securities using confidential information that was misappropriated in breach of a fiduciary duty to the source of the information is violates § 10(b) and Rule 10b–5.

James O'Hagan was a partner in the law firm of Dorsey & Whitney, and D&W was local Minnesota counsel for Grand Metropolitan PLC (Grand Met), which was a company based in London that was secretly preparing to launch a bid to acquire Pillsbury Company, located in Minneapolis, Minnesota. In the days before Grand Met announced its tender offer for Pillsbury, O'Hagan – who himself did not work with client Grand Met – bought call options for Pillsbury stock and Pillsbury common stock. After Grand Met announced its tender offer for Pillsbury, O'Hagan sold his Pillsbury stock and options for a profit of more than $4.3 million (the profits were used to replenish sums O'Hagan had embezzled from his clients; wait it gets worse, he embezzled those funds to pay off his bookies since he had a very bad gambling habit and, worse, he was not a very good gambler). A jury convicted O'Hagan of 57 counts of various sorts of fraud (including securities fraud), and a divided panel of the Court of Appeals for the Eighth

Circuit reversed all of O'Hagan's convictions. Specifically, the panel found that liability under Section 10(b) and Rule 10b-5 cannot be grounded in the "misappropriation theory" of liability.

The Supreme Court reversed, holding that:

> The "misappropriation theory" holds that a person commits fraud "in connection with" a securities transaction, and thereby violates § 10(b) and Rule 10b–5, when he misappropriates confidential information for securities trading purposes, in breach of a duty owed to the source of the information…. Under this theory, a fiduciary's undisclosed, self-serving use of a principal's information to purchase or sell securities, in breach of a duty of loyalty and confidentiality, defrauds the principal of the exclusive use of that information. In lieu of premising liability on a fiduciary relationship between company insider and purchaser or seller of the company's stock, the misappropriation theory premises liability on a fiduciary-turned-trader's deception of those who entrusted him with access to confidential information.

In teaching the case, you might begin by asking why the government won this case, but lost in *Chiarella*? Are the facts fundamentally different? The reason is that the jury was never instructed on the misappropriation theory in *Chiarella*. It was the basis for the case against Mr. O'Hagan.

Students then can be asked just what did the government have to show about Mr. O'Hagan to establish a violation per the misappropriation theory? Note here the fiduciary relationship lawyers have to their clients and to their employer. Technically Grand Metropolitan was not O'Hagan's client-he was not an M&A lawyer. But the firm had a relationship and as a partner in the firm O'Hagan has a duty to preserve the client's confidential information.

Students might be asked how the "in connection with" requirement was satisfied? The "in connection with" requirement "is satisfied because the fiduciary's fraud is consummated, not when the fiduciary gains the confidential information, but when, without disclosure to his principal, he uses the information to purchase or sell securities."

The following are some points that might be considered here:

1. What does this leave of *Chiarella?* Clearly Vincent Chiarella would be a misappropriator today after *O'Hagan.* This appears to be a full vindication of Burger's dissent in *Chiarella.*

2.. Was this not an appealing set of facts for the government to bring to the Supreme Court to resolve whether one could violate the disclose or abstain rule by misappropriating the information? At oral argument, several justices showed real interest in the fact O'Hagan had stolen from his clients. and that that was the reason for misappropriating the knowledge of Grand Metropolitan's intent to acquire Pillsbury. Furthermore, consider a case the court had earlier decided not to grant cert, *U.S. v. Bryan*. There a state government used advance knowledge of what firm the Virginia would use to operate its lottery. He lost money on the trade, not the most appealing case, or not as appealing.

3. How persuasive is the court's reasoning on the in connection with requirement? Or more fundamentally, why should it matter if he stole the information from the client or that if the client said, sure, instead of paying your outrageous fees, we'll let all the partners in the firm take a position in Pillsbury in advance of our public bid. This hardly would be a misappropriation but is the public interest any more jeopardized in the facts of the case than in the hypothetical? If the concern is that O'Hagan's trading if unregulated, would jeopardize Grand Metropolitan's bid, should that rise to the level of a securities law violation?

4. Time should be spent on Part III of the opinion, dealing with the scope of the Rule 14e-3. First, what was the issue here; it was the lack of a fiduciary relationship being part of Rule 14e-3. Second, how did the Court resolve this which should lead one back to the enabling statute, section 14(e), where the second sentence clearly authorizes rules "to prevent" fraudulent practices. Third, it is worth parsing part of the language of Rule 14e-3, beginning with what conduct is proscribed in (a)[trading] vs (d)[tipping], when do the prohibitions set in ["substantial step or steps to commence a tender offer] and who is under the prohibition [in (a) it is "any other person" and in (b) it is the group in (d)(2) with the broadest category being (iv)].

Note on Who's A Misappropriator

A possible starting point is to ask the students what the significance of *Chestman* is and how this gets changed in Rule 10b5-2? The block quote on who is a fiduciary does not fit well with the husband-wife or for that matter the father-daughter relationship. Neither are really an agent, so this may well explain why a bare majority in *Chestman* concluded that pillow talk does not involve a fiduciary relationship.

This moves matters to Rule 10b5-2. How would *Chestman* be resolved under this rule? We can speculate whether Rule 10b5-2 reverses *Chestman,* or does it merely change the presumptions or otherwise tilts the analysis to favor misappropriation? Rule 10b5-2(b)(3) still allows the defense "that the person receiving the information may demonstrate that no duty of trust or confidence existed with respect to the information."

Note that the Second Circuit in *Dorozhko* treated that as a misstatement case and not an omission case to circumvent the need for a fiduciary relationship; the misstatement was the use of a password to access the computer system, the implicit false statement being that Dorozhko was authorized to use the password.

The balance of the Note Who's a Misappropriator raises the question whether the theory essentially lays the foundation for insider trading not on public considerations (e.g., fairer markets) but private ones (unauthorized used of another's property, i.e., information). If this is the case, could, as raised earlier, Grand Metropolitan retain counsel by rewarding them with a license to trade in advance knowledge of a takeover?

Dirks v. Securities and Exchange Commission

Raymond Dirks, an officer of a New York broker-dealer firm, specialized in providing to institutional investors investment analysis of insurance company securities. He learned from a former Equity Funding of America officer, Ronald Secrist, that Equity Funding was a massive fraudulent enterprise, having fabricated thousands of policy holders to support its appearance as a very successful life insurance company. While Dirks sought to verify Secrist's tip, he selectively recommended that several funds he advised dispose of their Equity Funding shares. The funds dumped about $16 million in shares and this caused the market price to decline. Dirks also disclosed the fraud to a Wall Street Journal reporter, urging him to write a story to disclose the fraud (the reporter initially declined to write the story). Ultimately the California Commissioner of Insurance stepped in and soon thereafter trading in Equity Funding is suspended. The SEC shows its gratitude to Dirks by censuring him for having violated Section 10(b) and Rule 10b-5. An administrative law judge at the SEC ruled against Dirks, finding that he violated Section 10(b) as a tippee, having been tipped by Secrist and Equity Funding insiders and then tipping his own clients. The D.C. Circuit Court of Appeals affirmed the judgment against Dirks. Licking his wounds, Dirks vows to fight the censure, a mild reprimand, all the way to the Supreme Court. After all, this is America, and we love Davids that slew goliaths. Thus, to complete the story, he wins.

A good place to begin is to ask what is new in this case? The defendant is not himself a trader, but a tippor. He also got the information from another, so he is sort of second level tippor, really both a tippor and a tippee. What was the SEC's argument? It is that tippees, like Dirks, have a responsibility is derivative of that of the tippor, Ronald Secrist. Thus, since Secrist could not trade on his confidential knowledge he acquired via his employment position (he was a true insider, or at least an ex insider), then those who received the tip from him step into Secrist's shoes sort of speak. This was rejected by the court.

What then shields Dirks? It is that the disclosure to him by Secrist was not "improper" because it was not a violation of Secrist's fiduciary duty to Equity Funding. Note the influence here of *Chiarella* in anchoring the lore of insider trading around a fiduciary relationship. The court then defines when such a selective disclosure would be improper, i.e., a breach of fiduciary duty: when it is paid for, will result in a reputational benefit that will translate to a pecuniary gain, or is disclose to a friend or family member. Dirks is none of these. Does this make sense?

We should pause over whether under state law the field geologist in TGS would be acting in breach of his fiduciary duties as an employee if he had told all the dumb farmers in the Timmins Ontario area about the results of K-55-1 and warned them to beware of men offering to purchase their land. Clearly this conduct would be inconsistent with the fiduciary relationship an employee and certainly an officer has to treat confidential corporate information confidentially and use it only for corporate purposes. Thus, why did *Dirks* not similarly hold with respect to Secrist's abuse of trust to Equity Funding? Was it because Equity Funding was engaged in a massive fraud? The court's opinion applies regardless of the criminality of the issuer. The hint here is Powell's analysis in III C where he discusses the role of analysts; he appears to favor a rule that will encourage the aggressive pursuit of non public information by reporters and others.

That said, he accomplishes as much by holding a selective disclosure is not itself wrongful, unless paid for, or done for a reputational gain that would yield a pecuniary gain, or made to a friend or relative.

The Barry Switzer fact situation is a good point to push to students to verbalize just why Switzer was protected by *Dirks*.

SEC, Selective Disclosure and Insider Trading

A logical way to approach this material is to assign Reg. FD, it is mercifully short, and use the excerpt as background for working through the rule. After covering that it applies only to reporting companies and only when disclosure is made to certain specified parties, the students can then be moved to what it requires. This leads to the natural question whether the SEC has in Reg. FD essentially reversed in some ways *Dirks*? The Supreme Court prohibits selective disclosures in the rather narrow instances of disclosures for a pecuniary gain, to a friend or a relative. Can we justify Reg FD on any of these bases? The answer is not clear, but the release justifies the rule not just on the parity of information requirement, but also prophylactic considerations that selective disclosures to analysts (note the categories here of employees of broker-dealers, e.g., research analysts at Morgan Stanley, as well as advisors to mutual funds and mutual fund personnel) addressed an issue that was pervasive prior to Reg FD, namely using selective disclosures as a form of currency to curry favor with analysts, etc. We also see the category for a selective disclosure to a substantial stockholder where the circumstances suggest it is "reasonably foreseeable that the person will" trade. This too might be akin to the "friend" category. Thus, the regulation is not all that far afield. Also, there are no privately enforceable duties that flow from the Rule. As to compliance, it means that when the CEO/CFO is providing "earnings guidance" to a group that will include any of the four categories set forth in the rule it needs to do so in a very public fashion. You may wish to refer to the disclosure requirements in Form 8-K, Item 2.02, which calls for a reporting companies to file "any public announcements or release disclosing material nonpublic information regarding the registrants' results of operations or financial condition for a completed quarter or annual fiscal period" but the 8-K filing is suspended for among other reasons, if that announcement was made in a means that was broadly accessible via dial in conference call, web cast, etc. or was provided in conformity with Reg. FD. Hence, Form 8-K complements Reg FD in this area.

Note on Insider Trading Enforcement

Students might be asked why we don't see more class actions for insider trading violations? With respect to the breadth of the ceiling on liability, the quote from Langevoort, suggests that non-open market purchasers could sue for more than the insider's ill-gotten gains. Also, given the manner which insider trading is detected, namely from market surveillance efforts of the SRO's and tips to the SEC, centralized detection leads to centralized enforcement so that any private suit would largely be parasitic.

Section 3. Liability for Short-Swing Trading Under § 16(b) of the Securities Exchange Act.

Section 16 can be as complicated as one wishes to make the discussion. Over its life, the rules and allied interpretations, not to mention the development of exotic derivative securities, have in combination introduced a good deal of complexity to what Congress initially thought was a fairly straightforward goal of 1) requiring statutory insiders of reporting companies to report their trading in their company's shares and 2) discouraging insider trading by providing a private (not SEC) action to require disgorgement of any "short-swing profits."

In an introductory business organizations course, you can easily justify spending just enough time to allow the "bells to go off" when the student's future client has a statutory insider as a client who has traded. At the same time, you can use this material to illustrate the problems that courts and the regulated confront daily when Congress enacts broad prohibitions with no scienter requirement that can serve as a governor on the enforcement process.

In its most basic form, Section 16 is not rocket science. It applies only to Section 12 reporting companies (hence a need to review who these companies are) and only to a distinct subset of individuals, referred to in practice as "statutory insiders:" officers, directors or the *beneficial* owner of more than 10 percent. Later we can see that there is the so-called double transaction abuse requirement for the latter which the statute expressly requires that to be liable as a beneficial owner that person must have been such both at the moment of purchase and the moment of sale.

The new filing rules, (new in the sense that post Enron the filings were accelerated from what the statute provides) to now be made by the end of the second business following the date of the trade.

While the SEC can enforce failures to make these public filing, only shareholders, via derivative suit (which by the way is unimpaired by the demand requirement discussed in Chapter 14, Section 6), can seek on behalf of the corporation the short-swing profits. The quote from *Gollust* reflects that standing to initiate the suit is not limited to common shareholders. This too is a departure from the standard requirements for maintaining a derivative suit.

Report of the Task Force on Regulation of Insider Trading, Part II: Reform of Section 16

This is the last time the ABA weighed in on Section 16. We might wonder how they feel about the subject now with so many developments at the SEC with extensive rule making around derivatives and employee compensation plans. It may well be time to revisit Section 16, or at least Section 16(b). In any case, the excerpt crisply sets forth three historical bases for Section 16 which seem to boil down to ridding the temptation to abuse one's insider position by introducing the prophylaxis of disgorgement of gains made within short time of a purchase or sale. As the earlier data on the frequency of insider trading reflects, one might wonder if things could get that much worse if this provision did not exist. We might ponder the policy question whether the proof of the pudding is in the tasting of it. Thus, sampling some of the cases that follow with an eye toward whether those caught in the crosshairs of Section 16(b) are the same persons as Fogarty, Darke, Chiarella and O"Hagan may move this material out of the technical and into the more personal level.

Gratz v. Claughton

Students might be asked what Hand is explaining in the second full paragraph of the case? This seems to be explaining the justifications for Section 16(b) by pointing toward some of the problems of enforcement were we to depend on some other approach. Hand takes the difficult case where the officer or director is selling; this would likely be to one to whom prior to the sale there was no relationship on which the duty could be premised. What Hand seems to be arguing, however, is not that there as gap in the common law, but that on close examination he reasons that the buyer would presume the fiduciary would remain a fiduciary after the trade. This seems to overlook that it is the point of sale that matters, not what may happen after the point of sale. Hand moves on to say that those who control the company will also have privileged access and this may be more than single person.

The balance of the opinion emphasizes the prophylactic mission of compelling disgorgement of short-swing profits. Hence, we find that there is no need to match the precise shares sold with those their purchase. Rather the approach is to maximize the recoverable profits. Hand sets forth the example of an executive owning 10,000 shares before any sale. He learns important good news, and purchases an additional 1000 shares and disposes of those shares three months later. If the rule were either first in first out, or that there was absolute matching of shares sold with their purchase, the executive could use her secret knowledge to gain. Thus, in the earlier decision, *Smolowe v. Delendo Corporation* the Second Circuit held the preferred approach is to match shares so as to produce the greatest disgorgement possible. He supports this with reference to the ancient restitution case, the *Chimney Sweeper's Jewel Case.*

Hand emphasizes that intent has no role in the statute's construction. Not also that the sale can precede the purchase with which it is matched. Thus, what would be the purpose of doing that, assuming that we had a purchase of 1000 shares, a sale of 1000 shares, and the purchase of 1000 shares, each one month apart and the second purchase at a lower price than the first. How can it be consistent with the statute to match the second purchase with the preceding sale? The idea would be that there might not have been any inside knowledge before the first purchase or the sale. But with the second sale the insider knew that the stock had bottomed out.

Note on the Computation of Profits Under § 16(b)

The note further illustrates the maximum disgorgement approach to measuring the recoverable damages. The hypo number (iii) is interesting as the overall effect is that the statutory insider has seen her net worth decline as the stock plummeted. But we also may see that the executive may have minimized losses by selling shares on 3/1.

Note on the Interpretation of § 16(b)

The Note frames the question regarding how ambiguities in language are to be interpreted. That is, just what is a "sale" and who is an "officer." There will be instances in which textbook understanding of each of these terms does not apply because the transaction is unusual or the position someone holds is also unusual. We see that unorthodox transactions invite the "pragmatic" or "subjective" approach to the construction of Section 16(b). The opposite of this approach would be a literal approach. In the next case, the Supreme Court unequivocally commits to the pragmatic/subjective approach.

Kern County Land Co. v. Occidental Petroleum Corp.

Kern is one of the most complex cases for students to digest in the course materials. If you choose to teach it the first step is that the students understand that Occidental made two purchases of Kern stock: one purchase that increased its ownership above ten percent and a second purchases after that. By virtue of the section 16(b)'s express language providing that to be liable as a "beneficial owner" one must have been such, i.e., an owner of more than 10 percent both at the moment of purchase and moment of sale, Occidental was only exposed to short swing liability for the shares purchased after it had become an owner of more than 10 percent. This issue was later resolved in another matter in *Foremost McKesson*.

Occidental then loses to a white knight, Tenneco, and all parties agree it is time to go their separate ways. Occidental gets Tenneco preferred for the Kern shares it acquired within six months. Court holds this is an "unorthodox" transactions, i.e., not clearly a purchase or sale unless to deem it as such would fulfill the purpose of the statute. Since the statute is about discouraging abuse of inside information, and Occidental could not be said to have any information about Kern that was not already in the public domain, the court said this exchange will not be deemed a sale. The result would have been different if Occidental had sold its Kern shares in the market. That transaction would not be unorthodox. The involuntariness of Occidental's disposition, forced to accept Tenneco preferred as a consequence of the merger in which it was a loser for the battle for control, renders this an "unorthodox" transaction. Note also that Occidental did not want to own preferred in a rival, Tenneco. Thus the option was entered into giving Tenneco a right to acquire the preferred held by Occidental. The terms of the option priced the option price so it was not clear that it would be wise for Tenneco in more than six months to exercise the option. Thus, the court held that the option itself was not a sale; had the option price been set so that there would be no circumstance that the option would not have been exercised, the analysis would be somewhat different. That would likely be seen as a sale in that case and the question is whether it could be matched with a purchase within six months. The exchange of Kern common for Tenneco preferred, as seen earlier, posed no chance of abuse of inside information by Occidental. Hence, as an unorthodox transaction, this was not a purchase. However, the earlier purchase of Kern common within six months of the option would be a voluntary, non orthodox, transaction and could be matched up.

Perhaps the epilogue of this case is that section 16(b) can be seen as mischievous, perhaps too frequently snaring the unsuspecting in its grasp. This is where we find the greatest criticism of section 16(b).

NOTE ON WHO IS AN OFFICER UNDER § 16(b).

A good illustration of the current interpretation of who is an officer is *Livingston* where clearly honorific title is not sufficient to push one into either the reporting or short swing profit provision. Students might be asked why this is so, given the prophylactic purpose of section 16. The answer is overkill, people like Livingston who are brokers but not managers in Merrill Lynch just don't pose a threat. It is important to know who is an officer because the reporting function requires these reports to be filed, and promptly after SOX.

NOTE ON DEPUTIZATION

While a fairly arcane subject, it is not really all that rare an event for a company that has a substantial investment in another entity to place a "representative" on the other company's board. Bingo! Consider the venture capital firm that retains a stake in the company that has made its first IPO. Might not its continued presence on the startups board post going public lend itself to the reach of section 16(b) should it purchase and sell shares in the startup within six months?

Section 4.   Corporate Recoveries for Inside Trading Under State Law.

Diamond v. Oreamuno

The chapter closes where it opened, with state common law. What is different with the cases in Section 4 from those covered earlier in Section 1? Here the corporation is the moving party, not an investor as in *Goodwin v. Agassiz* or *Strong v. Repide*. What were the facts of *Diamond?* The allegation is that a number of the officers and directors of Management Assistance, Inc., a firm that financed the purchase of computers sold their MAI shares on their secret knowledge that MAI's expenses were rising so that its reported earnings would decline. Two of the defendants, Oreamuno and Gonzalez, avoided losses of $880,000 by dumping their shares on their secret knowledge.

Was New York making new law here? It relies heavily on the much earlier Delaware decision in *Brophy v. Cities Service Co.* and the Restatement (2d) of Agency on the agency principle that the agent cannot use for personal purposes information obtained through the agency. That is, the agent abuses his position of trust and confidence by using the principal's information for the agent's purposes.

How persuasive is the court's reasoning that this remedy is necessary even in the face of federal proscriptions of insider trading? Consider the following:

"In view of the practical difficulties inherent in an action under the Federal law, the desirability of creating an effective common-law remedy is manifest .... Only by sanctioning such a cause of action will there be any effective method to prevent the type of abuse of corporate office complained of in this case.... There is nothing in the Federal law which indicates that it was intended to limit the power of the States to fashion additional remedies to effectuate similar purposes."

There are, of course, many more government enforcement actions than private corporate actions based on insider trading. The corporate causes of action face issues covered in Chapter 14 related to the demand requirement. Moreover, as we've seen earlier, the private recoveries in insider trading cases are by and large limited to recovering the defendant's profits. Thus, there just may not be enough at stake to attract the entrepreneurial private counsel for this type of case. Nonetheless, it is hard to say that the agency relationship is not abused. While some courts do take the approach that absent harm there can be no recovery by the corporation, this reasoning defies the history of forbidding agents to use the principal's assets or the relationship to personal advantage. Disgorgement of gain by the agent has long been the disincentive for the agent to abuse the relationship.

In the *Pfeiffer v. Toll,* appearing after *Diamond*, the Delaware Chancery Court observes that disgorgement is historically appropriate in self-dealing cases and insider trading is not self-dealing. However, this does not render disgorgement inappropriate. The Vice-Chancellor provides a long list of items that could be recovered, most related to any internal investigation that followed the trading.

Chapter 14

Shareholder Suits

Chapter Overview: You likely will commit at least 4 class periods to this material. The core material is the Background Note, Note on Who Can Bring a Derivative Action and *Tooley v. Donaldson, Lufkin & Jenrette, Inc.* in the first class period. Class period two could open with the material in Section 4 and be joined by *Marx v. Akers.* Class 3 would be either *Auerbach v. Bennett* or *Zapata Corp. v. Maldonado* (the latter is a richer case for discussion), and an overview of the procedures followed under the Model Act. The final class period would be to cover the indemnification materials in Section 8. This would be the bare essentials. If you can increase the coverage by one or two days, you might consider adding *Barth v. Barth* (regarding derivative suits in close corporations), the Note on Independence (dealing with possible bias among board members), the materials in Section 9 (dealing with attorney conflict of interest, privilege, and work product), *Tandycrafts* (award of attorney fee), and Section 13 dealing with private ordering are all important topics for which an additional day or two can be easily justified to add to this chapter.

Section 1:   Introduction

In combination, the Background Note, the Macey and Miller excerpt, and the Note on the Empirical Studies of Shareholder Litigation allow you to engage the students around the following issues by way of an introductory discussion:

1. We've seen in earlier chapters that one problem with business organizations, and the public corporation especially, is agency costs that flow from the separation of ownership from management. How can we think of the derivative suit as a way to address agency costs?

2. Why might we think that the derivative suit itself is fraught with agency costs?

3. What makes a cost and benefit assessment of derivative suits problematic?

The following provides some background to each of the preceding three questions.

Shareholder suits covered in this chapter are derivative suits, and not class action suits. The latter can arise for misrepresentations, a subject covered in Chapter 12 as well as in the acquisition area where claims of unfairness can be raised by minority shareholders, a subject covered in Chapter 15. A common theme throughout the materials in this chapter is whether the derivative suit can be a way of not just redressing harm to the corporation, but at the same time disciplining managers and controlling stockholders for breaches of fiduciary duties owed to the corporation. Thus, we can well see the suits have both a compensatory and a deterrent effect; however, material in this chapter underscores the compensatory orientation of the legal rules that surround derivative suits.

Students should understand at the outset that derivative suits enforce rights the corporation has and is not about enforcing personal rights of the shareholders. Hence, materials in the early portion of the chapter probe what is and is not a corporate right, albeit one that a shareholder meeting certain requirements can assert on behalf of the corporation as a derivative suit. Because the subject of any derivative suit is a right of the corporation, there invariably is tension in the suit's maintenance with the policy underlying the business judgment rule, a subject studied in Chapter 10, regarding the prerogatives of the board of directors over the affairs of the corporation.

The vast preponderance of derivative suits focus on the breaches of fiduciary duties by officers, directors and controlling stockholders. Most of those suits entail claims of self-dealing, i.e., agency costs. What makes shareholder litigation interesting is the irony that such suits themselves are fraught with agency cost issues, a matter raised in the introductory portion of this chapter, and raised repeatedly throughout the materials as legislatures and courts have cast a critical eye to the suit's agent, counsel in the representative suit.

While fiduciary duty claims are the dominant focus of derivative suits, there is nothing in the definition of what constitutes a corporate cause of action (that can be asserted in derivatively) that restricts such suits to breaches of fiduciary duties. Indeed, it is theoretically possible for such suit to be brought against third party suppliers or customers. However, the reality of the demand requirement necessarily restricts suits as a practical matter to instances in which the board or a committee of the board is disabled from rendering an impartial view of whether the corporate interest is served by the suit's maintenance. These points are examined, later in the materials addressing the demand requirement, and its extension, the special litigation committee. More generally, this chapter reviews the variety of procedural hurdles the derivative suit plaintiff faces, such that we might well conclude that to prevail the plaintiff must win each of several events that await her.

The introductory material raises the intriguing question of what motivates the individual shareholder to institute derivative litigation? As the material reflects, most derivative suit plaintiffs have a relatively small stake in a corporation, such that the cost to them of instituting and pursuing a derivative suit would far outweigh any proportional benefit they gain if the corporation recovers in such litigation. This is an area that suggests the real engine behind the suit is the suit's counsel and not the suit's plaintiff.

Later materials in the chapter address topics such as the courts' role in reviewing settlements and the award of attorney fees. There we will question whether agency costs of the suit's counsel overwhelm the issues raised in the suit, because risk averse D & O insurance companies cooperate with counsel in supporting settlements that provide little recovery to the corporation but do provide awards that will cover all or a significant portion of the legal fees and other costs related to the suit's defense as well as fees for derivatives suit counsel. Here we might ask whether the process results not just in settling suits that if prosecuted to the end would have been dismissed, but also settling suits for too little compensation for the harm actually suffered by the alleged misconduct that was the subject of the suit.

Finally, the benefits of suits are hard to assess. We can measure costs – D & O premiums that ultimately feed the attorneys and the settlement awards are pretty measurable. If we focus on only the cash settlements wrested as a result of the derivative suit, we have a measurement of the suit's benefits. But is it likely to be an under inclusive measurement. The social calculus of representative suits admittedly is imperfect. But in the abstract we must at least recognize there is some value to the suits to compliance with norms generally. While we might conclude that in the individual suit the litigation costs overwhelm the benefits conferred on the corporation as a result of the suit. At the same time, just how do we measure the benefits of representative suits like *Van Gorkom*, *Gantler*, and *Caremark* via the principles and practices they produce?

That said, recent empirical literature might suggest that derivative litigation has been successfully used to achieve valuable corporate governance change, both in terms of deterrence (e.g. conveying to other directors what *not* to do with respect to fulfilling fiduciary duties) and in terms of direct relief (e.g. adopting new executive compensation procedures in order to settle derivative litigation).

Note on Who Can Bring a Derivative Suit

You might ask the student what is the good news and bad news regarding standing to bring a derivative suit that is captured in the first paragraph of the note? Well, the good news is that you need not own any particular amount of shares; the bad news is that if you are, for example, cashed out in a merger or otherwise dispose of the shares you do own, you lose your shares. Here you might wish to take time to discuss the full implications of *Lewis v. Anderson*. Also, you might wish to alert the students in this chapter to keep track how many times Harry Lewis' name appears; he was a professional derivative suit plaintiff who had small holdings in a large number of companies and circulated his holdings among several Delaware plaintiff firms with the instruction, to file suit if the counsel saw anything s/he believed was actionable.

The Note probes the distinction between whether one needs to be shareholder of record (not the earlier issues on this in Chapter 6, Section 1, regarding shares held in street name) or a beneficial owner. Clearly excluded from having standing are creditors and holders of derivatives including convertible bonds.

Here you might want to note the unusual New York provision that confers standing on a director to maintain a derivative suit.

Note on Personal Defenses

Students might be asked what we find in this Note? The suit is equitable and, hence, equitable defenses apply. This includes not just waiver and unclean hands, but you can actually find laches applied so that the suit might possibly be barred if the suit's plaintiff delay in bringing the suit caused harm to the suit's defendants.

Note on the Corporation as an Indispensable Party

So if the relief is to go to the corporation, assuming the suit is successful, how does the corporation become a party to the suit? It is named as a nominal defendant.

Section 2:   The Nature of the Derivative Action

Tooley v. Donaldson, Lufkin, & Jenrette, Inc.

To get the ball rolling, students might be asked what would be recovered if the suit were successful? Is a claim brought by plaintiff-stockholders regarding a 22-day delay is closing in a proposed merger (which is alleged to have caused harm due to the time value of money) a direct or a derivative claim?   From here you can move through the following points bearing on the issue of whether the claim was direct or derivative:

1. Why did it matter to the plaintiff how the suit was characterized? While the full discussion of various procedures for maintaining a derivative suit follow *Tooley*, the introductory material to this chapter allows the student to provide the answer: numerous procedural obstacles await the derivative suit plaintiff that do not await the direct suit. Hence, we don't find plaintiffs begging to have their suit characterized as a corporate cause of action that they can assert in derivative suit.

2. Why was this a class action and not a personal individual action? The claim of each litigant is small, so it would not be cost effective, even for a large institutional holder. The law of small numbers is that 22 days at the effective rate of interest is not likely to reward the individual plaintiff's lawyer.

3.   What result if the court had affirmed the notion that "special injury" was required?   This likely would have meant there would never be a class action. That is, just how could common questions of law and fact predominate and we still find there is a special injury to members of the class?

4. How predictable is the test the court articulates? Does this just invite clever pleading? For example, consider *Dodge v. Ford Motor Company*, discussed earlier in the course. Was that a direct or corporate law suit? Was the harm failing to maximize profits or was the intent here to prevent the Dodge boys from starting their own competing firm? Or, slightly different, what about another dividend case, *Smith v. Atlantic Properties, Inc.*, in Chapter 8, where dividends could not be paid without approval of all the directors and the holdout was a doctor who likely feared higher taxes if the dividend (then taxed at ordinary income rates) were paid. The company faced the excise tax (excess retained earnings tax). Is this a direct or corporate cause of action? In the close corporation setting, as in *Smith*, cases such as *Barth v. Barth,* courts dodge such ticklish questions by treating all claims as direct. Note here that the form of relief sought,

198

damages, restitution, or injunctive, appears not to matter under the *Tooley* formulation. Thus, while we might think what drives the characterization is protection of creditors, that is not an issue where the remedy is a mandatory order (even in the dividend case, ordering the majority to pay a dividend when the majority is seeking to freezeout the minority poses some threat to creditors but all suits that have considered the freezeout-non-payment-of-dividend cases have held they are direct not derivative).

5. Finally, note that the court ultimately rules against the plaintiff, holding there was no substantive right to the claim. Along the way, it does clarify some noise in its case law. Its decision on the direct vs. derivative issue is hardly dicta, however, since it could not render a holding on the contract's meaning until it decided that the substantive dispute was properly before the court

Barth v. Barth

To draw the students into the case you might consider the following:

1. Review the plaintiff's allegations to identify which are more likely direct (lowering dividend payments if allege he purpose was to drive out or otherwise punish the other holders) and which are more likely a corporate cause of action (all the others because appears the impact to the shareholders is incidental, or secondary, to the impact that occurs initially to the corporation).

2. What does the case tell us that is not discussed in *Tooley* regarding the derivative suit characterization issue? It is why we don't let all suits be direct, namely multiplicity of suits, possible harm to creditors, and one the court does not mention obeisance to the principle that it is the board, and not the shareholders, who manage the corporation and its assets, e.g., choses in action.

3. What then would have caused this suit to be treated as derivative so that the pre-suit procedures would be followed? If the firm were experiencing financial distress, then any monetary recovery that occurs pursuant to a direct suit characterization would bypass the creditors and, hence, harm them (for which perhaps they might have a claim under the fraudulent conveyance/transfer statutes, discussed later in Chapter 16.

4. Just what happens then when the exception followed in *Barth* does not apply? Presumably this would trigger an inquiry mostly around the demand requirement, discussed later. We believe this likely could be excused under the traditional basis of futility (and in a MBCA jurisdiction, as we will see, making the demand is required, but does not delay the bringing of a suit if the board is so badly divided that it cannot respond, albeit there is a period of time that must elapse after making the "universal demand" and bringing the suit).

5. Note here that concerns for creditors also is an important, but not determinative consideration, of the willingness of courts to authorize a pro-rata recovery in derivative suits, the next subject covered in the materials.

6. We might note that there is a somewhat more circumscribed ability in a direct action for attorney fees to be awarded from the corporation to the plaintiff - shareholder when the suit is transformed to a direct rather than a derivative action. This point is discussed later in the chapter and the right of recovery from the corporation in a direct action is illustrated in the *Tandycraft* case, *infra*.

Section 3:   Individual Recovery in Derivative Actions

Glenn v. Hoteltron Systems, Inc.

The facts of the case are fairly straightforward. There were two equal owners of the Ketek Electroc Corporation: Schachter and Kulik. Schacter was breached his fiduciary duty by diverting Ketek business to Hoteltron, a company wholly owned by Schacter. Kulik argued that Schachter should pay damages directly to him and not to Ketek Electric Corporation. The New York court rejected the request, reasoning that "An exception based on that fact alone would effectively nullify the general rule that damages for a corporate injury should be awarded to the corporation." Moreover, "The fruits of a diverted corporate opportunity are properly a corporate asset. Awarding hat asset directly to a shareholder could impair the rights of creditors whose claims may be superior to that of the innocent shareholder."

Is there any reason in this case to believe that Schachter should be eager to support Kulik's position? Would not Schachter prefer to write a check for fifty percent less than he would if the recovery were directed to Ketek? While he may share control of the recovered sum with Kulik, that nonetheless is shared control.

Nonetheless, the case demonstrates one reason for the direct-derivative distinction we saw earlier in *Tooley* and *Barth*, namely a concern for the protection of creditors. We might observe here that decisions such as *Barth v. Barth, supra*, obviate the question of direct recoveries in derivative suits in close corporations since they effectively transform corporate actions into direct actions.

The note material following the case captures several exceptions courts have invoked to allow the recovery to pass directly to the shareholders. The exception set forth in Item 4 where many of the shareholders have some personal defense is an interesting case for a pro rata recovery. Thus, if the conduct was ratified or perhaps even acquiesced in by some shareholders the court, peering through the derivative suit, could rule a pro rata recovery, albeit only for the proportionate shares of the non-ratifying shareholders.

Bottom line is that the form of the suit is equitable, thus inviting equitable arguments and approaches in many aspects of the suit, including whether the formalism of the suit vindicating the corporate right should give way when equitable considerations suggest recovery should be directed to individual shareholders.

Perlman v. Feldmann

Cross reference here should be to Chapter 11, Section 6. The court there, relying on Wilport continuing to control Newport, ordered a pro rata recovery of the control premium.

Section 4:   The Contemporaneous-Ownership Rule

The next case, and the contemporaneous ownership rule' raises the question of the purpose of shareholder suits, and the derivative suit in particular.   The contemporaneous ownership rule mandates that the plaintiff's ownership, of at least one share, overlap with the occurrence of the misconduct that is the subject of the wrongdoing. Thus, if the alleged wrong is embezzlement that occurred on January 15th and the plaintiff became a shareholder on February 1st via purchase, application of the rule bars the plaintiff from maintain the suit. The attorney needs to find someone who held the shares on January 15th, the date of the misconduct that is the subject of the suit. If such a holder is located, the suit can proceed, and, if successful, recovery will go to the corporation, indirectly benefitting all holders, regardless of whether the holders purchased their shares before or after January 15th. Does it make sense to restrict who can be the plaintiff but not who can reap the advantages of the suit's successful prosecution? Does this depend on whether we see the suits as serving a compensatory or deterrent function?   If the latter, does the contemporaneous ownership rule make sense? If the suit is compensatory, then why does not a large monetary recovery by the corporation not give rise to a windfall for shareholders acquiring their shares after the misconduct?   Does the answer to any of these questions turn on whether investors can price not the violation but the prospect of ultimate just desserts?

Bangor Punta Operations, Inc. v. Bangor & Aroostook R.R.

You might ask students at the outset, whether this was a derivative suit? No, it was a suit by the corporation against its former controlling stockholder. Then why is this case in this chapter? It illustrates the compensatory orientation of shareholder suits by the insights we gain from the "contemporaneous ownership" requirement of Fed. Rule Civ. Proc. 23.1(1) that the court invokes in much of its reasoning to bar the suit.

BAR sued in a derivative suit Bangor Punta, the corporation that formerly owned 98.3% of the BAR stock that it later sold to Amoskeag, now the 99% shareholder of BAR. It was alleged that Bangor Punta damaged BAR by way of mismanagement, misappropriation, and waste of BAR's assets, and damages of $7 million were sought.

The Supreme Court, relying on the reasoning of Pound's decision in *Home Insurance Co. v. Barber* establishing the vicarious incapacity defense, agreed with the District Court's, that since Amoskeag does not dispute that the interest it had purchased was not worth at least the $5 million it paid Bangor Punta, then to permit BAR to recover from Bangor Punta "would constitute a windfall."

Some possible questions for the students:

1. What moved the court here to pierce the veil so as to determine that Amoskeag was the ultimate beneficiary of the suit?

2. Do not derivative suit recoveries always give rise to a windfall with respect to holders who became such after the alleged wrongdoing? Would this not always be the case with public companies whose ownership changes daily and substantially over the course of the year?

3. Why not conclude that the issue is not whether recovery results in unjust enrichment to Amoskeag, but whether it is appropriate for Bangor Punta to retain the fruits of its misconduct? Answers to the above might all turn on whether the corporation's shares are priced in the market or the transaction so that they reflect the effects of the misconduct. If so, then those who purchase the shares after such misconduct is impounded in the company's share price will garner a windfall if the derivative suit subsequently yields a cash recovery. Certainly, if we had a pro rata recovery, it would be a good case could be made for limiting the recovery only to those who were holders prior to the misconduct, or at least prior to believing the misconduct was reflected (negatively) in the share price. This would support the conclusion reached by the majority in *Bangor Punta*. Note here this also is consistent with the approach taken by the ALI. *See* Note 1 following *Rifkin*. For the view that derivative suits, and shareholder suits generally, are ill-suited to serve a compensatory function, see Cox, Compensation, Deterrence, and the Markets as Boundaries for Derivative Suit Procedures, 52 Geo. Wash. L. Rev. 745 (1984)(because derivative suits focus out of necessity of the demand requirement on one-shot conflict of interest transactions they rarely produce recoveries that are significant vis-a-vis the firm's revenues or assets so that courts set the suit's up for failure by viewing their mission to be compensatory rather than deterrence of misconduct).

Rifkin v. Steele Platt

So, what connection does this case have with *Bangor Punta Operations*? Each involves a suit by the corporation against its former controlling stockholder. Each alleges a breach of fiduciary duty by the former controlling stockholder. And each had a new controlling stockholder who had purchased shares from the defendant. So, why did the suit succeed here and fail in *Bangor Punta Operations*?

The court distinguished Bangor Punta, holding that "the parties dispute whether the purchase price [paid by the new controlling shareholders] reflected the prior wrongdoings." Since the trial court did not make a finding on this issue, the case was remanded. We might wonder about this reasoning. If the purchase price did not reflect the prior misconduct, does that mean the plaintiff overpaid? If so, was that overpayment due to misrepresentation of the true state of Boiler Room? This would then suggest the suit should be for fraud, a direct action, not for embezzlement, a derivative suit.

Note on the Contemporaneous Ownership Rule

The contemporaneous ownership rule is fairly common. It is worth time reviewing, albeit this can be done quickly, the notable exceptions that appear in subparagraphs (a) – (c). You may also wish to take time to review the hypothetical and solution set forth in Item 3 of this note.

Section 5: Right to Trial by Jury in Derivative Actions

The topic of the role of a jury is steeped in history. The derivative suit was a creature of equity where the chancellor presided and juries did not exist. If the suit continued as such after the merger of law and equity courts in the U.S. we would expect juries not to be available in derivative suits. *Ross v. Bernhard* peers through the procedural format of the suit to conclude, at least within the federal courts, that it is the substance of the claim that is determinative and not the procedure. As the Note indicates, states are divided on whether they follow *Ross.*

Section 6: The Demand Requirement

We have seen some requirements the derivative suit plaintiff must meet: shareholder status, maintenance of shareholder status through completion of the suit, and in most jurisdictions there is a contemporaneous ownership requirement. By far the most formidable challenge facing the derivative suit plaintiff is "the demand requirement." While this is a procedural requirement it has significant substantive implications. An example of this requirement is Delaware Chancery Court Rule 23.1 states:

> "In a derivative action brought by 1 or more shareholders or members to enforce a right of a corporation... [the complaint shall allege] with particularity the efforts, if any, made by the plaintiff to obtain the action the plaintiff desires from the directors or comparable authority and the reasons for the plaintiff's failure to obtain the action or for not making the effort" in derivative litigation.

See FRCP 23.1 and Delaware state corollary. We also see this in the MBCA § 7.42.

There are several levels for thinking about why this requirement exists. You might ask the students why a legislature would condition maintaining a derivative suit on first making a demand on the board? Well, it is a corporate cause of action, so that within the broad statutory command that the 'affairs of the corporation are managed by or under the direction of the board of directors" we can logically conclude it is consistent with the structure of corporate law to seek the input of the board on whether a corporate cause of action should be asserted (note here it is as a theoretical matter possible that the suit is against a third party vendor or vendee or some other business matter and not just against a fiduciary). Second, if a suit is misguided, the corporate bears some cost (reputational harm, deflection of management time, role of counsel to monitor suit recalling the corporation is at least a nominal defendant) so have the board involved could be something of a governor on the entire process. That is, the demand serves as a filter of sorts. But, how reliable is this filter? And, does the skirmishing over whether a demand was excused just introduce another round of litigation within litigation to what is frequently an already complex litigation process? As we will see, the demand requirement is qualified, at least in non-Model Act jurisdictions, by exceptions. The subject of the next case.

A nice package here is to teach *Marx* (which has both interesting facts and a nice overview of the movement toward universal demand) and *Zapata* (which introduces the mechanics and issues surrounding the special litigation committee).

Marx v. Akers

The suit challenged as excessive compensation the IBM board of directors had approved for its CEO, Akers, as well as compensation the board voted for itself. More particularly, the plaintiff's derivative suit complaint alleged that the board committed waste and breached its fiduciary duties by awarding excessive compensation to IBM executives and outside directors.

Court of Appeals affirmed the appellate court, concluding that (a) the plaintiff was not excused from making demand with respect to the compensation of the senior officers and (b), even though demand was excused with respect to the directors' approval of their own compensation, this claim was dismissed because the plaintiff failed to state a cause of action for waste. As to the alleged excessiveness of the director's compensation, the failure was one of factual proof – the plaintiff's complaint did not "allege compensation rates excessive on their fact or other facts which call into question whether the compensation was fair to the corporation when approved, the good faith of the directors setting those rates, or that the decision to set the compensation could not have been a product of valid business judgment."

The Court provides a clear discussion of both Delaware's approach to demand futility and universal demand requirement that is now part of the Model Act. *Marx* clarifies that, in New York, demand is excuse because of futility when a complaint "alleges with particularity:"

(1) "that a majority of the board of directors is interested in the challenged transaction. Director interest may be either self-interest in the transaction at issue… or a loss of independence because a director with no direct interest in a transaction is 'controlled' by a self-interested director."

(2) "that the board of directors did not fully inform themselves about the challenged transaction to the extent reasonably appropriate under the circumstances…."

(3) "that the challenged transaction was so egregious on its face that it could not have been the product of sound business judgment of its directors."

Some teaching notes:

1. You might open this case by asking, "what does this case illustrate about the derivative suit." This leads to the demand requirement. So, you might ask, "so, why didn't the plaintiff make the demand?" The reply is that the board's answer is predictable, "No." So, what then happens?

The plaintiff could proceed to court, and challenge the "no" answer as not being in the corporation's best interest. If this is done, how should a court examine this? The answer is this appears to be a matter of the business judgment rule, unless there is some reason, obvious self interest or lack of reasonable investigation to remove the "no" decision from the presumptive protection of the business judgment rule.

2. Once we understand that the "no" answer shoves the plaintiff up against the business judgment rule, we might ask whether the court should be as deferential here as say whether the Cubs should play all their games in the daytime? There are lots of good reasons for according director and officer judgments a good deal of deference when the challenge is to a business decisions: courts are not chosen because of their sensitivity t marketing, accounting, and finance. This is what captains of industry have in their toolkits; this is not in the toolkit of the judiciary. Moreover, the consequence of judicial involvement in the day and night baseball type decision is that if the court substitutes its decision, e.g., night games, for that of the board's decision, e.g., day games, the consequence is not just an order that some games (how many? hmmmm!) will be played at night, but the second shoe to drop will be liability on the part of the directors for losses believed to have flown from their decision, e.g., play only daytime games where attendance is lower. Contrast this with the demand requirement context. Whether a suit has merits, how burdensome is the litigation, and what are the costs of on-going litigation, are each part of the daily fare of the court. That is, the courts more than the directors have experience in such questions, so that to the extent this is within their toolkit it would call for less deference. Second, a decision to reverse the board's "no" decision, only means the suit continues. It does not impose personal liability on the board for its conclusion that the suit was not in the corporation's best interest. It merely means the suit proceeds, perhaps just to the next level, e.g., discovery. Thus, there is less need for deference when considering the board's recommendation that the suit be dismissed than in the context of the board's substantive decision that the company play its games I the daytime only.

3. The preceding supports the ALI and Model Act approaches of universal demand. Also, under universal demand, we reduce the skirmishing over whether the facts support an excuse of demand. Demand is made and the skirmishing is on the real issue, namely whether the suit is in the best interest of the corporation.

4. You might consider getting the students to role play by placing them in the context of preparing a list of reasons why a suit, alleging excessive compensation to the CEO, is not in the best interests of the corporation. Note this can be linked to the role of the court per MBCA § 7.42(a) wherein the criteria for dismissal is "has determined in good faith, after conducting a reasonable inquiry . . . that the maintenance of the derivative suit proceeding is not in the best interests of the corporation." The list might include: 1) lacks merit, 2) harm to reputation of firm, 3) damage morale of the firm, 4) deflection of executive time, and 5) benefits to be obtained are dwarfed by the cost to defend for which the corporation is responsible. For such a list, you might ask students how many of these items could be raised in a motion to dismiss in say a patent infringement suit by Apple against Google? It would be only the former. Hard to think a court in such a suit would do more than roll its eyes if Google claimed that the suit by Apple had to be dismissed because it was costing Apple too much to defend, was a burden to its

executives or was harming its reputation. So, why is it different in the demand context? Because it is a suit brought on behalf of the corporation so we need to hear whether the suit is in the corporation's interest.

5. Now that almost half the states have adopted the MBCA derivative suit procedures, it is good to review the mechanics, particularly of section 7.44. For example, ask the students who has the burden of proof with respect to the criteria in paragraph (a)? This is answered in 7.44(d) where it turns on whether the majority of the board is independent.

Auerbach v. Bennett

So, another New York case, what's new? Auerbach filed a derivative action against the corporation's directors, auditors, and the corporation, invoking facts unearthed in a special investigation revealing that the company had carried out unlawful kickbacks. In response to the suit, the board established a special litigation committee "for the purpose of establishing a point of contact between the Board of Directors and the Corporation's General Counsel concerning the position to be taken by the Corporation in certain litigation involving shareholder derivative claims on behalf of the Corporation against certain of its directors and officers" and authorizing that committee "to take such steps from time to time as it deems necessary to pursue its objectives including the retention of special outside counsel." The special committee was made up of three directors who had joined the board *after* the complained-of transactions. The committee concluded that it would not be in the corporation's best interests for the derivative action to proceed and directed the corporation's general counsel to take that position in the litigation.

In response to the corporation's motion, the court dismissed the complaint. The court noted: "While the court may properly inquire as to the adequacy and appropriateness of the committee's investigative procedures and methodologies, it may not under the guise of consideration of such factors trespass in the domain of business judgment. At the same time those responsible for the procedures by which the business judgment is reached may reasonably be required to show that they have pursued their chosen investigative methods in good faith."

A further thought on *Auerbach*. We might question how significant the burden of proof is in any review of a report of the special litigation committee? This might well be what distinguishes *Auerbach* from *Zapata, infra*. A close review of the cases finds that derivative suit plaintiffs do about as well (or is that poorly) under either standard. What might be important is how the reviewing court interprets requirements such as "good faith" and "reasonable bases." Many courts accord "good faith" an expansive meaning so that this is the means by which the thoroughness of the investigation, reasoning, and independence of the process is scrutinized. Each of these gives the plaintiff a healthy shot at the committee's report, reasoning and conclusion. This is a vast improvement of where the law was say most of the last century in which courts were much less willing to entertain the derivative suit's plaintiff challenges to presumed director infallibility.

Zapata Corp. v. Maldonado

The central issue posed in *Auerbach,* and repeated in *Zapata Corporation,* is nicely framed by the Delaware Supreme Court in *Zapata Corporation*: "When, if at all, should an authorized board committee be permitted to cause litigation, properly initiated by a derivative stockholder in his own right, to be dismissed?... Even when demand is excusable, circumstances may arise when continuation of the litigation would not be in the corporation's best interests. Our inquiry is whether, under such circumstances, there is a permissible procedure under [Section] 141(a) by which a corporation can rid itself of detrimental litigation. If there is not, a single shareholder in an extreme case might control the destiny of the entire corporation." Thus, just how much deference should the court give to the SLC's recommendation? How much should the derivative suit plaintiff be allowed to probe the report or the members of the SLC?

It is worth drawing the students into the facts a bit to get the flavor of what prompted this suit and ask them whether the students believed the plaintiff had a strong case (if so, what does that tell us about the SLC's conclusions that dismissal was in the company's best interests)?

We might consider this spring loaded options. On the eve of Zapata Corporation making a self-tender for its shares at a price in the range of $25-30 per share, the board advanced the exercise date on options held by senior management from to July 2 from July 14. This would allow the options to be exercised at $19 per share, a price that was not influenced by the yet to announced much higher tender offer price. As a consequence, the managers avoided a tax hit. Whatever their taxable gain on the transaction would have been a deduction to the corporation (note the corporation in any case is parting with the same number of shares and causing to its shareholders the same dilution; hence, the corporation would benefit by a larger deduction).

Two years after the suit, the corporation created the SLC, appointed two newly installed directors to serve on the SLC, and charged the SLC with determining the corporate interest served by the suit.

The court holds that the board, although a majority of its members are implicated in the underlying misconduct, such that a demand on the board was earlier properly excused, can nonetheless resurrect the demand requirement by appointing, as the board did here, a SLC. It addresses any thought of self-interest, etc. with what it called a two-step test: "First, the Court should inquire into the independence and good faith of the committee and the bases supporting its conclusions," and the corporation will have the burden of proving "independence, good faith and a reasonable investigation." If the burden is not carried, the motion to dismiss will be denied. If the burden is carried, then the next step will be for the court to "appl[y] its own independent business judgment" and determine whether the motion to dismiss should be granted. In reality, this is one step test since no court has ever concluded that notwithstanding the satisfaction of the first step that the SLC's recommendation should be rejected.

Some thoughts for teaching the case:

1. It is useful to go over the substance of the plaintiff's complaint, namely the loss to the corporation and gain to the defendant executives by advancing the exercise date for the options. That is, by allowing the exercise date to be advanced, the executives avoided paying taxes on amount of gain in the stock's prices that was caused by announcement of the issuer's self tender. This reduced their taxes. If the date had not been advanced, and the executives exercised their options, they would have reported a taxable gain but the same amount could be deducted by the corporation. Thus, assume the option price was $15 and when the executives exercised their options the market price was $19. They reported a gain of $4 per share (for say 100,000 shares). This would result in a tax deduction to the corporation of $400,000. However, if the exercise date for the options was not accelerated, and the executives exercised their options at $25, a price influenced by the tender offer, they would have reported taxable gain of $1 million ($10 per share for 100,000 shares), and the corporation would have a tax deduction for the same amount. Under this set of assumptions, the board's decision to advance the exercise date cost the company the value of a $600,000 tax deduction. Moreover, the corporation faced the same dilution of its shareholders regardless of what the exercise date was, i.e., there was no gain to the corporation, whatever, by accelerating the exercise date.

2. Was this a demand required or demand excused case? It was the latter, so how would this be justified by *Aronson*? The answer is that appears the decision to advance the date was not justified by any reasonable interpretation of the business judgment rule since it produced benefits only to the benefitted executives and not to Zapata Corp.

3. How then did the demand return to the case? The board filled two vacant seats and appointed those new members to the special litigation Committee. See the power to fill seats and create committees in the Delaware 141(c).

4. What makes us shift the burden, as the court does, to the committee in this context? It was a demand excused case, so Delaware shifts the burden (this is very similar to the result reached in the MBCA because we excuse demand in Delaware when a majority of the board is either directly implicated in the suit or has made a decision for which there is a reasonable doubt the decision is protected by the business judgment rule. Also, note here the famous quote, "there but for the grace of God go I?" What is this about? Likely refers to the fact that directors empathize with the derivative suit defendants. Moreover, what else suggests there is cause for distrust? How about allowing the defending several years to shop for their jury as appears to be the case here?

5. Reviewing the elements of level one of the *Zapata* inquiry, what do you do if wish to make sure the special litigation committee's recommendation will be accepted? Who does the investigation (counsel with no historical relationship to the management/defendants). Who else is retained? Investment bankers, accountants and such other experts as the facts demand. And, a long lengthy report is likely the best assurance not just of reasonable grounds, but that there was a reasonable investigation, which most courts have subsumed within the good faith.

6. Note most courts authorize, at least, limited discovery of facts supporting the report as well as the process of preparing the report.

7. What do we make of level two of *Zapata's* scrutiny. It is discretionary, and no court has accepted the recommendation under level 1 but dismissed the suit under level 2.

8. Note, cleaning one's own stable is relevant under the Sentencing Guidelines (discretionary but followed after Booker). Thus, committee reports are very much part of the mix almost from day one of the violation or its discovery.

Aronson v. Lewis

The lens for determining in Delaware whether a demand is excused on the basis of futility is whether the complaint alleged with particularity sufficient facts to create "a reasonable doubt is created that: (1) the directors are disinterested and independent OR (2) the challenged transaction was otherwise the product of a valid exercise of business judgment."

The facts of *Aronson* were pretty extreme. The plaintiff was allowed to amend the complaint, did so with allegations that sufficiently impugned (i.e., created a reasonable doubt) the independence of the directors and whether the severance package awarded the aging controlling stockholder was outside the protection of the business judgment rule. Certainly it is not enough to merely allege that the defendant owned 54 percent of the stock and elected the entire board. More was needed to demonstrate that the directors so elected were financially or otherwise dependent on the defendant.

Note on Cuker v. Mikalauskas

The significance of *Cuker* is its adoption of the central provisions of the ALI's approach to demand. This included universal demand and the review standards to be followed by the derivative suit court. It is also noteworthy that the court appears to open the process up, whether it be a demand required or demand excused case, to scrutiny of a good many factors related to any (full board or SLC) determination that dismissal would be in the corporation's interest. The court observed:

> "In order to make the business judgment rule meaningful, the preliminary examination should be limited and precise so as to minimize judicial involvement when application of the business judgment rule is warranted.... Factors bearing on the board's decision will include whether the board or its special litigation committee was disinterested, whether it was assisted by counsel, whether it prepared a written report, whether it was independent, whether it conducted an adequate investigation, and whether it rationally believed its decision was in the best interests of the corporation (i.e., acted in good faith). If all of these criteria are satisfied, the business judgment rule applies and the court should dismiss the action."

Questions that arise are just how much discovery can the derivative suit plaintiff have regarding the board's or SLC's processes, etc.? That if discovery were limited, what would the reasonable factors to consider in so limiting discovery? Certainly we'd expect discovery and inquiry into the committee's independence including that of its advisors and counsel, processes followed, and any disconnects between findings and conclusions.

Note on Independence

The issue of whether directors who were friends or social acquaintances with the implicated CEO came up in the case of <u>Beam v. Martha Stewart, 845 A.2d 1040</u> (Del. Supr. 2004), which was a case regarding demand excusal, and the Delaware Supreme Court ruled in a way that was very generous to directors, declining to find that the directors at issue were disinterested due to their long-time social friendship with Martha Stewart. The court offered the following guidance:

> A variety of motivations, including friendship, may influence the demand futility inquiry. But, to render a director unable to consider demand, a relationship must be of a bias-producing nature. Allegations of mere personal friendship or a mere outside business relationship, standing alone, are insufficient to raise a reasonable doubt about a director's independence.... [For purposes of pre-suit demand futility, to] create a reasonable doubt about an outside director's independence, a plaintiff must plead facts that would support the inference that because of the nature of a relationship or additional circumstances other than the interested director's stock ownership or voting power, the non-interested director would be more willing to risk his or her reputation than risk the relationship with the interested director."

Cox & Munsinger, Bias in the Boardroom: Psychological Foundations and Legal Implications of Corporate Cohesion, 48 Law and Contemporary Problems 83 (1985), reviews the social and psychological forces that likely cause strong, albeit subtle, biases by the directors against the derivative suit plaintiff with the effect that board judgments regarding the suit's benefits are equally biased. These forces flow from the directors and the suit's defendants serving as members of the board where they share tasks together that essentially meld them into a team. The derivative suit plaintiff is a member of the other team. Neither *Beam* nor *Oracle* addresses these forces. As seen next, *Oracle's* reasoning appears to find a lack of independence only through financial dependency of the committee members, and not in their social or business interactions. One persuaded by the social and psychological literature would in all cases approach the director judgments regarding another colleague with some caution, if not skepticism.

In *Oracle,* the two committee members were professors at Stanford, and as such had strong ties to the defendant insiders/directors who were accused of insider. Vice Chancellor Strine concluded that there was a reasonable doubt about the impartiality of the SLC.

In *Martha Stewart*, the Delaware Supreme Court provided the following observation about *Oracle:*

> "[U]nlike the demand-excusal context [i.e., whether a demand on the board is excused for futility], where the board is presumed to be independent, the SLC has the burden of

establishing its own independence by a yardstick that must be 'like Caesar's wife'—'above reproach.' Moreover, unlike the presuit demand context, the SLC analysis contemplates not only a shift in the burden of persuasion but also the availability of discovery into various issues, including independence."

Is this a persuasive distinction? If all those on the board of Martha Stewart Omnimedia had connections to Martha Stewart like those of the two Stanford professors in *Oracle* would a demand still have been required? Probably not, so that the Supreme Court's distinction may not be all that probative of what is going on here. What we might surmise, and it is only surmise, is that running in the same social circle and interacting outside the boardroom goes with the turf. They are indeed birds of a feather and flock together.

Section 7: Demand on Shareholders

There is little life left to the earlier requirement that the plaintiff must either make a demand on the shareholders or allege why such a demand should be excused. As the note material points out, the exceptions now appear to have swallowed the rule so that most states, including the MBCA's provisions which is now heavily adopted, make no mention of this requirement.

Section 8: Indemnification and Insurance

A.   Indemnification

Indemnification refers to the corporation essentially bearing the cost of any financial burdens borne by its officer, director, employee or agent incurred in the discharge of his duties. This differs from insurance where the insurer, a third party, covers these costs.

Insurance and indemnification are always in the background of any settlement. The plaintiffs' lawyers, certainly one whose representation is on a contingency fee basis, will generally prefer the certainty of a settlement over the prolonged uncertainty of trial. The defense lawyers eye the D & O policy as their source of payment. Like the plaintiff's lawyer, they understand the standard policy is a wasting asset; the policy limit being reduced by periodic disbursements to the defense counsel. If there is less there, it is less for everyone, unless there is reason to believe the corporation through indemnification or the defendants themselves will cover the costs once the policy is depleted. The insurance company is the party whose concurrence in the settlement is not legally required, but a practical necessity seeks both a favorable settlement and certainty. These twin vectors point in the same direction - settlement. And, of course, the real defendants all appreciate the wisdom that it is always better if someone else pays. Rest assured that in this process, the real defendants wish a result that costs them little or nothing. This generally means a settlement, and it will be a settlement that is structured to fall within the coverage of any available D & O policy (i.e., settlement terms do not push the conduct into one of the areas of non coverage, e.g., willful misconduct). One has to appreciate as well that about 15 percent of all D&O claims are disputed by the insurance carrier. Thus, we frequently find litigation within litigation.

Students may be asked why should it be lawful for corporations to be able to indemnify its officers, directors, employees, and agents? Well, if the conduct that gave rise to the claim arose in the scope of carrying out the company's business, having the corporation pay is a way of requiring it to internalize the full costs of its operations. Moreover, indemnification encourages the most qualified people to assume positions with the company. Not surprisingly, every state has a statute authorizing indemnification. See, e.g., Delaware Gen. Corp. Law Section 145.

We customarily begin our coverage of this area by reviewing an indemnification statute. Delaware's statute has had a profound influence in the approach taken by other states so we use that here as an illustration of how the material might be approached.

Several items to note regarding the DGCL § 145:

1. We begin with DGCL 145 (c). This is a mandatory provision. If a present or former director is successful "on the merits or otherwise" in defense of a lawsuit against her, the corporation "shall" indemnify her against her expenses for her defense. Particularly when reflecting on agency law, this mandatory provision makes sense. The history of this provision is captured in the introductory paragraph to this section of the materials.

2. We next ask what the distinction is between DGCL 145(a) and (b). Note here that (b) deals with suits by the corporation (including derivative suits) and (a) covers all other bases for which indemnification is sought. We also make the point that this covers agents. Could a lawyer seek indemnification under this provision for work done for the client? The note material following *Waltuch* illustrates some case holdings regarding when an attorney can be an agent and more generally when one acts as an agent. The determining consideration is whether there is a master-servant relationship, or is the person acting as an independent contractor or just for himself. The facts in the Note case, *Stifel Financial Corp. v. Cochran*, arose from a discharged officer's refusal to repay some of his compensation as well as a promissory note he had executed for funds advanced as part of his wooing to join the firm. The court held the litigation costs in resisting the corporation's efforts to obtain this repayment were not related to his performance of company duties, but were personal in nature. On the overall approach to who's an agent under state indemnification statutes, *See* DeMott, ___ Law and Contemporary Problems (2011). Neither145(a) nor 145(b) provisions, however, are mandatory provisions. We ask the question whether a company that encourages its deliver truck drivers to exceed the speed limit can indemnify the speeding tickets that the delivery driver incur? This is covered by 145(a) and appears to be not permitted because the speeding driver must know that the conduct is unlawful. More generally, under Section 145(a), a corporation shall have the power (but is not required) to indemnify a person who is subject to action (in court, administratively, or otherwise – only excluding derivative actions) for any expenses, judgments, fines, settlement amounts, etc. incurred if the person "acted in good faith and in a matter such person reasonably believed to be in or not opposed to the best interests of the corporation, and, with respect to any criminal action or proceeding, had no reasonable cause to believe that such person's conduct was unlawful." Under Section 145(a), a corporation has the power to indemnify the person, if she is ultimately convicted of criminal conduct while performing her job duties, provided she can show that she

"had no reasonable cause" to believe that her conduct was unlawful.

3. As seen, DGCL 145(b) is permissive and empowers the corporation to indemnify an officer/director/agent/etc. in a *derivative action* for expenses reasonably incurred in defense or settlement. This power is conditioned, however, upon a determination that the person "acted in good faith and in a manner such person reasonably believed to be in or not opposed to the best interests of the corporation."

4. A further limitation in Section 145(b) is that if the matter went to judgment,, "no indemnification shall be made in respect of any claim, issue or matter as to which such person shall have been adjudged to be liable to the corporation," unless such person applies to the Court of Chancery for indemnification and the court deems such proper. Section 145(b), therefore, provides something of an incentive to settle.

5. Section (e) provides that a corporation has the power to advance any expenses for an officer/director in defending in an action (even in a derivative action), as long as the advanced party signs an undertaking in which he agrees to repay any advances "if it shall ultimately be determined that such person is not entitled to be indemnified" (presumably under DGCL 145(b)). Students may ask why the insurance policy does not cover this? Some policies are so written, but generally the D & O policy covers amounts the corporation is required (by statute, employment contract or otherwise) to indemnify the employee, so that advancements by the insurance company to the officer, director, etc. are beyond the standard policy.

6. Section 145(f) provides that indemnification and advancement of expenses provided in DGCL 145 "shall not be deemed exclusive" of any other rights under any by-law, agreement, vote of shareholders, etc. The question becomes, as we see in <u>Waltuch,</u> how far does 145(f) extend? Note here that a few states make their statute's the exclusive means by which indemnification and advances can occur.

Waltuch v. Conticommodity Services, Inc.

Question posed to the Court: Can DGCL 145(f) moot DGCL 145(a)'s "good faith" requirement? (No). A good preliminary point to raise with the students is what can "good faith" mean and whose good faith are we focused? You might try unraveling the case by asking the students as an initial matter whether Waltuch leaves the court empty handed. This leads to the easier part of the opinion, namely that he was successful, in part, with respect to the private suits where he never contributed anything toward the settlement so that he was thereby able to obtain mandatory indemnification under DGCL 145(c). From this you can move to how things were different with respect to the governmental prosecution. It is in this context that the meaning of "good faith" per the indemnification context can be discussed.

DGCL 145(c) requires a corporation to indemnify an officer/director who has been "successful on the merits." Waltuch was deeply involved in the manipulation of silver commodity futures. He was a defendant in both a government enforcement action and private suits by angry speculators. He incurred substantial legal fees with each: $1 million in fees with the CFTC which he paid a fine and was banned from the industry for 6 months and $1.2 million fees with the private suits from which he was dismissed as part of a $35 million settlement payment by his employer. Thus, what is the meaning of "successful on the merits?"?

Waltuch argued that he was "successful on the merits" in the private lawsuits, because he was dismissed from them, while Conti argues that Waltuch was only dismissed because Conti made a $35 million settlement payment. He prevailed on this part of the case. Note the strategic message here: always best to play with someone else's money, i.e. structure the settlement so that someone else, i.e., the corporate entity, contributes to the settlement but not the officer or director who later will seek indemnification. Under the indemnification contract that Waltuch had with Conti, he needed to avoid any adjudication of "negligence or misconduct." Thus, settle the case and have the company pay the settlement.

The other issue is whether he would be entitled to indemnification based on his employment contract which provided mandatory indemnification, except if Waltuch was "adjudged . . . to be liable." Note here the strong incentive to settle.

1.   Real purpose of studying Waltuch, and considering the subsequent note material, is 1) lawyers are deeply involved in drafting executive employment contracts for officers and directors. Some of what occurs in those contracts is in the shadow of the state indemnification procedures. Hence, we might wonder what does *Waltuch* allow you to do since it appears to strike down the avoidance of substantive limitations such as the "good faith" condition of DGCL 145(a)? Certainly you can tweak the procedures for making various determinations so that the manner for those determinations to be made can be broader and looser than set forth in the statute. Another area is to make advances of litigation costs mandatory. Advancement of costs is a hot area with a good deal of litigation. Note this likely does not fall on the "good faith" limitation since advances are made before there would have been any adjudication and anyone seeking an advancement is unlikely to stipulate, as Waltuch did in the case, that there conduct was not in good faith. Another reason to study *Waltuch* is to understand the strategy for settlements in government and private suits, namely not to take any steps in the settlement that makes life more difficult for the officer or director who will surely seek indemnification.

2. Waltuch avoids problems he confronted in the case if the insurance policy had covered his conduct. Presumably it did not or had been exhausted by the corporation's settlement. Hence, the empty coffers of the insurance policy likely drove his pursuit of indemnification under his employment contract.

3. The note material following the case includes further illustrations of courts denying indemnification for want of "good faith."

Section 9:   The Role of Corporate Counsel

Most students will be engaged in defending derivative suits than prosecuting them so some awareness of the conflicts in the defense of derivative suits will prove useful to them.

Bell Atlantic Corp. v. Bolger

Note there are two large issues, related, but distinct. First, whether the derivative suit corporation must have counsel separate from the real defendants. Second, regardless of how that question is resolved in the individual case, what defenses can the derivative suit corporation raise and what defenses to the suit can be raised only by the real defendants. *Bell Atlantic* addresses the first and from that we can speculate about the second. We might begin by asking why it matters to the plaintiff whether the same counsel represents the real defendants and the corporation? An easy answer is that there are conflicts at multiple stages of the suit. If the corporation is a beneficiary of the suit, should not it have an independent voice on whether to question the suit's continuance on procedural grounds, whether to settle, and more important what the contours of the settlement should look like (recall the lessons here of *Waltuch* and the importance to Waltuch to not contribute toward the settlement - meaning the Conti was a double loser-it paid all the settlement and therefore had to indemnify Waltuch, the true culprit of its travails). Regarding the second question, we should notice that since indemnification statutes, as seen in *Waltuch,* are not open ended, but rather have limitations on the corporation's power/obligation to indemnify its directors, officers and agents, allowing the corporation's counsel to carry the water on the suit's defense, particularly on substantive matters, invites a serious circumvention of the limits of the indemnification statute.

Nonetheless, *Bell Atlantic* reflects the mainstream view that separate counsel is not required when the suit is focused on manners of doing business (presumably this includes gouging the Pennsylvania phone customers) versus self-dealing type transaction. We might ask why this divide makes sense? Aren't the conflicts just as real in either case?

Students should be asked: if separate counsel is required, who gets new counsel? The answer invariably is the corporation, since the firm's traditional counsel will likely already have been advising and representing the real defendants (e.g., senior officers). Who then selects the counsel for the corporation? Who does that counsel advise? Not the real defendants. The best answer here is to create a subcommittee of the board to oversee the suit. If that is the case, then why not go the whole step and just create a special litigation committee? And, if one does have a special litigation committee, and believes there is a kernel, even a small one, of wisdom in the suit's allegations, then why would not the special litigation committee, through its counsel, not just settlement the claim? This leads to the next section of the materials, settlements.

Note on Problems Concerning the Law Governing Lawyers in Derivative Actions

Before heading off to settlements, it is useful to review who the client is in shareholder suits. For students bound to become litigators, and even transaction lawyers who will advise their clients on substantive matters that are privileged, a rich understanding of *Garner v. Wolfinbarger* in the note material is important. The case is widely followed, and holds that the attorney-client privilege is not a bar to derivative suit (and sometimes even class action suit) plaintiff obtaining corporate records related to the subject of the suit, provide good faith is established under a very long list of factors. The exception to this would be work product related to the derivative suit itself. On this point, the *Upjohn* decision reflects that work product includes intake interviews gathered in carrying out an internal investigation. Thus, work product would be beyond the scope of *Garner.* Just what is and what is not work product and when it must be shared is, as the note material points out, something over which the courts are divided.

Section 10: Settlement of Derivative Actions

Before a derivative action can be settled, court permission is required and notice must be given to all shareholders. *See e.g.,* FRCP 23.1. Courts tend to assess, before approving the settlement, whether it is "fair, reasonable, and adequate."

Clarke v. Greenberg

This brief case illustrates the issues that can arise in settlements whereby the narrow personal interests of the derivative suit plaintiff can be advanced by the settlement by dropping the corporate claim.

Background of the Purpose and Consequences of Court Approval of Settlements

Manufacturers Mutual Fire Ins. Co. v. Hopson illustrates the corruption of the corporate interests that could occur if judicial approval of a settlement was not required. Of special interest is the breadth of the settlement, illustrated by the facts of *Matsushita Electric Industrial Co. v. Epstein,* in which the Delaware Chancery Court's global settlement barred even federal securities law claims that could not be litigated before the settling court. Wow! And this all turned on the "adequacy" of the representation, which itself may give rise to how vigilant can a lawyer be expected to be for the interests of those who are not his own clients.

Desimone v. Industrial Bio-Text Laboratories, Inc.

This provides a laundry list of items to be considered in approving a settlement; While this is a thoughtful and customary list, we might wonder whether the breadth of the factors renders them too vacuous to be useful,

Background Note on Judicial Approval of Settlements

You may wish to assign either the Background Note or the excerpt from Macey & Miller. The message is fairly identical.

It is worth reviewing Henry Friendly's wise insight on the lack of an adversary process, when the settlement is before the court. Also, note here the troubling, but likely candid, insight from the settlement in *Warner Communications*. In combination, they suggest that settlement may well be the Achilles Heel of the representative suit. You might try drawing the students into this by asking what do we carry away from the note, and perhaps from that they may at least understanding that the strength of the trial depends on adversaries and an engaged judge. The note material suggests that these are absent when we forgo the trial and opt for settlement.

Macey and Miller Excerpt

Macey and Miller echo the insights of Henry Friendly and support the *Warner Communications* quote.

Note on Settlements Without the Plaintiff's Consent

Consider the issues raised in the note material in *Wolf v. Barkes* and *Clark v. Lomas & Nettleton*. In *Clark,* the corporation executed a release/settlement of the claim underlying the derivative suit. The Second Circuit held this was the prerogative of the corporation, and did not require approval by the derivative suit court since this was not a settlement of the suit. In *Clark,* the corporation sought to enter into a settlement of the suit over the plaintiff's objection. This was rejected by the Fifth Circuit on the grounds the directors acting for the corporation lacked independence. Minimally *Clark* illustrates that the court can, and should, look behind the settlement offer. But as the facts in the note point out, should it not also ask why the plaintiff is objecting (there appeared to be a not so well concealed private objective that the derivative suit plaintiff was pursuing, leverage for his individual claim). Thus, settlements of the suit challenge the presiding court who in an adversarial proceeding is dependent on the parties for the production of information by which its approval is dependent.

Section 11: Plaintiff's Counsel Fees

Tandycrafts, Inc. v. Initio Partners

No phrase is more important in the American legal system than that of "access to justice." We provide many ways for this to occur and they distinguish not just our legal system but our society. We reject the loser pay rule in favor of the American Rule. We provide class actions to allow small claims to be aggregated so that vindication of wrongs and restitution of harm can occur. We also permit contingency fee arrangements. Litigation would occur without these devices, but there would be much less of it. Each is important. But none more important than how we pay the engine that drives the suit, the class action and derivative suit entrepreneurial lawyer.

Tandycrafts is a very good case to illustrate the reason fees are not just awarded, but are assessed against the corporation. Students should first be asked whether this is a derivatives or class action suit. It was neither; it was an individual action but one that produced benefits to the shareholders of the company. It was the proof of this that supports the court requiring the corporation in a non-derivative suit context to pay plaintiff's counsel fee.

Note here no pot of money was created, so that the traditional salvage value approach was not available.

How are fees to be awarded to be determined? If a fund of money were created, we might assess a portion of the fund be paid to the suit's counsel. But no fund was created, so something akin to the Lodestar Approach, namely hours and costs sunk into the case with perhaps some multiplier greater than "1" to increase the award due to novelty, skill, complexity, and the like. Note here courts do still use the Lodestar approach, but more as a check or corroboration of the percentage of the benefits method.

The note material provides a rich tapestry of fee awards in the U.S. over time. We see here the conflicting moods and political forces that abound within the judiciary and American society as we grapple with whether there is truth to the rhetoric that we are a litigious society or one that believes in justice for all.

Sugarland Ind. Inc. v. Thomas

You may draw the students into this case by asking what justified the award of fees in this case? The plaintiffs engaged a lawyer to question the price the company's board of directors was considering for the sale of South Tract to White and Hill. Another bidder, offering a higher price arose, but the board remained committed to White and Hill. Suit was filed, the court ordered competitive (sealed) bidding, a higher price emerged as did offer to acquire other property, more sealed bids were ordered. Ultimately property was sold for $44 million. Now, how much credit should the plaintiff's lawyer get for this? They get a higher percentage for the increase of their first threats of suit ($23.8 to $27 million) and lower percentage of the gains after that including selling the other property.

Macey & Miller Excerpt

This provides a great pros and cons, mainly cons, of the loadstar versus percentage of recovery methods. Thus you can assign this material as background to discussing the pros and cons of each method for awarding fees.

We might add here that evidence from securities class action suits under the lead plaintiff provision reflect that institutional lead plaintiffs add value at least by negotiating ex ante fee arrangements with their counsel. Thus, we might believe a good approach for derivative suits is to incorporate a lead plaintiff type approach from securities laws.

Background Note on the Award of Counsel Fees to Successful Derivative-Action Plaintiffs

We see that the justification for award of fees has moved from the common fund/salvage value approach to compensating the private attorney general for the benefit conferred on the class, ala *Tandycraft, supra.*

The second part of the note provides the history on the lodestar approach. But as summarized in *Goodrich v. E.F. Hutton Group,* the very circuit that elevated the lodestar approach within a decade lowered its glimmering star by expressing a preference for the percentage of the fund approach.

Further Note on Plaintiff's Counsel Fees

We see that fees in the range of 30 percent of the recovered amount are the norm. We also must appreciate that there continues to be a role for the lodestar where, like in *Tandycraft, supra,* no fund is recovered but an ascertainable benefit was produced. But we need to be careful about these so-called therapeutic or governance settlements as they may be just mediums for letting the real defendants escape from the settlement by buying the plaintiff's lawyer off with an agreement not to oppose the fee request.

Section 12: Security for Expenses

West Hills Farms, Inc. v. RCO AG Credit, Inc.

Only a minority of the state statutes contain security for expense provisions that are applicable to derivative suits. Most are like the California provision interpreted here in that they permit fees to be recovered by the derivative suit defendants only to the extent security was posted. It is not, therefore, a pure loser pay rule. Indeed, loss of the suit does not cause fees to be automatically awarded to the derivative suit defendants. There is still a showing required by the statute for award from the security so posted.

Section 13. Private Ordering And Shareholder Suits

This is an area likely to expand, if not explode, before the next edition of this work appears. We appear to be in an era that loves private ordering and what better way than to choose the venue, and perhaps the forum, for disputes to resolved. Thus, can a California corporation identify not just that any dispute regarding internal affairs will be resolved in the Delaware Chancery Court? How about be subject to arbitration? How about according to the law of Delaware? Does it matter whether this provision is in the articles of incorporation or the bylaws, provided it is adopted by the shareholders? Can any of these occur via a bylaw adopted by the board of directors? Whether these are the right questions what is clear is that we don't know their answers.

Chapter 15

Corporate Combinations, Tender Offers and Defending Control

Chapter Overview: Over the past three decades, acquisition transactions have driven the events behind many of the decisions studied in the business organizations class. We have pondered whether the chapter devoted to acquisitions should appear earlier in the book, since an understanding of what is a merger vs. a tender, and even Unocal's demands, are the background for other areas studied (e.g., *Blasius*). We have decided, like so many choices in this book, to leave the decision as to the order of the material up to the individual instructor, so that we have chosen instead to take great care in this chapter, and particularly in other chapters, to make this and other chapters, as wells as every section within each chapter, modular so that the material can be arranged in any order that you find best for your course. Thus, this material can be taught earlier, indeed, as the first chapter, if that is your preference.

Because acquisitions are ubiquitous in the study and practice of business organizations, we allocate a fair amount of time to the area. We believe a minimum of 3 class hours could be justified, but we prefer much more, say 5-7 class hours, can be devoted to this chapter. There is a lot of material in this chapter and no class can, nor should it, cover all the material. You can pick and choose from the material, perhaps changing the selections year to year.

Section 1. Corporate Combinations

A. Sale of Substantially All Assets

Hollinger, Inc. v. Hollinger Int'l, Inc.

We begin by asking what is the issue here? Via super voting shares, Inc. holds a virtual veto (68% of the voting power) over any matter that comes to the International shareholders (although it holds just 18% of the equity). The issue here is whether the disposition of the *Telegraph* group triggers the rights of the International shareholder to vote under Delaware 271. Note here the facts get a bit messy in that as a technical matter the shareholder of the *Telegraph* Group is another corporation in the pyramid of ownership that persists within International. Strine side steps these niceties, concluding that even if we pierced the veil and ignored all the multiple levels of ownership that there would not be a vote 271.

We might ask why shareholders should have a vote at all, even if there was a sale of all the firm's assets? What makes us think they are competent to do this? Why not make all sales the prerogative of the board? We might try to pierce the language of 271, using the hypothetical whether a department store whose only asset is a downtown location. The store's management decides to liquidate its inventory, sell its fixtures, and sell its building needs a shareholder vote? Should it matter here why it is doing this? The answer to the latter is yes. If the company is moving its store to the "Burbs," believing that is a better location, then this looks like an ordinary business decision, which corporate law commends to the board of directors. Similarly, what if the company operates a small regional carrier, owning three planes that fly between Metro and Padooka. Because of declining traffic in February, it sells one of the three planes. In May, it sells another plane. And in August, it sells the last plane. A vote? When? Don't we need to know what it did with the proceeds? If it fulfilled the American Dream, using proceeds of each sale to acquire a McDonald's franchise, might we not believe that the company as evolved from an air carrier to an owner of McDonald franchises. Does the difference between evolution and revolution matter here? We might resolve each of these by asking whether the decision at hand appears to alter fundamentally the nature of the shareholder's investment, and do so quickly, and not in an evolutionary way. Thus, we do recognize that shareholders have the endowments to decide whether to invest in company A versus Company B. Hence, when a decision involves that kind of choice, do you want to liquidate the company or retain an interest in a department store company, this sounds like a matter that shareholders should be consulted. But if the question is where the company's store should be located, or how many square feet should be the size of the store, this does not look like an "investment" decision. It is more akin to the evolutionary decisions we find committed to the expertise of the board of directors.

Strine's opinion provides a great summary of the Delaware jurisprudence, and the notion of the vital character of the firm in terms of whether post disposition the firm retains qualitatively vital assets. We might probe what this means in light of the disposition of the *Telegraph* Group? Here we might contrast the language of Delaware § 271 with that of the MBCA § 12.02. Observe the innovation added by the MBCA regarding the safe harbor. You might also wish to pierce the distinctions made in the cases discussed in footnote 77, particularly the unique set of facts in *Katz*.

B. The Appraisal Remedy

Note on the Appraisal Remedy

The note material sets forth the history and varying scope of (some states apply in certain amendments to the articles) appraisal remedy. We also should observe that there are detailed procedures (an overview is set forth in the Unabridged edition) for the exercise of the appraisal remedy.

Note on Appraised Value: The Battling Experts

Bob Thompson's writings have documented that the appraisal remedy is resorted to largely in the self-interested acquisition setting. It is a remedy perhaps of desperation and frustration. Moreover, it can be expensive and uncertain. Professor Campbell provides terrific insight about the battling experts, and the likely reason that so many contrasting approaches to determining fair value is advance <u>by each side.</u> It is fun to speculate on the benefits that former Chancellor Allen saw in throwing out one side, rather than trying to cobble together a single approach from the different views of both sides. The strategic advantage of placing each side at risk that their input would be ignored is that this fear might draw them each closer to the center. Well, perhaps for baseball arbitrators, but the Delaware Supreme Court said no.

With respect to the "Delaware Block" method, which is still alive, how curious to attribute any weight to an untrustworthy figure, e.g., market price, as occurred in Piemonte. Note that the weight assigned to any one factor reflects two considerations, which may not have the same probabilities for each: how likely is that value will be realized via that method, e.g., liquidation versus going concern and how trustworthy is the estimated value.

Note on Discounts and Premiums in Appraisal Proceedings

The note sets the stage for the point that there is a difference between the value of the minority shares and the minority share in the firm. The former will, and should, embody a discount because of the threat of overreaching by the control person; the latter should not because the firm's value is unaltered by the composition of its ownership.

The note continues to the flip side as well, namely that firm with a dominant stockholder should not enjoy a premium over a firm without a dominant stockholder. This essentially is the complaint raised by Hammermesh, Wachter, Carney and Heimendinger with decisions such as *Rapid American.*

C. Statutory Mergers

To acquaint the students with the differences between types of acquisitions you may consider the following categories of information with respect to each manner of acquisition:

1. What assets and liabilities are transferred to survivor?

2. Does dissolution occur automatically with either company?

3. Approvals that are required

    a. which board

    b. which corporation's stockholders

4. Who gets appraisal

Experience has demonstrated that picking one statute, e.g., the MBCA, and working through the above is best initially. To do this in a comparative way, e.g., Delaware vs. MBCA as you move through it adds too many moving parts for the processing function of students. You likely will have a better experience if you go through the above with one statute. You can then double back to point out where another regime, e.g., Delaware, differs.

Some take away points from the above. With the merger form, items 1 and 2 transfer to the survivor by operation of law. This has the advantage over the purchase-sale structure where costly contracting and more costly changing of titles for all registered assets is involved. And, in some states, there is actually a transfer tax on assets involved in a purchase-sale, but not in a merger. However, with a merger, you get the dog with the fleas. All the assets and liabilities of the target firm are transferred by operation of law, so yikes for those contingent liability claims (e.g., environmental clean-up costs on Sludgeacre). Another point is that, in Delaware, there is no shareholder vote for the acquiring firm in all purchase-sale transactions, and the selling firm's shareholders get no appraisal. Hence in Delaware form matters, and a lot. Third, review of the philosophy of the small acquisition (less than 20 percent) takes us back to earlier discussions in *Hollinger* that in such a setting the acquisition (the survivor) looks like a normal business decision and can be for this reason commended to the board alone. Finally, you might consider introducing here the triangular merger material, where in Delaware this is a means to cut off a vote of the acquiring shareholders. This works not at all in the MBCA, if the consideration to be issued by the survivor triggers the shareholders vote under MBCA § 621(f) by increasing the outstanding shares by more than 20 percent.

If you choose not to assign *Terry v. Penn Central Corp.*, *infra*, you likely should assign in connection with the material in Section C the Note on Triangular Mergers and Share Exchanges.

D. Tax Aspects of Corporate Combinations

We suspect most choose not to cover this material. It can be assigned and briefly covered in light that tax considerations are always at least in the background for these transactions. The point is that tax free means that the acquiring firm obtains the carry-over basis on the acquired assets, and that shares exchanged for other shares give rise to no taxation for the seller. This is good news for the acquired shareholders, and less good news for the acquiring firm, since it likely paid a premium for the target and it would prefer to have, on its tax return, a stepped up basis to depreciate (for GAAP it is not tax free so the acquiring firm gets hammered with higher depreciation on the acquired assets).

E. The Stock Modes and the De Facto Merger Theory

This material has a single purpose: to illustrate different acquisition techniques. There has not been a de facto merger case in the U.S. for four decades. That doctrine is as a judicial principle is dead! It is, however, very much alive in the scheme of corporate statutes, e.g., California and the MBCA, where procedural differences that once existed between forms of transactions have consciously been removed in large measure by the codes' drafters.

Hariton v. Arco Electronics, Inc.

This classic case illustrates, in bold relief, an important doctrine of at least Delaware corporate law, but we find it elsewhere as well, the doctrine of independent legal significance. Delaware views the statute as a buffet of choices available to managers doing deals. These choices come with different procedural requirements and substantive limitations. The fact that some procedures apply to, e.g., mergers, but not to another, e.g., purchase of assets, does not mean that the gloss of the former will be applied to the latter, or vice versa.

Hence, the structuring of the acquisition as a purchase by Loral of Arco, and the contractual requirement that Arco thereafter dissolve and distribute the Loral common received as consideration of the its sale of all its assets (and the other consideration being Loral's assumption of Arco's debts), was not viewed by the court as merger. Had it been so viewed, the Arco shareholders would have an appraisal remedy, or more importantly in this case, entitled to notice of an appraisal remedy. Note here what the suit is about. The plaintiff first attacks the transaction for 1) unfair price and 2) failure to include notice of appraisal (arguing this was a merger in fact, i.e., de facto merger –this is why you took Latin in high school). The plaintiff drops the unfairness claim, and sticks with the nuisance/notice claim, arguing that they failed to give the right kind of notice to carry out this transaction. Thus, while generally it is much easier to raise procedural gaffs, than substantive claims of unfairness, it did not work here, because of the doctrine of independent legal significance.

Note on Another Approach: Rath v. Rath Packing Co.

The difference introduced here is that the Iowa Supreme court eschews the doctrine of independent legal significance and opts to read the statutes in pari materia so that the more specific applies to the more general. As a result, the recapitalization that was being carried out via multiple steps within the amendment of the articles was subjected to the two-thirds approval requirement that applied to merges. We might ask whether the uncertainty introduced by this approach is harmful, and if so, are the off-setting benefits of the uncertainty nonetheless worth that price?

Note on Heilbrunn v. Sun Chemical Corp.

Heilbrunn laid the ground work for *Hariton,* rejecting, on the basis of the doctrine of independent legal significance, the right of the purchasing firm's shareholders to an appraisal because the transaction yielded the same effects as a merger. So, form matters, but bear in mind that the earlier discussion showed that there is a legal difference in the acquisition of assets and liabilities between a acquisition carried out as a merger and an acquisition carried out as a purchase-sale (with the latter requiring much more effort regarding transfer of assets).

Farris v. Glen Alden Corp.

This classic case is a natural sequel to *Hariton*. It also is a great case to introduce how abuses in acquisitions can occur. You may wish to pull the rabbit out of the hat, the second point referred to about the case, after discussing the more straightforward portions of the case.

First, students should be asked to verbalize how this differs from *Hariton*? The court is unpersuaded by the doctrine of independent legal significance, and concludes that the transactions must be seen for its substance and not its form. This is not a sale by List, but really a sale by Glen Alden. The court emphasizes that the legislature appears to have provided that, when one company purchases the other "without more," the acquirer in a purchase structure (as contrasted with a merger structure) do not have appraisal rights. First the court concludes that there was more here: dissolution, assumption of liabilities and a transfer of executives from the seller to the buyer. Second, and perhaps equally, if not more, important, was that this was an upside down sale, i.e., the agreement structured the transaction so that the minnow swallowed the whale. Aha, but why should this matter?

Note that many of the considerations earlier emphasized by the court are not all that persuasive: after the transaction, the Glenn Alden shareholders will own shares in a larger company and one more diverse. Da, that is true for any combination of companies. What is telling is that the size differences between the two companies as well as the difference in book value for the Glen Alden shareholders after the exchange. These factors suggest that the deal might not be arm's length; worse, was a deal purposely structured to the disadvantage of the Glen Alden shareholders. But how could this happen? Now the rabbit comes out of the hat!

The first footnote to the case reveals that this is a bootstrap acquisition, where List borrowed the money to acquire its 38.5 percent stake in the firm. It then had three (out of how many?) of its people on the board. Once the acquisition is completed, the Glen Alden assets can be used to satisfy the loan. List appears to have twisted the transaction around to make the much smaller Glen Alden the purchaser. This is a good case to say the Glen Alden shareholders needed some mechanism for an independent determination of the value of their shares. Ta da, enter the appraisal remedy which comes with the court's holding.

Note the Pennsylvania statute now makes it even clearer that the de facto merger doctrine is dead in that state. Also the note reflects that there appears to have been some legitimate reasons for List placing itself as the seller.

Note on the Survivor's Liability to the Transferor's Creditors

Disgruntled stockholders are not the only ones that seek to invoke the de facto merger doctrine. Creditors from time-to-time try their hand to go after the successor company when the deal has been structured as a purchase. They meet with little success, save in the states that see this area as a matter of a products liability issue and not a corporate law issue. This reasoning is set forth in the quote from *Ray v. Alad Corp.* in the Unabridged edition.

F. Triangular Mergers and Share Exchanges

Share exchanges do not occur all that frequently. The procedure is authorized in most modern statutes, and it there should the parties wish to use this mechanism. Triangular mergers do occur frequently. The next case can be easily be omitted or substituted for *Farris*; since the de facto merger doctrine is moribund so that covering both *Terry* and *Farris* would likely be overkill. Of the two cases, *Farris* is likely to be of greater interest to the class.

Terry v. Penn Central Corp.

Plaintiffs seek declaratory relief that as holders of Penn Central they are entitled to a vote and appraisal on acquisitions that Penn Central plans to engage to as to harvest the large tax loss carried over from its colossal bankruptcy. Like Glenn Alden in *Farris v. Glenn Alden*, Penn Central is, true to its name, a Pennsylvania corporation. The key word in the statutory scheme was whether Penn Central was a "party" to the transaction between its wholly owned shell subsidiary and the third party target of the acquisition. The court refused to give "party" an expansive reading, except if the facts were like those in *Farris*, where, in footnote 7, the third party target was much larger than Penn Central. The Third Circuit appears to believe that the de facto merger doctrine is to be invoked when there is some evidence of overreaching, fraud or other abuse. Here the acquisitions were, unlike *Farris*, between strangers.

G. Freezeouts

Note on Freezeout Techniques

The introductory note material need not be covered, but can be assigned as background. What you might wish to do is ask which of the following paradigms should, as a matter of public policy, a court be most willing to take jurisdiction for the purpose of providing complaining shareholders with an independent forum to determine if they are being treated unfairly?

A. Alpha and Beta in an arms-length transaction agree to merger where Beta will be acquired and its shareholders will receive $21 per share.

B. Alpha acquired 50.5 percent of Beta through a cash tender offer paying $21 per share. Three years later, Alpha and Beta are to merge, whereby Beta will be acquired and its shareholders will receive $21 per share. At both the time of Alpha's initial acquisition of Beta shares and the proposed merger of Alpha and Beta the Beta shares traded on the NYSE at $14 per share.

C. In January, Alpha acquired 50.5 percent of Beta through a cash tender offer paying $21 per share, disclosing that if it acquired control of Beta it would soon follow up with a "clean up" merger at the same price. In late February, Alpha and Beta agree to merge whereby Beta will be acquired and its shareholders will receive $21 per share. At both the time of Alpha's initial acquisition of Beta shares the Beta shares traded on the NYSE at $14 per share.

We should agree that the situation with the greatest chance for abuse is B, since how do we know that the price of Beta shares on the NYSE reflects the intrinsic value of the Beta shares, and even more broadly based unlike A and C this is a clear self dealing transaction where we normally place on the fiduciary the duty of proving entire fairness. A and C are similar to each other. The A transaction is guided by the majority vote of the approving B shareholders. In a sense this is what occurred in C, where a majority of the shares were tendered in a non coercive tender offer. Thus, there is much less cause for judicial scrutiny in C than in A.

Note here that *Weinberger* is fact situation B. We should also note that the allegations in fact situation B are the type that in Chapter 11, per *Sinclair Oil v. Levien,* would be deemed self dealing (allegations that unfair price means an exclusive benefit to Alpha and a corresponding detriment to the minority holders). In this sense, *Weinberger* is old wine in a new bottle.

A side question is why isn't appraisal, if available, that forum? The short answer is that, with appraisal, the shareholders receive only their fair share of Beta. If a breach of controlling stockholder fiduciary duty action is brought, and the acquisition involves synergies, then recovery would be based on a fair sharing in the synergies as well as the value of Beta. Equally important, class action procedures are not part of the appraisal process (recall the individual steps that need to be taken to get to appraisal-and many of the minority shareholders might not have pursued these steps).

Weinberger v. UOP, Inc.

Good place to begin here is to make sure the students understand the facts. If you use the Alpha-Beta trilogy set forth above then filling in the facts around transaction sequel B is one way to do this.

Next, to reiterate the Alpha-Beta sequel B, what does this case have in common with the earlier covered case, *Sinclair Oil Co. v. Levien*? Both are self dealing. This leads to how this is self dealing, namely that Signal owned a bare majority of UOP, controlled the board, and engineered this transaction.

The next step you might follow is what steps did Signal (likely on the advice of its lawyers) take to overcome or address this obvious conflict of interest. First, they got an outside investment banker's opinion. Second, they had the Signal directors exit the UOP board meeting to let the non-Signal directors consider the deal. Third, the transaction was conditioned on a minority plebiscite. Why didn't these work to address the problem?

The investment bankers were sloppy. And, do we know this was a banker that did not have on-going ties with Signal? The blessing of the non-signal directors was believed without much force, since they were not aware of the Arledge and Chitea (those names!) report dealing with the minimal impact a substantially higher price would have had on Signals return on investment calculations. And, the minority plebiscite failed because the vote was not believed sufficiently informed, e.g., did not have the Arledge and Chitea information.

Going forward, does this mean that the controlling stockholder is always to be required to disclose its secret calculations? Hardly. First, this report was prepared by Signal officers who were also UOP directors. Thus, they had a fiduciary duty to inform their fellow UOP directors what they knew about the transaction, but such disclosure would conflict with their duty to Signal as Signal officers. The point is that they were not strangers to UOP, but fiduciaries, and their breach of disclosure tainted the independent director and shareholder approval. Second, the suggestion in note 7 is a template how to address this going forward: the independent negotiating committee.

What does the court say about the purpose test?

And, is the Delaware Block Method dead? No, just weakened as the court wisely opens up fair value determinations to any reasonably based system.

So going forward, what is the effect of *Weinberger?* The opinion puts a large "bulls eye" on self-dealing acquisitions, so that in such transactions the controlling stockholder is faced with the burden of proving entire fairness. This has two dimensions, each evolving and case specific: fair dealing and fair price. The latter really seeks some evidence that the price is in the zone of reasonableness. Fair dealing invites questions into procedures, such as the process by which the price was determined, the independence of that process including the advisors used, and most importantly did the outside directors provide a substantive and observable role consistent with independent bargaining.

Note on Substitutes, Opportunism and the Purpose Test

What was wrong with Coggin's purpose? He undertook the freezeout of the minority holders as a condition of getting the loan with which he acquired control. The loan was a personal loan, not one to the company, and hence the freezeout was for personal and not corporate purposes. The purpose that must be justified relates to the acquisition, and does not require an explanation why the minority are getting cash rather than a continuing equity interest. However, requiring an explanation for giving the minority cash rather than equity in the survivor would strike many as more demanding and meaningful.

Here we might want to consider just what is the harm of cashing someone out? One thought is that a cash out visits transaction costs on the cashed out shareholders. First, this is a taxable transaction so that if there is a gain on the shares there is a capital gains tax to pay. This deprives the shareholder of timing when s/he wishes to realize the gain (e.g., stepped up basis and large exemption from estate tax when die). Second, if the investor seeks a substitute, then there are search and brokerage costs. While each might be small, they are costs that the majority visits upon the minority. Second, how do we know the cash out is not timed at a moment that is most opportune for the majority. That is, we might think of cash outs as just a very large form of insider trading given the information asymmetries between the controlling stockholder and to be frozen out minority.

Corporations and Other Business Organizations

Glassman v. Unocal Exploration Corp.

The trilogy of *Glassman*, *Solomon* and *Pure Resources* are joined at the hip and should be assigned as a block; you can discuss each in the context of *Pure Resources* so that *Glassman* and *Solomon* are essentially background to *Pure Resources*.

Unocal proceeds on the assumption that *Weinberger* would apply to the short-form merger cashing out the minority. True to what has happened before this transaction, with numerous suits invoking *Weinberger* being filed upon announcement of a short-form merger, Unocal proceeded as though *Weinberger* applied. The complaint focused on whether the advisors and the committee were sufficiently diligent and independent. This is why, in deals in Delaware it is widely understood that money is kept aside to buy piece, via a very modest settlement.

The court reaches the sensible conclusion that the legislature's express authorization for a 90% holder to cash out the minority removes *Weinberger*.

Solomon v. Pathe

A tender offer by a dominant stockholder that gives it sufficient voting power to carry out a short-form merger is not subject to the *Weinberger's* entire fairness standard. Note here that the controlling stockholder was preparing itself for a *Weinberger* inquiry by assuring that subsidiary form a special committee to bless the transaction.

Students might be asked what justifies the exception? The idea is that the tender offer itself was voluntary with the individual shareholders. There was no alleged coercion or lack of disclosure.

In re Pure Resources Inc. Shareholder Litigation

So what is new here? Strine observes that tender offers are inherently coercive, due to the collective action problem among targeted shareholders. He points out the odd state that a cash out by a 51 percent holder is subject to *Weinberger* but if that holder can induce enough shareholders to raise its stake to at least 90 percent, it can then cash out the minority per *Glassman* without fear of *Weinberger*. And, *Solomon* suggests you can move from that 51 percent level to 90 percent level, outside of *Weinberger* too. Strine moves to square the circle.

Thus, to assure that the tender offer is not coercive, it needs to be one that is conditioned on an independent majority acceptance of the minority shares. This (likely later at the end of discussing the rest of Strine's formulation) failed in *Pure,* because the group defined into the denominator included company executives who were not independent. Second, there must be in that tender offer an undertaking to carry out the short-form merger at the same price in a short time. Third, there must not be any other coercion or retribution (e.g., if we fail, we will nonetheless seek to delist the shares or opt out of the SEC reporting requirements).

230

Note on "Going Dark"

Distinction between going private and going dark is worth emphasizing. Why might investors worry about a firm going dark? Recall the weak reporting standards of state law, discussed earlier in Chapter 6. Investors likely wish more than an annual financial statement. Also, their liquidity essentially disappears if the firm goes dark.

In discussing the material on Rule 13e-3, note the exception not only complements *Pure Resources* regarding the effects of a cash out merger within a short time (one year under Rule 13e-3), but also complements the earlier Alpha-Beta C sequel. What is the purpose of these disclosures? Well, if you fudge, you've invited a Rule 10b-5 suit. This likely has some disciplining effect, i.e., less likely to say the deal is fair if it is really not fair and you have to explain why it is fair.

Section 2.   Hostile Takeovers and Defending Control

The Lexicon of the Battle for Control

Expressions you might wish to refer to before beginning the cases are Raider, White Knight, Junk Bonds and Standstill. (Leverage and Poison Pills can be discussed later in *Revlon*)

Note on the Williams Act

Place to begin is section 13(d). What does it require and what must be disclosed and when. Contrast the when with section 14(d). From there you might wish to ponder what is the purpose of disclosure? Consider that, in connection with my cash above market offer for any and all shares the bidder discloses that that over three year average it had double earnings of companies acquired; or reverse, the bidder discloses it's a looter and offering just a modest premium for any and all shares? What disclosure is missing in each of these that investors need to determine whether to accept the bid? It is whether I will succeed in gaining control. In the first, if you knew I would fail, then you should tender your shares; if you knew I would succeed, you'd retain the shares. Similarly, in the second/looter case, you would tender if you thought I would be successful, but a modest premium would not be attractive in light of transaction costs if you thought I would not be successful.

You might wish to move to some of the other rules of engagement by asking what is the purpose that maybe links the following together:

Rule 14e-1 (duration)

Rule 14d-7 (withdrawal rights throughout duration)

Rule 14d-8 (proration)

Rule 14d-10 (best price)

One linkage of these rules is that of facilitating an auction. We wish the offer to stay open a reasonable period of time so competing bidders can enter, we allow broad withdrawal so if you accept on offer it does not lock up shares from a competing offer (which would discourage a competing bidder), and we would like shareholders to be patient and not jump on offers (their patience may be in seeing if other bids are forthcoming) so the proration and best price rules apply.

Tender offer definition is worth exploring. The reason for looking at this is to avoid the trap that is illustrated in *Field v. Trump*.

Finally, review the language in the first sentence of section 14(e). Have we seen something like this before? It is very similar to Rule 10b-5, sans a purchaser-seller requirement. Note that section 14(e) is not like section 10(b) as it has a fraud prohibition as well as broad enabling authority.

Unocal Corp. v. Mesa Petroleum Co.

To begin the discussion, students might be asked, what *Unocal* adds to the body of law we've covered thus far in the class. The case is the bedrock in Delaware and half the jurisdictions that have considered the question of how do we judge the propriety of a board's defense to another's effort to take over the firm.

Why did the Unocal board resist Mesa's efforts to acquire control of Unocal? The board argued Mesa's offer was unfair and coercive. What facts supported each of these claims? The coercion was on the face of the offer; $54 cash was offered for the shares needed to lift Mesa to a controlling stockholder. It was then going to cash out the minority a la *Weinberger* with "subordinated debt." Students might be asked what that expression means? It is more colloquially referred to as junk bonds and reflects the highly risky nature of the debt. So, why does this make the cash offer coercive? And what supports the view that $54 was an inadequate price? This was supported by the views of the investment bankers advising the board.

So, what are the chances the lawyers' advising the board were students of *Smith v. Van Gorkom*? Think of all the things this board did in reaching its defensive strategy that is just the opposite of what the board failed to do in *Smith*. First, they had two investment bankers advising the board. Second, their meeting lasted 9 and one-half hours, before adjourning for further consideration. And, the facts reveal they considered multiple strategies to address the Mesa offering (hence the length of the meeting).

What was the defensive measure and why was it effective? Hard to justify in your mind accepting $54, when you can sell them for $72.

Does the court assess this step through the lens of the business judgment rule? No, it introduces several major differences which should occupy the rest of the time discussing the case. In level one, the board has the burden of proving that it had, after reasonable investigation, a reasonable ground to believe that the offer posed a threat (coercion and unfair price here). Notice the burden is placed on the board. Why? Because as the court points out there is the omnipresent concern that the directors, both inside and outside, are acting to preserve their positions and allied perquisites.

How was this first level of *Unocal* satisfied? This relates back to the earlier question about how the lawyers advising on the defensive steps were students of *Smith*.

What is introduced in IV B? This is the second level of *Unocal,* which gets modified in *Unitrin,* infra. It requires that the defensive maneuver be reasonable in relation to the threat. So, how was that met here? Given that the threat was unfair price and coercion, hard not to see that offering the Unocal shareholders a choice of a higher price is not a response to each of these threats. How does the court justify excluding Mesa as being reasonable in relation to the threat? Court reasons, in part, that the threat was to the non-Mesa shareholders so no need to include Mesa to address that threat. Second, the court observed that including Mesa would provide funds with which Mesa could then continue its coercive, unfair offer. Thus, we see that if there is a purpose for non-pro rata treatment the law of Delaware allows different treatment across stockholders.

Note that Rule 14d-10, the all holders rule, now prevents exclusion of the bidder or anyone else from the tender offer.

Note on Unitrin, Inc. v. American General Corp.

How does *Unitrin* qualify *Unocal*? Whereas *Unocal's* second step appears to invite a close inspection of the relationship between the threat and the defensive maneuver, *Unitrin* instead appears to take a more compartmentalized approach. The first part of *Unitrin* asks whether the defensive measure is draconian, defined to be either coercive or preclusive. If it is neither, then the final inquiry is whether the defensive measure is "within the range of reasonableness." The latter does not appear to call for gauging the defense by the magnitude of the threat posed.

Just what was the defensive measure in *Unitrin*? The board undertook a buyback program with no intention of the insider selling any of their shares. The company's articles conditioned any merger with an interested party on obtaining 75 percent approval. The company insiders/directors collectively owned 23 percent before the buyback. Hence, the complaint was that this would be preclusive if the effect of the buyback was to lift the insiders/directors' ownership to greater than 25 percent. This appears to be how the Chancellor saw the question, as he granted a preliminary injunction, on the ground that the repurchase was not reasonable to the threat, since it was unnecessary given the high percentage ownership of the insiders/directors. The Supreme Court remanded so the Chancellor could consider the new formulation of the second step of *Unocal*. We might question whether the 3 factors set out near the end of the excerpt have much to do with preclusion or coercion as the Supreme Court appears to believe they do.

At several later locations, the topics of preclusion and coercion are more closely examined in the materials.

Moran v. Household International, Inc.

By way of introduction to the four pill cases, you might consider assigning the most recent, *Air Products,* which provides a nice discussion of preclusion and coercion as well as the more current issue with pills, namely their joinder with classified boards.

Regardless of where you decide to start, the subject that likely will require attention is just what is a pill. You can base this on the description of pills in the earlier Lexicon of the Battle for Control, supra). In bold relief, pills have really three features: the trigger, the catastrophic event, and redemption feature. The trigger is set forth as to what level of ownership or bid activates the catastrophic event. This is expressed as a percentage of ownership; historically it was in the 15-20 percent range but a more recent pill set it as low as 5 percent. If the trigger occurs, then the doomsday machine becomes engaged and cannot be stopped. This refers to the financially catastrophic event. Classic versions are the flip in right, which allows holders the option to convert their shares into short-term promissory notes of the issuer. One common conversion is for every $100 of value for the shares a note of $200 will be issued. The flip over right addresses the exchange ratio to be applied, if there is any merger or other transaction between the party activating the trigger (the "interested party"). This also is commonly expressed as providing not less than giving $200 of value in securities for each $100 given up by a target shareholder. Thus, the route to a takeover is to convince the board to redeem the pill; pills usually provide they can be repurchased by their issuer for some nominal amount, e.g., $0.05/right. Note that what the pill does is transform the tender offer mechanism for gaining control of a target into having to be a friendly deal, much along the lines of what was seen earlier was a requirement for a merger or purchase-sale transaction.

Moran v. Household International, Inc.

Moran continues to be historically important. It holds that a corporation's board of directors could validly adopt a "shareholder rights plan" – more colloquially, a poison pill. In issuing the shareholder rights, Household's board invoked the authority it enjoyed under the so-called "blank stock" authorization, by which in Delaware (Del. Gen. Corp L. § 157) and most states permit the articles of incorporation to contain a provision that empowers the board of directors to issue shares, rights and options with such rights, privileges and preferences as the board may from time to time establish. To the complaint that the rights plan usurped the shareholders' rights to receive tender offers by changing Household's fundamental structure, the court observed:

> There is little change in the governance structure as a result of the adoption of the Rights Plan. The Board does not now have unfettered discretion in refusing to redeem the Rights. The Board has no more discretion in refusing to redeem the Rights than it does in enacting any defensive mechanism.

Thus, *Unocal's* focus is not on the adoption, but whether the board acts properly in its decision not to redeem the pill. That is, the pill kicks the *Unocal* moment down the road to when there is an active suitor.

Note on Carmody v. Toll Brothers, Inc.

Pills provide important protection against unwanted suitors, but there is always the opportunity for the unwanted suitor to undertake a proxy contest to change the composition of the target board so that the pill will be redeemed. To this possibility, lawyers have been very innovative in their quest to make their client's pill bullet proof. The "dead hand" provision of a poison pill is one such innovation; it provides that the rights plan cannot be redeemed except by the incumbent directors who adopted the plan or were their designated successors. The dead hand provision seeks to reduce one obvious route for an unwanted suitor to ultimately overcome the pill: through a successful proxy contest install its nominees as the new majority of the target board who would then redeem the pill and do the deal. In *Carmody*, then Vice-Chancellor Jacobs declared the dead-hand pill invalid under Delaware law, on several grounds listed in the note. Of interest is that he did not find the pill preclusive, which could be argued since that appears to be the clear intent of the dead hand pill.

Quickturn Design Systems, Inc. v. Shapiro

Somewhat of a sequel to the dead-hand bill is the delayed redemption provision, which provides that if a majority of the directors are replaced by stockholder action, the newly elected board cannot redeem the rights for six months, if the purpose or effect of the redemption is to facilitate a transaction with an "interested person." The court holds that the delayed redemption provision is invalid under Delaware law. It does so, again not on the bases embraced in *Unitrin* – preclusive, coercive or beyond the range of reasonableness. Rather on fundamental corporate principles that the discretion of directors to discharge their board responsibilities cannot be contractually constrained. Observe that while the severable delayed redemption provision is invalid, the pill remains in place. Thus, Mentor wins only if successful in displacing a majority of the Quickturn board. This then sets the stage for considering whether taking this step, namely changing the board's composition, is where the real bulwark for the pill resides. The note material in the following *Quickturn* underscores the force of a classified board when coupled with a pill.

Air Products and Chemicals, Inc. v. Airgas, Inc.

To begin the discussion, we might ask how did Air Products try to overcome the pill? It was successful in launching a proxy contest and placing its three nominees on Air Gas' board. Why did this not work? They were indeed independent, maybe too independent at that, as they quickly joined the other six directors in deciding not to redeem the pill in the face of what they too concluded was an unfair price.

What other options were available to Air Products? It could invoke the rights in the articles to call a special meeting and with a two-thirds vote remove the entire board. Why is the court considering something that Air Products has decided not to do? This goes to the broad charge by Air Products that the pill joined with the classified board is preclusive. Whether it is preclusive in part depends on whether there are options to get around it. One option, remove the entire board. This the court concludes is, to be sure, a long shot but are the odds so slight that within the governing test, "realistically attainable" (borrowed in part from *Unitrin,* supra) it would be vulnerable. While the experts weighed in on this, neither satisfied the court. Why? They stuck to their knitting and did not canvass any of the Air Gas shareholders to see what would move the needle. The court was left with was testimony that, if a high enough price were offered, the shareholders would remove the board. That satisfied the court that the avenue of removing the entire board was "realistically attainable."

The court also dealt with another feature of the preclusivity-staggered board argument, reasoning that, yes, the staggered board did delay the moment when a bidder could wrest control of the board (two successive elections and after the prior Supreme Court decision, the second would have to be about a year after the first [see editor's note 1). But delay and making things more difficult are not the same as being preclusive. After all, as the Chancellor points out, that is what the pill is designed to do and the Supreme Court in *Moran* embraced the pill as legitimate defensive device. Thus, Air Products in some sense was hoisted by its own petard. It sought to change the board's composition. It got its three independent nominees elected. Transparently, it now sees that the only way to change its fortune is to raise substantially its bid or go through another couple rounds of nominating and electing less independent directors than in its first proxy contest, and finds neither of these attractive. This is not an appealing argument to persuade a skeptical Chancellor, and one bounded by fairly strong precedent, that is not supportive of Air Products.

The conclusion is revealing. There cannot be "just say never." But the court does recognize that the primacy of the board in this area to study and reflect on the manner, even if that is a staggered board.

The situation raised in dicta by Strine in *Yucaipa* is worth discussing. What separates that case from this? It is that the newly elected nominees of Air Products found, well not Jesus, but what the fair price had to be. If the facts were otherwise, what is Strine suggesting? It appears to be that a plebiscite has occurred with the election of the new directors, and once there, they had a full information package before them and could then continue to believe their patron, the bidder, was offering a fair price. In this context, refusal to redeem the pill looks different. All that redemption does is it allows the shareholders to decide whether to accept the offer.

In the note following the case, in the Unabridged edition, is the question whether there is an inconsistency in courts upholding bylaws that call on the board to remove the pill, when those resolutions or bylaws do not contain a fiduciary out clause Recall here CA Inc. calling, for on the board to reimburse successful insurgents but not subject to a fiduciary out? Is the case for the necessity of a fiduciary out clause stronger I the latter than the former?

Revlon, Inc. v. MacAndrews & Forbes Holdings, Inc.

You might wish to review each of the defensive steps and why they were defensive taken by Revlon:

1. Repurchase of shares = get the low hanging fruit, the remaining shares, although fewer in number will be needed to acquire control will with the upward sloping supply curve come at a higher price.

2. The issuance of a poison pill. So, if you did not cover pills in the material preceding this case, this is the moment to cover the trigger, catastrophic effect, and redemption features standard to pills. The pill here provides a concrete basis for discussing these features. Notice here that the rights were eventually redeemed by the Revlon board.

3. Repurchase of an additional 10 million shares. This purchase was via notes that had covenants that would make it impossible for a leveraged buyout to occur absent waiver of the not covenants. The Revlon board had the power to waive the covenants.

4. The board at the September 24th meeting authorized Revlon's management to seek a White Knight.

Why did Revlon's management prefer Forstmann to Pantry Pride? We could say the offer was higher. Initially this was because Forstmann was going to include the senior Revlon management in its purchase group; their equity investment would be from their golden parachutes.

Why did the note holders threaten to sue once the deal with Forstmann was announced? They lost significant value due to waiver of the covenants. Why? This was to be an LBO and this means their debt, combined with the new debt that would come from the Forstmann deal, would make the firm top heavy with debt, thus changing the risk of the earlier issued notes. What is the basis for their threat? It is that when the notes were issued for their shares (a purchase and sale of a security in connection with the misrepresentation, ala Rule 10b-5) they failed to disclose the intent to waive the covenants to entice a White Knight.

What then happened? Forstmann agreed to support the note's face value (thus protecting the Revlon directors from a securities fraud action), and to eliminate the clear appearance (if not fact) of self-interest to remove the Revlon management from participation in the special purpose vehicle set up to acquire Revlon. In exchange what did Forstmann get? A lock up-good to review what makes a lock up a deal protection measure.

So how is the analysis in Parts II A-C different from what happens after those three opening parts of Part II? The analysis starts out as vintage *Unocal* and the court easily finds that the board is armed with expert opinion that Pantry Pride's offer was inadequate.

The innovation of *Revlon* appears in IID as developed in III. This is the famous Revlon moment, meaning at some point the enhanced scrutiny shifts, from focusing on whether there was a ground for believing there was a threat such that actions could be taken to defend the firm to enhanced scrutiny, to whether the directors acted reasonably in obtaining the best offer for the firm. *Revlon* itself places this moment when the price got to the level, "in the mid 50 dollar range," at which the firm would have to be dismembered to fetch an even higher price. Over the years, as the following note material reflects, the court has grappled with what is the *Revlon* moment. With the benefit of hindsight, and in a burst of reconstructive history, we can say here that the Revlon directors were in the *Revlon* moment when they first supported a cash offer for the firm from Terry Forstmann, because it would thereafter mean that the offer they supported would be the last opportunity for the Revlon shareholders to share in a premium for control of Revlon.

So, what is the consequence of being in the Revlon moment? It meant that the lock up option granted Forstmann, because it stopped bidding <u>and</u> did not elicit a significantly higher bid from Forstmann was in violation of the Revlon directors' fiduciary duties.

Does this mean that a lock up is per se inconsistent with Revlon? Not at all. As the court points out, it may be the means to attract a new bidder or to extract a significantly higher bid from an existing bidder. It did neither in this case.

Paramount Communications, Inc. v. Time Inc.

This is a watershed case. After a factual development, particularly that Time had a strategic plan that led it to Warner, the following questions can be asked.

1. What was the defensive maneuver? The deal originally was based on Time purchasing Warner in an all stock deal. They changed the deal to a blended (cash and stock) deal. They tried to get relief from the NYSE rule that conditioned issuance of additional shares on there being a shareholder vote, i.e., this is not a matter determined by Delaware law but rather listing governance provisions of the NYSE. The NYSE refused to give them any relief. Thus, Time was forced to borrow a lot of money to do the deal. By the way, which was the larger firm? Why was the minnow swallowing the whale? This went to the preservation of journalistic quality (remember Time publishes many items, including Mad Magazine!) and thus the governance structure which was long holding up the deal worked best if Time were the acquiring company. Roughly after the deal Warner shareholders would own 62 percent of the combined company meaning it was about twice the size of Time.

2. Why? Paramount launched an all cash deal for Time, first at $175 and later raised to $200. Why did this upset the apple cart? Before Paramount's offer the deal for the Time shareholders was being priced at $126 in the market. Hmmm, $126 or $200, boy math is tough!

3. What was the threat? Was it low price? Coercion? What is significant about the case is that the threat was recognized to include a host of business considerations all point toward what

would be the best fit. Equally important, the court held that this is something it would not intrude by compelling the matter to be submitted to the shareholders.

4. So, what were those threats? First, the belief that the time culture would be better protected with the combination on the terms arranged with Warner. Second, that the Paramount offer was disruptive, coming in the throes of the proxy solicitation by Time so that the shareholders would be confused (estimates are that well over 95 percent of the Time shares were then held by arbitrageurs who were hardly confused about what was in their best interests, more money). And, the record supported the view that Time had considered a lot of options, including Paramount, and decided that the combination with Warner was best. Thus, business judgment considerations can support the threat, even under the heightened *Unocal* standard of review.

5. What result if *Revlon* had applied? Best offer was clearly Paramount's all cash deal of $200. But the court held *Revlon* did not apply. The Chancellor held that *Revlon* did not apply because there was no change of control; after the deal Time assets and Time shareholders would remain part of a larger "amorphous" group of shareholders and assets. The Supreme Court affirmed, reviewing some spotty case law that appears to talk about putting the company up for sale, breaking the company up and abandoning a long-term strategy. Certainly the fact that the company came into play because of a deal supported with another company is not enough according to *Time*.

6. How about the second prong of *Unocal*? Court finds that there is no preclusion. Paramount can still acquire Time, it is just that it needs to now swallow Warner as well.

Note on Revlon in Operation

Most important feature of this Note is the Black and Kraakman excerpt crisply setting forth the situations in which the Revlon duties attach. QVC illustrates this reasoning. It was not the bust up of the firm, but the fact that after the transaction the Paramount would be controlled by Sumner Redstone, even though the Paramount shareholders would obtain a continuing equity participation in Viacom.

Paramount Communications also sheds light on the demands *Revlon* makes on the directors. We might ask whether these are really new duties; what appears clear is that whether they are discharged is subject to closer scrutiny under *Revlon* in part because the burden of proof is on the board. Even so, with an immunity shield, *Ryan* appears to conclude they need only be reasonable and not perfect. We might also question why an immunity shield should change anything since it provides immunity only against damage claims and not an injunctive action that likely would be brought by a contesting disappointed suitor.

Note on Defensive Maneuvers Outside of Delaware

Delaware is truly important, but it is not the only source of law. The Note points out that the jurisdictions are about evenly divided in their following Delaware or instead applying the standard business judgment rule approach (where the complainant has the burden of proof). As the note points out here, a crucial variable in a state's choice between these two approaches is the content of the state's antitakeover statutes.

Section 3.   Protecting the Deal

Omnicare, Inc. v. NCS Healthcare, Inc.

To begin the discussion, you might consider asking what do we mean by "deal protection" provisions and what was the provision in this case?

Did the NCS board act unreasonably in entering into the deal protection provision with Genesis? Hard to believe they did, this was what Genesis was seeking, having lost deals in the past, and to Omnicare. There is a good deal of evidence of back and forth here and no clear basis to believe that Omnicare was on the cusp of providing its own option to NCS. This seems to be the point taken by Veasey in his dissent.

On what basis therefore did the majority strike down this provision? Court concludes the arrangement is coercive, i.e., violating the second prong of *Unocal-Unitrin*. It was coercive since with the voting agreement entered into by the majority holders the minority were locked in, having in the eyes of the majority no choice but to vote for the matter. It was predetermined the outcome and, hence, was deemed coercive.

The court also holds the provision invalid because of the absence of a fiduciary out clause.

Notice that the Delaware legislature after the decision enacted Delaware Corp. Law § 146 authorizing force the vote agreements.

As an aside, we might wonder if the majority would have viewed the case differently if the Outcalt and Shaw had not only controlled a majority of the shares but a majority of the equity in the firm. They held super voting shares and thus held a minority of the equity but a majority of the voting shares.

Note on Termination Fees

The Unabridged edition has information on the most popular deal protection provision, termination fees. The rule of thumb here is 2-4 percent of the target equity is well within the bounds of permissible liquidated damages-like provision.

Section 4.   State Takeover Statutes

The first question for the students is what's added by this section? Note that all of these matters found in a statute could easily be inserted into the company's articles of incorporation. So, why is it the legislatures provide this protection where if the shareholders wished the protection it could occur via the amendment to the articles process? The answer is likely that the shareholders don't want these protective provisions, but managers, or at least those who marched down to their legislature, do. Next question is what caused the court to uphold the takeover statute in *CTS Corp. v. Dynamics Corp. of America* after striking a state antitakeover statute down in *Edgar v. Mite*? The provisions challenged in *CTS* applied only to corporations incorporated in the enacting state, whereas *Edgar* was not so limited. Hence, the internal affairs doctrine carries the day akin to states mandating low or super votes for certain types of transactions. This is much of the reasoning of *Amanda*.

Since it is part of the current debate, you may wish to touch on the insights of Jarrell and Subramanian regarding the impact of the Delaware moratorium statute on takeover activity for Delaware companies.

Section 5. Restructuring and the Bondholders

The materials in this section provide a thumbnail sketch to the intersection of corporations and bond covenants. The leading cases on this subject are abstracted here with an idea that corporate lawyers deal with these principles as on a daily basis. Note the source of each issue is traced back to a bond covenant. The covenants trace their prose to the ABA efforts with respect to the Model Indenture provisions. There is very limited evidence of anyone rebuilding the wheel here. This is the realm of boilerplate.

Sharon Steel Corporation v. The Chase Manhattan Bank

Just what are the bond trustees arguing here? The trustees argue that the disposition to Sharon Steel was a sale of less than all or substantially all the assets. If this is the case, the covenant required payment of the entire outstanding debt. Note here that prevailing interest rates were substantially higher than the face rate on these bonds so this is not just standing on principle!

What are the arguments on both sides. For Sharon, when it purchased Mueller Brass, the mining properties and the remaining cash that UV had on hand, that was all the assets. The trustees argue that we need to look at the total sequence, going back at least to March 1979 shareholder approval of the orderly liquidation of UV.

Procedurally, how was this case resolved. The court sustained the grant of summary judgment in favor of the trustees. But weren't there facts in dispute? Yes indeed, and the meaning of words is such a dispute. But the Second Circuit affirmed the trial judge saying what was before it was a question of law, not fact or law and fact. Winter's opinion is the Bible in this area, holding that boilerplate requires uniform interpretation. Thus, extrinsic evidences of the parties' likely intention is not allowed. This is the domain of the judge.

We might ask whether this makes sense? Winter supports his analysis, and wisely, but pointing out that creditors extend credit to the firm that has multiple operations. To rule in favor of Sharon Steel would mean the creditors remain in place, even though the income stream on which they depend for payment has become less diversified, i.e., they had sold off prior to the Sharon Steel purchase, significant other operations. Thus, we can see that the successor obligation clause is a risk management provision.

What is important about the case is that provisions that come from the Model Indenture projects are entitled to a uniform interpretation notwithstanding the unique facts of the particular case.

Metropolitan Life Insurance Co. v. RJR Nabisco, Inc.

What is the argument raised by Metropolitan? They argue they had an implied covenant that RJR would not incur additional debt and destroy much of the value of the bonds they held. So, why did the bonds held by Metropolitan lose so much of their value? The $19 billion dollars of debt taken on by RJR to purchase its outstanding equity in what was then the largest LBO in history, rendered the AAA rated debt held by Metropolitan and others very risky.

What does the court say is required for there to be an implied covenant of good faith? The court holds it will imply such a covenant, if it is necessary to protect an explicitly bargained-for benefit. Thus courts may imply notice of an intent to liquidate the company if the bondholders have a conversion privilege and exercise of their conversion right would provide a great return. (see the court's discussion of *Van Gemert* as well as Zahn v. Transamerica Corp., Chapter 11, supra.). The court found that the fruits negotiated here was timely payment of interest and principle and there has been no allegation these benefits have been impeded by the leverage taken on by RJR.

Notice here that the plaintiff argued that the company implicitly undertook that it would never undertake a transaction of such dimensions that would place paying at risk. The court saw no basis in law or fact for this argument, and quickly dismissed it. Plaintiffs are not helped in any of their arguments by having earlier given up their covenants that barred additional debt and that the covenants that were in the indenture authorized mergers and the incurrence of new debt.

Katz v. Oak Industries, Inc.

Bond indentures do authorize covenants to be changed. The Trust Indenture Act sets a minimum vote required for some provisions and requires unanimity for some changes (principal, interest, and duration).

What is before the Chancellor? Notice that Signal needs to modify the debt covenants if it is going to carry out the refinancing of Oak Industries. This is because its offer if consummated without amendment of the covenants triggered protective provisions that would then require the full face amount of the debt to be paid (plus accrued interest). It wished to acquire the bonds at less than their face or even redemption amounts (albeit above their current market price). Thus, it conditioned its offer to repurchase on getting the holders' consents to the modification. The holder of one of the instruments sued, alleging the offer was coercive and therefore in violation of an implied covenant of good faith.

This builds on the reasoning in *Metropolitan Life Insurance* regarding when a court is willing to imply a covenant of good faith. Chancellor Allen also provides insight about coercion, the duties owed in these situations, and the vulnerability of bond holders.

First, note the clear unequivocal statement that the relationship between bond holders and the corporation is contractual, i.e., there is no fiduciary duty owed to them. Hence, the complaint that the exchange offer is designed to benefit the common at the expense of the bond holders falls on deaf ears. This antagonism is implicit in the relationship and that is what covenants are designed to address. It is finance's version of caveat emptor.

Was this offer coercive? Of course, and Allen observes as much, but wisely points out that there is lots of coercion in everyday life that is socially beneficial (kids do their homework before getting on the Internet). How do we decide what is permissible coercion? Allen suggests resort to the contract. This then leads him to consider when there is an implied covenant of good faith.

Is his formulation of finding a covenant of good faith the same as that in *Metropolitan Life*? No, he seems to be speaking not in defeating a bargained provision, as was the approach in *Metropolitan Life*, but rather that the court should imply this missing prohibition if from a review of the surrounding circumstances the court is convinced that the parties would have expressly agreed to proscribe the act had they thought to negotiate.

Thus, with this in mind, what conclusions did he reach? While the indenture did have provisions regarding procedures for modifying the terms, there was nothing in these provisions that would suggest the parties intended to prohibit the issuer or others offering incentives to bondholders to agree to a change.

And, the provision that barred the issuer from voting "treasury bonds" did not mean that a bondholder could not vote the bonds.

What about the redemption provision? This was seen as a non exclusive way in which bondholders could dispose of their bonds. Redemption is a word of art, covering the company's power to call the bonds. The transaction here was not a redemption, and there is no reason to believe that bondholders when they acquired the bonds intended to forego their right to dispose of the bonds, under whatever conditions they believed fair, to a third party.

The moral to this story: draft a better contract. But is it clear that the bondholders would ex ante want to prevent this type of transaction? Seems hardly likely as they each would like to encourage offers such as these, recognizing that there likely will be a lack of consensus over the life of the bonds but each likes the freedom to address that risk when it arises.

Chapter 16

Distributions to Shareholders

Chapter Overview: Never underestimate the students' aversion to numbers. Thus, one can never proceed too slowly through the material in this chapter. While there is a well-understood and much deserved temptation just to bag this material, skipping over it, that is not a wise strategy since lawyers invariably become engaged with this area of the corporate statute. Devoting two days to the material, centered on the Dividend Handout Exercise that appears as an Appendix to this chapter of the Teachers' Manual, is doable. You may wish to add to that exercise the material that is in Section 1 focused both on dividend policies of public companies and the role of the court in policing dividend policies.

Discussion of the topic of "distributions to shareholders" can be introduced by asking students to recall the structure of a corporation and the fact that a corporation is technically owned by its shareholders qua investors. Shareholders invest in a corporation presumably because they expect to receive a return from the corporation. The classic work of Modigliana and Miller developed the hypothesis that investors should be invariant to whether that return occurs via dividends or stock price appreciation which they can harvest via disposing of their shares. For example, for many years Microsoft was the darling of the investment community even though it paid no dividends; investors were attracted by the firm's growth in earnings that were reinvested that enhanced its share prices.

We should note that one of the assumptions underlying Modigliana and Miller is a world without taxation, or at least no differential in treatment between dividends and stock price gains. This differential was not true when they did their work; however, post the 2003 Bush tax cuts dividends and capital gains are pretty much treated the same by the IRC. In any case under the classic passive investor model, when the corporation becomes profitable and begins accumulating a stockpile of excess cash that is not needed for things like acquisitions, payroll, inventory, debt service, rent, etc., the corporation needs to do something with the excess money (such as issue dividends).

The most recognizable way (to students) that a corporation makes a distribution to shareholders is by way of a cash dividend. If Cisco has a good year and accumulates a cash surplus of $100 million dollars, Cisco's board of directors may declare and cause the payment. As a consequence, a dividend of 40 cents on each issued and outstanding share of common stock. A widow or orphan in Kansas who owns 100 shares of Cisco common stock will find in her mailbox a check from Cisco for $40.

In contrast, Cisco may instead resolve to purchase some of the shares that are held by investors (a/k/a "outstanding shares"). Thus, a corporation can make a distribution to its shareholders by repurchasing shares from them (at a premium). An important tax feature of dividends (and share repurchases) is that the payment is not a deductible expense to the corporation. As seen earlier, in the discussion of the motivations for leverage and thin capitalization, debt and not stock is the preferred instrument for financing the corporation, since interest on debt is a deductible business expense and dividends are not. This should strike the student as a curious result, since in each instance, interest or dividends payments, is really just the "rent" that is paid for the use of another's (lender or investor's) money. In part because of the non-deductibility of dividends, close corporations and LLCs sometimes make distributions by paying shareholders who are also employees inflated salaries or bonuses. This works quite naturally for the close corporation, and small LLC (where shareholders are often also employees), and they share a mutual desire to reduce taxes to the entity (where the LLC has opted for non-partnership taxation – given that salaries can be deducted before a corporation calculates its taxable income, but dividends cannot be deducted - there is a tax benefit to using salaries as opposed to dividends to distribute wealth to shareholders).

Section 1.   Dividend Policy

A.   The Elements of Dividend Policy

Brealey, Myers and Allen Excerpt and Brav, Graham, Harvey & Michaely Excerpt

By way of background, students can be asked which of the following is the most and least likely way that American businesses finance their growth: 1) from retained earnings, 2) borrowing from banks or investors (e.g., bonds), or 3) issuance of equity securities? This is the order with retained earnings dwarfing the other two combined! Now, ask the students why might some countries, as they do, require companies to pay 100% of their profits as a dividend? Why do those that believe in the disciplining effects of the market hold it is good public policy to require managers to yearly distribute all earnings as a dividend? By foreclosing managers from using retained earnings you force them to explain to another – a banker or an investors (in bonds or stock) - the intended uses of the funds sought by managers. Note this check on the managers is absent with retained earnings. Hence, the power that managers enjoy over the firm's dividend practices is an enormous one and hence we can see some the reason for institutions clamoring for greater payouts or the initiation of payouts.

The Brealey & Myers & Allen Excerpt provides a good summary of the classic study of dividend practices carried out by Lintner's in the1950's reporting that corporation's pursue dividend policies that reflect long-run target dividend payout ratios (i.e., a relative constant percentage of reported income), with mature companies with stable earnings paying out a higher proportion of earnings. Students could be asked why more mature companies would have a higher percentage on average of their income distributed as dividends? These companies, by definition of their being mature, have lower growth opportunities and, hence, less justification to apply earnings to expand the business. The survey by Brav, Graham, Harvey & Michaely, Payout Policy in the 21st Century, also reflects managers' desires to maintain the level of dividends. It also reports that the decision by non-paying firms to initiate a dividend is dominated by (a) demand by institutional investors and (b) a sustainable increase in earnings. We might ask why institutions are not guided by Miller and Modigliana's insights? Part of the answer is that requiring firm's to pay dividends makes them more accountable and likely addresses the concern of investors that managers may be engaging in empire building or other suboptimal strategies by not returning economic gains to the owners. Moreover, institutions face their own cash needs (redemptions, annuities to investors, etc.) so seek this cash.

Dividend practices have long been linked with signaling, which refers to a body of literature in the field of information economics that focuses on how discrete messages about the firm can be effectively communicated. Michael Spence's path breaking (ultimately earning him a Nobel Prize) rigorously demonstrated that the credibility of any message is linked to the costs of emitting the message. Thus, all firms can say they are doing well. But firms that are truly doing well can get a third party guaranty of their claim at much less cost than a firm that is not doing well. This is because the third-party certifier will charge an enormous amount to attest that Firm B is doing well, when it is doubtful it is, than the charge it would levy for Firm A, where there is abundant evidence by which the third-party certifier can believe Firm A is doing well. Firms do not hire third-party certifiers, but they do the same with several financial decisions. They attract high reputation underwriters when they undertake a public offering of their securities, they incur large amounts of debt (because the managers know they can meet the financial payments of such debt), and they have large dividend payout ratios reflecting the managers' belief that the firm will at least do enough in the future to maintain that level of dividends, regardless of the state of the economy. This indeed is the essence of much of what John Lintner documented in his classic study of dividend policies. Thus, it is believed that corporations signal i.e., communicate, information (to the market, to investors) about their financial health and long-term prospects through their dividend practices. Presumably managers would not issue dividends if not only (a) the corporation did not really have sufficient cash on hand but also (b) the corporation's managers believed that the firm was sufficiently solid in its finances and operations, so that it would under all foreseeable shifts in the economic cycle of the economy that the payout would be maintained. It is believed that the information communicated by way of dividends is more reliable than the information in an annual report (which can be manipulated), since real world financial repercussions would set in with an improvidently adopted dividend policy. Either a corporation has cash on hand to issue dividends or it does not. Interestingly, Brav et al. find that corporate managers themselves deny that this implicit communication motivates their dividend policies, and overall they believe their study results reject that executives act consciously to signal the firm's value. Nonetheless, much of their study results are consistent with the signaling theorem (e.g., executives do see that dividend and share repurchase decisions convey information to investors). Somewhat reassuring, perhaps, is that executives overwhelmingly see dividend payout decisions are secondary to investment decisions.

Some argue that by issuing dividends the corporation increases its value, whereas others reason that dividends reduces the firm's value, and some (most notably Miller and Modigliani) say that dividend policy is irrelevant to a corporation's value. Why would firm value increase when a company announces an increase in its dividend? This phenomenon is frequently observed and generally believed to reflect that the dividend increase is a credible signal by managers that the firm is doing well, hence poses lower risk/uncertainty regarding future earning levels.

Repurchases of stock (in order to use cash that is not needed rather than dividending the cash to shareholders) do not pose the same concerns for managers as dividends. That is, dividends once adopted are maintained, at least that is reflected first by Lintner and confirmed today by Brav et al. A firm with a hoard of cash may instead engage in an episodic share repurchase. This does not entangle them with investor expectations of future repurchases as occurs with dividends. Hence, the modern practice today reflects an ever-increasing resort to share repurchases among public companies. .

Because of the signaling effects associated with dividend announcements, corporate managers do not like to make changes – particularly unexpected and negative changes – in dividend payouts. Hence, dividend payouts are characterized as being "sticky."

Researchers have observed a "clientele" phenomenon whereby certain companies attract a class of investors seeking high dividend payouts. Some investors such as endowment funds and annuity insurance companies may prefer high-dividend stocks because dividends are regarded as "income" that the fund can spend (as opposed to non-spendable capital gains), and some investors such as retirees prefer to invest in stock that has a history of generating consistent dividends that the retirees can use as a source of cash for living expenses. For these investor groups, high dividend payout companies, such as utilities and drug companies, are very much sought. Note also that high payouts means that shareholders, not managers, control that cash. The firm that has a high payout signals that its managers are confident in their ability to not only identify positive investment opportunities, but confident in their ability to raise the funds to embrace such opportunities as they arise. Low payout firms may instead be managers that are empire builders, and do not have a persuasive case should they have to raise funds in the marketplace to embrace new opportunities.

Other reasons that corporation will repurchase stock are when good investments are harder to find and when they wish to offset option dilution.

Note that Brav et al. show that the company will borrow money or issue equity rather than reduce dividends to fund internal investment.

B.   Judicial Review of Dividend Policy

(1) Publicly Held Corporations With A Controlling Shareholder

Baron v. Allied Artists Pictures Corp.

Baron illustrates the deference accorded dividend decisions. And, placing the case in a contemporary context, it also illustrates a corporate governance concern of the duty of the

248

"constituent" director.

A provision in Allied's articles provided that the preferred shares became fully voting and have the right to elect a majority of the board of directors if six or more quarterly preferred dividends are not paid. Students may be asked where such a provision would be found (in the articles of incorporation is where all such preferences must be set forth) and why this kind of provision is desirable for the preferred? The provision is a protective device for the cumulative dividend to which the preferred was entitled. Because the preferred's dividend was cumulative, it was like a debt owed by the corporation. However, it cannot be sued upon and nonpayment does not empower the preferred to push Allied into bankruptcy. But the preferred can and did grab control of the board. Plaintiff sued the board of Allied maintaining that the board of directors fraudulently perpetuated itself in office by refusing to pay accumulated dividends due the preferred and did so for the purpose of retaining control of the company. Plaintiff supports his claim of fraudulent perpetuation by noting that the corporation has had positive net annual income or capital surplus in the most recent years.

Students can be asked to weigh in on the following:

1. What is the relevance of the factual issues regarding the dual positions and pay of Wolf, Ingis, Strauss and Prager? May well illustrate that Kalvex, shifted much of their pay and perquisites to Allied.

2. Why doesn't Miller and Modigliana also call for outright dismissal of the case? The thought being that, if investors should not pay a premium for dividend paying firms over non-dividend paying firms, then what is happening in *Baron* is really legally irrelevant. First, Miller and Modigliana would not themselves be neutral to the abuse suggesting in the preceding note. Second, in an efficient market, an assumption of M&M, would likely reflect the discount for the common because of not just the control held by the preferred/Kalvex but the omnipresent spectra of abuse by the control person.

3. Does the court say it would never intervene? No, the court observes: "While previous limitations on net income and capital surplus may offer a justification for the past, continued limitations in a time of greatly increased cash flow could well create new issues in the area of business discretion for the future. . . ." But note the complexity of this decision. Is Allied not to invest in new movies not withstanding that the tax deficiencies are not eliminated? If it is to so invest, is a court prepared to say you must raise that investment externally because profits must be paid toward eliminating the arrears on preferred? This is not an easy question of line drawing.

4. How is this different from the earlier studied case, Dodge v. Ford Motor Co.? In Allied there is a clear business purpose for non-payment of dividends. This business purpose is the bulwark against judicial intrusion, except if there is evidence of a duty of loyalty issue. This returns the facts to question No. 1 above. Thus, is there no other reliable means for judicial review other than the presence of a breach of duty of loyalty?

5. Why is this not just seen as bad drafting on the part of the common in their

"negotiations" with the preferred when the preferred stock was issued? Likely never entered the parties thought and in any case could easily see an implied term of good faith here whereby the preferred, once in control, were to use reasonable efforts to extract the firm from the conditions that caused the common to lose control.

6. Thus, the constituent director issue: what does this court say is the duty of the Allied directors who have been elected by the preferred? A fair reading of the case is that their duties are to the residual claimants, the common, but they have a good deal of discretion in how quickly/precipitously they are to eliminate the preferred stockholders' arrearages.

7. Note that the more recent *SV Investments Partners, LLC v. ThougtWorks, Inc.*, in the note following *Baron*, similarly to *Baron,* accords the board discretion on whether to repurchase shares even though such repurchase was mandated when there were "funds legally available." The court focused on the meaning of "funds" to distinguish this source from the legal benchmarks of the Delaware statute, "surplus," so that the absence of a enough cash to carry out the repurchase meant there was no duty to repurchase, notwithstanding there then being sufficient "surplus" (i.e., no capital impairment would ensue if the repurchase occurred) to support the repurchase.

(2) Close Corporations

As seen earlier in Chapter 8 and 9, in non-public companies, shareholders may derive their benefits as owners through their salaries and not dividends. Query, should this impact how the court approaches suits seeking dividends in a close corporation or LLC?

Consider here the reasoning of *Miller v. Magline* where the trial court held:

> ... To the extent that the management group, as directors, has adopted a nondividend policy, we are of the opinion that it has defeated one of the major purposes of a profit corporation, that is, to accumulate profits and divide them amongst the corporate owners when that is reasonable and proper.

The Michigan Court of Appeals affirmed, noting:

> Defendant contends that under the business judgment rule a court may not compel a dividend in the absence of clear and convincing proof of fraud, conspiracy, waste, or gross abuse of discretion by the board of directors.... Breach of this fiduciary duty amounts to a breach of trust, and has consistently been recognized in Michigan as a ground for court intervention. Under the circumstances here, their participating in a distribution to them of those profits and a squirreling away of the balance to meet future needs is, in our opinion, inequitable in not giving consideration properly to the needs and requirements of all of the stockholders of the corporation.

We might wonder just how different the facts in *Miller* are from *Baron*? First, there was no evidence of an IRS lien in the history of *Miller* as there was in *Baron.* Second, there was no wide variation in revenues or income reported in *Miller* as there was in *Baron*. Note that to some extent the facts may be stronger for non intervention in *Miller* because of repeated changes in the payout practices; we need to know whether the plaintiffs concurred or participated as directors in the change. Presumably they did not. Note also that there was ample surplus from which a dividend could be paid, whereas the record in *Baron* does not emphasize that the surplus was enormous, large or just ample. At the same time, we might also revisit why greater judicial involvement is justified in the close corporation? There is no ready exit for the plaintiffs in the close corporation. The absence of a market means that there is less chance for a market to discipline managers (note in *Baron* this too may be true since the preferred was heavily held by one holder, Kalvex, and the discipline would be evident in the disenfranchised common, the complaining parties). Also, in a close corporation, there may well be fewer externalities on creditors or the various constituencies dealing with the company since the company is generally smaller. In a close corporation, given the likely greater intimacy among owners, everything can become personal, thus tipping factual issues away from an allegation of care and in the direction of loyalty. Thus, the facts and the environment in *Miller* may just have been a stronger case for judicial involvement.

Section 2. Limitations on Dividends Under Creditors' Rights Law

While courts are asked to intervene to protect *shareholders* with respect to dividends, as noted above, the primary focus of dividend regulation is protecting creditors. There are various statutes that protect *creditors* of a corporation from dividend payments and share repurchases that are believed too prejudicial to the rights of the creditors. Each state in its corporate statute has its own regulatory protections for creditors that apply to dividends and share repurchases. For example, Section 510(a) of N.Y. Bus. Corp. Law prohibits a corporation from paying dividends when either the corporation is insolvent or the corporation would be made insolvent by paying the dividends. Section 102(a)(8) of N.Y. Bus. Corp. Law provides that "'[i]nsolvent' means being unable to pay debts as they become due...." (Note this is *not* the bankruptcy test of insolvency which assesses whether liabilities exceed assets.)

In addition, there are a variety of state statutes that generally protect creditors that can come into play for dividends and share repurchases. Foremost among these are the standard fraudulent conveyance/transfer statutes that are applicable to dividends and share repurchases whereby creditors can claw-back relevant dividends and amounts paid to repurchase shares. Indeed, there are many more suits for wrongful distributions brought under such statutes than corporate dividend regulation statutes.

To be noted here is that the statutes generally apply when the corporation is insolvent and that the remedy is against the recipient of the funds from the insolvent corporation, not the directors who approved the payment.

Corporations and Other Business Organizations

Section 3. Limitations on Dividends Under the Corporate Statutes

A.   Introduction

A reasonable place to begin discussing restrictions on dividends and repurchases imposed by corporate statutes is what do they add that is not found in state fraudulent conveyance and transfer statutes, discussed in the preceding section. This requires some knowledge of the mechanics of corporate statutes as they apply to such distributions. It is not a question for the uninitiated. But once those mechanics are understood the answer is something of a margin of safety; that is, corporate statutes, such as the capital impairment variety in Delaware or the surplus-based statutes such as New York, each add a measure of additional protection beyond a mere insolvency inquiry. That is, all corporate statutes provide that a dividend or repurchase cannot occur, if it would render the company unable to meet its bills as they mature. This duplicates the solvency test in the fraudulent conveyance and fraudulent transfer statutes. Corporate statutes also provide an additional measure of protection, namely that the net assets (assets less liabilities) cannot be reduced below the amount of the firm's legal capital. Legal capital thus is the additional buffer or protection corporate statutes provide. An additional impact of corporate statutes is that liability is first imposed on the directors declaring the illegal dividend or authorizing the share repurchase. As seen earlier, fraudulent conveyance and transfer statutes claw back the wrongful transfer from the shareholder but do not otherwise discipline the decision makers, the board of directors.

A final observation in this area is that dividend and share repurchase restrictions are virtually meaningless in the public company. This is because covenants in bonds or clauses in bank loans impose their own restrictions on corporate dividends and repurchases and in doing so are much more demanding and precise than what is found in a corporate statute. Thus, a covenant in a loan agreement, even with a single creditor, imposes limitations that benefit all the firm's creditors. This is free riding at its best.

B. Traditional Statutes – Capital Impairment Statutes

To illustrate the impairment of capital approach to dividend regulation, you should likely use the Delaware statutes. We see that Section 170 conditions dividends on there being surplus. This is a mysterious expression, but surplus is defined in Section 154 as the excess of net assets over capital. It is the latter that poses the challenge for students. Net assets are accounting derived figures, meaning the amount by which assets exceed liabilities. Both these items, as seen in Chapter 2, are balance sheet accounts. Capital is defined primarily in Section 154, and essentially refers to the aggregate par value of issued shares or, if those are no par shares, the amount that the board allocated to capital (if no formal allocation, then the full amount of the consideration received for the no-par shares will be capital). Thus, we see here that dividends cannot reduce the sum of all assets below the combined amount of the firm's liabilities and its capital. If a dividend does this, it "impairs" capital and is unlawful. Even Delaware 170 has exceptions, namely permits such impairment for nimble dividends, discussed later, and wasting asset companies.

252

This area can be reviewed with a few simple illustrations, using for example the Delaware or New York statute. The "Dividend Handout Exercise" that is included at the end of this chapter of the Teachers' Manual, has been used by Cox for several years.

To illustrate legal capital, what if the firm issued 1,000 shares of $1 common for $1? What if issued for $5 per share? What is the consequence of issuing for $ 0.50 per share? And what result if the shares are without par value? The predicate question here is what establishes the issuing price in each of these situations? It is not the par or no par figure; it is the investor's willingness to pay a certain price.

If a share's par value is unrelated to how much an investor will pay for the shares, what is the legal significance of the par value? The answer is found in provisions in Delaware and New York that provide that the shares having a par value are not fully paid and non assessable if less than the full par value is paid. Hence, the example above where $0.50 is paid for $1 par means the recipient of those shares can be required (most likely if the firm is insolvent and there is a trustee) to pay the deficiency.

What then is the legal capital? It is minimally the par value, but can be more 1) if more than par is paid and 2) the board resolves to allocate some portion or all of the excess above par to legal capital. In the case of no par shares, it is what the board has resolved to allocate to capital (presumably it must be something, and not zero).

Under the capital impairment statute, the legal benchmark for dividends and repurchases is principally (note six states do have nimble dividend statutes and some states permit capital to be eroded to a certain extent for companies in the mineral extraction business, i.e., so-called wasting asset firms) the amount by which net assets (assets less liabilities) exceeds the amount deemed legal capital (e.g., at least the aggregate par value of issued shares). Hence,

Assets – Liabilities = Net Assets

Net Assets – Liabilities =Legal Benchmark for Maximum Dividend or Share Repurchase (a/k/a Surplus)

Note on Revaluation of Assets and Klang v. Smith's Food and Drug Centers, Inc.

As captured in the note, New York and Delaware allow their dividend statutes to incorporate fair market value, in contrast to historically cost of assets (that are the bedrock of generally accepted accounting principles). The note questions this on public policy grounds. First, if dividend and repurchases are regulated for the protection of creditors would we 1) want to let the regulated determine the critical inputs for such regulation and 2) is this not an area where conservatism should prevail? Second, the example in the Note regarding the upward valuation of the firm's copper inventory shows that such a gain is not a true economic profit, because if the firm is to continue in operations it must replace that inventory once sold at the higher prevailing market price. That is, if dividends are to be permitted, because the amount to be distributed represents profits of operation, distributing assets that have appreciated in value due to inflation is not what the economist view as distributing profits if the firm's continuation is dependent on replacing the asset, copper inventory, once it is sold in operations. But the highest courts of Delaware and New York have spoken on this subject so to complain is a bit futile. And, as will be seen, the Model Act now expressly authorizes deviation from cost in measuring the firm's assets.

It should be noted that Delaware does not discriminate where the "surplus" came from, whereas statues following New York do distinguish between surplus flowing from profitable operations ("earned surplus") and that arising from the sale of shares ("capital surplus"). New York imposes some limitations on the use of capital surplus that do not apply if the board of directors relied instead on earned surplus.

C.   Traditional Statutes – Earned Surplus Statutes

The New York statute best illustrates the "earned surplus" test for dividends. Where Delaware characterizes the total excess of net assets over capital as surplus, the New York statute distinguishes between surplus that arose from profitable operations (earned surplus) and surplus (paid-in surplus or capital surplus) that arises from other activities, such as a reduction of capital or selling shares for in excess of par (or some allocation of the consideration received for no-par shares). With this distinction, the statute then proceeds to allow the board of directors much greater discretion with respect to distributions from earned surplus than paid-in surplus.

Section 4.   The Modern Dividend Statutes

In 1977, California enacted statutory provisions that significantly departed from the traditional approaches to dividend regulation. To be sure, dividends were still authorized to the extent of "retained earnings," the accounting profession's terminology for earned surplus. However, the new California provision also authorized dividends based on the relationship of assets to liabilities, casting aside the archaic "surplus" terminology.

The overall effect of both California and the Model Act is that there no longer any relevance of par value within the corporate statute. That is, in California and the Model Act all shares are without par value and there is no concept of legal capital embedded in the statutes.

Do note that in the Model Act, there is express statutory authority when applying its asset and liability test to use any reasonable method of determining amount of assets or liabilities.

Section 5.   Contractual Restrictions on the Payment of Dividends

As examined earlier, creditors normally receive minimal protection from the courts and corporate statutes and the protection they receive under fraudulent conveyance and transfer statutes is also somewhat constrained. However, creditors frequently protect themselves when they do business with corporations by way of contract provisions. For example, when a large institutional lender loans $1 million to GE the loan documents themselves can specify that, so long as the loan is outstanding, GE shall not issue and pay any dividends without first notifying and securing the consent of the lender. As seen earlier, these provisions are much more demanding than the restrictions found in state statutes and have the effect of benefitting all the firm's creditors since such a contractual limitation constrains the firm's dividends or repurchases across the board. Thus, the contractual restrictions imposed by a single lender on its creditor redound to the benefit of all creditors; this is a classic illustration of free riding by creditors.

Section 6.   Liability of Directors for Improper Dividends

It is interesting to note that corporate law customarily places the first level of liability for any improperly paid dividends on directors whereas, as seen earlier, creditors' rights laws focus on the recipient of the improper transfer. With respect to corporate statutes, the director is typically accorded the defense of good-faith reliance on defined financial statements, and also can obtain contribution against shareholders who received the distribution with knowledge of its illegality.

Section 7.   Liability of Shareholders for Improper Dividends

Both common law and statutory provisions exist to address the liability of shareholders for improper dividends.

In this area, we note that generally shareholder liability under corporate statutes runs only to the directors who, if liable to creditors for an unlawful dividend, can obtain reimbursement against a shareholder who received the dividend with knowledge of its illegality. In contrast, creditors have a direct action under fraudulent conveyance/transfer statutes against the transferee, and in many instances knowledge of the illegality is not a defense. For example, the Uniform Fraudulent Transfer Act § 5 renders fraudulent a transfer that is made without receiving in exchange a reasonably equivalent transfer when the transferor was or thereby became insolvent. Under Section 7, a creditor can avoid a fraudulent transfer and can seek to attach the asset transferred. Moreover, the Bankruptcy Code allows a bankruptcy trustee to avoid any transfers by a bankrupt corporation that are "voidable under applicable law by a creditor holding an unsecured claim," which means that a trustee can recover an improper distribution of dividends directly from shareholders if a creditor could have avoided the distribution.

Section 8.   Repurchase By A Corporation of Its Own Stock

A.   Financial Limitations on Stock Repurchases

While likely the point was made earlier, it can be repeated here that there is no sensible distinction from the potential harm to creditors' perspective between the payment of a dividend and the payment for shares. In each case, assets leave the corporation, it receives nothing in return that is of tangible benefit to the creditors, and the money winds up in the pocket of a shareholder. Thus, California paved the way and that path is now followed by the Model Act in broadly treating both dividends and share repurchase as a distribution subject to the same regulatory provisions. There are some wrinkles that we can find in corporate statutes for very unique transactions such as (a) eliminating fractional shares, (b) paying dissenting shareholders for their shares pursuant to the exercise of appraisal rights, and (c) redeeming or purchasing redeemable stock.

Thus, you might focus on the differing treatment of share repurchases between the Model Act and Delaware (which regulates repurchases under Section 160 with very obtuse language which is no more than the surplus standard studied earlier).

The installment repurchases is tricky. Thus, if the shareholder agrees to the repurchase of her shares over three annual payments and the company is insolvent or lacks surplus when the final payment is due, can the payment be made? This depends on whether we view the installment repurchase as a series of separate transactions so that each must meet the surplus and solvency test, or do we apply those tests at the outset, or apply surplus at the outset and solvency on a payment-by-payment plan. At common law states varied in their approach. Note here the second sentence of MBCA § 6.40(g) adopts the payment-by-payment approach.

B. Non-Financial Rules Concerning Stock Repurchases

You may wish to ask what the significance is of *Italo Petroleum Corp. v. Producers Oil Corp.*? It reflects the view that the subsidiary cannot vote the shares it might own in its parent, a perfectly sensible outcome. Students should understand here that "treasury shares" refers to reacquired shares that have not been formally cancelled. Under the Model Act reacquired shares are automatically restored to the status of authorized but unissued. Treasury shares are authorized, issued but not outstanding. They are therefore accounted for on the balance sheet in the equity section as a negative item.

The Note reviews numerous ways shares repurchases may occur: open market purchase, open market purchase preceded by an announcement, and issuer tender offer. Note also there are concerns for green mail where a steep excise tax can be imposed. Going private transactions were examined earlier in Chapter 15.

Section 9. Liability for Watered Stock and Related Issues

This is an area that is rarely covered in business organizations classes. The rise of no par shares and the broad influence of the Model Act, not to mention the presence of Blue Sky administrators has caused this subject to vanish. It does have some historical value in knowing the tortured route that led to the Model Act and an understanding behind the archaic impairment of capital/surplus approach to dividend regulation.

Appendix to Chapter 16 Teachers' Manual

Roadmap for Understanding Legal Capital Requirements

I. Issuance of Shares

    A. Eligible forms of consideration

        Compare narrower Del. § 152 (lines8-10) with MBCA § 6.21(b)

    B. Determinations required of board when shares issued

        Compare stricter Del. §152 (second sentence) and § 153 (a) vs. (b) with MBCA §6.27(c)

    C. What is the purpose of MBCA § 6.21(f)

        See regarding acquisition procedures

    C. The meaning of a "preemptive right"

        See MBCA 6.30

        1. What must be done to provide this "right?"

        2 What does this mean?

            Hypo: Four equal holders of all the company's 1000 shares. Proposal is to issue 100 additional shares. If the articles provide a preemptive right, what does this mean for each of the present stockholders?

        3. What is the purpose of MBCA §§ 6.30(b)(3)?

        i.e., why might this be helpful to the lazy lawyer?

II. Dividend and Share Repurchase Regulation

A. The Balance Sheet

Assets	1500	Liabilities	900
		Equity	
		100 shares $5 par	500

Corporations and Other Business Organizations

Retained Earnings   100

B. The Model Act Regime

1. What meant by distribution" as used in MBCA § 6.40? See §1.40(6)

2. How does the determination under §6.40(c)(1) differ from that in (c)(2)?

3. Do you add or subtract to figure out the maximum distribution that can be made under MBCA § 6.40(c)(2)

4. What is the maximum distribution under the above that company can make?

5. What result if assets have reasonable value of $1800?

6. Is it likely that assets will have a value greater than those reflect in its accounting records?

7. Who decides to declare a dividend?

C. The Delaware Regime

1. Relevance of 170(a)(1) vs. 160(a)(1)

2. "Surplus"?

a. See the last three sentences of Del. § 154. What is not defined?

b. What is relevance of "par" value in this equation? See Del. §154 (first sentence) (what does this mean?)

c. What is "capital" if no-par shares?

d. What is the capital in the above illustration?

e. What is the amount that can be declared as a dividend in the above illustration?

f. In dollars, what is the maximum amount the company can spend to acquire its own shares?

Chapter 17

The Public Distribution of Securities

Chapter Overview: This chapter provides a broad overview of the Operation of the Securities Act of 1933. Because all schools offer a separate Securities Regulations course, we leave to that course the details within the regulatory framework covered in this chapter. We include this material because many students do not enroll in Securities Regulations but nonetheless will enter a general corporate practice. Thus, a working familiarity of the framework of the '33 Act would prove most useful for the students. Our experience is that the materials in this chapter can be covered reasonably well in 3 to 4 class hours. Earlier chapters covered the proxy rules, antifraud rule, insider trading regulation, and Williams Act provisions.

Section 1: Introduction

A. An Overview of the Securities Markets

The excerpt from Cox, Hillman and Langevoort acquaints students with the difference between issuer and trading transactions. Students can be asked why each is important to the other and how each is necessary for a developed economy. Trading markets provide liquidity for investors. Shares can be successfully issued by firms, but without an active and trustworthy trading market for the purchased shares investors would purchase illiquid shares at a deep discount. Indeed, we will see later that a downside to many of the exemptions from registration is the significant discount issuers incur for their placed securities due to their illiquidity, i.e., they are restricted securities. Trading markets also are a good indication of the risk-return relationship. Hence, economic theorists have repeatedly argued that trading markets do affect the allocation of capital in market economies. And, without issuer transactions there would be no shares for investors to trade. Students should understand that what they hear reported each day regarding market results is a report on trading transactions. Students should be asked to name the three largest trading markets (not in the material). They certainly will name two of them, the NYSE and Nasdaq. The third largest is the Pink Sheet Market (not the Over-the Counter Bulletin Board market overseen by FINRA).

B. An Overview of the Securities Act

Students should be asked what appears to be the purpose of the securities laws and how is that purpose accomplished. The purposes (note there is some healthy overlap) are 1) facilitate informed choices among securities by investors, 2) enhance the allocation of capital among competing investments in securities, 3) reduce fraudulent offerings of securities and 4) render firms and more importantly their managers more accountable to investors and markets generally.Students should be asked how this is accomplished. Disclosure, at least at the federal level, is the method by which these goals are accomplished. Students could be asked to verbalize how this occurs based on the readings provided here.

C. An Overview of the Underwriting Process

One way to draw the students into this material is to ask whether they would be neutral between two offerings that appear very similar to one another but one is a firm commitment and the other is a best efforts underwriting. The wise investors will prefer the firm commitment offering, much like the discriminating diner prefers the restaurant where the chef eats his own cooking. That is, studies repeatedly show that firm commitment underwritings involve larger issuers, whose offerings are larger and that ultimately a successful (survive 1, 3 and 5 years later/ have overall better returns) than do best efforts. This is expected namely because underwriters are not likely to commit their capital to an offering unless they believe they can quickly resell the shares and quick resell means it has to appeal to investors.

Since roughly one fourth of the total underwriting commission in a firm commitment offering is for underwriting (the remainder is the management fee to the lead underwriter(s) and the selling concession (commission for shares actually sold), what does a member of the underwriting syndicate do to earn this portion of the commission? Students may ponder this. We might reinforce the question by saying can one get paid part of the underwriting commission even though you are not the lead underwriter (who provides important advisory business to the issuer) and sells no shares? The answer is the underwriting commission portion of the total commission is for standing ready to purchase the shares in the event all the shares cannot be sold.

A final question is why is there a syndicate for most offerings? One answer is more salesmen in the breach means a way to manage the underwriting risk, i.e., risk that the securities will not "go out the window." Another answer is that this spreads that risk among the capital of several firms. Why might we think syndicates today have fewer members than say 20 or so years ago? Answer here is that the major investment banking firms, i.e., underwriters, have gotten bigger and are able to better absorb the risk. Along with this is that the industry has consolidated since 1975 so that by acquisition firms have gotten bigger. Third, more and more the shares are placed with institutions and not the retail trade so that the rise of institutions as a player, even in IPOs, means a large selling staff is less important than it was years earlier.

Section 2: What Constitutes A "Security"

McGinty's excerpt provides useful background for the definition of a security. Reviewing section 2(a)(1) with respect to locating therein "stock," "bond," "note" and "investment contract" would help reinforce that this area of law at least begins with a statute.

SEC v. W.J. Howey. From there it is useful to ask what part of section 2(a)(1) is being interpreted in *W.J. Howey* and what exactly was being offered to investors. For effect, you might draw a square and then horizontal parallel lines to illustrate the typical configuration of strips of land within a larger parcel. This illustrates the great difficulty investors can encounter cultivating their own tract of 48 or so orange trees (consider here the skill of a crop duster retained to spray on one of the contiguous strips). From this factual background, you can move to why the court deemed the offering to be that of an investment contract. Does the Court's definition have three or is it four elements. If three, it is (as *Glenn Turner* and a small group of cases have done) because common enterprise and efforts of others are treated as one element. What is pernicious about doing this? Why have most courts required horizontal (i.e., some pooling among investors) and not such vertical commonality? The likely answer to this is, if we can satisfy common enterprise via reliance on the efforts of another, many simple business arrangements will be a security. For example, P, who speculates in real estate, retains A to travel to California and purchase land. A is therefore an undisclosed agent. If A purchases land, and receives a kickback from the seller and fails to disclose the kickback to P, is this not just fraud on the principal P, but is it also securities fraud? One way to demonstrate the distinction between horizontal and vertical commonality is with the hypo of a condominium project at the beach. Individuals are encouraged to but a condo and place their unit up for rent. The promoters of the project operate a management company and assure purchasers that they can rent the unit out when not in use; this is attractive because the rental income can be used to make the mortgage payments on the unit. The managers obtain one-half of the rental income. This looks like a standard agency arrangement. But the ability to profit from the experience is dependent on the efforts of the management company. And the management company does have a stake in being successful since the management company garners one-half of the rents. But is this enough? It would be a stronger case if all the rents were "pooled" so that all the unit owners had an undivided interest in the rents that were received so that even if some units rented more often (better view) than others all share proportionately. This would be deemed a security as we would have sufficient interdependence among investors/owners so that horizontal commonality would be present. This appears more like the facts of *Howey,* where there was such interdependence among purchasers of tracts since it was not economically feasible to cultivate the strips of land individually. They were efficient only if cultivated as a unit.

Int'l Brotherhood of Teamsters v. Daniel. This case likely failed because there was really no real investment gain and there was no investment. This was a defined benefit plan, where if the union member worked a certain number of years a fixed pension would be available. Here the court held there was no "investment" as this was a noncontributory plan. Moreover, since this was a defined benefit, i.e., payments to beneficiaries not depending on the performance of the investment, there was no expectation of profits. Note this case illustrates that one reason a litigant may argue s/he purchased a security is to bring the complaint under the antifraud rules such as Rule 10b-5. Thus, if it is a security, it might run afoul of the failure to register the public offering under the '33 Act, or if it is a security, any material misrepresentation in connection with its purchase or sale would give rise to a claim under the antifraud rule.

United Housing Foundation, Inc. v. Forman. Students might ask how *Forman* differs from the vacation condo at the beach that is part of a rental pool (discussed above)? This case again illustrates parties may seek to characterize a transaction as a security so as to invoke the antifraud provision. Here the claim was misrepresentations of the cost of housing in Co-op City. The court held the primary motive was not price appreciation or income, but rather housing. Thus, if an investor's principal motivation for a transaction is personal consumption of the item being purchased, e.g., housing, this is not "an expectation of profits." The court also rejected the argument that since the certificate memorializing the reservation of house was labeled "stock" that this was an independent basis for being a security. As discussed later, the name of the certificate representing the transaction is not determinative. If labeled stock, then it must have the indicia of stock, such as being freely transferable, carrying voting rights, providing holders to a share of profits, and the like. If it does not walk like a duck, quack like a duck, then it is not stock.

Marine Bank v. Midland. Students might be asked what this Supreme Court case adds. It holds that a certificate of deposit issued by a thrift institution is not a security, reasoning that banks are subject to a separate regulatory regime so the purchasers of CDs do not need the protection of the securities laws. This holding appears fairly limited to profit sharing instruments issued by banks and the like, where state or federal regulation of thrift institutions, banks, etc. is seen as providing protection needed for investors.

Landredth Timber Co. v. Landreth

Students might be drawn into this case by asking what did the unsuccessful defense in this case have to do with *Howey*? The court holds that "stock" is a separate item within the definition of a security and defining what is stock is not done by applying the "investment contract" gloss of *Howey*. What then does the Court's approach to determining whether an instrument labeled "stock" is in fact a security have to do with: if it looks like a duck, quacks like a duck and walks like a duck, it's a duck? This gets into the Court's rejection of a strict literal approach, whereby if it is labeled stock then it will be so treated. This failed in *Forman,* and it failed here. The court instead peered through the label to inquire if the instrument had the indicia we normally associate with shares of stock: transferability, right to pledge, voting rights, economic rights. What was the defense actually used in this case that was unsuccessful? Before *Landredth,* many lower courts applied the "sale of business" doctrine which essentially applied *Howey* to conclude that if the purchaser of an instrument labeled "stock" had acquired a security, concluding it was not a security if the purchaser obtained control of the business, as was the case in *Landredth.* Those courts reasoned that if control was so acquired, it can hardly be said that the purchaser's profits were from the efforts of the promoter; they would be your efforts or those you appointed. While the SOB doctrine was widely followed before *Landredth*, the Court holds that the various instruments within the definition of a security are sui generis and that their meaning is not to be interpreted by what are the elements for determining another item listed in section 2(a)(1).

Reves v. Young illustrates how notes can be a security. Students should begin by looking closely at section 2(a)(1) and being asked what does section 3(a)(3) do. The legislative intent of the latter clearly expresses the intent to exempt (section 3 authorizes securities exemptions) commercial paper. This likely is the intent behind the "current transaction" clause of the provision. What if they are not commercial paper but less than 9 months? This question is not resolved by *Reves*. Observe these were demand notes and arguably would be excluded if deemed to have a maturity of less than 9 months as provided in both Securities Act section 3(a)(3) and Exchange Act section 3(a)(10). However, the court avoided determining what the significance of the 9 month duration is by concluding that these notes were to be deemed longer than nine months even though demand notes. The court accepts the Second Circuit's family resemblance test. But it seeks to introduce rigor to that test by its four factors to be considered. Under Friendly's development of the family resemblance test, a note longer than nine months is presumed to be a security, and a note for a shorter duration is presumed not to be. The presumption in both instances was rebuttable by demonstrating the note fell within a bundle of case decisions that characterized that type of note/transaction as a financing-investment decision and not a borrowing-commercial one. Thus, notes given to purchase a car or home are not securities; those representing, as here, advances to finance a business are investments. A search through the case law reveals the cases that group notes into these two pots and the litigants seek to push the note in question into one group or the other depending whether the litigant is the plaintiff or defendant. It is worth reviewing the four factors so students get a feel for them and then applying each factor to the note issued by the Co-Op.

Section 3: What Constitutes A "Sale" and An "Offer to Sell"

Until a registration statement is filed, section 5(c) prohibits both sales and offers to sell (as well as offers to buy). And, under section 5(a)(1) no sale of security can occur until the registration statement is effective. Each of these statements is qualified: "unless either the security is exempt or there is an applicable exemption for the transaction. As will be seen later, offer to sell is broadly interpreted so as to include any communication that has the effect of conditioning investor interest.

Corporations and Other Business Organizations

Section 4: The Requirements of Registration

A. The Broad Sweep of Section 5

The keys to the breadth of the securities laws are 1) broad definition of a security, 2) broad concept, explore later of offer and sale, 3) broad prohibition of any offer to sell and sale prior to filing a registration statement, and 4) once a registration statement is filed we find that by virtue of section 2(a)(10) any non-oral offer is a prospectus and section 5(b)(1) permits only prospectuses that meet the requirements of section 10 of the act. Thus, absent an exempt security or a transaction exemption, a written communication can only occur after a registration is filed if that communication is one deemed a prospectus by one of the SEC's rules. Thus, exemptions are of great importance to issuers, particularly small companies seeking to raise capital via the offer and sale of securities.

B. The Intrastate Exemption

You might begin this section by asking the students where this exemption is found. Next, if we have a Texas company (what does that mean?) seeking to raise capital under the intrastate exemption, how should those conducting the offering be instructed regarding who they might approach and what other concerns are there? The answer is the statutory exemption and its safe harbor, Rule 147, are each focused on the qualities of the offerees. Thus, the company can only approach those who are residents of Texas. Moreover what happens if X, Y and Z are approached, and while Z looks like a Texan (pickup with hunting hound, Levis, and boots), turns out she lives in Oklahoma? This destroys the entire offering, even though we ultimately do not sell shares to Z. Thus, Oklahoma in this case is not OK. Next, assume that we only approach X and Y who are Texans and sell shares to each. But shortly thereafter Y sells to Z? This focuses on the need for the offering to come to rest in the hands of only those who meet the criteria of the exemption (they're all Texans) so that resells or offers to resell to non Texans destroys the exemption. Just when an offering comes to rest is hard to pin down. Certainly, if the resale occurred a year or more after purchase from the issuer, this would indicate that the offering has come to rest (making analogy to Rule 144 which is a safe harbor for resales and provides that its longest holding period is one year). Sales within one year are problematic with respect to whether the offering has come to rest. Notice a substantial offering portion of the offering's proceeds must also be deployed by the issuer in Texas. Note Rule 147 requires that for the issuer's exemption there must be restrictions on transfer for 9 months.

What policy justifies the intrastate exemption? It may well be that, if everything is local, to a single state this better assures that investors, who must be residents of that state, can carry out their own due diligence. Second, it might be the view that, if everything is happening in a single state, it is appropriate to let the investors' protection depend on the state blue sky administrator.

Students should be asked how does Rule 147 relate to this subject? This is the SEC's intrastate safe harbor rule. What does this mean? It means that compliance with Rule 147 assures that the offering will be exempt as an intrastate offering. What then does Rule 147 provide that is not provided by section 3(a)(11) itself. First, it is precise on such matters as what we mean by doing business in a state, how do you determine an issuer's residency, and how much of the offering proceeds must be dedicated to activities in the home state. Note also that Rule 147(e) sets a nine month time period during which sales are not to be made to non residents. Also, while examined more later, Rule 147(b) has an integration safe harbor (something the statutory exemption in section 3(a)(11) does not have). This provides some assurance that if no other sale occurs within six months of the Rule 147 offering that the validity of the Rule 147 offering will not be in doubt because the other offering was made to non residents. Note also that Rule 147 mandates specific requirements in paragraph (f) to assure that resales do not occur to non eligible purchasers (i.e., non Texans).

C. Private Placements

Students may be asked where this exemption is found? Section 4(2) talks about an offering that is not a "public offering." What does this mean? The next case sheds light on the intent behind this exemption.

SEC v. Ralston Purina Co.

What was Ralston's argument for why this was a private placement? Being limited to "key employees," it was hardly available to anyone who wished to acquire the stock. Thus, why was this outside section 4(2). *Ralston's* holding is that the exemption is not available if not all the offerees could "fend for themselves." Look at the list of purchasers. Who on that list might we have doubts could fend for himself?

What does fend for yourself mean? This certainly speaks to having information on which to make an informed investment decision. The court repeatedly stated that the various offerees were deprived of information of the *type* that registration would make available. Does this mean the exemption must provide information that is the mirror image of what would be disclosed if the offering to the chow loading foreman and other Ralston employees was registered? Type refers to the category of information but not the format and detail. Registration compels much more detailed disclosures; private placements provide less.

What do we learn about the "fend for yourself" litmus from the accompanying note material? The court in *Doran* reflects the general view on the demands of the private placement exemption; to wit, section 4(2) requires offerees to be sophisticated. That is, making gobs of objectively useful information to the chow loading foreman in *Ralston* is part of the answer, but we also would require that the foreman be able to understand the information and thereby be able to assess the risks and return of the security in light of that information. Hence, offeree sophistication is widely believed embedded in *Ralston's* fend for yourself criteria.

Notice this exemption, as was the case with the intrastate exemption and Rule147, is focused on the qualities of the offeree. One non-*Ralston* qualified offeree destroys the exemption for that offering.

We might puzzle how the information requirement gets satisfied. One is by the issuer and its representatives making the information available to potential investors. This is the "disclose" part of the *Doran* formulation. Such disclosure customarily occurs through a detailed private placement memorandum. Another way the information requirement can be satisfied is via the investors' access to the relevant information. This may work well for securities sold to management, certainly senior management, whose positions and experience enable them to extract information relevant to considering the offering. We might also believe that family members of the promoters would, through that relationship, provide *access*. Also, a very experienced investor with significant resources, not just financial but also perhaps a staff, can extract information of the type registration would make available.

D. Limited Offerings

Students can be asked where Regulation D can be found and what is it? This is a collection of three issuer safe harbors set forth in Rules 504, 505 and 506. Students can be asked which poses the least regulation? Which allows the most to be raised? Indeed, Rule 506 is used by all sized companies, since it has no dollar limit. It is generally the first step in a Rule 144A syndication, discussed later. Rule 504 is the least regulated, allowing $1 million to be raised during any 12 month period without federal restrictions on how the offering occurs. Rule 505 has a 5 million cap and is largely ignored due to the more attractive Regulation offerings discussed later.

How are Rule 505 and 506 different in their operation from either the intrastate or private offering exemption? Note that unlike the exemptions studied earlier, with Regulation D, it is the quality of the *purchaser* and not the offeree that is relevant. Why is this a positive step? Note that Rules 505 and 506 each have a numerical limit of 35 non accredited purchasers. Moreover, Rule 506 requires each non accredited purchaser to be sophisticated or be represented by a purchaser representative (who satisfies the sophistication requirement). With eligibility for each of the exemptions teeing off from purchasers, it allows the issuer and its representatives to learn a good deal (are they accredited and/or sophisticated) from targeted investors before actually closing the sale. This allows the issuer and its representatives to structure the offer to meet the criteria of the
266

exemption. As seen earlier, under an offeree-based regime an approach to an ineligible offeree destroys the exemption for the offering.

You might want to review who qualifies as an "accredited investors." Note that after Dodd-Frank one's home is not taken into consideration in determining net worth for individuals.

Students can be asked whether Rule 505 or 505 have an information requirement. The answer is yes, but the extent of the mandatory disclosure is scaled to the size of the offering

E. Regulation A

Students can be drawn into discussing Regulation A by asking why is it that issuers and their advisors prefer Regulation A over Rule 505 of Regulation D? That is, very few Rule 505 offerings occur in any year, while there are hundreds of Reg A offerings. The following are the advantages, captured in the materials, that explain the wonders of Reg. A:

1. Shares are not restricted thus avoiding issuance discount for illiquidity during restricted period;

2. There are no limits on qualities of offerees, purchasers, or number of either;

3. The offering can be widely publicized, i.e., there is no restriction as there is with all Reg. D. offerings on general solicitation and general advertisement;

4. Broad integration protection (e.g., does not integrate with offers made prior to the Reg. A offering);

5. If audited financial statements are not available for the Offering Statement then can proceed with unaudited statements;

6. Can test the waters before taking the more formal step of preparing and filing an Offering Statement (does require written materials used in such a market test to be filed with SEC);

7. The Offer Statement is rather abbreviated disclosures in a user-friendly plain English question-and-answer style for ease of completion by issuers; and

8. Provides a moving 12-month window during which issuers can raise $5 million (and others, e.g., control persons $1.5 million.

What is the downside? It is not available to reporting companies and in today's world, $5 million is not a lot of money. The SEC does have authority to increase the section 3(b) limit, but as preparing this manual has chosen not to exercise this authority that Congress granted in 1996 per section 28 (the legislative history is quite clear this was one of the purposes of the exemptive authority of this provision).

The Note on Integration is brief because we believe this not being a full securities regulations course it is sufficient for students to understand that with transaction exemptions, such as those covered in this section, it is important to define the transaction. Hence the five factors of integration and we have seen that Rules 147(b), 502(a) and 251(c) set forth integration safe harbors for the intrastate, Regulation D and Regulation A safe harbors, respectively. Most importantly, the concept of integration means that exemptions are not cumulative within the same transaction, i.e., you cannot graft a private offering exemption to and intrastate exemption. You have to choose one or the other.

Omitted from these materials is Regulation S. This is a complex safe harbor for identifying when an offering is "off shore", i.e., outside the "in interstate commerce" jurisdictional provision of section 5. Regulation S allows offerings to occur abroad, provided one of the Regulation S safe harbors are complied with and that offering will not be subject to section 5 and will not be integrated with even a simultaneous exempt offering carried out in the U.S. Hence, with Regulation S a foreign tranche can occur at the same time as, for example, an intrastate offering is occurring in Texas.

Section F: Transactions Not Involving An Issuer, Underwriter, or Dealer

1. Who Is A Statutory Underwriter

The most complicated area of the '33 Act is resales. It begins with the breadth of section 2(a)(11) whose multiple clauses need to be examined. You might ignore the last sentence dealing with control persons until you deal with subsection 2. Most of the analysis in this area begins with section 4(1) which exempts all God's children save those engaged in a *transaction* by an issuer, underwriter or dealer. Each of these are defined separately in section 2(a). The most important and sweeping is section 2(a)(11)'s definition of underwriter. Note the exemption is a transaction exemption. Hence, if the transaction is NOT exempt then all whose participation is necessary for that transaction would not be exempt (unless they can invoke a separate exemption, e.g., the broker's transaction exemption in section 4(4) protects the broker even though her client may not enjoy an exemption).

SEC v. Chinese Consolidated Benevolent Ass'n broadly holds that we do not need a contract or even understanding between the issuer and one selling on its behalf to render the soliciting party an underwriter. Students can be asked whether this is consistent with the language and likely intent of Congress. The answer in each case has to be yes. The strict construction used by the Second Circuit appears entirely appropriate for the reasons stated in the opinion, i.e., investor protection is eroded by the gratuitous as well as the highly paid underwriter. Thus, one who leans over the backyard fence to encourage her neighbor to purchase an issuer's shares is clearly an underwriter. As such, the broad transaction exemption in section 4(1) would not be applicable.

The most difficult area for students to grasp is section 2(a)(11)'s, which provides that one who has purchased from an issuer with a view to the distribution of a security. This is illustrated best by the leading case, *Gilligan Will & Co.* Students might be asked how the brokerage firm violated section 5. It purchased privately placed securities and ten months later sold the shares into a market. It thereby met both the "view to" and "distribution" language of section 2(a)(11). Students might be asked what is the connection between the "view to" and what was discussed earlier in connection with exemptions regarding the offering coming to rest when all purchasers have "investment intent." "View to" sets up the "investment intent" focus that we saw earlier because when a security is offered pursuant to an exemption we focus on whether all offerees (or in the case of Reg. D, purchasers) meet the criteria of that exemption. This means that those taking the security, if they meet the applicable criteria of the exemption, must absorb the risks of that security for the indefinite future. This lacks any precise meaning, but historically this meant you had to hold the security two to three years to establish the bona fides of your intent when you acquired the security. That is, holding period is circumstantial evidence of your intent when you acquired the security. With changes in the resale safe harbor rule, Rule 144, we likely find the holding period is now shorter than 2-3 years since that rule now has a 1 year holding period for restricted securities. If you have a sale within the one-year period, as in *Gilligan Will*, you might argue, as did Gilligan, that things changed, i.e., there was a change in circumstances, post purchase, i.e., you had the required intent when you bought it but changed that intent. Why did this not work in *Gilligan?* Because the circumstances that must change are the investor's not the issuer's circumstance. Gilligan argued that Crowell Collier's performance declined from what Gilligan sought when it initially invested. But this is a risk of the investment that the initial buyer is to absorb so not sufficient. Now, if Gilligan had entered into bankruptcy or serious financial distress so that it needed to raise case, then its circumstances would have changed and that would be a sufficient justification for selling earlier than what would otherwise be the necessary holding period to establish initial investment intent.

Note that one does not become an underwriter solely because you lack investment intent. The resale must be in connection with a "distribution." What does that mean? What did it mean in *Gilligan?* It means selling restricted securities to someone who the issuer could not have sold pursuant to the exemption the issuer relied. Thus, Crowell-Collier used the private offering exemption. Thus, all offerees must meet the *Ralston* criteria. A market, such as the one Gilligan sold the shares, is made up of all kinds of investors, not all are *Ralston* qualified. To state this more positively, even with no investment intent, Gilligan could have sold the shares, and not been an underwriter, if the sale were to a sophisticate investor with access or disclosure of the type of information registration would have made available.

Thus, a Texas issuer who sells to X and Y (Texans) pursuit to section 3(a)(11) does not lose its exemption if Y resells to Z who is also a Texan, even if Y never had investment intent. But if Y sold the shares to a sophisticated Oklahoman the issuer's intrastate exemption would be destroyed, and hence there would be a "distribution," unless the offering had come to rest before Y's resale.

2. Sales by Controlling Persons

An initial question is who is a control person? Rule 405 broadly defines this to include those who can influence the managerial policies of the firm. This would clearly the senior officers, likely members of the board of directors and general partner in a partnership. The legislative history of the '33 Act clearly shows that a control person at least includes someone who had enough influence to compel the filing of a registration statement.

If we have a control person, then students should observe the effect of the last sentence of section 2(a)(11). That effect means that one returns to the first sentence and substitutes "control person" everywhere an issuer appears.

How then did Ira Haupt violate section 5? How about Wolfson? The brokerage firm Ira Haupt was selling large quantities of shares for a control person, and the dividend in liquor announcement can be seen as a solicitation. As such, the exemption in section 4(4) was not available. Since the shares were sold into a market, and *Gilligan Will* tells us a distribution is the opposite of a private placement a la section 4(2), we have one selling for a control person in connection with a distribution. *Wolfson* (notice this is a criminal prosecution) is a bit more complicated, because while the facts are very similar, namely a large number of shares being sold into a market. Wolfson's brokers were each able to invoke the broker's transaction exemption per the safe harbor, former Rule 154, that then existed. Notwithstanding the broker's exemption, their collective resales was seen as selling for an issuer in connection with a distribution so that Wolfson was thereby implicated in an underwriter transaction what was not exempt per section 4(1). Hence, Wolfson goes to jail.

3. Rules 144 and 144A

The challenge in this subsection is how much depth to accord each of these safe harbors. Each entails at least a day in the standard Securities Regulations course. In the context of a business organization course, perhaps only half a class period is appropriate. What is important here is that in practice resales are considered first under Rule 144, and not the more amorphous questions of "investment intent" and "distribution."

The basic orientation to Rule 144 begins with (b) where we find different treatment of affiliates (control person resales) and non affiliates. Note that with respect to affiliates, the safe harbor applies to both restricted and non restricted securities. What is restricted is defined in (a)(3) and noticeably excludes intrastate securities.

Sales by or on behalf of (i.e. by a broker) an affiliate must comply with the information, volume and manner of sale requirements. And, if the security is also a restricted one, then the holding period requirement must be met as well.

Sales by non affiliate pose resale problems only if the security is restricted. If within the definition of restricted security in 144(a)(3) then the holding period requirement must be met (as long as one year in the case of a non-reporting company's shares). There also is an information requirement that needs to be met for the first year the securities were acquired from the issuer or an affiliate of the issuer.

The information requirements are set forth in 144(a)(c), and counsel for a non-reporting company is well advised to counsel the issuer to make sure its website sets forth information that satisfies (c)(2) so that those holding restricted securities of that issuer can resell their shares.

Where do these various requirements come from? Information requirement is consistent with *Ralston*, volume requirement for control resales is consistent with *Wolfson* and *Ira Haupt*, and manner of sale is consistent with *Ira Haupt*. And the holding period requirement is imbedded with "view to" and the investment intent lore.

Rule 144A is designed to facilitate the syndication/distribution of non registered securities to financial institutions. The students may gain insight to this area by understanding that much more is raised via Rule 144A transactions in any year than is registered pursuant to section 5. The standard 144A transaction commences with a Rule 506 offering (note not dollar limit) to an investment banker. That investment banker then invokes 144A (purely a resale safe harbor and one not available to an issuer) to distribute the securities among financial institutions who meet the definition of a Qualified Institutional Investors per Rule 144A(a)(1). Note the security to be distributed cannot be fungible with on listed on a U.S. exchange. Rule 144A(b)(3). For a reporting company there is no substantial information requirement, see (b)(4), but practice is to prepare a "10b-5 disclosure package" for QIBs akin to the private offering memorandum.

QIBs can resell to other QIBs pursuant to Rule 144A; there is no holding period required by Rule 144A itself. Reselling outside of Rule 144A could occur pursuant to Rule 144, see here Rule 144(a)(3)(iii) which treats such securities as "restricted" for Rule 144 purposes.

The 4 1-1/2 exemption applies to sales by a control person where the issuer's shares have been either earlier registered or the issuer earlier issued pursuant to an exemption and that offering has come to rest. Thus, we are focused only on whether someone is either selling for or purchasing from a control person is an underwriter. In this area, the analogy is made to section

4(2) (recall this is only for issuers, hence the analogy only) to determine whether the resell is a "distribution." As seen earlier, the leading case defining what this otherwise undefined term means is *Gilligan Will*. Hence, does the resale have properties akin to those that would qualify the sale, if made by an issuer, a private offering?

Section 5: Mechanics of Registration

Students can be directed to review a sample form for S-1 or S-3. There we find that completing the form is a bit like following directions in a cookbook. That is, each of the forms refers to information that is required by Regulation S-K where elaborate instructions can be found on just what has to be supplied. Thus completing a registration statement is not one begins without a lot of guidance. There is a good deal of guidance provided in Regulation S-K.

Students should be aware of the difference between the "registration statement" and a "prospectus." The latter includes all the information in the former except the exhibits. You might consider pulling up on the Web a filed registration statement and reviewing the lengthy list of exhibits. The content of the other parts of the registration statement is discussed in the material of this chapter.

Students should also understand the three distinct periods in the registration process: pre filing, waiting and post effective. Much of the concern is what can be said and one in the pre filing period without appearing to "jump the gun," a topic later covered.

Students should be asked what is meant by "integrated disclosure?" Note the real benefits of being an S-3 eligible issuer is not incorporation of material from '34 Act reports but rather the dispensations that are accorded issuers eligible to use Form S-3, i.e., this is a short-hand way of identifying who in a rule can have some regulatory slack cut to them. Students might be asked why might we do this for some companies and not others? There likely is less need for paternalism for companies that are held largely by institutions and followed closely by analysts, WorldCom and Enron notwithstanding.

Students can be asked what is meant by shelf registration? Why is this process not only desirable but necessary? Issue with shelf registration is that it essentially disconnects the act of registration from the act of either sale or issuance. In the case of catching market windows this unhinging greatly reduces market risk and, therefore, reduces the cost of offerings, likely increases the aggregation of capital, and hence is allocationally efficient.

Section 6: Duties and Prohibitions When A Security Is In Registration

A. Overview

This introduces the three stages of the registration period. Notice that post 2005 that much of the regulatory hand was lifted for the post effective period; no longer must a final prospectus accompany the confirmation or delivery of the certificates. Moreover, as we will see, post 2005 much more information can be circulated outside the registration statement/prospectus during the waiting period.

B. Pre-Filing Period

Students can be asked why this period is referred to as the "quiet period." How did Carl M. Loeb, Rhoades & Co. run afoul of section 5? Which part of section 5? And why was not the statements released of the type covered by Securities Act Release 5180?

Clearly the statements released by Arvida under Loeb, Rhoades guidance were designed to attract investor interest, even mentioning the forthcoming public offering. The case illustrates the continuing SEC position that any communication that will have the effect (whether intended or not) of conditioning investor interest is an offer to sell a security. As such, absent the filing of a registration statement or an applicable safe harbor, section 5(c) is violated. Hence, when in registration, which begins at least as early as talking with the underwriters, mum's the word.

How would *Loeb, Rhoades* fair today under the various safe harbors listed in the readings?

Many of the statements were made within the 30 day period and if made more than 30 days within the registration period we would ask whether made by the issuer or did they mention the forthcoming public offering.

While much of the information appears factual, was it part of the regular practice of releasing such information? Not likely so this safe harbor is not available. Moreover, the target appears to be investors not customers and suppliers as permitted by Rule 169.

While some of the information was a forecast or talked about the future, this is not a reporting company and also we wonder if this was consistent with its earlier practice. Moreover the safe harbor is only available to releases by the issuer and must not mention the forthcoming public offering.

Arvida is not a well-known seasoned issuer. By the way, why create a blanket exemption for this type of company?

C. The Waiting Period

Students can be asked what changes once the registration statement is filed? There can be actually selling efforts and no regulation applies to oral offers at all (provided not on television or radio). Here the operative concept is the prospectus, defined in section 2(a)(1) so that it includes not just paper but as the SEC rules now define, email, and other items via the Internet (as a "graphic written communication").

Students can be asked what is a "free writing prospectus?" What might be circulated to investors that is not already in the registration statement and hence would be in the preliminary prospectus? One idea would be forecasts or pro forma information that fear of section 11 liability might cause the information to be excluded from the more regulated registration statement. Brokers promoting the offering customarily circulate term sheets regarding the offering. These are essentially outlines presenting a skeletal view of the offering and its potential. Indeed, most filed free writing prospectus are term sheets. A free writing prospectus faces minimal requirements, such as filing the free writing material with the SEC and a legend. In the case of an "unseasoned" company, the free writing material must be accompanied or preceded by a preliminary prospectus.

D. The Post-Effective Period

Since the offering reform rules in 2005, the regulatory hand has been substantially lifted in the post-effective period. As the Loss & Seligman quote reflects, this seemed like an easy step to take. Confirmations, although expressly referred to in section 2(a)(1) as a "prospectus" now need not be accompanied or preceded by a final prospectus by virtue of rule 172. Similarly, the securities can be mailed, etc. without being accompanied by a final prospectus. All that the dealer must do, if not otherwise exempt from doing so, is either provide a final prospectus within two days of sale or send the customer a notice that the security was registered.

Section 7: Liabilities Under the Securities Act

Private suits are expressly provided under sections 11, 12 and 15. The latter applies to recoveries against a person that controls someone who is liable under either section 11 or 12. It is not vicarious liability (respondeat superior liability does survive the enactment of the Securities Act so that if a master-servant relationship exists the master will be liable for the amount recoverable under either section 11 or 12).

No private action has been recognized under the antifraud provision, section 17(a).

A review of section 12(a)(1) should invite students to answer how this remedy is designed to assure compliance with section 5? The remedy is rescission, does not have any reliance, causation or scienter requirement. Liability is absolute. Thus, one who violates section 5 essentially proves the security's holder with a put option for the statute of limitations period. Few issuers wish to guaranty the offering price of their securities for the 1-3 year period.

In contrast, section 12(a)(2) provides relief for misrepresentations in connection with a "prospectus." The recovery is, per section 12(b), the out of pocket, not rescission, measure of damages. Due to what is at best a curious interpretative approach by Justice Kennedy in *Gustafson v. Alloyd*, recovery is limited to offers that are public in nature. This excludes, as it did in the fact of *Gustafson*, private offerings. It applies clearly to intrastate, section 3(b)-based offerings, and of course registered public offerings. Hence, a free writing prospectus used in a registered offering or an Offering Statement in a Reg. An offering each would give rise to a section 12(a)(2) suit if carried out via a material misstatement. Note the defense is that the defendant did not know and in the exercise of reasonable care could not learn of the untruth of the misrepresented fact. Finally, *Pinter v. Dahl*, while a section 12(a)(1) case applies has correctly been interpreted to apply to both causes of action under section 12; hence, suit must be against the plaintiff's seller (interpreting the "from him" language).

Section 11 imposes serious liability on an exclusive list of defendants. You might consider reviewing the list of defendants, asking who is in the best position to protect the public interest? Arguably either those that are experts, e.g., accountants, or the underwriters. Others have much less independence. We might prefer between these two outsiders the underwriters since they have reputations to protect and they are liable for the entire registration statement whereas the experts are only responsible for that part prepared on their authority as an expert.

Note the issuer and senior officers become defendants as signers, ala section 6 of the act and implementing rules.

Note the tracing problem identified in *Barnes v. Osofsky*, flowing from the "such securities" language.

Also, a cause of action only exists for material misrepresentations that existed when the registration statement became effective. If something occurs during the post effective period that makes a statement in the registration statement materially misleading that might give rise to a causation of action under section 12(a)(2) or Rule 10b-5, but not section 11.

Finally, as a preliminary matter, note the issuer has no defense while others do under section 11(b)(3).

Escott v. BarChris Constr. Corp.

We might begin by asking what generally appears to be the problem that caused BarChris to fail as a business? It was oversupply. Demand for anything is satiable, and even more so for bowling allies. Its business models was built on there being an increasing demand for bowling allies? Why? Because it sold each alley on credit, sold the resulting promissory notes to a factor, Talcott, got back less than the face amount of the paper. At the same time, material and labor providers needed to be paid. Hence, it had to borrow to keep in business. Thus, it needed to have a constant demand, if not rising demand, to provide the cash (from selling notes to Talcott) to stay in business. It also went to credit markets by selling bonds which required proof of an ability to repay which meant cash, you guessed it, from Talcott on factored notes). When demand slackened, the house of cards collapsed upon itself.

We generally begin by reviewing the table of 9 items that summarize the various material misrepresentations that existed in the registration statement when it became effective. We can ask the students what was the source of the misrepresentation for each of the following.

1. Income Statement: inflated sales by including among sales completed bowling allies that were merely transferred to a wholly owned BarChris subsidiary and not disposed to a third party.

2. Current Asset Overstatement: Incorrectly included receivable for allies not sold to third person.

3 Contingent liability. Failure to reflect that the contingent liability on factored notes had changed to full recourse from 25 percent recourse.

4. Same as item No. 3, but this was for the quarter.

5. Same as item No. 1, but this relates to the quarter.

6. Backlog. Students may be asked what does it mean to have something "backordered?" This is the vendor's side of that phenomenon, except for BarChris there was no firm order for allies. Why would this be material? Backlog reflects future sales and hence future cash flow. This is very relevant to investors in either bonds or stock.

7 Officers' Loans. Officers had made loans to BarChris. This was not disclosed. Why is this material? May implicate use of proceeds and officers making loans to their corporation is not a ringing endorsement of the stability of the issuer.

8. Use of Proceeds. Registration statement identified proceeds would be used for working capital in operations for construction of more allies. In fact, events had deteriorated and funds

would be used to cover negative (overdrafts) balances in banking accounts and payment of maturing debts. Not where one wishes to see their investment deployed.

9. Customer Delinquencies. This material because on the factored notes this gives rise to a matured obligation to pay Talcott and for any non factored notes it means a receivable that will not be collected. In this regard, this item also relates to item No. 2 above.

10. Operation of Bowling Allies. This reflects it could not move its product and hence was not a vendor but an operator of allies. Thus, the business plan has changed.

From this sketch of what went wrong we move to how each of the defendants did with their defenses under section 11(b). The short answer is, bad.

Before reviewing the defendants, ask the students which portion is prepared on the authority of an expert (Items 1, 2 & 3)? Why is this relevant? It is relevant to the expert but also to others since as to items 1-3 they then have a lower defense, "had no reasonable ground to believe and did not believe) that any statement in the expertised portion was materially misleading.

In reviewing the following, we ask how each became a defendant. Some signed, others were directors and still others were either an underwriter or expert.

Note how all the insiders - Russo, Vitolo, Pugliese and Kircher (with the exception of Birnbaum-one of our own) - never established a defense with respect, even as to the expertise portion of the registration statement. They must have known. Why did Birnbaum escape? He had been there only a couple of months. We like to ask our students whether after reading this case they as a young or later more senior lawyer would like to earn a place in the history of the law, as did Birnbaum, by signing a registration statement?

Birnbaum. Why was he liable? He failed to show any investigation.

Auslander. First, how did he become subject to section 11? Second, why did he become a director? Note the glee in the eyes of plaintiff's counsel when they discovered that Auslander wanted the funds for his bank, not that he thought serving on company boards was good for America! Did not Auslander carry out an investigation? What was wrong with it? The short answer, it was not focused on the representations in the registration statement.

Grant. Why is grant like us? What do we learn from this part of the opinion? Court rejects Grant's argument that reasonable investigation as viewed by the court required an "audit." What does audit mean? It means independent verification of each representation. What did the court require, for example, with respect to the backlog? The contingent liabilities? The use of the proceeds? Each of these the court required Grant to look behind the representations to some documents that would support the representation. Is this not an audit?

Underwriters. What result here if Drexel was deemed to have carried out a reasonable investigation and the other members of the syndicate did nothing? They are a partnership (technically a joint venture) and Drexel's efforts are on behalf of all syndicate members. Hence, they all stand or fall on what Drexel did. What result? Drexel through its counsel was deemed not to have carried out anything that resembled a reasonable investigation.

Peat Marwick. Court essentially blasts the auditor, Bernardi, performing the work for Peat Marwick, finding he went through the motions, but did not act or think critically when finding inconsistencies. While finding he failed to carry out a reasonable investigation, one wonders if there were not enough warning signs ignored by him to at least give rise to negligence. This is evident in his handling of the Heavenly and Capitol lanes, believing they were different when in fact they were one and the same (not sold to a third party but operated as a division of BarChris).

Note it is worth discussing that the auditors do look at the period post financial statement date to see if any events in that period suggest corrections to statements speaking of the statement's date. Had this investigation been done with a critical eye he would have seen clear evidence of BarChris' rapid financial deterioration which would have caused a recalibration of assumptions and conclusions made earlier about BarChris, including whether it could be seen as a going concern.

Section 9: Blue Sky Laws

Since 1996, Congress has constricted the scope of state regulation of public offerings. That occurs now largely in intrastate, Regulation A and Rule 504 and 505 offerings. All others, particularly section 4(2), Rule 506 and registered offerings (because a listing usually is part of that process) are beyond the permitting authority of the state.

What is different about Blue Sky registration? It is both disclosure and merit oriented. When a permit is required, the states do have a process of coordinated review so that one of the states in which the offering is to be made takes the lead in reviewing the permit application.